Implementing Cisco IP Switched Networks (SWITCH) Foundation Learning Guide

Richard Froom, CCIE No. 5102
Erum Frahim, CCIE No. 7549

Cisco Press

800 East 96th Street

Indianapolis, IN 46240

Implementing Cisco IP Switched Networks (SWITCH) Foundation Learning Guide

Richard Froom, CCIE No. 5102
Erum Frahim, CCIE No. 7549

Published by:
Cisco Press
800 East 96th Street
Indianapolis, IN 46240 USA

Printed in the United States of America

First Printing May 2015

Library of Congress Control Number: 2015934731

ISBN-13: 978-1-58720-664-1

ISBN-10: 1-58720-664-1

Warning and Disclaimer

Trademark Acknowledgments

All terms mentioned in this book that are known to be trademarks or service marks have been appropriately capitalized. Cisco Press or Cisco Systems, Inc., cannot attest to the accuracy of this information. Use of a term in this book should not be regarded as affecting the validity of any trademark or service mark.

Special Sales

For information about buying this title in bulk quantities, or for special sales opportunities (which may include electronic versions; custom cover designs; and content particular to your business, training goals, marketing focus, or branding interests), please contact our corporate sales department at corpsales@pearsoned.com or (800) 382-3419.

For government sales inquiries, please contact governmentsales@pearsoned.com.

For questions about sales outside the U.S., please contact international@pearsoned.com.

Feedback Information

At Cisco Press, our goal is to create in-depth technical books of the highest quality and value. Each book is crafted with care and precision, undergoing rigorous development that involves the unique expertise of members from the professional technical community.

Readers' feedback is a natural continuation of this process. If you have any comments regarding how we could improve the quality of this book, or otherwise alter it to better suit your needs, you can contact us through email at feedback@ciscopress.com. Please make sure to include the book title and ISBN in your message.

We greatly appreciate your assistance.

Publisher: Paul Boger

Associate Publisher: Dave Dusthimer

Business Operations Manager, Cisco Press: Jan Cornelssen

Executive Editor: Mary Beth Ray

Managing Editor: Sandra Schroeder

Development Editor: Box Twelve Communications

Project Editor: Mandie Frank

Copy Editor: Keith Cline

Technical Editor: Sean Wilkins

Editorial Assistant: Vanessa Evans

Designer: Mark Shirar

Composition: Bronkella Publishing LLC

Indexer: Tim Wright

Proofreader: The Wordsmithery LLC

ılıılıı
CISCO.

Americas Headquarters
Cisco Systems, Inc.
San Jose, CA

Asia Pacific Headquarters
Cisco Systems (USA) Pte. Ltd.
Singapore

Europe Headquarters
Cisco Systems International BV
Amsterdam, The Netherlands

Cisco has more than 200 offices worldwide. Addresses, phone numbers, and fax numbers are listed on the Cisco Website at www.cisco.com/go/offices.

CCDE, CCENT, Cisco Eos, Cisco HealthPresence, the Cisco logo, Cisco Lumin, Cisco Nexus, Cisco StadiumVision, Cisco TelePresence, Cisco WebEx, DCE, and Welcome to the Human Network are trademarks; Changing the Way We Work, Live, Play, and Learn and Cisco Store are service marks; and Access Registrar, Aironet, AsyncOS, Bringing the Meeting To You, Catalyst, CCDA, CCDP, CCIE, CCIP, CCNA, CCNP, CCSP, CCVP, Cisco, the Cisco Certified Internetwork Expert logo, Cisco IOS, Cisco Press, Cisco Systems, Cisco Systems Capital, the Cisco Systems logo, Cisco Unity, Collaboration Without Limitation, EtherFast, EtherSwitch, Event Center, Fast Step, Follow Me Browsing, FormShare, GigaDrive, HomeLink, Internet Quotient, IOS, iPhone, iQuick Study, IronPort, the IronPort logo, LightStream, Linksys, MediaTone, MeetingPlace, MeetingPlace Chime Sound, MGX, Networkers, Networking Academy, Network Registrar, PCNow, PIX, PowerPanels, ProConnect, ScriptShare, SenderBase, SMARTnet, Spectrum Expert, StackWise, The Fastest Way to Increase Your Internet Quotient, TransPath, WebEx, and the WebEx logo are registered trademarks of Cisco Systems, Inc. and/or its affiliates in the United States and certain other countries.

All other trademarks mentioned in this document or website are the property of their respective owners. The use of the word partner does not imply a partnership relationship between Cisco and any other company. (0812R)

About the Authors

Richard Froom, CCIE No. 5102, is a manager within the Solution Validation Services (SVS) team at Cisco. Richard previously worked as a network engineer in the Cisco TAC and in various customer-facing testing organizations within Cisco. Richard holds CCIEs in Routing and Switching and in Storage Networking. Richard currently focuses on expanding his team's validation coverage to new technologies in the data center, including Application Centric Infrastructure (ACI), OpenStack, Intercloud Fabric, and big data solutions with Hadoop.

Erum Frahim, CCIE No. 7549, is a technical leader working in the Solution Validation Services (SVS) group at Cisco. In her current role, Erum is leading efforts to test data center solutions for several Cisco high-profile customers and leading all the cross-business units interlock. Most recently, she is working on Application Centric Infrastructure (ACI), UCS Director, OpenStack, and big data. Before this, Erum managed the Nexus platform escalation group and served as a team lead for the data center storage-area network (SAN) test lab under the Cisco data center business unit. Erum joined Cisco in 2000 as a technical support engineer. Erum has a Master of Science degree in electrical engineering from Illinois Institute of Technology and also holds a Bachelor of Engineering degree from NED University, Karachi, Pakistan. Erum also authors articles in *Certification Magazine* and on Cisco.com and has participated in many CiscoLive Events. In her spare time, Erum enjoys her time with her husband and child.

About the Technical Reviewer

Sean Wilkins is an accomplished networking consultant for SR-W Consulting (http://www.sr-wconsulting.com) and has been in the field of IT since the mid-1990s, working with companies such as Cisco, Lucent, Verizon, and AT&T, in addition to several other private companies. Sean currently holds certifications with Cisco (CCNP/CCDP), Microsoft (MCSE), and CompTIA (A+ and Network+). He also has a Master of Science degree in Information Technology with a focus in network architecture and design, a Master of Science degree in Organizational Management, a Masters Certificate in Network Security degree, a Bachelor of Science degree in Computer Networking, and an Associate of Applied Science in Computer Information Systems degree. In addition to working as a consultant, Sean spends a lot of his time as a technical writer and editor for various companies.

Dedications

From Richard:

This book is dedicated to my wife, Elizabeth, and my son, Nathan. Thank you for your encouragement and patience as I completed this effort.

From Erum:

This book is dedicated to my daughter, my hubby, and my parents, for their love and patience all throughout this process.

Acknowledgments

We want to thank many people for helping to put this book together.

The Cisco Press team: Mary Beth Ray, the executive editor, coordinated the whole project, steered the book through the necessary processes, and understood when the inevitable snags appeared. Sandra Schroeder, the managing editor, brought the book to production. Vanessa Evans was once again wonderful at organizing the logistics and administration. Jeff Riley, the development editor, has been invaluable in coordinating and ensuring that we all focused on producing the best manuscript.

We also want to thank Mandie Frank, the project editor, and Keith Cline, the copy editor, for their excellent work in getting this book through the editorial process.

The Cisco Switch course development team: Many thanks to the members of the team who developed the Switch course. The course was a basis for this book, and without it, we would never have completed the text in short order.

The technical reviewers: We want to thank the technical reviewer of this book, Sean Wilkins, for his thorough review and valuable input.

Our families: Of course, this book would not have been possible without the endless understanding and patience of our families. They have always been there to motivate and inspire us, and we are forever grateful.

Contents at a Glance

Contents

Icons Used in This Book

 Router

 Switch

 Multilayer Switch

 Cisco IOS Firewall

 Route/Switch Processor

 Access Server

 PIX Firewall

 Laptop

 Server

 PC

 Authentication Server

Camera PC/Video

Ethernet Connection

Serial Line Connection

 Network Cloud

 IP Phone

   Analog Phone

Command Syntax Conventions

The conventions used to present command syntax in this book are the same conventions used in the IOS Command Reference. The Command Reference describes these conventions as follows:

- **Boldface** indicates commands and keywords that are entered literally as shown. In actual configuration examples and output (not general command syntax), boldface indicates commands that are manually input by the user (such as a **show** command).

- *Italic* indicates arguments for which you supply actual values.

- Vertical bars (|) separate alternative, mutually exclusive elements.

- Square brackets ([ ]) indicate an optional element.

- Braces ({ }) indicate a required choice.

- Braces within brackets ([{ }]) indicate a required choice within an optional element.

Introduction

This book starts you down the path toward attaining your CCNP or CCDP certification, providing in-depth information to help you prepare for the SWITCH exam (300-115).

The commands and configuration examples presented in this book are based on Cisco Catalyst IOS for the Catalyst 3750 and 6500.

In terms of content, campus networks continue to evolve, scale, and require minimal convergence and downtime. As these campus networks grow to need these parameters, Cisco has created new switching features to support growth of the networks. Features found in spanning-tree enhancements, port channeling, and trunking all drive the evolving campus networks and are discussed in this book, among other features.

Moreover, as with Internet security, security within the campus network is paramount. Most enterprises focus heavily on security at the Internet edge, but focus is also needed on internal security. Rogue access by hackers to either create a denial-of-service attack or steal data is an example where internal security is needed. This book covers the basic building blocks of campus networks, with a new and heavy emphasis placed on campus network security.

In terms of the structure, configuration examples and sample verification outputs throughout this book demonstrate troubleshooting techniques and illustrate critical issues surrounding network operation. Chapter-ending review questions illustrate and will help solidify the concepts presented in this book.

Who Should Read This Book?

This book is intended for network architects, network designers, systems engineers, network managers, and network administrators who are responsible for implementing and troubleshooting campus networks.

If you are planning to take the SWITCH exam toward your CCNP or CCDP certification, this book provides you with in-depth study material. To fully benefit from this book, you should have your CCNA Routing and Switching certification or possess the same level of knowledge, including an understanding of the following topics:

- A working knowledge of the OSI reference model and networking fundamentals
- The ability to operate and configure a Cisco router/switch, including the following:
  - Displaying and interpreting a router's or switch's routing table
  - Configuring management IP address
  - Configuring static and default routes
  - Enabling a switch interface
  - Configuring IP standard and extended access lists
  - Managing network device security

- Configuring network management protocols and managing device configurations and Cisco Catalyst IOS images and licenses

- Verifying router and switch configurations with available tools, such as **show** and **debug** commands

- Working knowledge of the TCP/IP stack and IPv6

- The ability to configure, verify, and troubleshoot basic IP connectivity and switching problems

If you lack this knowledge and these skills, you can gain them by completing the Interconnecting Cisco Network Devices Part 1 (ICND1) and Interconnecting Cisco Network Devices Part 2 (ICND2) courses or by reading the related Cisco Press books.

Switch Exam Topic Coverage

The Cisco website has the following information on the exam topics page for the SWITCH exam (300-115) (available at https://learningnetwork.cisco.com/docs/DOC-24499):

"The following topics are general guidelines for the content that is likely to be included on the practical exam. However, other related topics may also appear on any specific delivery of the exam. In order to better reflect the contents of the exam and for clarity purposes, the following guidelines may change at any time without notice."

The referenced list of exam topics available at the time of this writing is provided in Table I-1.

The Cisco SWITCH course does not cover all the listed exam topics and may not cover other topics to the extent needed by the exam, because of classroom time constraints. The Cisco SWITCH course is not created by the same group that created the exam.

This book does provide information on each of these exam topics (except when the topic is covered by prerequisite material as noted), as identified in the "Where Topic Is Covered" column in Table I-1. This book provides information related to all the exam topics to a depth that should be adequate for the exam. Note, however, that because the wording of the topics is quite general in nature and the exam itself is Cisco proprietary and subject to change, the authors of this book cannot guarantee that all the details on the exam are covered.

As mentioned, some of the listed SWITCH exam topics are actually covered by the prerequisite material. You may already be familiar with this material, and so this book provides pointers to the relevant chapters of the *ICND1* and *ICND2 Foundation Learning Guide* (ISBN: 978-1587143762 and 978-1587143779) Cisco Press books for these topics.

Table I-1   *SWITCH Exam Topic Coverage*

Topic #	Topic	Where Topic Is Covered
1.0	Layer 2 Technologies	
1.1	Configure and Verify Switch Administration	
	SDM Templates	Chapter 8
	Managing MAC Address Table	Chapters 1–10
	Troubleshoot Err-Disable Recovery	Chapter 10
1.2	Configure and Verify Layer 2 Protocols	
	CDP, LLDP	Chapter 8
	UDLD	Chapter 8
1.3	Configure and Verify VLANs	
	Access Ports	Chapter 3
	VLAN Database	Chapter 3
	Normal, Extended VLAN, Voice VLAN	Chapter 3
1.4	Configure and Verify Trunking	
	VTPv1, VTPv2, VTPv3, VTP Pruning	Chapter 3
	Dot1Q	Chapter 3
	Native VLAN	Chapter 3
	Manual Pruning	Chapter 3
1.5	Configure and Verify EtherChannels	
	LACP, PAgP, Manual	Chapter 3
	Load Balancing	Chapter 3
	EtherChannel Misconfiguration Guard	Chapter 3
1.6	Configure and Verify Spanning Tree	
	PVST+, RPVST+, MST	Chapter 4
	Switch Priority, Port Priority, Path Cost, STP Timers	Chapter 4
	PortFast, BPDU Guard, BPDU Filter	Chapter 4
	Loop Guard and Root Guard	Chapter 4
1.7	Configure and Verify Other LAN Switching Technologies	
	SPAN, RSPAN	Chapter 8

Topic #	Topic	Where Topic Is Covered
1.8	Describe Chassis Virtualization and Aggregation Technologies	
	StackWise	Chapter 9
2.0	Infrastructure Security	
2.1	Configure and Verify Switch Security Features	
	DHCP Snooping	Chapter 10
	IP Source Guard	Chapter 10
	Dynamic ARP Inspection	Chapter 10
	Port Security	Chapter 10
	Private VLAN	Chapter 10
	Storm Control	Chapter 10
2.2	Describe Device Security Using Cisco IOS AAA with TACACS+ and RADIUS	
	AAA with TACACS+ and RADIUS	Chapter 7
	Local Privilege Authorization Fallback	Chapter 7
3.0	Infrastructure Services	
3.1	Configure and Verify First-Hop Redundancy Protocols	
	HSRP	Chapter 6
	VRRP	Chapter 6
	GLBP	Chapter 6

How This Book Is Organized

The chapters and appendix in this book are as follows:

Chapter 1, "Fundamentals Review," begins with a review of basic switching terminology and previews a couple of terms used in later chapters. The chapter attempts to prevent excessive cross-referencing, because many switching technologies are applicable to all chapters.

Chapter 2, "Network Design Fundamentals," covers campus network design fundamentals, including campus network structure, Cisco Catalyst switches, and Layer 2 versus multilayer switches. A brief on Catalyst switching hardware functions is also included.

Chapter 3, "Campus Network Architecture," introduces VLANs, VTP, trunking, and port channeling.

Chapter 4, "Spanning Tree in Depth," goes into detail about spanning tree and its enhancements that are useful in today's network.

Chapter 5, "Inter-VLAN Routing," discusses the fundamentals of routing between VLANs and associated network designs and best practices. In addition, it also discusses Dynamic Host Configuration Protocol (DHCP) services and layer 3 Portchannels.

Chapter 6, "First-Hop Redundancy," covers the protocols leveraged by Cisco Catalyst switches to support first-hop redundancy, including Hot Standby Router Protocol (HSRP), Gateway Load Balancing Protocol (GLBP), and Virtual Router Redundancy Protocol (VRRP).

Chapter 7, "Network Management," covers AAA (authentication, authorization, and accounting), Network Time Protocol (NTP), 802.1X, and Simple Network Management Protocol (SNMP) to present a holistic view of network management and Cisco Catalyst device security.

Chapter 8, "Switching Features and Technologies for the Campus Network," describes how campus networks use advanced features to add resiliency and availability. Network monitoring using Switched Port Analyzer (SPAN) and Remote SPAN (RSPAN) is also covered, in addition to the Cisco IOS IP SLA (Service Level Agreement) feature.

Chapter 9, "High Availability," discusses switch physical redundancy using StackWise, Virtual Switching System (VSS), or redundant supervisors.

Chapter 10, "Campus Network Security," delves into a plethora of network security features, such as Dynamic Host Configuration Protocol (DHCP) snooping, IP Source Guard, dynamic ARP inspection (DAI), port security, private VLANs, and storm control.

Appendix A, "Answers to Chapter Review Questions," contains the answers to the review questions that appear at the end of each chapter.

Chapter 1

Fundamentals Review

Before journeying into Cisco campus networks and detail technology readouts to prepare for CCNP: Switch, this chapter quickly reviews several topics covered in CCNA and briefly introduces a few topics to ease comprehension of this book. Because each technology covered, such as spanning tree or virtual LANs (VLANs), can exist by itself, the short technology highlights in the chapter reduce cross-referencing of chapters.

If you have a very good understanding of switching terminology and a basic understanding of switching technology, you may want to skip this chapter and begin with Chapter 2, "Network Design Fundamentals."

This chapter covers the following basic switching topics as a review to CCNA and serves as a teaser for topics covered later in chapter:

- Hubs and switches
- Bridges and switches
- Switches of today
- Broadcast domains
- MAC addresses
- The basic Ethernet frame format
- Basic switching function
- VLANs
- The Spanning Tree Protocol
- Trunking
- Port channels
- Multilayer switching (MLS)

Switching Introduction

The term *LAN switching* is becoming legacy. LAN switching was a popular term to describe LANs built on Cisco Catalyst switches in the 1990s to mid-2000s. In today's networks, LANs have been segmented into distinct functional areas: data centers and campus networks.

This book focuses on campus networks. Campus networks generally take a more conservative approach to architectures, using Cisco Catalyst switches and leveraging traditional Layer 2 and Layer 3 hierarchical designs. Data centers are in a state of evolution, with the focus on applications, dev/ops, and software programmability. These architectures use bleeding-edge technologies such as FabricPath, Dynamic Fabric Allocation (DFA), Application Centric Infrastructure (ACI), and so on.

The remainder of this chapter focuses on a couple of key switching concepts in relation to campus networks that are found throughout this text. Many of these concepts are discussed in more detail in later chapters, but a quick review and definition will help you understand the following chapters. Moreover, because all campus network features are heavily intertwined, it is difficult to present topics in a serial fashion. Definitions in this chapter will ease reading in that manner as well.

Hubs and Switches

Hubs are archaic, and the terminology should be avoided. Even the simplest multiport Ethernet devices for the home are switches.

In review, hubs died off as a product because they are shared-bandwidth devices. Switches introduced dedicated bandwidth. A hub allows multiple devices to be connected to the same network segment. The devices on that segment share the bandwidth with each other. As an example with a 100-Mbps hub, and there are six devices connected to six different ports on the hub, all six devices share the 100 Mbps of bandwidth with each other. A 100-Mbps hub shares 100 Mbps of bandwidth among the connected devices. In terms of the OSI reference model, a hub is considered a Layer 1 (physical layer) device. It hears an electrical signal on the wire and passes it along to the other ports.

A switch allows multiple devices to be connected to the same network, just like a hub does, but this is where the similarity ends. A switch allows each connected device to have dedicated bandwidth instead of shared bandwidth. The bandwidth between the switch and the device is reserved for communication to and from that device alone. Six devices connected to six different ports on a 1-Gbps switch each have 1 Gbps of bandwidth to work with, instead of shared bandwidth with the other devices. A switch can greatly increase the available bandwidth in your network, which can lead to improved network performance. Switches also support additional capabilities beyond what hubs support. Later sub-sections describe some of these features.

Bridges and Switches

A basic switch is considered a Layer 2 device. When we use the word *layer*, we are referring to the seven-layer OSI reference model. A switch does not just pass electrical signals along, like a hub does; instead, it assembles the signals into a frame (Layer 2), and then decides what to do with the frame. A switch determines what to do with a frame by borrowing an algorithm from a previously common networking device: a transparent bridge. Logically, a switch acts just like a transparent bridge would, but it can handle frames much faster than a transparent bridge could (because of special hardware and architecture). Once a switch decides where the frame should be sent, it passes the frame out the appropriate port (or ports). You can think of a switch as a device creating instantaneous connections between various ports, on a frame-by-frame basis.

Switches of Today

Today's switches have evolved beyond just switching frames. Most modern switches can actually route traffic. In addition, switches can prioritize traffic, support no downtime through redundancy, and provide convergence services around IP telephony and wireless networks.

In summary, to meet evolving network needs of today, Cisco Catalyst switch designs include support for the following industry-leading features beyond the legacy features found in all switches:

- **Application intelligence:** This helps networks recognize many types of applications and secure and prioritize those applications to provide the best user experience.

- **Unified network services:** Combining the best elements of wireless and wired networking allows you to consistently connect to any resource or person with any device. 10 Gigabit Ethernet technology and Power over Ethernet (PoE) technology support new applications and devices.

- **Nonstop communications:** Features such as redundant hardware, and nonstop forwarding and stateful switchover (NSF/SSO) technology support more-reliable connections.

- **Integrated security:** LAN switches provide the first line of defense against internal network attacks and prevent unauthorized intrusion.

- **Operational manageability:** To more easily manage the network, IT staff must be able to remotely configure and monitor network devices from a central location.

Broadcast Domains

In a review from CCNA material, a broadcast domain is a set of network devices that receive broadcast frames originating from any device within the group. Routers typically bound broadcast domains because routers do not forward broadcast frames. VLANs are an example of broadcast domain. Broadcast domains are generally limited to a specific Layer 2 segment that contains a single IP subnet. The next section discusses the addresses used within broadcast domains.

MAC Addresses

MAC addresses are standardized data link layer addresses that are required for every port or device that connects to a LAN. Other devices in the network use these addresses to locate specific ports in the network and to create and update routing tables and data structures. MAC addresses are 6 bytes long and are controlled by the IEEE. MAC addresses are also known as a hardware address, MAC layer address, and physical address.

A MAC address is also applied to virtual devices. Virtual machines on a server may all contain individual MAC addresses. Moreover, most devices have more than one MAC address. A simple example is your laptop; it has both a LAN MAC address and a wireless MAC address. The next section covers the basic frame structure used in Ethernet.

The Basic Ethernet Frame Format

The IEEE 802.3 standard defines a basic data frame format that is required for all MAC implementations, plus several additional optional formats that are used to extend the protocol's basic capability. The basic data frame format contains the following seven fields, as shown in Figure 1-1.

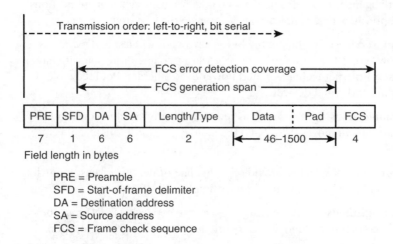

Figure 1-1   *The Basic IEEE 802.3 MAC Data Frame Format*

- **Preamble (PRE):** Consists of 7 bytes. The PRE is an alternating pattern of 1s and 0s that tells receiving stations that a frame is coming, and that provides a means to synchronize the frame-reception portions of receiving physical layers with the incoming bit stream.

- **Start-of-frame delimiter (SOF):** Consists of 1 byte. The SOF is an alternating pattern of 1s and 0s, ending with two consecutive 1 bits, indicating that the next bit is the leftmost bit in the leftmost byte of the destination address.

■ **Destination address (DA):** Consists of 6 bytes. The DA field identifies which station(s) should receive the frame. In the first byte of the DA, the 2 least significant bits are used to indicate whether the destination is an individual address or group address (that is, multicast). The first of these 2 bits indicates whether the address is an individual address (indicated by a 0) or a group address (indicated by a 1). The second bit indicates whether the DA is globally administered (indicated by a 0) or locally administered (indicated by a 1). The remaining bits are a uniquely assigned value that identifies a single station, a defined group of stations, or all stations on the network.

■ **Source addresses (SA):** Consists of 6 bytes. The SA field identifies the sending station. The SA is always an individual address, and the leftmost bit in the SA field is always 0.

■ **Length/Type:** Consists of 2 bytes. This field indicates either the number of MAC-client data bytes that are contained in the data field of the frame, or the frame type ID if the frame is assembled using an optional format. If the Length/Type field value is less than or equal to 1500, the number of LLC bytes in the Data field is equal to the Length/Type field value. If the Length/Type field value is greater than 1536, the frame is an optional type frame, and the Length/Type field value identifies the particular type of frame being sent or received.

■ **Data:** Is a sequence of *n* bytes of any value, where *n* is less than or equal to 1500. If the length of the Data field is less than 46, the Data field must be extended by adding a filler (a pad) sufficient to bring the Data field length to 46 bytes.

Note that jumbo frames up to 9000 bytes are supported on the current-generation Cisco Catalyst switches.

■ **Frame check sequence (FCS):** Consists of 4 bytes. This sequence contains a 32-bit cyclic redundancy check (CRC) value, which is created by the sending MAC and is recalculated by the receiving MAC to check for damaged frames. The FCS is generated over the DA, SA, Length/Type, and Data fields.

Basic Switching Function

When a switch receives a frame, it must decide what to do with that frame. It could ignore the frame, it could pass the frame out one other port, or it could pass the frame out many other ports.

To know what to do with the frame, the switch learns the location of all devices on the segment. This location information is placed in a content addressable memory table (CAM, named for the type of memory used to store these tables). The CAM table shows, for each device, the MAC address of the device, out which port that MAC address can be found, and with which VLAN this port is associated. The switch continually performs this learning process as frames are received into the switch. The CAM table of the switch is continually updated. The next chapter discusses the CAM table in more detail.

This information in the CAM table is used to decide how a received frame is handled. To decide where to send a frame, the switch looks at the destination MAC address in a received frame and looks up that destination MAC address in the CAM table. The CAM table shows the port that the frame must be sent out for that frame to reach the specified destination MAC address. In brief, the basic switching function at Layer 2 adheres to these rules for determining forwarding responsibility:

- If the destination MAC address is found in the CAM table, the switch sends the frame out the port that is associated with that destination MAC address in the CAM table. This process is called *forwarding*.

- If the associated port to send the frame out is the same port that the frame originally came in on, there is no need to send the frame back out that same port, and the frame is ignored. This process is called *filtering*.

- If the destination MAC address is not in the CAM table (that is, unknown unicast), the switch sends the frame out all other ports that are in the same VLAN as the received frame. This is called *flooding*. It does not flood the frame out the same port on which the frame was received.

- If the destination MAC address of the received frame is the broadcast address (FFFF.FFFF.FFFF), the frame is sent out all ports that are in the same VLAN as the received frame. This is also called *flooding*. The only exception is the frame is not sent out the same port on which the frame was received.

The next section introduces a widely popular feature leveraged by Cisco Catalyst switches and Nexus switches to segment groups of ports into their own LAN segments.

VLANs

Because the switch decides on a frame-by-frame basis which ports exchange data, it is a natural extension to put logic inside the switch to allow it to choose ports for special groupings. This grouping of ports is called a *virtual local-area network* (VLAN). The switch makes sure that traffic from one group of ports never gets sent to other groups of ports (which would be routing). These port groups (VLANs) can each be considered an individual LAN segment.

VLANs are also described as broadcast domains. This is because of the transparent bridging algorithm, which says that broadcast packets (packets destined for the *all devices* address) be sent out all ports that are in the same group (that is, in the same VLAN). All ports that are in the same VLAN are also in the same broadcast domain.

The next section introduces the legacy spanning tree technology used to build Layer 2 domains.

The Spanning Tree Protocol

As discussed previously, the switch forwarding algorithm floods unknown and broadcast frames out of all the ports that are in the same VLAN as the received frame. This causes a potential problem. If the network devices that run this algorithm are connected together in a physical loop, flooded frames (like broadcasts) are passed from switch to switch, around and around the loop, forever. Depending on the physical connections involved, the frames can actually multiply exponentially because of the flooding algorithm, which can cause serious network problems.

There is a benefit to a physical loop in your network: It can provide redundancy. If one link fails, there is still another way for the traffic to reach its destination. To allow the benefits derived from redundancy, without breaking the network because of flooding, a protocol called the *Spanning Tree Protocol* (STP) was created. Spanning tree was standardized in the IEEE 802.1D specification.

The purpose of STP is to identify and temporarily block the loops in a network segment or VLAN. The switches run STP, which involves electing a root bridge or switch. The other switches measure their distance from the root switch. If there is more than one way to get to the root switch, there is a loop. The switches follow the algorithm to determine which ports must be blocked to break the loop. STP is dynamic; if a link in the segment fails, ports that were originally blocking can possibly be changed to forwarding mode.

Spanning tree is covered in more detail later in this book. The next section covers how to pass multiple VLANs on a single port.

Trunking

Trunking is a mechanism that is most often used to allow multiple VLANs to function independently across multiple switches. Routers and servers can use trunking, as well, which allows them to live simultaneously on multiple VLANs. If your network only has one VLAN in it, you might never need trunking; but if your network has more than one VLAN, you probably want to take advantage of the benefits of trunking.

A port on a switch normally belongs to only one VLAN; any traffic received or sent on this port is assumed to belong to the configured VLAN. A trunk port, however, is a port that can be configured to send and receive traffic for many VLANs. It accomplishes this when it attaches VLAN information to each frame, a process called *tagging* the frame. Also, trunking must be active on both sides of the link; the other side must expect frames that include VLAN information for proper communication to occur. As with all the section briefs in this chapter, more information is found later in this book.

Port Channels

Utilizing port channels (EtherChannels) is a technique that is used when you have multiple connections to the same device. Rather than each link functioning independently, port channels group the ports together to work as one unit. Port channels distribute traffic across all the links and provide redundancy if one or more links fail. Port channel settings must be the same on both sides of the links involved in the channel. Normally, spanning tree would block all of these parallel connections between devices because they are loops, but port channels run *underneath* spanning tree, so that spanning tree thinks all the ports within a given port channel are only a single port. Later chapters discuss port channels in more detail.

Multilayer Switching

Multilayer switching (MLS) is the ability of a switch to forward frames based on information in the Layer 3 and sometimes Layer 4 header. Almost all Cisco Catalyst switches model 3500 or later support MLS. MLS is becoming a legacy term due to the wide support. The most important aspect to MLS is recognizing that switches can route or switch frames at wire-rate speeds using specialized hardware. This effectively bundles the routing function into the switch and is specifically useful for routing between VLANs in the core of the network. The next chapter discusses this capability in more detail.

Summary

This chapter briefly reviewed several common technology topics pertaining to switching. The remaining chapters of this book cover these topics and other (newer) switching technology related to security.

Chapter 2

Network Design Fundamentals

Every time you go to an office to work or go to class at school, college, or university, you will use a campus network to access critical applications, tools, the Internet, and so on over wired or wireless connections. Often, you may even gain access by using a portable device such as an Apple iPhone connected on a corporate Wi-Fi to reach applications such as e-mail, calendaring, or instant messaging over a campus network. Therefore, the persons responsible for building this network need to deploy sound fundamentals and design principles for the campus networks to function adequately and provide the necessary stability, scalability, and resiliency necessary to sustain interconnectivity with a 100 percent uptime.

This chapter begins the journey of exploring campus network design fundamentals by focusing on a few core concepts around network design and structure and a few details about the architecture of Cisco switches. This is useful knowledge when designing and building campus networks. Specifically, this chapter focuses on the following two high-level topics:

- Campus network structure
- Introduction to Cisco switches and their associated architecture

Campus Network Structure

A campus network describes the portion of an enterprise infrastructure that interconnects end devices such as computers, laptops, and wireless access points to services such as intranet resources or the Internet. Intranet resources may be company web pages, call center applications, file and print services, and almost anything end users connect to from their computer.

In different terms, the campus network provides for connectivity to company applications and tools that reside in a data center for end users. Originally, prior to around 2005, the term *campus network* and its architectures were relevant for application server farms and computing infrastructure as well. Today, the infrastructure that interconnects server farms, application servers, and computing nodes are clearly distinguished from campus networks and referred to as *data centers*.

Over the past few years, data center architectures have become more complex and require sophistication not required in the campus network due to high-availability, low-latency, and high-performance requirements. Therefore, data centers may use bleeding-edge technologies that are not found in the campus network, such as FabricPath, VXLAN, and Application Centric Infrastructure (ACI). For the purpose of CCNP Switch at the time of this writing, these technologies, as well as data center architectures, are out of scope. Nevertheless, we will point out some of the differences as to avoid any confusion with campus network fundamentals.

The next subsection describes the hierarchical network design with the following subsections breaking down the components of the hierarchical design in detail.

Hierarchical Network Design

A flat enterprise campus network is where all PCs, servers, and printers are connected to each other using Layer 2 switches. A flat network does not use subnets for any design purposes. In addition, all devices on this subnet are in the same broadcast domain, and broadcasts will be flooded to all attached network devices. Because a broadcast packet received by an end device, such as tablet or PC, uses compute and I/O resources, broadcasts will waste available bandwidth and resources. In a network size of ten devices on the same flat network, this is not a significant issue; however, in a network of thousands of devices, this is a significant waste of resources and bandwidth (see Figure 2-1).

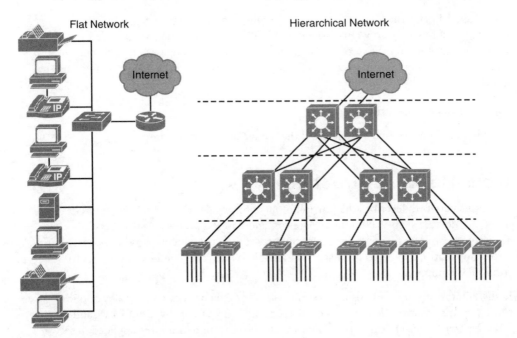

Figure 2-1 *Flat Versus Hierarchical Network Design*

As a result of these broadcast issues and many other limitations, flat networks do not scale to meet the needs of most enterprise networks or of many small and medium-size businesses. To address the sizing needs of most campus networks, a hierarchical model is used. Figure 2-2 illustrates, at a high level, a hierarchical view of campus network design versus a flat network.

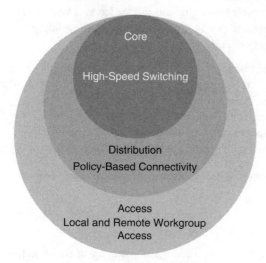

Figure 2-2   *The Hierarchical Model*

Hierarchical models for network design allow you to design any networks in layers. To understand the importance of layering, consider the OSI reference model, which is a layered model for understanding and implementing computer communications. By using layers, the OSI model simplifies the task that is required for two computers to communicate. Leveraging the hierarchical model also simplifies campus network design by allowing focus at different layers that build on each other.

Referring to Figure 2-2, the layers of the hierarchical model are divided into specific functions categorized as core, distribution, and access layers. This categorization provides for modular and flexible design, with the ability to grow and scale the design without major modifications or reworks.

For example, adding a new wing to your office building may be as simple as adding a new distribution layer with an access layer while adding capacity to the core layer. The existing design will stay intact, and only the additions are needed. Aside from the simple physical additions, configuration of the switches and routes is relatively simple because most of the configuration principles around hierarchy were in place during the original design.

By definition, the access, distribution, and core layer adhere to the following characteristics:

- **Access layer:** The access layer is used to grant the user access to network applications and functions. In a campus network, the access layer generally incorporates switched LAN devices with ports that provide connectivity to workstations, IP phones, access points, and printers. In a WAN environment, the access layer for teleworkers or remote sites may provide access to the corporate network across WAN technologies.

- **Distribution layer:** The distribution layer aggregates the access layer switches wiring closets, floors, or other physical domain by leveraging module or Layer 3 switches. Similarly, a distribution layer may aggregate the WAN connections at the edge of the campus and provides policy-based connectivity.

- **Core layer (also referred to as the backbone):** The core layer is a high-speed backbone, which is designed to switch packets as fast as possible. In most campus networks, the core layer has routing capabilities, which are discussed in later chapters of this book. Because the core is critical for connectivity, it must provide a high level of availability and adapt to changes quickly. It also provides for dynamic scalability to accommodate growth and fast convergence in the event of a failure.

The next subsections of this chapter describe the access layer, distribution layer, and core layer in more detail.

Access Layer

The access layer, as illustrated in Figure 2-3, describes the logical grouping of the switches that interconnect end devices such as PCs, printers, cameras, and so on. It is also the place where devices that extend the network out one more level are attached. Two such prime examples are IP phones and wireless APs, both of which extend the connectivity out one more layer from the actual campus access switch.

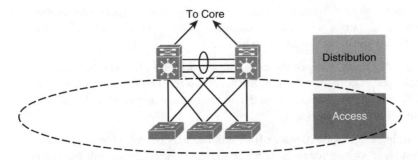

Figure 2-3 *Access Layer*

The wide variety of possible types of devices that can connect and the various services and dynamic configuration mechanisms that are necessary make the access layer one of the most capable parts of the campus network. These capabilities are as follows:

- **High availability:** The access layer supports high availability via default gateway redundancy using dual connections from access switches to redundant distribution layer switches when there is no routing in the access layer. This mechanism behind default gateway redundancy is referred to as *first-hop redundancy protocol* (FHRP). FHRP is discussed in more detail in later chapters of this book.

- **Convergence:** The access layer generally supports inline Power over Ethernet (PoE) for IP telephony, thin clients, and wireless access points (APs). PoE allows customers to easily place IP phones and wireless APs in strategic locations without the need to run power. In addition, the access layers allow support for converged features that enable optimal software configuration of IP phones and wireless APs, as well. These features are discussed in later chapters.

- **Security:** The access layer also provides services for additional security against unauthorized access to the network by using tools such as port security, quality of service (QoS), Dynamic Host Configuration Protocol (DHCP) snooping, dynamic ARP inspection (DAI), and IP Source Guard. These security features are discussed in more detail in later chapters of this book.

The next subsection discusses the upstream layer from the access layer, the distribution layer.

Distribution Layer

The distribution layer in the campus design has a unique role in which it acts as a services and control boundary between the access layer and the core. Both the access layer and the core are essentially dedicated special-purpose layers. The access layer is dedicated to meeting the functions of end-device connectivity, and the core layer is dedicated to providing nonstop connectivity across the entire campus network. The distribution layer, in contrast, serves multiple purposes. Figure 2-4 references the distribution layer.

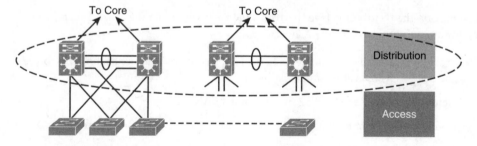

Figure 2-4 *Distribution Layer*

Availability, fast path recovery, load balancing, and QoS are all important considerations at the distribution layer. Generally, high availability is provided through Layer 3 redundant paths from the distribution layer to the core, and either Layer 2 or Layer 3 redundant paths from the access layer to the distribution layer. Keep in mind that Layer 3 equal-cost load sharing allows both uplinks from the distribution to the core layer to be used for traffic in a variety of load-balancing methods discussed later in this chapter.

Note   Equal-cost multipathing (ECMP) is another term used to describe equal-cost load sharing. However, the term ECMP is typically used with respect to data center architectures and not campus architectures. This book uses both terms, equal-cost load sharing and ECMP, interchangeably.

With a Layer 2 design in the access layer, the distribution layer generally serves as a routing boundary between the access and core layer by terminating VLANs. The distribution layer often represents a redistribution point between routing domains or the demarcation between static and dynamic routing protocols. The distribution layer may perform tasks such as controlled routing decision making and filtering to implement policy-based connectivity, security, and QoS. These features allow for tighter control of traffic through the campus network.

To improve routing protocol performance further, the distribution layer is generally designed to summarize routes from the access layer. If Layer 3 routing is extended to the access layer, the distribution layer generally offers a default route to access layer switching while leveraging dynamic routing protocols when communicating with core routers.

In addition, the distribution layer optionally provides default gateway redundancy by using a first-hop routing protocol (FHRP) such as Host Standby Routing Protocol (HSRP), Gateway Load Balancing Protocol (GLBP), or Virtual Router Redundancy Protocol (VRRP). FHRPs provide redundancy and high availability for the first-hop default gateway of devices connected downstream on the access layer. In designs that leverage Layer 3 routing in the access layer, FHRP might not be applicable or may require a different design.

In summary, the distribution layer performs the following functions when Layer 3 routing is not configured in the access layer:

- Provides high availability and equal-cost load sharing by interconnecting the core and access layer via at least dual paths

- Generally terminates a Layer 2 domain of a VLAN

- Routes traffic from terminated VLANs to other VLANs and to the core

- Summarizes access layer routes

- Implements policy-based connectivity such as traffic filtering, QoS, and security

- Provides for an FHRP

Core Layer (Backbone)

The core layer, as illustrated in Figure 2-5, is the backbone for campus connectivity, and is the aggregation point for the other layers and modules of an enterprise network. The core must provide a high level of redundancy and adapt to changes quickly.

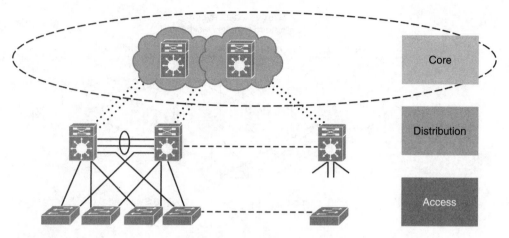

Figure 2-5 *Core Layer*

From a design point-of-view, the campus core is in some ways the simplest yet most critical part of the campus. It provides a limited set of services and is designed to be highly available and requires 100 percent uptime. In large enterprises, the core of the network must operate as a nonstop, always-available service. The key design objectives for the campus core are based on providing the appropriate level of redundancy to allow for near-immediate data-flow recovery in the event of the failure of any component (switch, supervisor, line card, or fiber interconnect, power, and so on). The network design must also permit the occasional, but necessary, hardware and software upgrade or change to be made without disrupting any network applications. The core of the network should not implement any complex policy services, nor should it have any directly attached user or server connections. The core should also have the minimal control plane configuration that is combined with highly available devices that are configured with the correct amount of physical redundancy to provide for this nonstop service capability. Figure 2-6 illustrates a large campus network interconnected by the core layer (campus backbone) to the data center.

From an enterprise architecture point-of-view, the campus core is the backbone that binds together all the elements of the campus architecture to include the WAN, the data center, and so on. In other words, the core layer is the part of the network that provides for connectivity between end devices, computing, and data storage services that are located within the data center, in addition to other areas and services within the network.

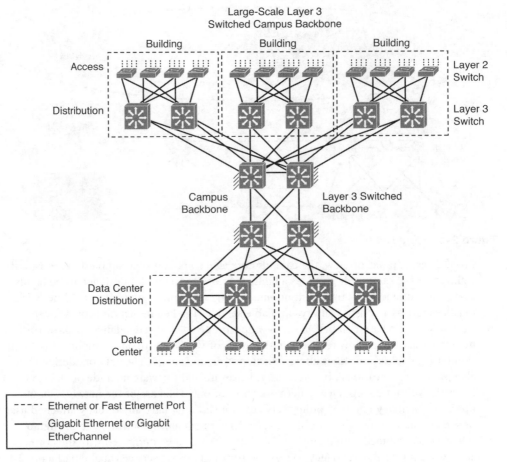

Figure 2-6 *Large Campus Network*

Figure 2-7 illustrates an example of the core layer interconnected with other parts of the enterprise network. In this example, the core layer interconnects with a data center and edge distribution module to interconnect WAN, remote access, and the Internet. The network module operates out of band from the network but is still a critical component.

In summary, the core layer is described as follows:

- Aggregates the campus networks and provides interconnectivity to the data center, the WAN, and other remote networks

- Requires high availability, resiliency, and the ability to make software and hardware upgrades without interruption

- Designed without direct connectivity to servers, PCs, access points, and so on

- Requires core routing capability

- Architected for future growth and scalability

- Leverages Cisco platforms that support hardware redundancy such as the Catalyst 4500 and the Catalyst 6800

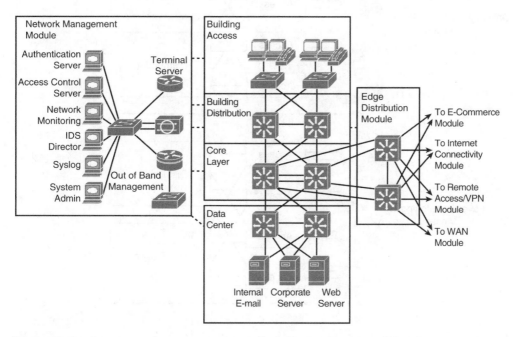

Figure 2-7 *Core Layer Interconnecting with the Enterprise Network*

Layer 3 in the Access Layer

As switch products become more commoditized, the cost of Layer 3 switches has diminished significantly. Because of the reduced cost and a few inherit benefits, Layer 3 switching in the access layer has become more common over typical Layer 2 switching in the access layer. Using Layer 3 switching or traditional Layer 2 switching in the access layer has benefits and drawbacks. Figure 2-8 illustrates the comparison of Layer 2 from the access layer to the distribution layer with Layer 3 from the access layer to the distribution layer.

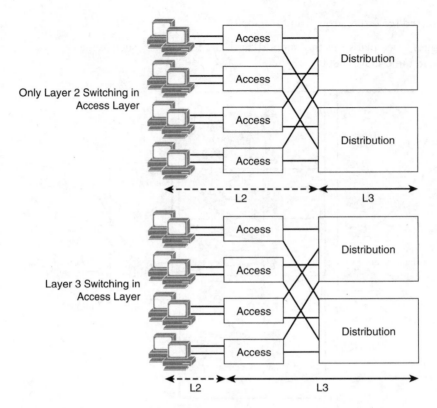

Figure 2-8 *Layer 3 in the Access Layer*

As discussed in later chapters, deploying a Layer 2 switching design in the access layer may result in suboptimal usage of links between the access and distribution layer. In addition, this method does not scale as well in very large numbers because of the size of the Layer 2 domain.

Using a design that leverages Layer 3 switching to the access layer VLANs scales better than Layer 2 switching designs because VLANs get terminated on the access layer devices. Specifically, the links between the distribution and access layer switches are routed links; all access and distribution devices would participate in the routing scheme.

The Layer 2-only access design is a traditional, slightly cheaper solution, but it suffers from optimal use of links between access and distribution due to spanning tree. Layer 3 designs introduce the challenge of how to separate traffic. (For example, guest traffic should stay separated from intranet traffic.) Layer 3 designs also require careful planning with respect to IP addressing. A VLAN on one Layer 3 access device cannot be on another access layer switch in a different part of your network because each VLAN is globally significant. Traditionally, mobility of devices is limited in the campus network of the enterprise in Layer 3 access layer networks. without using an advanced mobility networking features.

Note   Modern technologies such as Dynamic Fabric Allocation (DFA) and ACI enable simplified mobility of devices while maintaining a scalable and resilient architecture. At the time of this writing, DFA and ACI were data center only technologies and beyond the scope of CCNP.

In summary, campus networks with Layer 3 in the access layer are becoming more popular. Moreover, next-generation architectures will alleviate the biggest problem with Layer 3 routing in the access layer: mobility.

The next subsection of this chapter applies the hierarchical model to an enterprise architecture.

The Cisco Enterprise Campus Architecture

The Cisco enterprise campus architecture refers to the traditional hierarchical campus network applied to the network design, as illustrated in Figure 2-9.

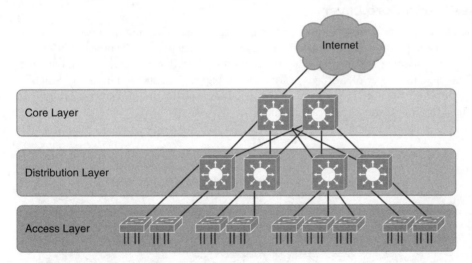

Figure 2-9   *Cisco Enterprise Campus Network*

The Cisco enterprise campus architecture divides the enterprise network into physical, logical, and functional areas while leveraging the hierarchical design. These areas allow network designers and engineers to associate specific network functionality on equipment that is based on its placement and function in the model.

Note that although the tiers do have specific roles in the design, no absolute rules apply to how a campus network is physically built. Although it is true that many campus networks are constructed by three physical tiers of switches, this is not a strict requirement. In a smaller campus, the network might have two tiers of switches in which the core and distribution elements are combined in one physical switch: a collapsed distribution and core. However, a network may have four or more physical tiers of switches because the scale, wiring plant, or physical geography of the network might require that the core be extended.

The hierarchy of the network often defines the physical topology of the switches, but they are not the same thing. The key principle of the hierarchical design is that each element in the hierarchy has a specific set of functions and services that it offers and a specific role to play in the design.

In reference to CCNP Switch, the access layer, the distribution layer, and core layer may be referred to as the *building access layer*, the *building distribution layer*, and the *building core layer*. The term *building* implies but does not limit the context of layers as physical buildings. As mentioned previously, the physical demarcation does not have to be a building; it can be a floor, group of floors, wiring closets, and so on. This book will solely use the terms *access layer*, *distribution layer*, and *core layer* for simplicity.

In summary, network architects build Cisco enterprise campus networks by leveraging the hierarchical model and dividing the layers by some physical or logical barrier. Although campus network designs go much further beyond the basic structure, the key takeaway of this section is that the access, distribution, and core layers are applied to either physical or logical barriers.

The Need for a Core Layer

When first studying campus network design, persons often question the need for a core layer. In a campus network contained with a few buildings or a similar physical infrastructure, collapsing the core into the distribution layer switches may save on initial cost because an entire layer of switches is not needed. Figure 2-10 shows a network design example where the core layer has been collapsed into the distribution layer by fully meshing the four distinct physical buildings.

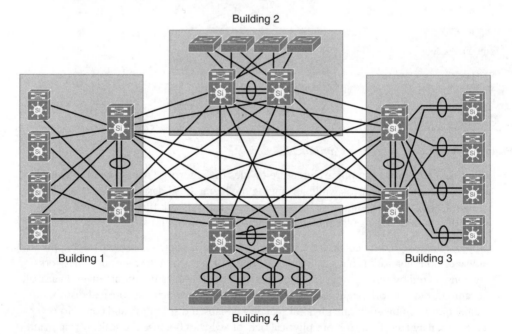

Figure 2-10 *Collapsed Core Design*

Despite a possible lower cost to the initial build, this design is difficult to scale. In addition, cabling requirements increase dramatically with each new building because of the need for full-mesh connectivity to all the distribution switches. The routing complexity also increases as new buildings are added because additional routing peers are needed.

With regard to Figure 2-10, the distribution module in the second building of two interconnected switches requires four additional links for full-mesh connectivity to the first module. A third distribution module to support the third building would require 8 additional links to support the connections to all the distribution switches, or a total of 12 links. A fourth module supporting the fourth building would require 12 new links for a total of 24 links between the distribution switches.

As illustrated in Figure 2-11, having a dedicated core layer allows the campus to accommodate growth without requiring full-mesh connectivity between the distribution layers. This is particularly important as the size of the campus grows either in number of distribution blocks, geographical area, or complexity. In a larger, more complex campus, the core provides the capacity and scaling capability for the campus as a whole and may house additional services such as security features.

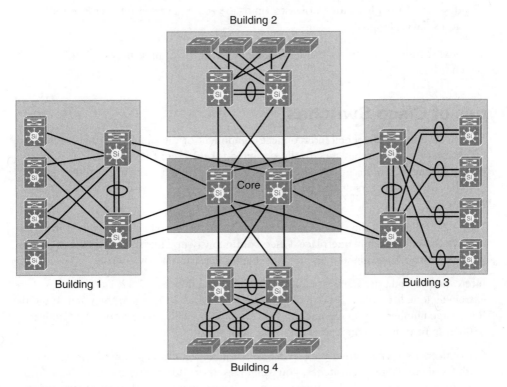

Figure 2-11 *Scaling with a Core Layer*

The question of when a separate physical core is necessary depends on multiple factors. The ability of a distinct core to allow the campus network to solve physical design challenges is important. However, remember that a key purpose of having a distinct campus core is to provide scalability and to minimize the risk from (and simplify) moves, adds, and changes in the campus network. In general, a network that requires routine configuration changes to the core devices does not yet have the appropriate degree of design modularization. As the network increases in size or complexity and changes begin to affect the core devices, it often points out design reasons for physically separating the core and distribution functions into different physical devices.

In brief, although design networks without a core layer may work at small scale, medium-sized to enterprise-sized networks, they require a core layer for design modularization and scalability.

In conclusion of the hierarchical model presented in this section, despite its age, the hierarchical model is still relevant to campus network designs. For review, the layers are described as follows:

■ The access layer connects end devices such as PCs, access points, printers, and so on to the network.

■ The distribution layer has multiple roles, but primarily aggregates the multiple access layers. The distribution may terminate VLANs in Layer 2 to the access layer designs or provide routing downstream to the access layer with Layer 3 to the access layer designs.

The next section delves into a major building block of the campus network: the Cisco switch itself.

Types of Cisco Switches

Switches are the fundamental interconnect component of the campus network. Cisco offers a variety of switches specifically designed for different functions. At the time of this writing, Cisco designs the Catalyst switches for campus networks and Nexus switches for data centers. In the context of CCNP, this book focuses mostly on Catalyst switches.

Figure 2-12 illustrates the current recommended Catalyst switches. However, in the competitive campus switch marketplace, Cisco continuously updates the Catalyst switches with new capabilities, higher performance, higher density, and lower cost.

Interesting enough, the Catalyst 6500 was not detailed in Figure 2-12. Despite its extremely long life cycle, Cisco marketing has finally shifted focus to the Catalyst 6800. For a large number of you reading this book, you have likely come across the Catalyst 6500 at some point in your career.

Cisco offers two types of network switches: fixed configuration and modular switches. With fixed configuration switches, you cannot swap or add another module, like you can with a modular switch. In enterprise access layers, you will find fixed configuration switches, like the Cisco Catalyst, 2960-X series. It offers a wide range of deployments.

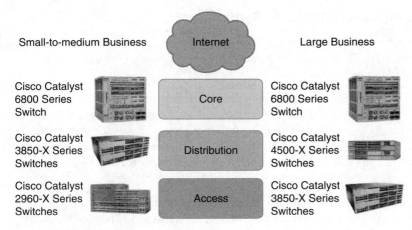

Figure 2-12 *Cisco Catalyst Switches*

In the enterprise distribution layer, you will find either fixed or modular switches depending on campus network requirements. An example of a modular switch that can be found in the distribution layer is the Cisco Catalyst 3850-X series. This series of switches allows you to select different network modules (Ethernet or fiber optic) and redundant power supply modules. In small businesses without a distribution layer, the 3850-X can be found in the core layer. In large enterprise networks, you might find 3850-X in the access layer in cases where high redundancy and full Layer 3 functionality at the access layer are requirements.

In the enterprise core layer, you will often find modular switches such as the Cisco Catalyst 6500 or the Catalyst 6800 series. With the 6800 switch, nearly every component, including the route processing/supervisor module and Ethernet models to power supplies) is individually installed in a chassis. This individualization allows for customization and high-availability options when necessary.

If you have a network where there is a lot of traffic, you have the option to leverage the Cisco Catalyst 4500-X series switches into the distribution layer. The Catalyst 4500-X supports supervisor/route process redundancy and supports 10 Gigabit Ethernet.

All switches within the 2960-X, 3850-X, 4500-X, and 6800-X series are managed. This means that you can configure an IP address on the device. By having a management IP address, you can connect to the device using Secure Shell (SSH) or Telnet and change device settings. An unmanaged switch is only appropriate for a home or very small business environment. It is highly recommended not to use an unmanaged switch in any campus network.

This section just described a few examples of Cisco switches and their placement in the network. For more information, go to http://www.cisco.com/c/en/us/products/switches/index.html.

The next section compares Layer 2 and Layer 3 (multilayer switches).

Comparing Layer 2 and Multilayer Switches

A Layer 2 Ethernet switch operates at the Data Link Layer of the OSI model. These types of switches make decisions about forwarding frames based on the destination MAC addresses found within the frame.

Recalling basic networking: A switch collision domain is only port to port because each switch port and its associated end device is its own collision domain. Because there is no contention on the media, all hosts can operate in full-duplex mode, which means that they can receive and transmit data at the same time. The concept of half duplex is legacy and applies only to hubs and older 10/100-Mbps switches, because 1 Gbps operates by default at full duplex.

When a switch receives in store-n-forward mode, the frame is checked for errors, and frames with a valid cyclic redundancy check (CRC) are regenerated and transmitted. Some models of switches, mostly Nexus switches, opt to switch frames based only on reading the Layer 2 information and bypassing the CRC check. This bypass, referred to as cut-through switching, lowers the latency of the frame transmission as the entire frame is not stored before transmission to another port. Lower switching latency is beneficial for low-latency applications such as algorithm trading programs found in the data center. The assumption is that the end device network interface card (NIC) or an upper-level protocol will eventually discard the bad frame. Most Catalyst switches are store-n-forward.

MAC Address Forwarding

To figure out where a frame must be sent, the switch will look up its MAC address table. This information can be told to the switch or it can learn it automatically. The switch listens to incoming frames and checks the source MAC addresses. If the address is not in the table already, the MAC address, switch port, and VLAN will then get recorded in the forwarding table. The forwarding table is also called the *CAM table*.

What happens if the destination MAC address of the frame is unknown to the switch? The switch then forwards the frame through all ports within a VLAN except the port the frame was received on. This is known as *unknown unicast flooding*. Broadcast and multicast traffic is destined for multiple destinations, so it will get flooded by default.

Referring to Figure 2-13, in the first example, the switch receives a frame on port 1. The destination MAC address for the frame is 0000.0000.5555. The switch will look up its forwarding table and figure out that MAC address 0000.0000.5555 is recorded on port 5. The switch will then forward the frame through port 5.

In the second example, the switch receives a broadcast frame on port 1. The switch will forward the frame through all ports that are within the same VLAN except port 1. The frame was received on port 1, which is in VLAN 1; therefore, the frame is forwarded through all ports on the switch that belong to VLAN 1 (all ports except port 3).

The next subsection discusses Layer 2 switch operation from a mechanics point of view.

CAM Table

MAC Address	Port	VLAN
0000.0000.1111	1	1
0000.0000.2222	2	1
0000.0000.6666	6	1
0000.0000.5555	5	1
0000.0000.3333	3	20
0000.0000.4444	4	1

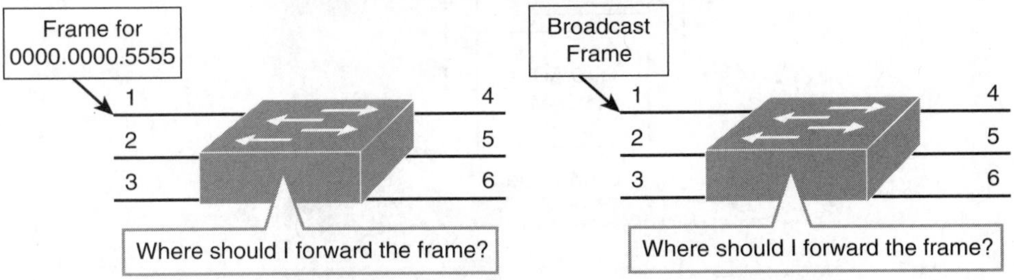

Figure 2-13 *Layer 2 Switching Operation: MAC Address Forwarding*

Layer 2 Switch Operation

When a switch receives a frame, it places the frame into an ingress queue. A port can have multiple ingress queues, and typically these queues are used to service frames differently (for example, apply quality of service [QoS]). From a simplified viewpoint, when the switch selects a frame from a queue to transmit, the switches need to answer a few questions:

- Where should the frame be forwarded?

- Are there restrictions preventing the forwarding of the frame?

- Is there any prioritization or marking that needs to be applied to the frame?

Decisions about these three questions are answered, respectively, as illustrated in Figure 2-14 and described in the list that follows.

- **Layer 2 forwarding table:** The Layer 2 forwarding table, also called the *MAC table*, contains information about where to forward the frame. Specifically, it contains MAC addresses and destination ports. The switches reference the destination MAC address of the incoming frame in the MAC table and forward the frames to the destination ports specified in the table. If the MAC address is not found, the frame is flooded through all ports in the same VLAN.

- **ACLs:** Access control lists (ACLs) do not only apply to routers. Switches can also apply ACLs based on MAC and IP addresses. Generally only higher-end switches support ACLs based on both MAC and IP addresses, whereas Layer 2 switches support port ACLs only with MAC addresses.

- **QoS:** Incoming frames can be classified according to QoS parameters. Traffic can then be marked, prioritized, or rate-limited.

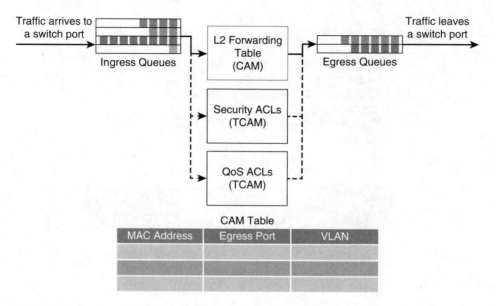

Figure 2-14   *Layer 2 Switch Operation: Mechanics*

Switches use specialized hardware to house the MAC table, ACL lookup data, and QoS lookup data. For the MAC table, switches use content-addressable memory (CAM), whereas the ACL and QoS tables are housed in ternary content-addressable memory (TCAM). Both CAM and TCAM are extremely fast access and allow for line-rate switching performance. CAM supports only two results: 0 or 1. Therefore, CAM is useful for Layer 2 forwarding tables.

TCAM provides three results: 0, 1, and don't care. TCAM is most useful for building tables for searching on longest matches, such as IP routing tables organized by IP prefixes. The TCAM table stores ACL, QoS, and other information generally associated with upper-layer processing. As a result of using TCAM, applying ACLs does not affect the performance of the switch.

This section only touches on the details and implementation of CAM and TCAM needed for the CCNP certification. For a more detailed description, review the following support document at Cisco.com:

> https://supportforums.cisco.com/document/60831/cam-vs-tcam
>
> https://www.pagiamtzis.com/cam/camintro

The next subsection discusses Layer 3 (multilayer) switch operation in more detail.

Layer 3 (Multilayer) Switch Operation

Multilayer switches not only perform Layer 2 switching but also forward frames based on Layer 3 and 4 information. Multilayer switches not only combine the functions of a switch and a router but also add a flow cache component.

Multilayer switches apply the same behavior as Layer 2 switches but add an additional parallel lookup for how to route a packet, as illustrated in Figure 2-15.

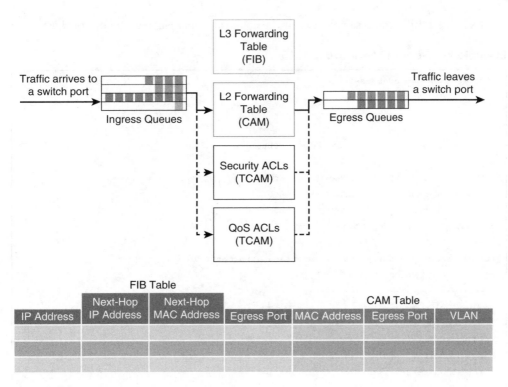

Figure 2-15 *Multilayer Switch Operation*

The associated table for Layer 3 lookups is called a *FIB table*. The FIB table contains not only egress ports and VLAN information but also MAC rewrite information. The ACL and QoS parallel lookups happen the same as Layer 2 switches, except there may be additional support for Layer 3 ACLs and QoS prioritization.

For example, a Layer 2 switch may only be able to apply to rate-limiting frames based on source or destination MAC addresses, whereas a multilayer switch generally supports rate-limiting frames on IP/MAC addresses.

Unfortunately, different models of Cisco switches support different capabilities, and some Layer 2-only switches actually support Layer 3 ACLs and QoS lookups. It is best to consult the product documentation at Cisco.com for clear information about what your switch supports. For the purpose of CCNP Switch and the context of this book, Layer 2 switches support ACLs and QoS based on MAC addresses, whereas Layer 3 switches support ACLs and QoS based on IP or MAC addresses.

Useful Commands for Viewing and Editing Catalyst Switch MAC Address Tables

There is one command for viewing the Layer 2 forwarding table on Catalyst and Nexus switches: **show mac address-table**. The table has many optional parameters to narrow the output to a more manageable result in large networks. The full command options are as follows: **show mac-address-table [aging-time | count | dynamic | static] [address** *hw-addr*] **[interface** *interface-id*] **[vlan** *vlan-id*] **[| {begin | exclude | include}** *expression*].

Example 2-1 illustrates sample uses of the command and several useful optional uses.

Example 2-1 *Layer 2 Forwarding Table*

```
Switch1# show mac address-table
          Mac Address Table
-------------------------------------------


Vlan    Mac Address        Type        Ports
----    -----------        --------    -----
   1    0000:0c00.9001     DYNAMIC     Et0/1
   1    0000.0c00.9002     DYNAMIC     Et0/2
   1    0000.0c00.9002     DYNAMIC     Et0/3
Total Mac Addresses for this criterion: 3


Switch1# show mac address-table interface ethernet 0/1
          Mac Address Table
-------------------------------------------


Vlan    Mac Address        Type        Ports
----    -----------        --------    -----
   1    0000:0c00.9001     DYNAMIC     Et0/1
Total Mac Addresses for this criterion: 1


Switch1# show mac address-table | include 9001
   1    0000:0c00.9001     DYNAMIC     Et0/1
```

Frame Rewrite

From your CCNA studies, you know that many fields of a packet must be rewritten when the packets are routed between subnets. These fields include both source and destination MAC addresses, the IP header checksum, the TTL (Time-to-Live), and the trailer checksum (Ethernet CRC). See Chapter 1, "Fundamentals Review," for an example.

Distributed Hardware Forwarding

Network devices contain at least three planes of operation:

- Management plane
- Control plane
- Forwarding plane

The management plane is responsible for the network management, such as SSH access and SNMP, and may operate over an out-of-band (OOB) port. The control plane is responsible for protocols and routing decisions, and the forwarding plane is responsible for the actual routing (or switching) of most packets.

Multilayer switches must achieve high performance at line rate across a large number of ports. To do so, multilayer switches deploy independent control and forwarding planes. In this manner, the control plane will program the forwarding plane on how to route packets. Multilayer switches may also employ multiple forwarding planes. For example, a Catalyst 6800 uses forwarding planes on each line module, with a central control plane on the supervisor module.

To continue the example of the Catalyst 6800, each line module includes a microcoded processor that handles all packet forwarding. For the control plane on the supervisor to communicate with the line module, a control layer communication protocol exists, as shown in Figure 2-16.

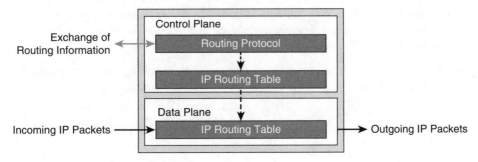

Figure 2-16 *Distributed Hardware Forwarding*

The main functions of this control layer protocol between the control plane and the forwarding plane are as follows:

- Managing the internal data and control circuits for the packet-forwarding and control functions

- Extracting the other routing and packet-forwarding-related control information from the Layer 2 and Layer 3 bridging and routing protocols and the configuration data, and then conveying the information to the interface module for control of the data path

- Collecting the data path information, such as traffic statistics, from the interface module to the route processor

- Handling certain data packets that are sent from the Ethernet interface modules to the route processor (for example, DCHP requests, broadcast packets, routing protocol packets)

Cisco Switching Methods

The term *Cisco switching methods* describes the route processor behavior found on Cisco IOS routers. Because multilayer switches are capable of routing and, in fact, contain a routing process, a review of these concepts is necessary.

A Cisco IOS-based router uses one of three methods to forward packets: process switching, fast switching, and Cisco Express Forwarding (CEF). Recall from your study of

routers that process switching is the slowest form of routing because the router processor must route and rewrite using software. Because speed and the number of cores limit
the route processor, this method does not scale. The second method, fast switching, is
a faster method by which the first packet in a flow is routed and rewritten by a route
processor using software, and each subsequent packet is then handled by hardware. The
CEF method uses hardware forwarding tables for most common traffic flows, with only
a few exceptions. If you use CEF, the route processor spends its cycles mostly on other
tasks.

The architecture of the Cisco Catalyst and Nexus switches both focus primarily on the
Cisco router equivalents of CEF. The absolute last-resort switching method for Cisco
Catalyst or Nexus switches is process switching. The route processors of these switches
were never designed to switch or route packets, and by doing so, this will have an
adverse effect on performance. Fortunately, the default behavior of these switches is to
use fast switching or CEF, and process switching occurs only when necessary.

With Cisco Catalyst switching terminology, fast switching is referred to as *route caching*, and the application of CEF with distributed hardware forwarding is referred to as
topology-based switching.

As a review, the following list summarizes route caching and topology-based forwarding
on Cisco Catalyst switches:

- **Route caching:** Also known as *flow-based* or *demand-based switching*, route caching describes a Layer 3 route cache that is built within the hardware functions as the
  switch detects traffic flow into the switch. This method is functionally equivalent to
  fast switching in Cisco IOS Software.

- **Topology-based switching:** Information from the routing table is used to populate
  the route cache, regardless of traffic flow. The populated route cache is the FIB,
  and CEF is the facility that builds the FIB. This method is functionally equivalent to
  CEF in Cisco IOS Software.

The next subsections describe route caching and topology-based switching in more
detail.

Route Caching

Route caching is the fast switching equivalent in Cisco Catalyst switches. For route
caching to operate, the destination MAC address of an incoming frame must be that of
a switch interface with Layer 3 capabilities. The first packet in a stream is switched in
software by the route processor, because no cache entry exists yet for the new flow.
The forwarding decision that is made by the route processor is then programmed into a
cache table (the hardware forwarding table), and all subsequent packets in the flow are
switched in the hardware, commonly referred to as using *application-specific interface
circuits* (ASICs). Entries are created only in the hardware forwarding table as the switch
detects new traffic flows, and entries will time out after they have been unused for a
period of time.

Because entries are created only in the hardware cache as flows are detected by the switch, route caching will always forward at least one packet in a flow using software.

Route caching carries many other names, such as NetfFow LAN switching, flow-based or demand-based switching, and route once, switch many.

Figure 2-17 briefly highlights this concept from a hardware perspective.

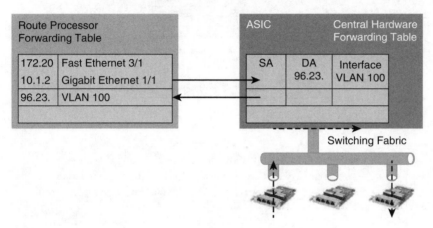

Figure 2-17   *Route Caching*

Topology-Based Switching

Topology-based switching is the CEF equivalent feature of Cisco Catalyst switches. Topology-based switching is ideal for Layer 3 switching over route caching because it offers the best performance and scalability. Fortunately, all Cisco Catalyst switches capable of Layer 3 routing leverage topology-based switching / CEF. For the purpose of CCNP Switch, focus primarily on the benefits and operation of topology-based switching.

CEF uses information in the routing table to populate a route cache (known as an FIB), without traffic flows being necessary to initiate the caching process. Because this hardware FIB exists regardless of traffic flow, assuming that a destination address has a route in the routing table, all packets that are part of a flow will be forwarded by the hardware. The FIB even handles the first packet of a flow. Figure 2-18 illustrates this behavior.

In addition, CEF adds enhanced support for parallel paths and thus optimizes load balancing at the IP layer. In most current-generation Catalyst switches, such as the Catalyst 4500 and 6800, CEF supports both load balancing based on source IP address and destination IP address combination and source and destination IP plus TCP/UDP port number.

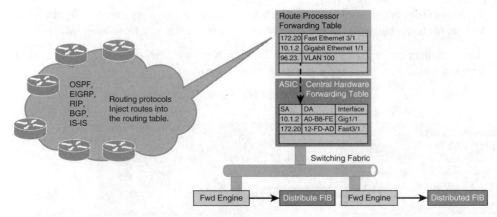

Figure 2-18   *Topology-Based Switching*

Note   The load-balancing options and default behavior varies between different Catalyst switch models and software versions. Consult Cisco.com for the particular Catalyst switch you have in question for supported load-balancing methods and default configurations.

CEF load-balancing schemes allow for Layer 3 switches to use multiple paths to achieve load sharing. Packets for a given source-destination host pair are guaranteed to take the same path, even if multiple paths are available. This ensures that packets for a given host pair arrive in order, which in some cases may be the desired behavior with legacy applications.

Moreover, load balancing based only on source and destination IP address has a few shortcomings. Because this load-balancing method always selects the same path for a given host pair, a heavily used source-destination pair, such as a firewall to web server, might not leverage all available links. In other words, the behavior of this load-balancing scheme may "polarize" the traffic by using only one path for a given host pair, thus effectively negating the load-balancing benefit of the multiple paths for that particular host pair.

So, optimal use of any load-balancing scheme depends on the statistical distribution of traffic because source and destination IP load sharing becomes more effective as the number of source-destination IP pairs increases. In an environment where there is a broad distribution of traffic among host pairs, polarization is of minimal concern. However, in an environment where the data flow between a small number of host pairs creates a disproportionate percentage of the packets traversing the network, polarization can become a serious problem.

A popular alternative that is now the default behavior in new Catalyst switches is load balancing based on source and destination IP to include TCP/UDP port numbers. The more additional factors added to the load-balancing scheme, the less likely polarization will exist.

Cisco Catalyst supports additional load-balancing methods and features by which to tune load balancing based on hardware model and software version. Consult Cisco.com for such configuration optimizations if necessary.

Hardware Forward Details

The actual Layer 3 switching of packets occurs at two possible different locations on Catalyst switches. These possible locations are in a centralized manner, such as on a supervisor module, or in distributed fashion, where switching occurs on individual line modules. These methods are referred to as *centralized switching* and *distributed switching*, respectively.

The Catalyst 6500 was a perfect example where there was an option to centralize switch everything on the supervisor or place specific hardware versions of line modules in the chassis to gain distributed switching capability.

The benefits of centralized switching include lower hardware cost and lower complexity. For scaling and large enterprise core networks, distributed switching is optimal. Most small form-factor switches leverage centralized switching.

Note   Some small form-factor switches may leverage a switch-on-chip (SOC) concept, where the entire intelligence and processing of the switch happens on a single low-cost ASIC. This practice has now become an industry standard for low-feature and low-cost switches and is found on specific fixed-port Cisco Catalyst and Nexus switches. In addition, newer generation modular switches such as the Nexus 9000 may leverage SOC in a hybrid capacity, whereas line modules may contain their own SOC and leverage distributed switching concepts.

In conclusion, the subsections of this chapter pertaining to switching methods and hardware forwarding included many specific details about routing and switching operations on Cisco switches. Among all the lengthy explanations and details, conclude this section with the following concepts:

- The control plane (CPU/route processor) of a Cisco Catalyst was never designed to route or switch frames. The control plane is intended only to populate hardware tables with routing information and maintain routing protocols. The control plane may route frames in a few exception conditions.

- Medium- to high-end Cisco Catalyst switches were designed based on the distributing forward model to scale to demands of campus and data center networks.

- Cisco Catalyst switches leverage CEF (topology-based switching) for routing of frames as a means to implement a distributing hardware forwarding model.

- Cisco Catalyst switches use either a centralized method or a distributed line module method of hardware forwarding, depending on specific platform model and configuration.

Study Tips

- The **show mac address-table** command displays the Layer 2 forwarding table of a Cisco switch.

- Layer 2 switches forward traffic based on the destination MAC address of a frame.

- Campus network designs are still built upon the hierarchical model, where end devices connect to the access layer, the distribution layer aggregates the access layer, and the core aggregates the entire enterprise network.

- Cisco switches leverage CEF (topology-based switching) for Layer 3 forwarding.

Summary

This chapter briefly introduced some concepts about campus networks, including the hierarchical model, benefits of Layer 3 routing the access, Cisco switches, and some hardware details related to Cisco Catalyst switches. The next chapters of this book go into more detail about specific feature and design elements of the campus network, such as VLANs, spanning tree, and security. The information in this chapter is summarized as follows:

- Flat Layer 2 networks are extremely limited in scale and in most cases will only scale to 10 to 20 end users before adverse conditions may occur.

- Despite its age, the hierarchical model continues to be a key design fundamental of any network design, including campus network designs.

- The hierarchical model consists of an access, distribution, and core layer, thus allowing for scalability and growth of a campus network in a seamless manner.

- The different models of Cisco Catalyst switches provide for a range of capabilities depending on need and placement within the hierarchical model.

- Cisco Catalyst switches leverage CAM for Layer 2 forwarding tables and TCAM for Layer 3 forwarding tables to achieve line-rate performance.

- Cisco Catalyst switches leverage CEF (topology-based switching) for routing, utilizing a distributed hardware forwarding model that is centralized or distributed per line card.

Review Questions

Use the questions in this section as a review of what you have learned in this chapter. The correct answers are found in Appendix A, "Answers to Chapter Review Questions."

1. Which of the following statements is true about campus networks?

    a. The campus network describes the interconnections of servers in a data center.

    b. The campus network describes the WAN interconnectivity between two remote sites and head office.

    c. The campus network describes the network devices that interconnect end users to applications such as e-mail, the intranet, or the Internet over wire or wireless connections.

2. Which of the following is a disadvantage to using flat Layer 2 networks?

    a. Broadcast packets are flooded to every device in the network.

    b. No IP boundary to administer IP-based access control.

    c. A host flooding traffic onto the network effects every device.

    d. Scalability is limited.

    e. All the above

3. Why are networks designed with layers?

    a. Allows focus within specific layers due to grouping, segmentation, and compartmentalization

    b. Simplification of network design

    c. Optimizes use of physical interconnects (links)

    d. Optimizes application of policies and access control

    e. Eases network management

    f. All of the above

4. Identify the three layers of the hierarchical model for designing networks.

    a. Core

    b. Access

    c. Distribution

    d. Enterprise edge

    e. WAN

    f. Wireless

5. What is another common name for the core layer?

 a. Backbone

 b. Campus

 c. Data center

 d. Routing layer

6. In newer terminology, what layers are referred to as the spine layer and the leaf layer?

 a. The spine layer is the equivalent to the core layer, and the leaf layer is equivalent to the distribution layer.

 b. The spine layer is equivalent to the access layer, and the leaf layer is equivalent to the distribution layer.

 c. The spine layer is equivalent to the distribution layer, and the leaf layer is equivalent to the access layer.

 d. The spine layer is equivalent to the core layer, and the leaf layer is equivalent to the access layer.

7. Match each layer to its definition.

 a. Core

 b. Distribution

 c. Access

   1. Connects PCs, wireless access points, and IP phones

   2. High-speed interconnectivity layer that generally supports routing capability

   3. Aggregates access layer switches and provides for policy control

8. Which of the following are generally true about recommended core layer designs?

 a. Requires high-availability and resiliency

 b. Connects critical application servers directly for optimal latency and bandwidth

 c. Leverages fixed form factor switches in large enterprises

9. In which layer are you most likely to find fixed Catalyst switches?

 a. Access layer

 b. Core layer

 c. Distribution layer

10. In which layer are you most likely to find modular Catalyst switches?

   a. Access layer

   b. Backbone layer

   c. Core layer

11. Which of the following are benefits to using Layer 3 in the access layer? (Choose two.)

   a. Reduced cost

   b. Reduced Layer 2 domain

   c. Reduced spanning-tree domain

   d. Mobility

12. Which of the following is the biggest disadvantage with using Layer 3 in the access layer using current technologies?

   a. More difficult troubleshooting

   b. Lack of broadcast forwarding

   c. Native mobility without additional features

   d. Lack of high availability

13. A Layer 2-only switch makes forwarding decisions based on what?

   a. Source MAC address

   b. Destination MAC address

   c. Source IP address

   d. Destination IP address

14. What does a switch do when it does not know how to forward a frame?

   a. Drops the frame

   b. Floods the frames on all ports in the same Layer 2 domain except the source port

   c. Stores the frame for later transmission

   d. Resends the frame out the port where it was received

15. The Layer 2 forwarding table of Cisco switches is also referred to as which of the following?

   a. CAM table

   b. Routing table

   c. MAC address table

   d. FIB table

16. Which of the following lookups does a Layer 2-only Cisco Catalyst switch perform on an ingress frame?

   a. Layer 2 forwarding for destination port

   b. ACL for access control

   c. NetFlow for statistics monitoring

   d. QoS for classification, marking, or policing

17. Which of the following are true about CAM and/or TCAM? (Choose three.)

   a. TCAM stands for ternary content-addressable memory.

   b. CAM provides three results: 0, 1, and don't care.

   c. Leveraging CAM and TCAM ensures line-rate performance of the switch.

   d. CAM and TCAM are software-based tables.

   e. TCAM is leveraged by QoS and ACL tables.

18. Why is TCAM necessary for IP routing tables over CAM?

   a. TCAM supports longest matching instead of match or not match.

   b. TCAM is faster than CAM.

   c. TCAM memory is cheaper than CAM.

19. Cisco Catalyst switches leverage which of the following technologies for Layer 3 forwarding?

   a. Route caching

   b. Processor/CPU switching

   c. NetFlow

   d. CEF

20. Cisco Catalyst switches relay routing information to hardware components for additional performance and scalability (line-rate forwarding). What are the two common hardware types that receive relayed routing information?

   a. Centralized

   b. Distributed

   c. Aggregated

   d. Core-based

21. With regard to load balancing, what term describes the situation where less than optimal use of all links occurs?

   a. Reverse path forwarding (RPF)

   b. Polarization

   c. Inverse routing

   d. Unicast flooding

22. What is the default load-balancing mechanism found on Cisco Catalyst switches?

   a. Per-flow

   b. Per-destination IP address

   c. Per-packet

   d. Per-destination MAC address

Chapter 3

Campus Network Architecture

This chapter covers the following topics:

- Implementing VLANs and trunks in campus switched architecture
- Understanding the concept of VTP and its limitation and configurations
- Implementing and configuring EtherChannel

This chapter covers the key concepts of VLANs, trunking, and EtherChannel to build the campus switched networks. Knowing the function of VLANs and trunks and how to configure them is the core knowledge needed for building a campus switched network. VLANs can span across the whole network, or they can be configured to remain local. Also, VLANs play a critical role in the deployment of voice and wireless networks. Even though you might not be a specialist at one of those two fields, it is important to understand basics because both voice and wireless often rely on a basic switched network.

Once VLANs are created, their names and descriptions are stored in a VLAN database, with the exception of specific VLANs such as VLANs in the extended range in Cisco IOS for the Catalyst 6500. A mechanism called *VLAN Trunking Protocol* (VTP) dynamically distributes this information between switches. However, even if network administrators do not plan to enable VTP, it is important to consider its consequences.

EtherChannel can be used to bundle physical links in one virtual link, thus increasing throughput. There are multiple ways traffic can be distributed over the physical link within the EtherChannel.

Implementing VLANs and Trunks in Campus Environment

Within the switched internetwork, VLANs provide segmentation and organizational flexibility. VLANs help administrators to have the end node or workstations group that are segmented logically by functions, project teams, and applications, without regard to the physical location of the users. In addition, VLANs allow you to implement access and security policies to particular groups of users and limit the broadcast domain.

In addition, the voice VLAN feature enables access ports to carry IP voice traffic from an IP phone. Because the sound quality of an IP phone call can deteriorate if the data is unevenly sent, the switch supports quality of service (QoS).

This section discusses in detail how to plan, implement, and verify VLAN technologies and address schemes to meet the given business and technical requirements along with constraints. This ability includes being able to meet these objectives:

- Describe the different VLAN segmentation models
- Identify the basic differences between end-to-end and local VLANs
- Describe the benefits and drawbacks of local VLANs versus end-to-end VLANs
- Configure and verify VLANs
- Implement a trunk in a campus network
- Configure and verify trunks
- Explain switchport mode interactions
- Describe voice VLANs
- Configure voice VLANs

VLAN Overview

A VLAN is a logical broadcast domain that can span multiple physical LAN segments. Within the switched internetwork, VLANs provide segmentation and organizational flexibility. A VLAN can exist on a single switch or span multiple switches. VLANs can include (hosts or endnotes) stations in a single building or multiple-building infrastructures. As shown in Figure 3-1, sales, human resources, and engineering are three different VLANs spread across all three floors.

The Cisco Catalyst switch implements VLANs by only forwarding traffic to destination ports that are in the same VLAN as the originating ports. Each VLAN on the switches implements address learning, forwarding, and filtering decisions and loop-avoidance mechanisms, just as though the VLAN were a separate physical switch.

Ports in the same VLAN share broadcasts. Ports in different VLANs do not share broadcasts, as illustrated in Figure 3-2, where a PC 3 and PC 4 cannot ping because they are in different VLANs, whereas PC 1 and PC 2 can ping each other because they are part of the same VLAN. Containing broadcasts within a VLAN improves the overall performance of the network. Because a VLAN is a single broadcast domain, campus design best practices recommend mapping a VLAN generally to one IP subnet. To communicate between VLANs, packets need to pass through a router or Layer 3 device.

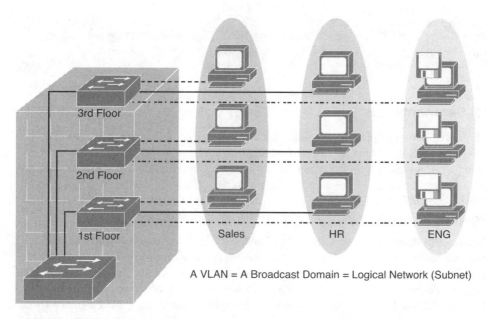

Figure 3-1   *VLAN Overview*

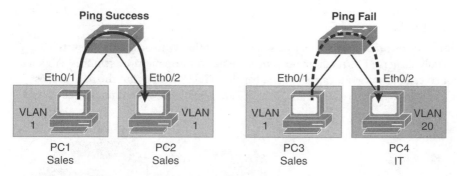

- VLAN is an independent LAN network.
- VLAN = broadcast domain.
- VLAN maps to logical network (subnet).
- VLANs provide segmentation, security, and network flexibility.

Figure 3-2   *VLAN Broadcast Domain*

Note   Inter-VLAN routing is discussed in detail in Chapter 5, "Inter-VLAN Routing." Generally, a port carries traffic only for the single VLAN. For a VLAN to span multiple switches, Catalyst switches use trunks. A trunk carries traffic for multiple VLANs by using Inter-Switch Link (ISL) encapsulation or IEEE 802.1Q. This chapter discusses trunking in more detail in later sections. Because VLANs are an important aspect of any campus design, almost all Cisco devices support VLANs and trunking.

> **Note**   Most of the Cisco products support only 802.1Q trunking because 802.1Q is the industry standard. This book focuses only on 802.1Q.

VLAN Segmentation

Larger flat networks generally consist of many end devices in which broadcasts and unknown unicast packets are flooded on all ports in the network. One advantage of using VLANs is the capability to segment the Layer 2 broadcast domain. All devices in a VLAN are members of the same broadcast domain. If an end device transmits a Layer 2 broadcast, all other members of the VLAN receive the broadcast. Switches filter the broadcast from all the ports or devices that are not part of the same VLAN.

In a campus design, a network administrator can design a campus network with one of two models: end-to-end VLANs or local VLANs. Business and technical requirements, past experience, and political motivations can influence the design chosen. Choosing the right model initially can help create a solid foundation upon which to grow the business. Each model has its own advantages and disadvantages. When configuring a switch for an existing network, try to determine which model is used so that you can understand the logic behind each switch configuration and position in the infrastructure.

End-to-End VLANs

The term *end-to-end VLAN* refers to a single VLAN that is associated with switch ports widely dispersed throughout an enterprise network on multiple switches. A Layer 2 switched campus network carries traffic for this VLAN throughout the network, as shown in Figure 3-3, where VLANs 1, 2, and 3 are spread across all three switches.

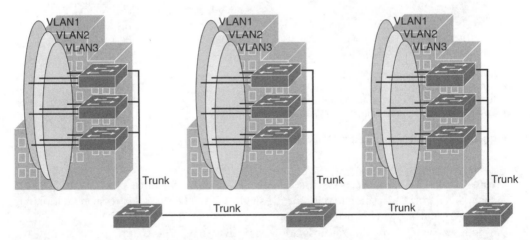

Figure 3-3   *End to End VLAN*

If more than one VLAN in a network is operating in the end-to-end mode, special links (Layer 2 trunks) are required between switches to carry the traffic of all the different VLANs.

An end-to-end VLAN model has the following characteristics:

- Each VLAN is dispersed geographically throughout the network.

- Users are grouped into each VLAN regardless of the physical location.

- As a user moves throughout a campus, the VLAN membership of that user remains the same, regardless of the physical switch to which this user attaches.

- Users are typically associated with a given VLAN for network management reasons. This is why they are kept in the same VLAN, therefore the same group, as they move through the campus.

- All devices on a given VLAN typically have addresses on the same IP subnet.

- Switches commonly operate in a server/client VTP mode.

Local VLANs

The campus enterprise architecture is based on the local VLAN model. In a local VLAN model, all users of a set of geographically common switches are grouped into a single VLAN, regardless of the organizational function of those users. Local VLANs are generally confined to a wiring closet, as shown in Figure 3-4. In other words, these VLANs are local to a single access switch and connect via a trunk to an upstream distribution switch. If users move from one location to another in the campus, their connection changes to the new VLAN at the new physical location.

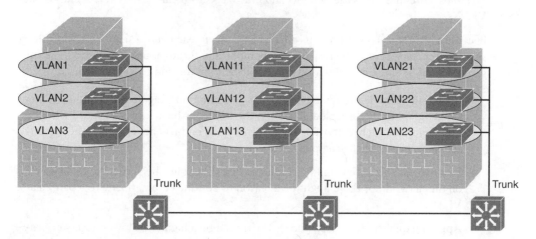

Figure 3-4 *Local VLANs*

In the local VLAN model, Layer 2 switching is implemented at the access level, and routing is implemented at the distribution and core level, as shown in Figure 2-4, to enable users to maintain access to the resources they need. An alternative design is to extend routing to the access layer, and links between the access switches and distribution switches are routed links.

The following are some local VLAN characteristics and user guidelines:

■ The network administrator should create local VLANs with physical boundaries in mind rather than the job functions of the users on the end devices.

■ Generally, local VLANs exist between the access and distribution levels.

■ Traffic from a local VLAN is routed at the distribution and core levels to reach destinations on other networks.

■ Configure the VTP mode in transparent mode because VLANs on a given access switch should not be advertised to all other switches in the network, nor do they need to be manually created in any other switch VLAN databases.

Note   VTP is discussed in more detail later in this chapter.

■ A network that consists entirely of local VLANs can benefit from increased convergence times offered via routing protocols, instead of a spanning tree for Layer 2 networks. It is usually recommended to have one to three VLANs per access layer switch.

Comparison of End-to-End VLANs and Local VLANs

This subsection describes the benefits and drawbacks of local VLANs versus end-to-end VLANs.

Because a VLAN usually represents a Layer 3 segment, each end-to-end VLAN enables a single Layer 3 segment to be dispersed geographically throughout the network. The following could be some of the reasons for implementing the end-to-end design:

■ **Grouping users:** Users can be grouped on a common IP segment, even though they are geographically dispersed. Recently, the trend has been moving toward virtualization. Solutions such as those from VMware need end-to-end VLANs to be spread across segments of the campus.

■ **Security:** A VLAN can contain resources that should not be accessible to all users on the network, or there might be a reason to confine certain traffic to a particular VLAN.

■ **Applying quality of service (QoS):** Traffic can be a higher- or lower-access priority to network resources from a given VLAN. Note that QoS may also be applied without the use of VLANs.

■ **Routing avoidance:** If much of the VLAN user traffic is destined for devices on that same VLAN, and routing to those devices is not desirable, users can access resources on their VLAN without their traffic being routed off the VLAN, even though the traffic might traverse multiple switches.

■ **Special-purpose VLAN:** Sometimes a VLAN is provisioned to carry a single type of traffic that must be dispersed throughout the campus (for example, multicast, voice, or visitor VLANs).

■ **Poor design:** For no clear purpose, users are placed in VLANs that span the campus or even span WANs. Sometimes when a network is already configured and running, organizations are hesitant to improve the design because of downtime or other political reasons.

The following list details some considerations that the network administrators should consider when implementing end-to-end VLANs:

■ Switch ports are provisioned for each user and associated with a given VLAN. Because users on an end-to-end VLAN can be anywhere in the network, all switches must be aware of that VLAN. This means that all switches carrying traffic for end-to-end VLANs are required to have those specific VLANs defined in each switch's VLAN database.

■ Also, flooded traffic for the VLAN is, by default, passed to every switch even if it does not currently have any active ports in the particular end-to-end VLAN.

■ Finally, troubleshooting devices on a campus with end-to-end VLANs can be challenging because the traffic for a single VLAN can traverse multiple switches in a large area of the campus, and that can easily cause potential spanning-tree problems.

Based on the data presented in this section, there are many reasons to implement end-to-end VLANs. The main reason to implement local VLANs is simplicity. Local VLAN configures are quick and easy for small-scale networks.

Mapping VLANs to a Hierarchical Network

In the past, network designers have attempted to implement the 80/20 rule when designing networks. The rule was based on the observation that, in general, 80 percent of the traffic on a network segment was passed between local devices, and only 20 percent of the traffic was destined for remote network segments. Therefore, network architecture used to prefer end-to-end VLANs. To avoid the complications of end-to-end VLANs, designers now consolidate servers in central locations on the network and provide access to external resources, such as the Internet, through one or two paths on the network because the bulk of traffic now traverses a number of segments. Therefore, the paradigm now is closer to a 20/80 proportion, in which the greater flow of traffic leaves the local segment; so, local VLANs have become more efficient.

In addition, the concept of end-to-end VLANs was attractive when IP address configuration was a manually administered and burdensome process; therefore, anything that reduced this burden as users moved between networks was an improvement. However, given the ubiquity of Dynamic Host Configuration Protocol (DHCP), the process of configuring an IP address at each desktop is no longer a significant issue. As a result, there are few benefits to extending a VLAN throughout an enterprise (for example, if there are some clustering and other requirements).

Local VLANs are part of the enterprise campus architecture design, as shown in Figure 3-4, in which VLANs used at the access layer should extend no further than their associated distribution switch. For example, VLANs 1, 10 and VLANs 2, 20 are confined to only a local access switch. Traffic is then routed out the local VLAN as to the distribution layer and then to the core depending on the destination. It is usually recommended to have two to three VLANs per access block rather than span all the VLANs across all access blocks. This design can mitigate Layer 2 troubleshooting issues that occur when a single VLAN traverses the switches throughout a campus network. In addition, because Spanning Tree Protocol (STP) is configured for redundancy, the switch limits the STP to only the access and distribution switches that help to reduce the network complexity in times of failure.

Implementing the enterprise campus architecture design using local VLANs provides the following benefits:

- **Deterministic traffic flow:** The simple layout provides a predictable Layer 2 and Layer 3 traffic path. If a failure occurs that was not mitigated by the redundancy features, the simplicity of the model facilitates expedient problem isolation and resolution within the switch block.

- **Active redundant paths:** When implementing Per-VLAN Spanning Tree (PVST) or Multiple Spanning Tree (MST) because there is no loop, all links can be used to make use of the redundant paths.

- **High availability:** Redundant paths exist at all infrastructure levels. Local VLAN traffic on access switches can be passed to the building distribution switches across an alternative Layer 2 path if a primary path failure occurs. Router redundancy protocols can provide failover if the default gateway for the access VLAN fails. When both the STP instance and VLAN are confined to a specific access and distribution block, Layer 2 and Layer 3 redundancy measures and protocols can be configured to failover in a coordinated manner.

- **Finite failure domain:** If VLANs are local to a switch block, and the number of devices on each VLAN is kept small, failures at Layer 2 are confined to a small subset of users.

- **Scalable design:** Following the enterprise campus architecture design, new access switches can be easily incorporated, and new submodules can be added when necessary.

Implementing a Trunk in a Campus Environment

A trunk is a point-to-point link that carries the traffic for multiple VLANs across a single physical link between the two switches or any two devices. Trunking is used to extend Layer 2 operations across an entire network, such as end-to-end VLANs, as shown in Figure 3-5. PC 1 in VLAN 1 can communicate with the host in VLAN 21 on another switch over the single trunk link, the same as a host in VLAN 20 can communicate with a host in another switch in VLAN 20.

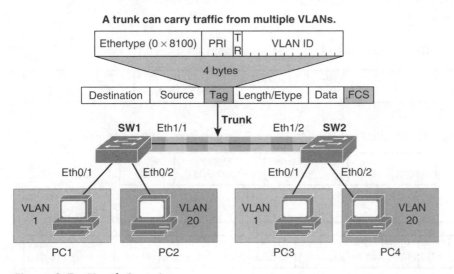

Figure 3-5   *Trunk Overview*

As discussed earlier in this chapter, to allow a switch port that connects two switches to carry more than one VLAN, it must be configured as a trunk. If frames from a single VLAN traverse a trunk link, a trunking protocol must mark the frame to identify its associated VLAN as the frame is placed onto the trunk link. The receiving switch then knows the frame's VLAN origin and can process the frame accordingly. On the receiving switch, the VLAN ID (VID) is removed when the frame is forwarded on to an access link associated with its VLAN.

A special protocol is used to carry multiple VLANs over a single link between two devices. There are two trunking technologies:

■ **Inter-Switch Link (ISL):** A Cisco proprietary trunking encapsulation

■ **IEEE 802.1Q:** An industry-standard trunking method

Note   ISL is a Cisco proprietary implementation. It is not widely used anymore.

When configuring an 802.1Q trunk, a matching native VLAN must be defined on each end of the trunk link. A trunk link is inherently associated with tagging each frame with a VID. The purpose of the native VLAN is to enable frames that are not tagged with a VID to traverse the trunk link. Native VLAN is discussed in more detail in a later part of this section.

Because the ISL protocol is almost obsolete, this book focuses only on 802.1Q. Figure 3-6 depicts how ISL encapsulates the normal Ethernet frame. Currently, all Catalyst switches support 802.1Q tagging for multiplexing traffic from multiple VLANs onto a single physical link.

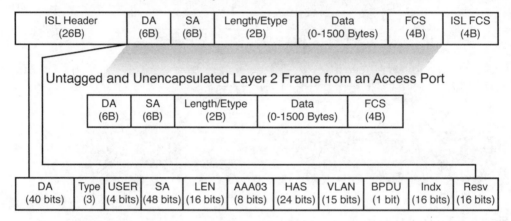

ISL Encapsulated Layer 2 Frame from an ISL Trunk Port

ISL Header (26B)	DA (6B)	SA (6B)	Length/Etype (2B)	Data (0-1500 Bytes)	FCS (4B)	ISL FCS (4B)

Untagged and Unencapsulated Layer 2 Frame from an Access Port

DA (6B)	SA (6B)	Length/Etype (2B)	Data (0-1500 Bytes)	FCS (4B)

DA (40 bits)	Type (3)	USER (4 bits)	SA (48 bits)	LEN (16 bits)	AAA03 (8 bits)	HAS (24 bits)	VLAN (15 bits)	BPDU (1 bit)	Indx (16 bits)	Resv (16 bits)

Figure 3-6 *ISL Frame*

IEEE 802.1Q trunk links employ the tagging mechanism to carry frames for multiple VLANs, in which each frame is tagged to identify the VLAN to which the frame belongs. Figure 3-7 shows the layout of the 802.1Q frame.

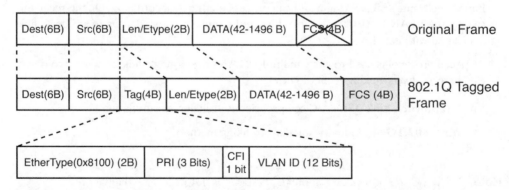

Dest(6B)	Src(6B)	Len/Etype(2B)	DATA(42-1496 B)	FCS(4B)	Original Frame

Dest(6B)	Src(6B)	Tag(4B)	Len/Etype(2B)	DATA(42-1496 B)	FCS (4B)	802.1Q Tagged Frame

EtherType(0x8100) (2B)	PRI (3 Bits)	CFI 1 bit	VLAN ID (12 Bits)

Figure 3-7 *802.1Q Frame*

The IEEE 802.1Q/802.1p standard provides the following inherent architectural advantages over ISL:

- 802.1Q has smaller frame overhead than ISL. As a result, 802.1Q is more efficient than ISL, especially in the case of small frames. 802.1Q overhead is 4 bytes, whereas ISL is 30 bytes.
- 802.1Q is a widely supported industry standard protocol.
- 802.1Q has the support for 802.1p fields for QoS.

The 802.1Q Ethernet frame header contains the following fields:

- **Dest:** Destination MAC address (6 bytes)
- **Src:** Source MAC address (6 bytes)
- **Tag:** Inserted 802.1Q tag (4 bytes, detailed here)
  - **EtherType(TPID):** Set to 0x8100 to specify that the 802.1Q tag follows.
  - **PRI:** 3-bit 802.1p priority field.
  - **CFI:** Canonical Format Identifier is always set to 0 for Ethernet switches and to 1 for Token Ring-type networks.
  - **VLAN ID:** 12-bit VLAN field. Of the 4096 possible VLAN IDs, the maximum number of possible VLAN configurations is 4094. A VLAN ID of 0 indicates priority frames, and value 4095 (FFF) is reserved. CFI, PRI, and VLAN ID are represented as Tag Control Information (TCI) fields.
- **Len/Etype:** 2-byte field specifying length (802.3) or type (Ethernet II)
- **Data:** Data itself
- **FCS:** Frame check sequence (4 bytes)

IEEE 802.1Q uses an internal tagging mechanism that modifies the original frame (as shown by the X over FCS in the original frame in Figure 3-7), recalculates the cyclic redundancy check (CRC) value for the entire frame with the tag, and inserts the new CRC value in a new FCS. ISL, in comparison, wraps the original frame and adds a second FCS that is built only on the header information but does not modify the original frame FCS.

IEEE 802.1p redefined the three most significant bits in the 802.1Q tag to allow for prioritization of the Layer 2 frame.

If a non-802.1Q-enabled device or an access port receives an 802.1Q frame, the tag data is ignored, and the packet is switched at Layer 2 as a standard Ethernet frame. This allows for the placement of Layer 2 intermediate devices, such as unmanaged switches or bridges, along the 802.1Q trunk path. To process an 802.1Q tagged frame, a device must enable a maximum transmission unit (MTU) of 1522 or higher.

Baby giants are frames that are larger than the standard MTU of 1500 bytes but less than 2000 bytes. Because ISL and 802.1Q tagged frames increase the MTU beyond 1500 bytes, switches consider both frames as baby giants. ISL-encapsulated packets over Ethernet have an MTU of 1548 bytes, whereas 802.1Q has an MTU of 1522 bytes.

Understanding Native VLAN in 802.1Q Trunking

The IEEE 802.1Q protocol allows operation between equipment from different vendors. All frames, except native VLAN, are equipped with a tag when traversing the link, as shown in Figure 3-8.

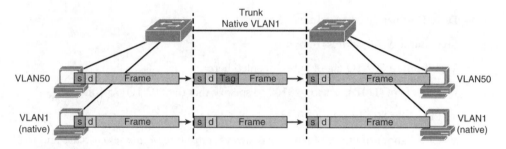

Figure 3-8   *Native VLAN in 802.1Q*

A frequent configuration error is to have different native VLANs. The native VLAN that is configured on each end of an 802.1Q trunk must be the same. If one end is configured for native VLAN 1 and the other for native VLAN 2, a frame that is sent in VLAN 1 on one side will be received on VLAN 2 on the other. VLAN 1 and VLAN 2 have been segmented and merged. There is no reason this should be required, and connectivity issues will occur in the network. If there is a native VLAN mismatch on either side of an 802.1Q link, Layer 2 loops may occur because VLAN 1 STP BPDUs are sent to the IEEE STP MAC address (0180.c200.0000) untagged.

Cisco switches use Cisco Discovery Protocol (CDP) to warn of a native VLAN mismatch. On select versions of Cisco IOS Software, CDP may not be transmitted or will be auto-matically turned off if VLAN 1 is disabled on the trunk.

By default, the native VLAN will be VLAN 1. For the purpose of security, the native VLAN on a trunk should be set to a specific VID that is not used for normal operations elsewhere on the network.

```
Switch(config-if)# switchport trunk native vlan vlan-id
```

Note   Cisco ISL does not have a concept of native VLAN. Traffic for all VLANs is tagged by encapsulating each frame.

Understanding DTP

All recent Cisco Catalyst switches, except for the Catalyst 2900XL and 3500XL, use a Cisco proprietary point-to-point protocol called *Dynamic Trunking Protocol* (DTP) on trunk ports to negotiate the trunking state. DTP negotiates the operational mode of directly connected switch ports to a trunk port and selects an appropriate trunking protocol. Negotiating trunking is a recommended practice in multilayer switched networks because it avoids network issues resulting from trunking misconfigurations for initial configuration, but best practice is when the network is stable, change to permanent trunk.

Cisco Trunking Modes and Methods

Table 3-1 describes the different trunking modes supported by Cisco switches.

Table 3-1 *Trunking Modes*

Mode in Cisco IOS	Function
Access	Puts the interface into permanent nontrunking mode and negotiates to convert the link into a nontrunk link. The interface becomes a nontrunk interface even if the neighboring interface does not agree to the change.
Trunk	Puts the interface into permanent trunking mode and negotiates to convert the link into a trunk link. The interface becomes a trunk interface even if the neighboring interface does not agree to the change.
Nonegotiate	Prevents the interface from generating DTP frames. You must configure the local and neighboring interface manually as a trunk interface to establish a trunk link. Use this mode when connecting to a device that does not support DTP.
Dynamic desirable	Makes the interface actively attempt to convert the link to a trunk link. The interface becomes a trunk interface if the neighboring interface is set to trunk, desirable, or auto mode.
Dynamic auto	Makes the interface willing to convert the link to a trunk link. The interface becomes a trunk interface if the neighboring interface is set to trunk or desirable mode. This is the default mode for all Ethernet interfaces in Cisco IOS.

Note   The Cisco Catalyst 4000 and 4500 switches run Cisco IOS or Cisco CatOS depending on the Supervisor Engine model. The Supervisor Engines for the Catalyst 4000 and 4500 do not support ISL encapsulation on a per-port basis. Refer to the product documentation on Cisco.com for more details.

Figure 3-9 shows the combination of DTP modes between the two links. A combination of DTP modes can either make the port as an access port or trunk port.

	Dynamic Auto	Dynamic Desirable	Trunk	Access
Dynamic Auto	Access	Trunk	Trunk	Access
Dynamic Desirable	Trunk	Trunk	Trunk	Access
Trunk	Trunk	Trunk	Trunk	Limited Connectivity
Access	Access	Access	Limited Connectivity	Access

Figure 3-9   *Output from the SIMPLE Program*

VLAN Ranges and Mappings

ISL supports VLAN numbers in the range of 1 to 1005, whereas 802.1Q VLAN numbers are in the range of 1 to 4094. The default behavior of VLAN trunks is to permit all normal and extended-range VLANs across the link if it is an 802.1Q interface and to permit normal VLANs in the case of an ISL interface.

VLAN Ranges

Cisco Catalyst switches support up to 4096 VLANs depending on the platform and software version. Table 3-2 illustrates the VLAN division for Cisco Catalyst switches. Table 3-3 shows VLAN ranges.

Note   The Catalyst 2950 and 2955 support as many as 64 VLANs with the Standard Software image, and up to 250 VLANs with the Enhanced Software image. Cisco Catalyst switches do not support VLANs 1002 through 1005; these are reserved for Token Ring and FDDI VLANs. Furthermore, the Catalyst 4500 and 6500 families of switches do not support VLANs 1006 through 1024. In addition, several families of switches support more VLANs than the number of spanning-tree instances. For example, the Cisco Catalyst 2970 supports 1005 VLANs but only 128 spanning-tree instances. For information on the number of supported spanning-tree instances, refer to the Cisco product technical documentation.

Table 3-2 *VLAN Support Matrix for Catalyst Switches*

Type of Switch	Maximum Number of VLANs	VLAN ID Range
Catalyst 2940	4	1–1005
Catalyst 2950/2955	250	1–4094
Catalyst 2960	255	1–4094
Catalyst 2970/3550/3560/3750	1005	1–4094
Catalyst 2848G/2980G/4000/4500	4094	1–4094
Catalyst 6500	4094	1–4094

Table 3-3 *VLAN Ranges*

VLAN Range	Range Usage	Propagated via VTP
0, 4095	Reserved for system use only. You cannot see or use these VLANs.	—
1	Normal Cisco default. You can use this VLAN, but you cannot delete it.	Yes
2–1001	Normal For Ethernet VLANs. You can create, use, and delete these VLANs.	Yes
1002–1005	Normal Cisco defaults for FDDI and Token Ring. You cannot delete VLANs 1002–1005.	Yes
1006–1024	Reserved for system use only. You cannot see or use these VLANS.	—
1025–4094	Extended for Ethernet VLANs only.	Not supported in VTP Versions 1 and 2. The switch must be in VTP transparent mode to configure extended-range VLANS. This range is only supported in Version 3.

Configuring, Verifying, and Troubleshooting VLANs and Trunks

This section provides the configuration, verification, and troubleshooting steps for VLANs and trunking.

To create a new VLAN in global configuration mode, follow these steps:

Step 1.   Enter global configuration mode:

```
Switch# configure terminal
```

Step 2.   Create a new VLAN with a particular ID number:

```
Switch(config)# vlan vlan-id
```

Step 3.   (Optional.) Name the VLAN:

```
Switch(config-vlan)# name vlan-name
```

Example 3-1 shows how to configure a VLAN in global configuration mode.

Example 3-1   *Creating a VLAN in Global Configuration Mode in Cisco IOS*

```
Switch# configure terminal
Switch(config)# vlan 5
Switch(config-vlan)# name Engineering
Switch(config-vlan)# exit
```

To delete a VLAN in global configuration mode, delete the VLAN by referencing its ID number:

```
Switch(config)# no vlan vlan-id
```

Note   After a VLAN is deleted, the access ports that belong to that VLAN move into the inactive state until the ports are moved to another VLAN. As a security measure, ports in the inactive state do not forward traffic.

Example 3-2 demonstrates deletion of a VLAN in global configuration mode.

Example 3-2   *Deleting a VLAN in Global Configuration Mode*

```
Switch# configure terminal
Switch(config)# no vlan 3
Switch(config)# end
```

To assign a switch port to a previously created VLAN, follow these steps:

Step 1.   From global configuration mode, enter the configuration mode for the particular port you want to add to the VLAN:

```
Switch(config)# interface interface-id
```

Step 2.   Specify the port as an access port:

```
Switch(config-if)# switchport mode access
Switch(config-if)# switchport host
```

Note   The **switchport host** command effectively configures a port for a host device, such as a workstation or server. This feature is a macro for enabling spanning-tree PortFast and disabling EtherChanneling on a per-port basis. These features are discussed in later chapters. The **switchport mode access** command is needed so that the interface doesn't attempt to negotiate trunking.

Step 3.   Remove or place the port in a particular VLAN:

```
Switch(config-if)# [no] switchport access vlan vlan-id
```

Example 3-3 illustrates configuration of an interface as an access port in VLAN 200.

Example 3-3   *Assigning an Access Port to a VLAN*

```
Switch# configure terminal
Enter configuration commands, one per line. End with CNTL/Z.
Switch(config)# interface FastEthernet 5/6
Switch(config-if)# description PC A
Switch(config-if)# switchport
Switch(config-if)# switchport host
Switch(config-if)# switchport mode access
Switch(config-if)# switchport access vlan 200
Switch(configif)# no shutdown
Switch(config-if)# end
```

Note   Use the **switchport** command with no keywords to configure interfaces as Layer 2 interfaces on Layer 3 switches. After configuring the interface as a Layer 2 interface, use additional **switchport** commands with keywords to configure Layer 2 properties, such as access VLANs or trunking.

Verifying the VLAN Configuration

As previously discussed, after you configure the VLANs, one of the important steps is to be able to verify the configuration. To verify the VLAN configuration of a Catalyst switch, use **show** commands. The **show vlan** command from privileged EXEC mode displays information about a particular VLAN. Table 3-4 documents the fields displayed by the **show vlan** command.

Table 3-4 *show vlan Field Descriptions*

Field	Description
VLAN	VLAN number
Name	Name, if configured, of the VLAN
Status	Status of the VLAN (active or suspended)
Ports	Ports that belong to the VLAN
Type	Media type of the VLAN
SAID	Security association ID value for the VLAN
MTU	Maximum transmission unit size for the VLAN
Parent	Parent VLAN, if one exists
RingNo	Ring number for the VLAN, if applicable
BridgNo	Bridge number for the VLAN, if applicable
Stp	Spanning Tree Protocol type used on the VLAN
BrdgMode	Bridging mode for this VLAN
Trans1	Translation bridge 1
Trans2	Translation bridge 2
AREHops	Maximum number of hops for All-Routes Explorer frames
STEHops	Maximum number of hops for Spanning Tree Explorer frames

Example 3-4 displays information about a VLAN identified by number in Cisco IOS.

Example 3-4 *Displaying Information About a VLAN by Number in Cisco IOS*

```
SW1#show vlan id 3

VLAN Name                             Status    Ports
---- -------------------------------- --------- -------------------------------
3    VLAN0003                         active    Et1/1


VLAN Type  SAID       MTU   Parent RingNo BridgeNo Stp  BrdgMode Trans1 Trans2
---- ----- ---------- ----- ------ ------ -------- ---- -------- ------ ------
3    enet  100003     1500  -      -      -        -    -        0      0


Primary Secondary Type              Ports
------- --------- ----------------- -----------------------------------------


SW1#
```

Example 3-5 displays information about a VLAN identified by name in Cisco IOS.

Example 3-5   *Displaying Information About a VLAN by Name in Cisco IOS*

```
SW1# show vlan name VLAN0003

VLAN Name                             Status    Ports
---- -------------------------------- --------- -------------------------------
3    VLAN0003                         active    Et1/1

VLAN Type  SAID       MTU   Parent RingNo BridgeNo Stp  BrdgMode Trans1 Trans2
---- ----- ---------- ----- ------ ------ -------- ---- -------- ------ ------
3    enet  100003     1500  -      -      -        -    -        0      0

Primary Secondary Type              Ports
------- --------- ----------------- -------------------------------------------

SW1#
```

To display the current configuration of a particular interface, use the **show running-config interface** *interface-type slot/port* command. To display detailed information about a specific switch port, use the **show interfaces** command. The command **show interfaces** *interface-type slot/port* with the **switchport** keyword displays not only a switch port's characteristics but also private VLAN and trunking information. The **show mac address-table interface** *interface-type slot/port* command displays the MAC address table information for the specified interface in specific VLANs. During troubleshooting, this command is helpful in determining whether the attached devices are sending packets to the correct VLAN.

Example 3-6 displays the configuration of a particular interface. Example 3-6 shows that the interface Ethernet 5/6 is configured with the VLAN 200 and in an access mode so that the port does not negotiate for trunking.

Example 3-6   *Displaying Information About the Interface Config*

```
Switch# show running-config interface FastEthernet 5/6
Building configuration... !
Current configuration :33 bytes
interface FastEthernet 5/6
switchport access vlan 200
switchport mode access
end
```

Example 3-7 displays detailed switch port information as the port VLAN and operation modes. As shown in Example 3-7, the Ethernet port 4/1 is configured as the switch port means Layer 2 port, working as an access port in VLAN 2.

Example 3-7   *Displaying Detailed Switch Port Information*

```
BXB-6500-10:8A# SW1# show int ethernet 4/1 switchport
Name: Et4/1
Switchport: Enabled
Administrative Mode: static access
Operational Mode: static access
Administrative Trunking Encapsulation: negotiate
Operational Trunking Encapsulation: native
Operational Dot1q Ethertype:  0x8100
Negotiation of Trunking: Off
Access Mode VLAN: 200 (Inactive)
Trunking Native Mode VLAN: 1 (default)
Administrative Native VLAN tagging: enabled
Operational Native VLAN tagging: disabled
Voice VLAN: none
Administrative private-vlan host-association: none
Administrative private-vlan mapping: none
Operational private-vlan: none
Trunking VLANs Enabled: ALL
Pruning VLANs Enabled: 2-1001
Capture Mode Disabled
Capture VLANs Allowed: ALL


Voice VLAN: none (Inactive)
Appliance trust: none
```

Example 3-8 displays the MAC address table information for a specific interface in VLAN 1.

Example 3-8   *Displaying MAC Address Table Information*

```
Switch# show mac-address-table interface GigabitEthernet 0/1 vlan 1
SW1# show mac address-table interface Gigabitethernet 0/1
          Mac Address Table
-------------------------------------------


Vlan    Mac Address      Type        Ports
----    -----------      --------    -----
   1    aabb.cc01.0600   DYNAMIC     Gi0/1
Total Mac Addresses for this criterion: 1
```

> **Note**   In this book, the configuration and verification are shown as the part of the scenarios that will be shown in a particular topology.

To configure the VLANs on switches SW1 and SW2 and enable trunking between the switches, use the topology shown in Figure 3-10.

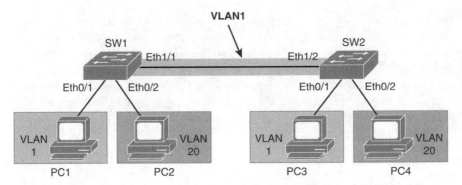

Figure 3-10   *Topology to Configure VLAN and Trunking*

Table 3-5 outlines the IP addressing scheme that will be used for this topology.

Table 3-5   *IP Addressing*

Device	Device IP	Device Interface	Device Neighbor	Interface on the Neighbor
PC1	192.168.1.100	Eth0/0	SW1	Eth0/1
PC2	192.168.20.101	Eth0/0	SW1	Eth0/2
PC3	192.168.1.110	Eth0/0	SW2	Eth0/1
PC4	192.168.20.110	Eth0/0	SW2	Eth0/2

Configuring VLANs and Trunks

To configure a port to belong to a certain VLAN, you have the following two options:

- Static VLAN configuration
- Dynamic VLAN configuration

With static VLAN configuration, switch ports are assigned to a specific VLAN. End devices become members in a VLAN based on the physical port to which they are connected. The end device is not even aware that a VLAN exists. Each port that is assigned to a VLAN receives a port VLAN ID (PVID).

With dynamic VLAN configuration, membership is based on the MAC address of the end device. When a device is connected to a switch port, the switch must query a database to figure out what VLAN needs to be configured. With dynamic VLANs, you need to assign a user's MAC address to VLAN in the database of a VLAN Management Policy Server (VMPS). With dynamic VLANs, users can connect to any port on the switch, and they will be automatically assigned into the VLAN they belong to.

Note   This book focuses only on configuring VLANs statically. All Cisco Catalyst switches support VLANs. That said, each Cisco Catalyst switch supports a different number of VLANs, with high-end Cisco Catalyst switches supporting as many as 4096 VLANs. Table 3-2 notes the maximum number of VLANs supported by each model of Catalyst switch. With static VLAN configuration, you first need to create a VLAN on the switch, if it does not yet exist. VLANs are identified by the VLAN number that runs 1 through 4094.

Step 1.   Create VLAN 20 on both switches.

```
SW1(config)# vlan 20
SW1(config-vlan)# exit
% Applying VLAN changes may take few minutes.  Please
wait...SW1(config)#
```

Step 2.   As shown in Figure 3-10, on SW1 configure port Ethernet 0/2 to be an access port and assign it to VLAN 20. By default, it is part of VLAN 1:

```
SW1(config)# interface ethernet 0/2
SW1(config-if)# switchport mode access
SW1(config-if)# switchport access vlan 20
```

The **switchport mode access** command explicitly tells the port to be assigned only a single VLAN, providing connectivity to an end user. When you assign a switch port to a VLAN using this method, it is known as a *static access port*.

Step 3.   On SW1, verify membership of port Ethernet 0/2.

Use the **show vlan** command to display information on all configured VLANs. The command displays configured VLANs, their names, and the ports on the switch that are assigned to each VLAN:

```
SW1# show vlan

VLAN Name                             Status    Ports
---- -------------------------------- --------- -------------------------------
1    default                          active    Et0/0, Et0/1, Et0/3, Et1/0
                                                Et1/2, Et1/3, Et2/0, Et2/1
                                                Et2/2, Et2/3, Et3/0, Et3/1
                                                Et3/2, Et3/3, Et4/0, Et4/1
```

```
                                       Et4/2, Et4/3, Et5/0, Et5/1
                                       Et5/2, Et5/3
20   IT                        active  Et0/2
1002 fddi-default              act/unsup
1003 token-ring-default        act/unsup
1004 fddinet-default           act/unsup
1005 trnet-default             act/unsup


VLAN Type  SAID       MTU   Parent RingNo BridgeNo Stp  BrdgMode Trans1 Trans2
---- ----- ---------- ----- ------ ------ -------- ---- -------- ------ ------
1    enet  100001     1500  -      -      -        -    -        0      0
20   enet  100020     1500  -      -      -        -    -        0      0
1002 fddi  101002     1500  -      -      -        -    -        0      0
1003 tr    101003     1500  -      -      -        -    -        0      0
1004 fdnet 101004     1500  -      -      -        ieee -        0      0
1005 trnet 101005     1500  -      -      -        ibm  -        0      0


Primary Secondary Type              Ports
------- --------- ----------------- -------------------------------------------
```

In the **show vlan** output, you can see that VLAN 20, named IT, is created. Also notice that Ethernet 0/2 is assigned to VLAN 20.

Use the **show vlan id** *vlan-number* or the **show vlan name** *vlan-name* command to display information about a particular VLAN.

Note   If you do not see a port listed in the output, this is probably because it is not configured as an access port.

Step 4.   Ping from PC 1 to PC 3. The ping should be successful:

```
PC1# ping 192.168.1.110
Type escape sequence to abort.
Sending 5, 100-byte ICMP Echos to 192.168.1.110, timeout is 2 seconds:
..!!!
Success rate is 60 percent (3/5), round-trip min/avg/max = 1/1/1 ms
```

First few pings might fail because of the Address Resolution Protocol (ARP) process.

PC 1 and PC 3 belong to the same VLAN. The configuration on the two ports that connect switches SW1 and SW2 is default; both ports belong to VLAN 1. So PCs 1 and 3 belong to the same LAN-Layer 2 network.

Step 5.   Ping from PC 2 to PC 4. The ping should not be successful.

The ping should not be successful because the link between SW1 and SW2 is an access link and carries only data for VLAN 1:

```
PC2# ping 192.168.20.110
Type escape sequence to abort.
Sending 5, 100-byte ICMP Echos to 192.168.20.110, timeout is 2 seconds:
.....
Success rate is 0 percent (0/5)
```

Step 6.   Configure ports that connect SW1 and SW2 as trunks. Use the dot1Q encapsulation. Allow only VLANs 1 and 20 to traverse the trunk link.

Trunk configuration on SW1:

```
SW1(config)# interface Ethernet 1/1
SW1(config-if)# switchport trunk encapsulation dot1q
SW1(config-if)# switchport trunk allowed vlan 1,20
SW1(config-if)# switchport mode trunk
```

Trunk configuration on SW2:

```
SW2(config)# interface Ethernet 1/2
SW2(config-if)# switchport trunk encapsulation dot1q
SW2(config-if)# switchport trunk allowed vlan 1,20
SW2(config-if)# switchport mode trunk
```

If you do not explicitly allow VLANs to traverse the trunk, all traffic will be allowed to cross the link. This includes broadcasts for all VLANs, using unnecessary bandwidth.

Step 7.   Verify that Ethernet 1/1 on SW1 is now trunking:

```
SW1# show interfaces trunk

Port            Mode            Encapsulation   Status          Native vlan
Et1/1           on              802.1q          trunking        1

Port            Vlans allowed on trunk
Et1/1           1,20

Port            Vlans allowed and active in management domain
Et1/1           1,20

Port            Vlans in spanning tree forwarding state and not pruned
Et1/1           1,20
```

Also notice that only VLANs 1 and 20 are allowed on the trunk.

Step 8.   Issue a ping from PC2 to PC4. The ping should be successful.

You have configured the link between SW1 and SW2 to carry data for both VLAN 1 and VLAN 20:

```
PC2# ping 192.168.20.110
Type escape sequence to abort.
Sending 5, 100-byte ICMP Echos to 192.168.20.110, timeout is 2 seconds:
..!!!
Success rate is 60 percent (3/5), round-trip min/avg/max = 1/1/1 ms
```

Best Practices for VLANs and Trunking

Usually, network designers design and implement the VLANs and their components depending on the business needs and requirements, but this section provides general best practices for implementing VLAN in a campus network.

Following are some of the practices for VLAN design:

■ For the Local VLANs model, it is usually recommended to have only one to three VLANs per access module and, as discussed, limit those VLANs to a couple of access switches and the distribution switches.

■ Avoid using VLAN 1 as the black hole for all unused ports. Use any other VLAN except 1 to assign all the unused ports to it.

■ Try to always have separate voice VLANs, data VLANs, management VLANs, native VLANs, black hole VLANs, and default VLANs (VLAN 1).

■ In the local VLANs model, avoid VTP; it is feasible to use manually allowed VLANs in a network on trunks.

■ For trunk ports, turn off DTP and configure it manually. Use IEEE 802.1Q rather than ISL because it has better support for QoS and is a standard protocol.

■ Manually configure access ports that are not specifically intended for a trunk link.

■ Prevent all data traffic from VLAN 1; only permit control protocols to run on VLAN 1 (DTP, VTP, STP bridge protocol data units [BPDUs], Port Aggregation Protocol [PAgP], Link Aggregation Control Protocol [LACP], Cisco Discovery Protocol [CDP], and such.).

■ Avoid using Telnet because of security risks; enable Secure Shell (SSH) support on management VLANs.

■ In a hierarchical design, access layer switches connect to distribution layer switches. This is where the trunks are implemented, as illustrated in Figure 3-11, where the links from each access switch to the distribution switches are the trunk links because they must carry two VLANs from each switch. Links between distribution and core layers are usually Layer 3. Also, to avoid spanning-tree problems, it is usually recommended not to link the two distribution switches as Layer 2 trunk links or have no link between them. In this way, the access layer switches are configured as a

spanning-tree, loop-free V topology if one distribution link fails, using the Hot
Standby Router Protocol (HSRP) or Virtual Router Redundancy Protocol (VRRP)
for creating a virtual default gateway. Spanning tree, HSRP, and VRRP are discussed
more in later chapters.

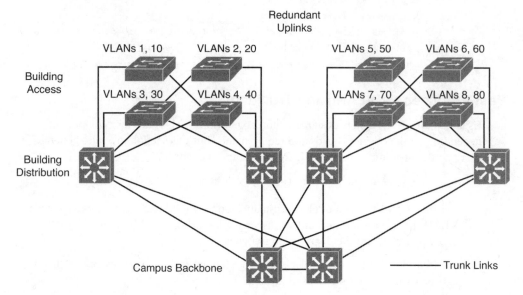

Figure 3-11   *Trunk Implementations*

- DTP is useful when the status of the switch on the other end of the link is uncer-
  tain or might be changing over time. When the link is to be set to trunk in a stable
  manner, changing both ends to trunk nonegotiate accelerates the convergence time,
  saving up to 2 seconds upon boot time. We recommend this mode on stable links
  between switches that are part of the same core infrastructure.

- On trunk links, it is recommended to manually prune the VLANs that are not used.
  You can use VTP pruning if VTP is in use, but manual pruning (using a switchport trunk allowed VLAN) is a secure way of allowing only those VLANs that are
  expected and allowed on the link. In addition to this, it is also a good practice to
  have an unused VLAN as a native VLAN on the trunk links to prevent DTP spoofing.

- If trunking is not used on a port, you can disable it with the interface level command **switchport host**. This command is a macro that sets the port to access mode
  (switchport mode access) and enables portfast.

Voice VLAN Overview

Some Cisco Catalyst switches offer a unique feature called *voice VLAN*, which lets you overlay a voice topology onto a data network. You can segment phones into separate logical networks even though the data and voice infrastructure are physically the same.

The voice VLAN feature places the phones into their own VLANs without any end-user intervention. These VLAN assignments can be seamlessly maintained even if the phone is moved to a new location.

The user simply plugs the phone into the switch, and the switch provides the phone with the necessary VLAN information. By placing phones into their own VLANs, network administrators gain the advantages of network segmentation and control. Furthermore, network administrators can preserve their existing IP topology for the data end stations. IP phones can be easily assigned to different IP subnets using standards-based DHCP operation.

With the phones in their own IP subnets and VLANs, network administrators can more easily identify and troubleshoot network problems. In addition, network administrators can create and enforce QoS or security policies.

With the voice VLAN feature, Cisco enables network administrators to gain all the advantages of physical infrastructure convergence while maintaining separate logical topologies for voice and data terminals. This ability offers the most effective way to manage a multiservice network.

Multiservice switches support a new parameter for IP telephony support that makes the access port a multi-VLAN access port. The new parameter is called a *voice* or *auxiliary VLAN*. Every Ethernet 10/100/1000 port in the switch is associated with two VLANs:

- A native VLAN for data service that is identified by the PVID

- A voice VLAN that is identified by the voice VLAN ID (VVID)

During the initial CDP exchange with the access switch, the IP phone is configured with a VVID.

The IP phone is also supplied with a QoS configuration using CDP.

Data packets between the multiservice access switch and the PC or workstation are on the native VLAN. All packets going out on the native VLAN of an IEEE 802.1Q port are sent untagged by the access switch. The PC or workstation connected to the IP phone usually sends untagged packets, as shown in Figure 3-12, whereas a PC VLAN that connected directly to the phone sends untagged packets because this considers the native VLAN and voice VLAN as VVID 110. The IP phone tags voice packets based on the CDP information from the access switch.

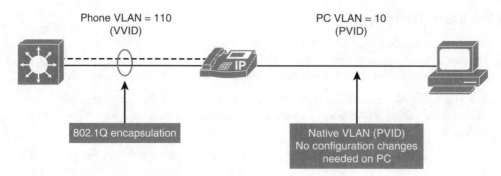

Figure 3-12   *Voice VLAN Overview*

The multi-VLAN access ports are not trunk ports, even though the hardware is set to the dot1Q trunk. The hardware setting is used to carry more than two VLANs, but the port is still considered an access port that is able to carry one native VLAN and the voice VLAN.

The **switchport host** command can be applied to a multi-VLAN access port on the access switch.

As shown in Figure 3-13, interface Fa0/1 is configured to set data devices in data VLAN 10 and VoIP devices in voice VLAN 110.

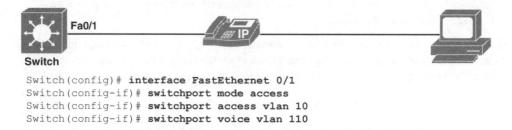

```
Switch(config)# interface FastEthernet 0/1
Switch(config-if)# switchport mode access
Switch(config-if)# switchport access vlan 10
Switch(config-if)# switchport voice vlan 110
```

Figure 3-13   *Voice VLAN Configuration*

When you run the **show vlan** command, both the voice and the data VLAN are seen applied to the interface Fa0/1 as demonstrated in Example 3-9.

Example 3-9   *show vlan Command Output Provides Information About the Voice and Data VLAN*

```
Switch# show vlan


VLAN  Name                            Status     Ports
----  ------------------------------- ---------- -----------------
1     default                         active Fa0/6,Fa0/7,Fa0/8,Fa0/9,Fa0/10

10    VLAN0010                        active     Fa0/1
110   VLAN0110                        active     Fa0/1
<... output omitted ...>
```

Verify the switchport mode and the voice VLAN by using the **show interface** *interface-slot/number* **switchport** command.

Switch Configuration for Wireless Network Support

Cisco offers the following two WLAN implementations:

- The standalone WLAN solution is based on autonomous (standalone) access points (APs).

- The controller-based WLAN solution is based on controller-based APs and WLCs (Wireless LAN Controllers).

In the autonomous (or standalone) solution, each AP operates independently and acts as a transition point between the wireless media and the 802.3 media. The data traffic between two clients flows via the Layer 2 switch when on the same subnet from a different AP infrastructure. As the AP converts the IEEE 802.11 frame into an 802.3 frame, the wireless client MAC address is transferred to the 802.3 headers and appears as the source for the switch. The destination, also a wireless client, appears as the destination MAC address. For the switch, the APs are relatively transparent, as illustrated in Figure 3-14.

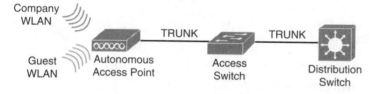

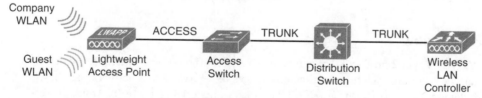

Figure 3-14 *Wireless Configurations Options*

In a controller-based solution, management, control, deployment, and security functions are moved to a central point: the wireless controller, as shown in Figure 3-14. Controllers are combined with lightweight APs that perform only the real-time wireless operation. Controllers can be standalone devices, integrated into a switch, or a WLC can be virtualized.

Both standalone and lightweight APs connect to a switch. It is common that the switch is Power over Ethernet (PoE)-able and so APs get power and data through the Ethernet cable. This makes the wireless network more scalable and easier to manage.

To implement a wireless network, APs and switches need to be configured. APs can be configured directly (autonomous APs) or through a controller (lightweight APs). Either way, configuring APs is a domain of the WLAN specialist. On the switch side, just configure VLANs and trunks on switches to support WLAN.

VLAN Trunking Protocol

VTP is a protocol that is used to distribute and synchronize information about VLAN databases configured throughout a switched network. VTP minimizes misconfigurations and configuration inconsistencies that might result in various problems, such as duplicate VLAN names, incorrect VLAN-type specifications, and security violations.

This section discusses in detail how to plan, implement, and verify VTP in campus networks. The following subsections cover these topics:

- VTP overview
- VTP modes
- VTP versions
- VTP pruning
- VTP authentication
- VTP advertisements
- VTP configuration and verifications
- VTP configuration overwriting
- VTP best practices

VTP Overview

VTP is a Layer 2 protocol that maintains VLAN configuration consistency by managing the additions, deletions, and name changes of VLANs across networks, as shown in Figure 3-15. Switches transmit VTP messages only on 802.1Q or ISL trunks. Cisco switches transmit VTP summary advertisements over the management VLAN (VLAN 1 by default) using a Layer 2 multicast frame every 5 minutes. VTP packets are sent to the destination MAC address 01-00-0C-CC-CC-CC with a logical link control (LLC) code of Subnetwork Access Protocol (SNAP) (AAAA) and a type of 2003 (in the SNAP header).

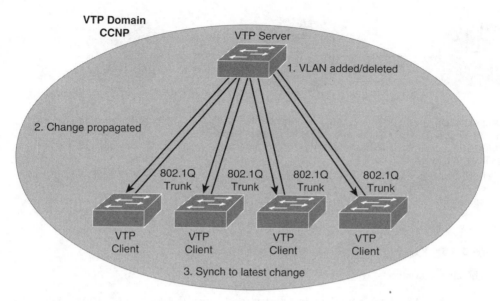

Figure 3-15 *VTP Overview*

In Figure 3-15, configurations made to a single VTP server propagate across trunk links to all connected switches in the network in the following manner:

Step 1.   An administrator adds a new VLAN definition.

Step 2.   VTP propagates the VLAN information to all switches in the VTP domain.

Step 3.   Each switch synchronizes its configuration to incorporate the new VLAN data.

VTP domain is one switch or several interconnected switches sharing the same VTP environment but switch can be only in one VTP domain at any time. By default, a Cisco Catalyst switch is in the no-management-domain state or <null> until it receives an advertisement for a domain over a trunk link or until you configure a management domain. Configurations that are made on a single VTP server are propagated across trunk links to all of the connected switches in the network. Configurations will be exchanged if VTP domain and VTP passwords match.

VTP is a Cisco proprietary protocol.

VTP Modes

VTP operates in one of three modes: server, transparent, or client. On some switches, VTP can also be completely disabled. Figure 3-16 shows the brief description of each of the VTP modes.

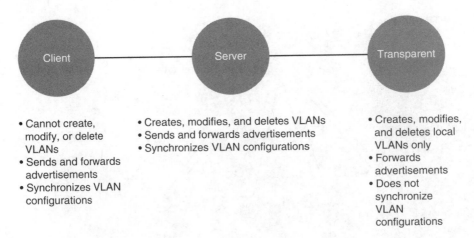

Figure 3-16 *VTP Modes and Its Characteristics*

The characteristics of the three VTP modes are as follows:

- **Server:** The default VTP mode is server mode, but VLANs are not propagated over the network until a management domain name is specified or learned. When you make a change to the VLAN configuration on a VTP server, the change is propagated to all switches in the VTP domain. VTP messages are transmitted out of all the trunk connections.

- **Transparent:** When you make a change to the VLAN configuration in VTP transparent mode, the change affects only the local switch. The change does not propagate to other switches in the VTP domain. VTP transparent mode does forward VTP advertisements that it receives within the domain.

- **Client:** A VTP client behaves like a VTP server and transmits and receives VTP updates on its trunks, but you cannot create, change, or delete VLANs on a VTP client. VLANs are configured on another switch in the domain that is in server mode.

Note In VTP Version 3, there is a concept of a primary server and a secondary server. VTP Version 3 is not within the scope of this book; for more information, refer to documents on Cisco.com.

In the server, transparent, and client modes, VTP advertisements are received and transmitted as soon as the switch enters the management domain state. In the VTP off mode, switches behave the same as in VTP transparent mode with the exception that VTP advertisements are not forwarded. Off mode is not available in all releases.

By default, Cisco IOS VTP servers and clients save VLANs to the vlan.dat file in flash memory, causing them to retain the VLAN table and revision number.

Switches that are in VTP transparent mode display the VLAN and VTP configurations in the **show running-config** command output because this information is stored in the configuration text file. If you perform **erase startup-config** on a VTP transparent switch you will delete its VLANs.

Note The **erase startup-config** command does not affect the vlan.dat file on switches in VTP client and server modes. Delete the vlan.dat file and reload the switch to clear the VTP and VLAN information. See documentation for your specific switch model to determine how to delete the vlan.dat file.

VTP Versions

Cisco Catalyst switches support three different versions of VTP: 1, 2, and 3. It is important to decide which version to use because they are not interoperable. In addition, Cisco recommends running only one VTP version for network stability. This chapter emphasizes VTP Versions 1 and 2 because VTP Version 3 is not the most frequently used version of the VTP. ·

The default VTP version that is enabled on a Cisco switch is Version 1. If you do need to change the version of VTP in the domain, the only thing that you need to do is to enable it on the VTP server; the change will propagate throughout the network.

VTP Version 2 offers the following features that Version 1 does not:

- **Version-dependent transparent mode:** In VTP Version 1, a VTP transparent network device inspects VTP messages for the domain name and version, and forwards a message only if the version and domain name match. Because only one domain is supported in the Supervisor Engine software, VTP Version 2 forwards VTP messages in transparent mode, without checking the version.

- **Consistency check:** In VTP Version 2, VLAN consistency checks, such as VLAN names and values, are performed. However, this is only done when you enter information through the command-line interface (CLI) or Simple Network Management Protocol (SNMP). Consistency checks are not performed when new information is obtained from a VTP message or when information is read from NVRAM. If the digest on a received VTP message is correct, its information is accepted without consistency checks.

- **Token ring support:** VTP Version 2 supports Token Ring LAN switching and VLANs.

- **Unrecognized type-length-value support:** VTP Version 2 switches propagate received configuration change messages out other trunk links, even if they are not able to understand the message. Instead of dropping the unrecognized VTP message, Version 2 still propagates the information and keeps a copy in NVRAM.

VTP Version 3 brings the following properties:

- **Extended VLAN support:** VTP also can be used to propagate VLANs with numbers 1017–4094 (1006–1017 and 4095–2096 are reserved).

- **Domain name is not automatically learned:** With VTPv2, a factory default switch that receives a VTP message will adapt the new VTP domain name. Because this is a very dangerous behavior, VTPv3 forces manual configuration.

- **Better security:** VTP domain password is secure during transmission and in the switch's database.

- **Better database propagation.** Only the primary server is allowed to update other devices and only one server per VTP domain is allowed to have this role.

- **Multiple Spanning Tree (MST) support:** VTPv3 adds support for propagation of MST instances.

Note   VTPv3 is not compatible with VTPv1. VTPv3 is compatible with VTPv2 as long as you are not using it to propagate private or extended VLANs.

Note   This book focuses only on VTP Versions 1 and 2 because VTP Version 3 is still not common in the field and is not the focus of the exam.

VTP Pruning

VTP pruning uses VLAN advertisements to determine when a trunk connection is flooding traffic needlessly. By default, a trunk connection carries traffic for all VLANs in the VTP management domain. Commonly, some switches in an enterprise network do not have local ports configured in each VLAN. In Figure 3-17, Switches 1 and 4 support ports statically configured in the red VLAN.

VTP pruning increases available bandwidth by restricting flooded traffic to those trunk links that the traffic must use to access the appropriate network devices. Figure 3-17 shows a switched network with VTP pruning enabled. The broadcast traffic from Hosts or workstation in red VLAN is not forwarded to Switches 3, 5, and 6, because traffic for the red VLAN has been pruned on the links indicated on Switches 2 and 4.

Regardless of whether you use VTP pruning support, Catalyst switches run an instance of STP for each VLAN. An instance of STP exists for each VLAN even if no ports are active in the VLAN or if VTP pruning removes the VLANs from an interface. As a result, VTP pruning prevents flooded traffic from propagating to switches that do not have members in specific VLANs. However, VTP pruning does not eliminate the switches' knowledge of pruned VLANs.

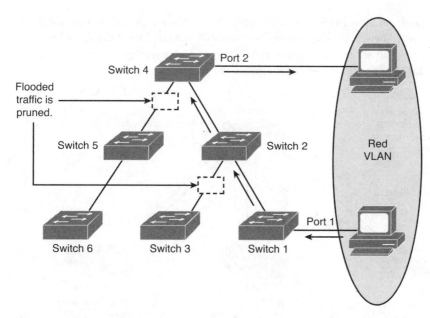

Figure 3-17   *VTP Pruning*

VTP Authentication

VTP domains can be secured by using the VTP password feature. It is important to make sure that all the switches in the VTP domain have the same password and domain name; otherwise, a switch will not become a member of the VTP domain. Cisco switches use the message digest 5 (MD5) algorithm to encode passwords in 16-byte words. These passwords propagate inside VTP summary advertisements. In VTP, passwords are case sensitive and can be 8 to 64 characters in length. The use of VTP authentication is a recommended practice.

VTP Advertisements

VTP advertisements are flooded throughout the management domain. VTP advertisements are sent every 5 minutes or whenever there is a change in VLAN configurations. Advertisements are transmitted (untagged) over the native VLAN (VLAN 1 by default) using a multicast frame. A configuration revision number is included in each VTP advertisement. A higher configuration revision number indicates that the VLAN information being advertised is more current than the stored information.

One of the most critical components of VTP is the configuration revision number. Each time a VTP server modifies its VLAN information, the VTP server increments the configuration revision number by one. The server then sends out a VTP advertisement with the new configuration revision number. If the configuration revision number being advertised is higher than the number stored on the other switches in the VTP domain, the switches overwrite their VLAN configurations with the new information that is being advertised. As shown in Figure 3-18, when the VLAN was added into the database on the VTP server switch, it increased the revision to 4 and advertised the rest of the domain switches that are in client or server VTP mode. However, the switch in transparent mode does not change its revision number or its database.

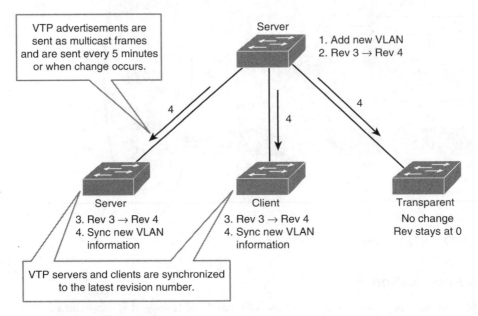

Figure 3-18   *VTP Advertisement*

The configuration revision number in VTP transparent mode is always zero. Because a VTP-transparent switch does not participate in VTP, that switch does not advertise its VLAN configuration or synchronize its VLAN database upon receipt of a VTP advertisement.

Note   In the overwrite process, if the VTP server were to delete all the VLANs and have the higher revision number, the other devices in the VTP domain would also delete their VLANs.

A device that receives VTP advertisements must check various parameters before incorporating the received VLAN information. First, the management domain name and password in the advertisement must match those values that are configured on the local switch. Next, if the configuration revision number indicates that the message was created after the configuration currently in use, the switch incorporates the advertised VLAN information.

Note   On many Cisco Catalyst switches, you can change the VTP domain to another name and then change it back to reset the configuration revision number; alternatively, you can change the mode to transparent and then back to the previous setting.

VTP Messages Types

VTP uses various message types for its communication. The subsections that follow describe the message types for VTP.

Summary Advertisements

By default, Catalyst switches issue summary advertisements in 5-minute increments. Summary advertisements inform adjacent Catalysts of the current VTP domain name and the configuration revision number.

When the switch receives a summary advertisement packet, the switch compares the VTP domain name to its own VTP domain name. If the name differs, the switch simply ignores the packet. If the name is the same, the switch then compares the configuration revision to its own revision. If its own configuration revision is higher or equal, the packet is ignored. If it is lower, an advertisement request is sent.

Subset Advertisements

When you add, delete, or change a VLAN in a Catalyst server, the Catalyst server where the changes are made increments the configuration revision and issues a summary advertisement. One or several subset advertisements follow the summary advertisement. A subset advertisement contains a list of VLAN information. If there are several VLANs, more than one subset advertisement can be required to advertise all the VLANs.

Advertisement Requests

A switch needs a VTP advertisement request in these situations:

- The switch has been reset.

- The VTP domain name has been changed.

- The switch has received a VTP summary advertisement with a higher configuration revision than its own.

- Upon receipt of an advertisement request, a VTP device sends a summary advertisement. One or more subset advertisements follow the summary advertisement.

Configuring and Verifying VTP

When creating VLANs, one must decide whether to use VTP in your network. With VTP, changes made on one or more switches propagate automatically to all other switches in the same VTP domain.

Note   The domain name and password are case sensitive.

The VTP domain name can be specified or learned. By default, the domain name is <null>. You can specify the password for the VTP management domain. However, if the same password for each switch is not used in the domain, VTP will not function properly. MD5 hashing is used for VTP passwords.

Note   The domain name cannot be reset to <null> except if the database is deleted. The domain name can only be reassigned.

To configure VTP, use the topology layout shown in Figure 3-19. In this scenario, Switch 1 will be configured as client, Switch 2 as server, and Switch 3 for transparent mode.

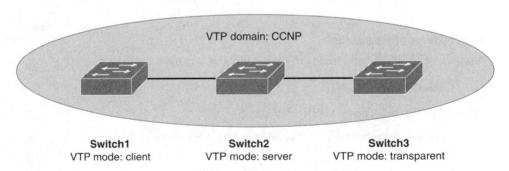

Figure 3-19   *VTP Configuration Topology*

Complete the following steps to configure the VTP on the switches shown in the topology in Figure 3-19:

Step 1.   Configure VTP on all the switches, Switch 1 and Switch 3 as client mode
where as Switch2 as server mode

```
Switch1(config)# vtp password Cisco
Switch1(config)#vtp mode client
Switch1(config)#vtp domain CCNP
Switch1(config)#vtp version 1
------
Switch3(config)# vtp password Cisco
Switch3(config)#vtp mode client
Switch3(config)#vtp domain CCNP
Switch3(config)#vtp version 1
-----
Switch2(config)# vtp password Cisco
Switch2(config)#vtp mode server
Switch2(config)#vtp domain CCNP
Switch2(config)#vtp version 1
```

Note   By default the switches run VTP Version 1. Vtp Version 2 is not covered in this
book. You can look on Cisco.com for more information and capabilities of Version 2.

Step 2.   Issue the **show vtp status** command on Switch 1 to view the default configuration.

Switch 1 is configured as a VTP client.

Switch 1 is in VTP domain CCNP:

```
Switch1# show vtp status
VTP Version capable              : 1 to 3
VTP version running              : 1
VTP Domain Name                  :CCNP
VTP Pruning Mode                 : Disabled
VTP Traps Generation             : Disabled
Device ID                        : aabb.cc00.5600
Configuration last modified by 0.0.0.0 at 0-0-00 00:00:00

Feature VLAN:
--------------
VTP Operating Mode               : Client
Maximum VLANs supported locally  : 1005
Number of existing VLANs         : 5
```

```
Configuration Revision          : 0
MD5 digest                      : 0x57 0xCD 0x40 0x65 0x63 0x59 0x47
0xBD
                                  0x56 0x9D 0x4A 0x3E 0xA5 0x69 0x35
0xBC
```

As you notice, there are only five default VLANs present on the switch. VLAN 1 and 1002–1005. The VTP revision is 0. Revision 0 means that no changes were made to the VLAN database on this switch so far. Every time that you make a change to the VLAN database (add, remove, modification), the revision will increase by one.

Step 3.   Issue the **show vtp status** command on Switch 2.

Switch 2 is configured as VTP server.

Like on Switch 1, only default VLANs are present, VTP revision is 0, and the VTP domain is set to CCNP:

```
Switch2# show vtp status
VTP Version capable             : 1 to 3
VTP version running             : 1
VTP Domain Name                 :CCNP
VTP Pruning Mode                : Disabled
VTP Traps Generation            : Disabled
Device ID                       : aabb.cc00.6300
Configuration last modified by 0.0.0.0 at 0-0-00 00:00:00
Local updater ID is 0.0.0.0 (no valid interface found)


Feature VLAN:
--------------

VTP Operating Mode              : Server
Maximum VLANs supported locally : 1005
Number of existing VLANs        : 5
Configuration Revision          : 0
MD5 digest                      : 0x57 0xCD 0x40 0x65 0x63 0x59 0x47
0xBD
                                  0x56 0x9D 0x4A 0x3E 0xA5 0x69 0x35
0xBC
```

Step 4.   Issue the **show vtp status** command on Switch 3.

Switch 3 is configured for VTP transparent mode.

Like on Switch 1 and Switch 2, only default VLANs are present, VTP revision is 0, and the VTP domain is set to CCNP:

```
Switch3# show vtp status
VTP Version capable             : 1 to 3
VTP version running             : 1
```

```
VTP Domain Name                :CCNP
VTP Pruning Mode               : Disabled
VTP Traps Generation           : Disabled
Device ID                      : aabb.cc00.6400
Configuration last modified by 0.0.0.0 at 0-0-00 00:00:00


Feature VLAN:
--------------
VTP Operating Mode             : Transparent
Maximum VLANs supported locally : 1005
Number of existing VLANs       : 5
Configuration Revision         : 0
MD5 digest                     : 0x57 0xCD 0x40 0x65 0x63 0x59 0x47
0xBD
                                 0x56 0x9D 0x4A 0x3E 0xA5 0x69 0x35
0xBC
```

Step 5.   Create VLAN 10 on Switch 2.

Switch 2 is in VTP server mode. You should be allowed to add VLAN 10 to the Switch 2 database:

```
Switch2# configure terminal
Switch2(config)# vlan 10
```

Note   If you try to add a VLAN on a VTP client, you will not be allowed. For example, if you try to add VLAN 5 to Switch 1, you will get the following message:

Switch1(config)# **vlan 5**

VTP VLAN configuration not allowed when device is in client mode.

Step 6.   Verify VLAN database and VTP status on Switch 2.

Use the commands **show vlan** and **show vtp status**.

Switch 2 now has VLAN 10 in the database:

```
Switch2# show vlan

VLAN Name                            Status    Ports
---- -------------------------------- --------- -------------------------------
1    default                          active    Et0/0, Et0/3, Et1/0, Et1/1
                                                Et1/2, Et1/3, Et2/0, Et2/1
```

```
                                                  Et2/2, Et2/3, Et3/0, Et3/1
                                                  Et3/2, Et3/3, Et4/0, Et4/1
                                                  Et4/2, Et4/3, Et5/0, Et5/1
                                                  Et5/2, Et5/3
10    VLAN0010                                active
1002  fddi-default                            act/unsup
1003  token-ring-default                      act/unsup
1004  fddinet-default                         act/unsup
1005  trnet-default                           act/unsup


VLAN Type  SAID       MTU   Parent RingNo BridgeNo Stp  BrdgMode Trans1 Trans2
---- ----- ---------- ----- ------ ------ -------- ---- -------- ------ ------
1    enet  100001     1500  -      -      -        -    -        0      0
10   enet  100010     1500  -      -      -        -    -        0      0
1002 fddi  101002     1500  -      -      -        -    -        0      0
1003 tr    101003     1500  -      -      -        -    -        0      0
1004 fdnet 101004     1500  -      -      -        ieee -        0      0
1005 trnet 101005     1500  -      -      -        ibm  -        0      0


Primary Secondary Type             Ports
------- --------- ---------------- ----------------------------------------
```

The revision number increased by one on Switch 2:

```
Switch2# show vtp status
VTP Version capable             : 1 to 3
VTP version running             : 1
VTP Domain Name                 :
VTP Pruning Mode                : Disabled
VTP Traps Generation            : Disabled
Device ID                       : aabb.cc00.6300
Configuration last modified by 0.0.0.0 at 9-23-13 08:33:48
Local updater ID is 0.0.0.0 (no valid interface found)


Feature VLAN:
--------------

VTP Operating Mode              : Server
Maximum VLANs supported locally : 1005
Number of existing VLANs        : 6
Configuration Revision          : 1
MD5 digest                      : 0xB1 0xBE 0x72 0x49 0x96 0x6D 0x99
0xA4
                                  0xB4 0xDC 0x94 0x56 0xD4 0xC2 0x6A
0xBB
```

But the real question now is did changes in Switch 2's database propagate to Switch 1 and Switch 3?

Step 7.   Verify changes in VLAN database and VTP status on Switch 1.

Use the commands **show vlan** and **show vtp status**.

Because Switch 1 is a VTP client, VLAN 10 got replicated from Switch 2:

```
Switch1# show vlan

VLAN Name                             Status    Ports
---- -------------------------------- --------- -------------------------------
1    default                          active    Et0/0, Et0/2, Et0/3, Et1/0
                                                Et1/1, Et1/2, Et1/3, Et2/0
                                                Et2/1, Et2/2, Et2/3, Et3/0
                                                Et3/1, Et3/2, Et3/3, Et4/0
                                                Et4/1, Et4/2, Et4/3, Et5/0
                                                Et5/1, Et5/2, Et5/3
10   VLAN0010                         active
1002 fddi-default                     act/unsup
1003 token-ring-default               act/unsup
1004 fddinet-default                  act/unsup
1005 trnet-default                    act/unsup

VLAN Type  SAID       MTU   Parent RingNo BridgeNo Stp  BrdgMode Trans1 Trans2
---- ----- ---------- ----- ------ ------ -------- ---- -------- ------ ------
1    enet  100001     1500  -      -      -        -    -        0      0
10   enet  100010     1500  -      -      -        -    -        0      0
20   enet  100020     1500  -      -      -        -    -        0      0
1002 fddi  101002     1500  -      -      -        -    -        0      0
1003 tr    101003     1500  -      -      -        -    srb      0      0

VLAN Type  SAID       MTU   Parent RingNo BridgeNo Stp  BrdgMode Trans1 Trans2
---- ----- ---------- ----- ------ ------ -------- ---- -------- ------ ------
1004 fdnet 101004     1500  -      -      -        ieee -        0      0
1005 trnet 101005     1500  -      -      -        ibm  -        0      0


Primary Secondary Type              Ports
------- --------- ----------------- -------------------------------------------
```

The revision number on Switch 1 is now the same as on Switch 2. This indicates that they have an identical VLAN database:

```
Switch1# show vtp status
VTP Version capable             : 1 to 3
VTP version running             : 1
```

```
VTP Domain Name                        : CCNP
VTP Pruning Mode                       : Disabled
VTP Traps Generation                   : Disabled
Device ID                              : aabb.cc00.5600
Configuration last modified by 0.0.0.0 at 9-23-13 08:59:42


Feature VLAN:
--------------
VTP Operating Mode                     : Client
Maximum VLANs supported locally        : 1005
Number of existing VLANs               : 6
Configuration Revision                 : 1
MD5 digest                             : 0xDF 0x2B 0x3B 0x5D 0x0E 0x8E 0x10
0x17
                                         0x6D 0xDD 0xE2 0x45 0x7F 0x91 0x95
0x9E
```

Step 8.   Verify changes in VLAN database and VTP status on Switch 3.

Use the commands **show vlan** and **show vtp status**.

Switch 3 is in VTP transparent mode. A switch in transparent mode never synchronizes its database to that of the VTP server. In essence, enabling VTP transparent mode disables VTP.

Notice that there is no VLAN 10 on Switch 3:

```
Switch3# show vlan

VLAN Name                             Status    Ports
---- -------------------------------- --------- -------------------------------
1    default                          active    Et0/0, Et0/2, Et0/3, Et1/0
                                                Et1/1, Et1/2, Et1/3, Et2/0
                                                Et2/1, Et2/2, Et2/3, Et3/0
                                                Et3/1, Et3/2, Et3/3, Et4/0
                                                Et4/1, Et4/2, Et4/3, Et5/0
                                                Et5/1, Et5/2, Et5/3
1002 fddi-default                     act/unsup
1003 token-ring-default               act/unsup
1004 fddinet-default                  act/unsup
1005 trnet-default                    act/unsup

VLAN Type  SAID       MTU   Parent RingNo BridgeNo Stp  BrdgMode Trans1 Trans2
---- ----- ---------- ----- ------ ------ -------- ---- -------- ------ ------
1    enet  100001     1500  -      -      -        -    -        0      0
1002 fddi  101002     1500  -      -      -        -    -        0      0
```

```
1003 tr    101003   1500  -      -       -       -    -    0    0
1004 fdnet 101004   1500  -      -       -     ieee   -    0    0
1005 trnet 101005   1500  -      -       -      ibm   -    0    0


Primary Secondary Type             Ports
------- --------- ---------------- -------------------------------------------
```

The revision number on a VTP transparent switch will always be at zero:

```
Switch3# show vtp status
VTP Version capable             : 1 to 3
VTP version running             : 1
VTP Domain Name                 : CCNP
VTP Pruning Mode                : Disabled
VTP Traps Generation            : Disabled
Device ID                       : aabb.cc00.6400
Configuration last modified by 0.0.0.0 at 0-0-00 00:00:00


Feature VLAN:
--------------
VTP Operating Mode              : Transparent
Maximum VLANs supported locally : 1005
Number of existing VLANs        : 5
Configuration Revision          : 0
MD5 digest                      : 0xC8 0x7E 0xBB 0x23 0xCB 0x0D 0xFA
0xCE
                                  0xDB 0xC1 0x0F 0x96 0xF6 0xCA 0x8B
0xAA
```

Step 9.   Create VLAN 20 on Switch 3:

```
Switch3(config)# vlan 20
```

Step 10.   Investigate VLAN databases on all three switches. Is VLAN 20 present on all three?

Use the **show vlan** command:

```
Switch1# show vlan


VLAN Name                             Status    Ports
---- -------------------------------- --------- -------------------------------
1    default                          active    Et0/0, Et0/2, Et0/3, Et1/0
                                                Et1/1, Et1/2, Et1/3, Et2/0
                                                Et2/1, Et2/2, Et2/3, Et3/0
                                                Et3/1, Et3/2, Et3/3, Et4/0
                                                Et4/1, Et4/2, Et4/3, Et5/0
                                                Et5/1, Et5/2, Et5/3
```

```
10   VLAN0010                          active
1002 fddi-default                      act/unsup
<... output omitted ...>


Switch2# show vlan

VLAN Name                             Status    Ports
---- -------------------------------- --------- ------------------------------
1    default                          active    Et0/0, Et0/3, Et1/0, Et1/1
                                                Et1/2, Et1/3, Et2/0, Et2/1
                                                Et2/2, Et2/3, Et3/0, Et3/1
                                                Et3/2, Et3/3, Et4/0, Et4/1
                                                Et4/2, Et4/3, Et5/0, Et5/1
                                                Et5/2, Et5/3
10   VLAN0010                          active
1002 fddi-default                      act/unsup
1003 token-ring-default                act/unsup
1004 fddinet-default                   act/unsup
1005 trnet-default                     act/unsup
<... output omitted ...>


Switch3# show vlan

VLAN Name                             Status    Ports
---- -------------------------------- --------- ------------------------------
1    default                          active    Et0/0, Et0/1, Et0/3, Et1/0
                                                Et1/1, Et1/2, Et1/3, Et2/0
                                                Et2/1, Et2/2, Et2/3, Et3/0
                                                Et3/1, Et3/2, Et3/3, Et4/0
                                                Et4/1, Et4/2, Et4/3, Et5/0
                                                Et5/1, Et5/2, Et5/3
20   VLAN0020                          active
1002 fddi-default                      act/unsup
1003 token-ring-default                act/unsup
1004 fddinet-default                   act/unsup
1005 trnet-default                     act/unsup
<... output omitted ...>
```

While a switch is in VTP transparent mode, it can create and delete VLANs that are local only to itself. These VLAN changes are not propagated to any other switch.

In this example, VLAN 20 is only present in the VLAN database of Switch 3 (the VTP transparent switch, on which you created the VLAN).

Overwriting VTP Configuration (Very Common Issue with VTP)

One of the common issues with VTP is that if you are not careful you can easily wipe out the configuration of the VLAN database across the entire network. Therefore, when a switch is added to a network, it is important that it does not inject spurious information into the domain. Let's review the scenarios illustrated in Figure 3-20, where the SW1 is a VTP server, and SW2 and SW3 are in the VTP client mode. They are all synced to the same configuration revision number '12' and have VLANs 10, 20, 30, and 40. In addition, each switch has hosts connected to multiple VLANs, like SW1 has hosts in VLAN 10 and 20, as depicted in Figure 3-20.

Example 3-10 shows the VTP and VLAN configuration of the switch SW1. Note that SW2 and SW3 would have the similar revision number and VLANs because they are completely synced.

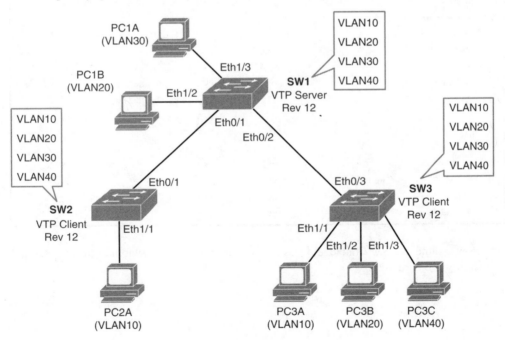

Figure 3-20 *Overwriting VTP Configuration*

Example 3-10   *VLAN and VTP Outputs from Switch SW1*

```
SW1# show vtp status
VTP Version capable          : 1 to 3
VTP version running          : 1
VTP Domain Name              : CCNP
VTP Pruning Mode             : Disabled
VTP Traps Generation         : Disabled
Device ID                    : aabb.cc00.5a00
Configuration last modified by 0.0.0.0 at 9-24-13 07:33:33
Local updater ID is 0.0.0.0 (no valid interface found)


Feature VLAN:
--------------
VTP Operating Mode           : Server
Maximum VLANs supported locally   : 1005
Number of existing VLANs     : 9
Configuration Revision       : 12
MD5 digest                   : 0x11 0x31 0x4F 0x6A 0x96 0x0D 0xB6 0xB9
                               0xAE 0xF4 0xD4 0x85 0x4D 0x58 0xC8 0x4D
SW1# show vlan


VLAN Name                             Status     Ports
---- -------------------------------- ---------  -------------------------------
1    default                          active     Et0/0, Et1/0, Et2/0, Et2/1
                                                 Et2/2, Et2/3, Et3/0, Et3/1
                                                 Et3/2, Et3/3, Et4/0, Et4/1
                                                 Et4/2, Et4/3, Et5/0, Et5/1
                                                 Et5/2, Et5/3
10   VLAN0010                         active
20   VLAN0020                         active     Et1/2
30   VLAN0030                         active     Et1/3
40   VLAN0040                         active
```

Now assume that SW2 failed and was replaced by another new switch in the closet, as shown in Figure 3-21.

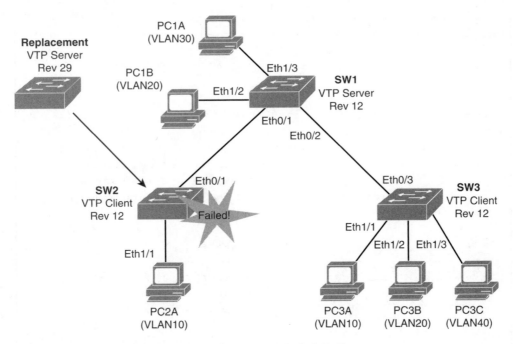

Figure 3-21 *Overwriting VTP Configuration: Switch Failure*

However, the network administrator forgot to erase the configuration and VLAN database.

The replacement switch has the same VTP domain name configured as the other two switches. The VTP revision number on the replacement switch is 29, higher than the revision on the other two switches.

Note The VTP revision number is stored in NVRAM and is not reset if you erase switch configuration and reload it.

Example 3-11 shows the output of VLANs and VTP on the new replacement switch to show the revision number and its VLAN database.

Example 3-11 *VTP and VLAN Output from the New Replacement Switch*

```
Replacement# show vtp status
VTP Version capable             : 1 to 3
VTP version running             : 1
VTP Domain Name                 : CCNP
VTP Pruning Mode                : Disabled
VTP Traps Generation            : Disabled
Device ID                       : aabb.cc00.5a00
```

```
Configuration last modified by 0.0.0.0 at 9-24-13 08:15:44
Local updater ID is 0.0.0.0 (no valid interface found)

Feature VLAN:
--------------

VTP Operating Mode                 : Server
Maximum VLANs supported locally    : 1005
Number of existing VLANs           : 10
Configuration Revision             : 29
MD5 digest                         : 0x29 0xF2 0x1F 0xA5 0x41 0x44 0x04 0xAC
                                     0x08 0x3B 0x9A 0x2C 0x73 0x8A 0xA2 0xBD
! The replacement switch does not have VLANs 20, 30, and 40 in its database.
Replacement# show vlan

VLAN Name                          Status    Ports
---- ------------------------------ --------- ------------------------------
1    default                        active    Et0/0, Et0/1, Et0/2, Et1/0
                                              Et2/0, Et2/1, Et2/2, Et2/3
                                              Et3/0, Et3/1, Et3/2, Et3/3
                                              Et4/0, Et4/1, Et4/2, Et4/3
                                              Et5/0, Et5/1, Et5/2, Et5/3
10   VLAN0010                       active    Et1/1
11   VLAN0011                       active
22   VLAN0022                       active
33   VLAN0033                       active
44   VLAN0044                       active
<... output omitted ...>
```

Because SW2 has a higher revision number, SW1 and SW3 will sync to the latest revision.

The consequence is that VLANs 20, 30, and 40 no longer exist on SW1 and SW2. This leaves the clients that are connected to ports belonging to nonexisting VLANs without connectivity, as shown in Figure 3-22.

Example 3-12 shows the output of show vtp status and show vlan of the SW1 and SW3 to show how the VLAN database is updated with new switch database.

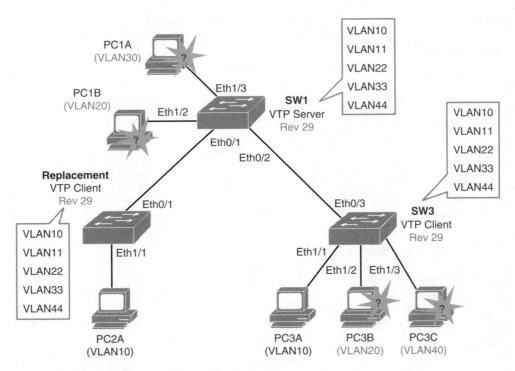

Figure 3-22 *VTP Overwriting Advertisement*

Example 3-12 *Show VTP Status and Show VLAN Outputs from SW1 and SW3*

```
SW1# show vtp status
VTP Version capable             : 1 to 3
VTP version running             : 1
VTP Domain Name                 : CCNP
VTP Pruning Mode                : Disabled
VTP Traps Generation            : Disabled
Device ID                       : aabb.cc00.5900
Configuration last modified by 0.0.0.0 at 9-24-13 08:15:44
Local updater ID is 0.0.0.0 (no valid interface found)


Feature VLAN:
--------------
VTP Operating Mode              : Server
Maximum VLANs supported locally : 1005
Number of existing VLANs        : 10
Configuration Revision          : 29
```

```
MD5 digest                          : 0x29 0xF2 0x1F 0xA5 0x41 0x44 0x04 0xAC
                                      0x08 0x3B 0x9A 0x2C 0x73 0x8A 0xA2 0xBD
SW1# show vlan

VLAN Name                           Status    Ports
---- -------------------------------- --------- -------------------------------
1    default                         active    Et0/0, Et1/0, Et2/0, Et2/1
                                               Et2/2, Et2/3, Et3/0, Et3/1
                                               Et3/2, Et3/3, Et4/0, Et4/1
                                               Et4/2, Et4/3, Et5/0, Et5/1
                                               Et5/2, Et5/3
10   VLAN0010                        active
11   VLAN0011                        active
22   VLAN0022                        active
33   VLAN0033                        active
44   VLAN0044                        active
<... output omitted ...>
SW3# show vtp status
VTP Version capable          : 1 to 3
VTP version running          : 1
VTP Domain Name              : CCNP
VTP Pruning Mode             : Disabled
VTP Traps Generation         : Disabled
Device ID                    : aabb.cc00.5600
Configuration last modified by 0.0.0.0 at 9-24-13 08:15:44


Feature VLAN:
--------------
VTP Operating Mode           : Client
Maximum VLANs supported locally  : 1005
Number of existing VLANs     : 10
Configuration Revision       : 29
MD5 digest                   : 0x29 0xF2 0x1F 0xA5 0x41 0x44 0x04 0xAC
                               0x08 0x3B 0x9A 0x2C 0x73 0x8A 0xA2 0xBD
SW3# show vlan

VLAN Name                           Status    Ports
---- -------------------------------- --------- -------------------------------
1    default                         active    Et0/0, Et0/2, Et1/0, Et2/0
                                               Et2/1, Et2/2, Et2/3, Et3/0
                                               Et3/1, Et3/2, Et3/3, Et4/0
                                               Et4/1, Et4/2, Et4/3, Et5/0
```

```
                                             Et5/1, Et5/2, Et5/3
10    VLAN0010                    active     Et1/1
11    VLAN0011                    active
22    VLAN0022                    active
33    VLAN0033                    active
44    VLAN0044                    active
<... output omitted ...>
```

Also, when the new switch is added with a VTP client with a higher revision number, it can cause the same havoc as a switch with the VTP server, as discussed earlier. The VTP client, as a general rule, just listens to VTP advertisements from VTP servers, and it does not do its own advertisements. However, when the switch with the VTP client is added to a network, it will send a summary advertisement from its own stored database. If the VTP client gets an inferior advertisement from the VTP server, it will assume it has better, more current information. The VTP client will now send out advertisements with a higher revision number. The VTP server and all directly connected VTP clients will accept these as more current. This will not only delete the old VLANs but also can add new VLANs into the network and create network instability.

Remember the revision configuration and how to reset it each time a new switch is inserted so that it does not bring down the entire network. Following are some of the key points:

- Avoid, as much as possible, VLANs that span the entire network.

- The VTP revision number is stored in NVRAM and is not reset if you erase the switch configuration and reload it. To reset the VTP revision number to zero, use the following two options:

  - Change the switch's VTP domain to a nonexistent VTP domain, and then change the domain back to the original name.

  - Change the switch's VTP mode to transparent and then back to the previous VTP mode.

Best Practices for VTP Implementation

VTP is often used in a new network to facilitate the implementation of VLANs. However, as the network grows larger, this benefit can turn into a liability. If a VLAN is deleted by accident on one server, it is deleted throughout the network. If a switch that already has a VLAN database defined is inserted into the network, it can hijack the VLAN database by deleting added VLANs. Because of this, it is the recommended practice to configure all switches to transparent VTP mode and manually add VLANs as needed, especially in a larger campus network. VTP configuration is usually good for small environments.

Implementing EtherChannel in a Switched Network

In networks where resources may be located far from where users might need them, some links between switches or between switches and servers become heavily solicited. The speed of these links can be increased, but only to a certain point. EtherChannel is a technology that allows you to circumvent the bandwidth issue by creating logical links that are made up of several physical links.

This section examines the benefits of EtherChannel and the various technologies available to implement it and also the types of EtherChannel protocol. In addition, it explains how to configure Layer 2 EtherChannels and how to load balance traffic between physical links inside a given EtherChannel bundle. EtherChannels can also operate in a Layer 3 mode, but this is discussed later in Chapter 5. The following topics are discussed in detail in the following subsections:

- The need for EtherChannel technology

- Port aggregation negotiation protocols

- Configuration steps for bundling interfaces into a Layer 2 EtherChannel

- Configuring EtherChannel

- Changing EtherChannel load-balancing behavior

- How EtherChannel load-balancing works

- The role of EtherChannel Guard

The Need for EtherChannel

Any-to-any communications of intranet applications, such as video to the desktop, interactive messaging, Voice over IP (VoIP), and collaborative whiteboard use, are increasing the need for scalable bandwidth within the core and at the edge of campus networks. At the same time, mission-critical applications call for resilient network designs. With the wide deployment of faster switched Ethernet links in the campus, users need to either aggregate their existing resources or upgrade the speed in their uplinks and core to scale performance across the network backbone.

In Figure 3-23, traffic coming from several VLANs at 100 Mbps aggregate on the access switches at the bottom and need to be sent to distribution switches in the middle. Obviously, bandwidth larger than 100 Mbps must be available on the link between two switches to accommodate the traffic load coming from all the VLANs. A first solution is to use a faster port speed, such as 1 or 10 Gbps. As the speed increases on the VLANs links, this solution finds its limitation where the fastest possible port is no longer fast enough to aggregate the traffic coming from all VLANs. A second solution is to multiply the numbers of physical links between both switches to increase the overall speed of the switch-to-switch communication. A downside of this method is that there must be a strict consistency in each physical link configuration. A second issue is that spanning tree may block one of the links, as shown in Figure 3-23.

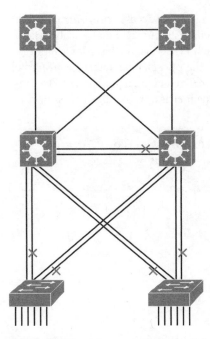

Figure 3-23   *Network Without EtherChannel*

EtherChannel is a technology that was originally developed by Cisco as a LAN switch-to-switch technique of grouping several Fast or Gigabit Ethernet ports into one logical channel. This technology has many benefits:

- It relies on the existing switch ports. There is no need to upgrade the switch-to-switch link to a faster and more expensive connection.

- Most of the configuration tasks can be done on the EtherChannel interface instead of on each individual port, thus ensuring configuration consistency throughout the switch-to-switch links.

- Load balancing is possible between the links that are part of the same EtherChannel. Depending on the hardware platform, you can implement one or several methods, such as source-MAC to destination-MAC or source-IP to destination-IP load balancing across the physical links.

Keep in mind that the logic of EtherChannel is to increase the speed between switches, as illustrated in Figure 3-24. This concept was extended as the EtherChannel technology became more popular, and some hardware nonswitch devices support link aggregation into an EtherChannel link. In any case, EtherChannel creates a one-to-one relationship. You can create an EtherChannel link between two switches or between an EtherChannel-enabled server and a switch, but you cannot send traffic to two different switches through the same EtherChannel link. One EtherChannel link always connects the same two devices only. The individual EtherChannel group member port configuration must be consistent on both devices. EtherChannel technology only bundles ports of the same type. On a Layer 2 switch, EtherChannel is used to aggregate access ports or trunks. For example, if the physical ports of one side are configured as trunks, the physical ports of the other side must also be configured as trunks. Each EtherChannel has a logical port channel interface. A configuration that is applied to the port channel interface affects all physical interfaces that are assigned to that interface. (Such commands can be STP commands or commands to configure a Layer 2 EtherChannel as a trunk or an access port.)

Note   Using new technologies like VSS (Virtual Switching System) and vPC (Virtual Port Channel), a port channel can be created across two aggregation switches from the same access layer to provide better redundancy.

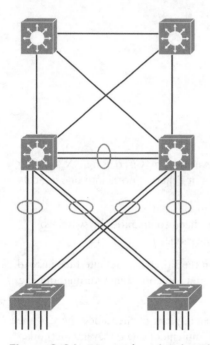

Figure 3-24   *Network with EtherChannel*

Keep in mind that EtherChannel creates an aggregation that is seen as one logical link. When several EtherChannel bundles exist between two switches, spanning tree may block one of the bundles to prevent redundant links. When spanning tree blocks one of the redundant links, it blocks one EtherChannel, thus blocking all the ports belonging to this EtherChannel link. Where there is only one EtherChannel link, all physical links in the EtherChannel are active because spanning tree sees only one (logical) link. If one link in EtherChannel goes down, the bandwidth of the EtherChannel will be automatically updated, and thus the STP cost will change as well.

Note   On Layer 3 switches, you can convert switched ports to routed ports. You can also create EtherChannel links on Layer 3 links. Layer 3 port channels are discussed in more detail in Chapter 5.

Note   Also, with technologies like VSS and VPC (which are discussed in more detail in Chapter 9, "High Availability," you can create the EtherChannel between the access layer and two different aggregation switches.

EtherChannel Mode Interactions

EtherChannel can be established using one of the following three mechanisms, as shown in Figure 3-25:

- **LACP:** IEEE's negotiation protocol
- **PAgP:** Cisco's negotiation protocol
- **Static persistence:** No negotiation protocol

LACP	Active	Passive
Active	Yes	Yes
Passive	Yes	No

PAgP	Desirable	Auto
Desirable	Yes	Yes
Auto	Yes	No

Static Persistance		On
	On	Yes

Figure 3-25   *EtherChannel Modes Interactions*

LACP

Link Aggregation Control Protocol (LACP) is part of an IEEE specification (802.3ad) that allows several physical ports to be bundled together to form a single logical channel. LACP allows a switch to negotiate an automatic bundle by sending LACP packets to the peer. Because LACP is an IEEE standard, you can use it to facilitate EtherChannels in mixed-switch environments. LACP checks for configuration consistency and manages link additions and failures between two switches. It ensures that when EtherChannel is created, all ports have the same type of configuration speed, duplex setting, and VLAN information. Any port modification after the creation of the channel will also change all the other channel ports.

LACP packets are exchanged between switches over EtherChannel-capable ports. Port capabilities are learned and compared with local switch capabilities. LACP assigns roles to EtherChannel's ports. The switch with the lowest system priority is allowed to make decisions about what ports actively participate in EtherChannel. Ports become active according to their port priority. A lower number means higher priority. Commonly up to 16 links can be assigned to an EtherChannel, but only 8 can be active at a time. Nonactive links are placed into a standby state and are enabled if one of the active links goes down.

The maximum number of active links in an EtherChannel varies between switches.

These are the LACP modes of operation:

- **Active:** Enable LACP
- **Passive:** Enable LACP only if an LACP device is detected

The following are some additional parameters that you can use when configuring LACP:

- **System priority:** Each switch running LACP must have a system priority. The system priority can be specified automatically or through the CLI. The switch uses the MAC address and the system priority to form the system ID.
- **Port priority:** Each port in the switch must have a port priority. The port priority can be specified automatically or through the CLI. The port priority and the port number form the port identifier. The switch uses the port priority to decide which ports to put in standby mode when a hardware limitation prevents all compatible ports from aggregating.
- **Administrative key:** Each port in the switch must have an administrative key value, which can be specified automatically or through the CLI. The administrative key defines the capability of a port to aggregate with other ports, determined by these factors: the port's physical characteristics, such as data rate, duplex capability, and point-to-point or shared medium.

All the preceding options of LACP are optional to configure. Usually, defaults are the best to use. To configure any of these options, refer to your configuration guide.

PAgP

Port Aggregation Protocol (PAgP) provides the same negotiation benefits as LACP. PAgP is a Cisco proprietary protocol, and it will work only on Cisco devices. PAgP packets are exchanged between switches over EtherChannel-capable ports. Neighbors are identified and capabilities are learned and compared with local switch capabilities. Ports that have the same capabilities are bundled together into an EtherChannel. PAgP forms an EtherChannel only on ports that are configured for identical VLANs or trunking. PAgP will automatically modify parameters of the EtherChannel if one of the ports in the bundle is modified. For example, if configured speed, duplex, or VLAN of a port in a bundle is changed, PAgP reconfigures that parameter for all ports in the bundle. PAgP and LACP are not compatible.

These are the following two PAgP modes of operation:

- **Desirable:** Enable PAgP
- **Auto:** Enable PAgP only if a PAgP device is detected

Note Negotiation with either LACP or PAgP introduces overhead and delay in initialization. As an alternative, you can statically bundle links into an EtherChannel. This method introduces no delays but can cause problems if not properly configured on both ends.

Layer 2 EtherChannel Configuration Guidelines

Before implementing EtherChannel in a network, plan the following steps necessary to make it successful:

- The first step is to identify the ports that you will use for the EtherChannel on both switches. This task helps identify any issues with previous configurations on the ports and ensures that the proper connections are available.

- Each interface should have the appropriate protocol identified (PAgP or LACP), have a channel group number to associate all the given interfaces with a port group, and be configured whether negotiation should occur.

- After the connections are established, make sure that both sides of the EtherChannel have formed and are providing aggregated bandwidth.

Follow these guidelines and restrictions when configuring EtherChannel interfaces:

- **EtherChannel support:** All Ethernet interfaces on all modules support EtherChannel, with no requirement that interfaces be physically contiguous or on the same module.

- **Speed and duplex:** Configure all interfaces in an EtherChannel to operate at the same speed and in the same duplex mode. Also, if one interface in the bundle is shut down, it is treated as a link failure, and traffic will traverse other links in the bundle.

- **VLAN match:** All interfaces in the EtherChannel bundle must be assigned to the same VLAN or be configured as a trunk.

- **Range of VLANs:** An EtherChannel supports the same allowed range of VLANs on all the interfaces in a trunking Layer 2 EtherChannel.

If the allowed range of VLANs is not the same, the interfaces do not form an EtherChannel, even when set to auto or desirable mode. For Layer 2 EtherChannels, either assign all interfaces in the EtherChannel to the same VLAN or configure them as trunks.

- **STP path cost:** Interfaces with different STP port path costs can form an EtherChannel as long as they are compatibly configured. Setting different STP port path costs does not, by itself, make interfaces incompatible for the formation of an EtherChannel.

- **Port channel versus interface configuration:** After you configure an EtherChannel, any configuration that you apply to the port channel interface affects the EtherChannel. Any configuration that you apply to the physical interfaces affects only the specific interface that you configured.

Note   If you do not specify any protocol, it will be static binding. That topic is not within the scope of this book.

EtherChannel Load-Balancing Options

EtherChannel load balances traffic across links in the bundle. However, traffic is not necessarily distributed equally among all the links.

Frames are forwarded over an EtherChannel link that is based on results of a hashing algorithm. Options that switch can use to calculate this hash depends on the platform.

Table 3-6 shows the comment set of options for EtherChannel load balancing.

Table 3-6   *EtherChannel Load-Balancing Options*

Hash Input Code	Hash Input Decision	Switch Model
dst-ip	Destination IP address	All models
dst-mac	Destination MAC address	All models
src-dst-ip	Source and destination IP address	All models
src-dst-mac	Source and destination MAC address	All models
src-ip	Source IP address	All models
src-mac	Source MAC address	All models
src-port	Source port number	4500, 6500
dst-port	Destination port number	4500, 6500
src-dst-port	Source and destination port number	4500, 6500

To verify load-balancing options available on the device, use the **port-channel load-balance ?** global configuration command.

The hash algorithm calculates a binary pattern that selects a link within the EtherChannel bundle to forward the frame.

Note   Default configuration can differ from switch to switch, but commonly the default option is src-dst-ip. It is not possible to have different load-balancing methods for different EtherChannels on one switch. If the load-balancing method is changed, it is applicable for all EtherChannels.

If only one address or port number is hashed, a switch looks at one or more low-order bits of the hash value. The switch then uses those bits as index values to decide over which links in the bundle to send the frames.

If two or more addresses or port numbers are hashed, a switch performs an XOR operation.

A four-link bundle uses a hash of the last 2 bits. A bundle of eight links uses a hash of the last 3 bits.

Table 3-7 shows results of an XOR on a two-link bundle, using the source and destination addresses.

Table 3-7   *XOR for Two-Link EtherChannels*

Example IP Addresses	IPs in Binary	XOR Result	Forward Frame over Link with Index
Source: 192.168.1.2	Source: ...xxxxx0	...xxxxx0	0
Destination: 192.168.1.4	Destination: ...xxxxx0		
Source: 172.16.1.20	Source: ...xxxxx0	...xxxxx1	1
Destination: 172.16.1.21	Destination: ...xxxxx1		
Source: 192.168.1.1	Source: ...xxxxx1	...xxxxx1	1
Destination: 192.168.1.2	Destination: ...xxxxx0		
Source: 10.1.1.101	Source: ...xxxxx1	...xxxxx0	0
Destination: 10.1.1.103	Destination: ...xxxxx1		

A conversation between two devices is sent through the same EtherChannel link because the two endpoint addresses stay the same. Only when a device talks to several other devices does traffic get distributed evenly over the links in the bundle.

When one pair of hosts has a much greater volume of traffic than the other pair, one link will be much more utilized than others. To fix the imbalance, consider using some other load-balancing mechanisms, such as source and destination port number, that will redistribute traffic much differently.

If most of the traffic is IP, it makes sense to load balance according to IP addresses or port numbers. For non-IP traffic, the hash uses MAC addresses to calculate the path.

To achieve the optimal traffic distribution, always bundle an even number of links. For example, if you use four links, the algorithm will take the last 2 bits. These 2 bits mean four indexes: 00, 01, 10, and 11. Each link in the bundle will get assigned one of these indexes. If you bundle only three links, the algorithm still needs to use 2 bits to make decisions. One of the three links in the bundle will be used more than the other two. With four links, the algorithm strives to load balance traffic in a 1:1:1:1 ratio. A three-link algorithm strives to load balance traffic in a 2:1:1 ratio.

> **Note**   You cannot control the port that a particular flow uses. You can only influence the load balance with a frame distribution method that results in the greatest variety.

Configuring EtherChannel in a Switched Network

This section shows you how to configure the Layer 2 EtherChannel and explains its load-balancing behavior. Configure a port channel between SW1 and SW2 shown in Figure 3-26.

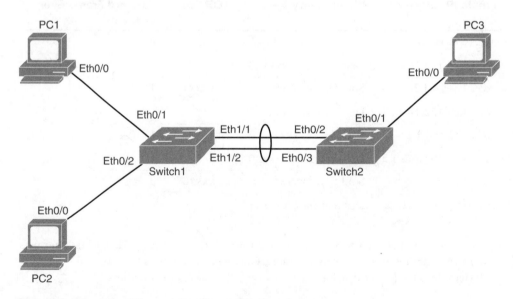

Figure 3-26   *EtherChannel Configuration Topology*

Table 3-8 shows device information.

Table 3-8 *Device Information*

Device	IP Address	Interface	Neighbor	Interface on the Neighbor
PC 1	172.16.1.101/24	Ethernet 0/0	Switch 1	Ethernet 0/1
PC 2	172.16.1.102/24	Ethernet 0/0	Switch 1	Ethernet 0/2
PC 3	172.16.1.203/24	Ethernet 0/0	Switch 2	Ethernet 0/1
Switch 1	*No IP address*	Ethernet 1/1	Switch 2	Ethernet 0/2
Switch 1	*No IP address*	Ethernet 1/2	Switch 2	Ethernet 0/3

EtherChannel Configuration and Load Balancing

Complete the following steps to configure EtherChannel on Switch 1. Switch 2 has
EtherChannel preconfigured.

Step 1. On Switch 1, configure the two ports that connect to Switch 2 to use channel
group 1 and LACP active mode:

```
Switch1# configure terminal
Switch1(config)# interface range Ethernet 1/1-2
Switch1(config-if-range)# channel-group 1 mode active
Creating a port-channel interface Port-channel 1
```

Now the two interfaces are bundled into channel group 1. Because you
chose the **active** keyword, LACP will work as the negotiation protocol.
Because Switch 2 has its ports bundled and activated for LACP passive mode,
EtherChannel should come right up.

%LINEPROTO-5-UPDOWN: Line protocol on Interface Port-channel1,
changed state to up

Notice that by assigning the two ports to a port channel, the switch has created a port channel 1 interface.

Issue the **show ip interface brief** command. Port channel 1 will be listed as
just another interface at the very bottom of the list.

Step 2. Enter interface configuration mode for the newly created port channel interface and configure it for trunk mode using dot1Q:

```
Switch1(config)# interface port-channel 1
Switch1(config-if)# switchport trunk encapsulation dot1q
Switch1(config-if)# switchport mode trunk
```

The configuration applied to the port channel will also reflect on physical interfaces that are bundled into that port channel. You can investigate the running configuration and see that EtherChannel 1/1 and EtherChannel 1/2 both have had the trunking configuration applied.

Step 3.   On Switch 1, enter the **show etherchannel summary** command:

```
Switch1# show etherchannel summary
Flags:  D - down         P - bundled in port-channel
        I - stand-alone s - suspended
        H - Hot-standby (LACP only)
        R - Layer3       S - Layer2
        U - in use       f - failed to allocate aggregator

        M - not in use, minimum links not met
        u - unsuitable for bundling
        w - waiting to be aggregated
        d - default port


Number of channel-groups in use: 1
Number of aggregators:           1

Group  Port-channel  Protocol    Ports
------+-------------+-----------+-------------------------------------
1      Po1(SU)        LACP        Et1/1(P)    Et1/2(P)
```

Group 1 port channel is a Layer 2 EtherChannel that is in use (SU flag). The negotiation protocol in use is LACP, and the ports bundled (notice the P flag) are Ethernet 1/1 and Ethernet 1/2.

If a port comes up but cannot join the port channel, it is denoted with an I flag (for "independent").

Step 4.   Enter the **show etherchannel load-balance** command to verify which information EtherChannel uses to load balance traffic:

```
Switch1# show etherchannel load-balance
EtherChannel Load-Balancing Configuration:
        src-dst-ip


EtherChannel Load-Balancing Addresses Used Per-Protocol:
Non-IP: Source XOR Destination MAC address
  IPv4: Source XOR Destination IP address
  IPv6: Source XOR Destination IP address
```

Notice that the default configuration for load balancing is src-dst-ip. This means the source and destination IP address are used for hash input.

Step 5. For testing how much traffic goes over each link, as shown in Figure 3-27, clear interface counters on Switch 1 using the **clear counters** command:

```
Switch1# clear counters
Clear "show interface" counters on all interfaces [confirm] [Enter]
```

By clearing the counters, you are setting up to test how much traffic goes over each link.

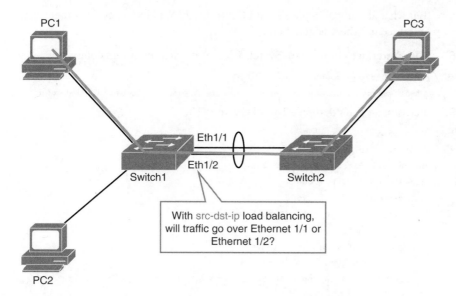

Figure 3-27 *EtherChannel Load-Balancing Configuration Option*

Step 6. Perform an extended ping from PC 1 to PC 3:

```
PC1# ping
Protocol [ip]: [Enter]
Target IP address: 172.16.1.203
Repeat count [5]: 10000
Datagram size [100]: 1500
Timeout in seconds [2]: [Enter]
Extended commands [n]: [Enter]
Sweep range of sizes [n]: [Enter]
Type escape sequence to abort.
Sending 10000, 1500-byte ICMP Echos to 172.16.1.203, timeout is 2 sec-
onds:
!!!!!!!!!!!!!!!!!!!!!!!!!!!!!!!!!!!!!!!!!!!!!!!!!!!!!!!!!!!!!!!!!!!!!!!!!!
<... output omitted ...>
```

In the next step, you check over which interface all the traffic went.

Step 7. Verify counters on Switch 1 for both interfaces:

```
Switch1# show interface ethernet 1/1 | i packets output
    10094 packets output, 15146494 bytes, 0 underruns
Switch1# show interface ethernet 1/2 | i packets output
    13 packets output, 1664 bytes, 0 underruns
```

Notice that most of the traffic went over the Ethernet 1/1 interface.

But what about if you ping from PC 2 to PC 3? Will traffic go over the other interface in EtherChannel bundle?

Step 8. Clear interface counters on Switch 1 using the **clear counters** command:

```
Switch1# clear counters
Clear "show interface" counters on all interfaces [confirm] [Enter]
```

Step 9. Perform an extended ping from PC 2 to PC 3:

```
PC2# ping
Protocol [ip]: [Enter]
Target IP address: 172.16.1.203
Repeat count [5]: 10000
Datagram size [100]: 1500
Timeout in seconds [2]: [Enter]
Extended commands [n]: [Enter]
Sweep range of sizes [n]: [Enter]
Type escape sequence to abort.
Sending 10000, 1500-byte ICMP Echos to 172.16.1.203, timeout is 2
  seconds:
!!!!!!!!!!!!!!!!!!!!!!!!!!!!!!!!!!!!!!!!!!!!!!!!!!!!!!!!!!!!!!!!!!!!!!!
<... output omitted ...>
```

Step 10. Verify counters on Switch 1 for both interfaces:

```
Switch1# show interface ethernet 1/1 | i packets output
    29 packets output, 2201 bytes, 0 underruns
Switch1# show interface ethernet 1/2 | i packets output
    10003 packets output, 15140537 bytes, 0 underruns
```

So, with the ping from PC 1 to PC 3, traffic went over Ethernet 1/1. With the ping from PC 2 to PC 3, traffic went over Ethernet 1/2. This is for the default load-balancing method that takes destination and source IP address for calculating the hash.

Step 11. Change the load-balancing behavior on Switch 1 from src-dst-ip to dst-ip:

```
Switch1(config)# port-channel load-balance dst-ip
```

How will traffic get distributed over the two links now?

Step 12. Verify that the load-balancing behavior has changed:

```
Switch1# show etherchannel load-balance
EtherChannel Load-Balancing Configuration:
        dst-ip

EtherChannel Load-Balancing Addresses Used Per-Protocol:
Non-IP: Source XOR Destination MAC address
  IPv4: Source XOR Destination IP address
  IPv6: Source XOR Destination IP address
```

Step 13. Clear the interface counters on Switch 1 by using the **clear counters** command:

```
Switch1# clear counters
Clear "show interface" counters on all interfaces [confirm] [Enter]
```

Step 14. Perform an extended ping from PC 1 to PC 3:

```
PC1# ping
Protocol [ip]: [Enter]
Target IP address: 172.16.1.203
Repeat count [5]: 10000
Datagram size [100]: 1500
Timeout in seconds [2]: [Enter]
Extended commands [n]: [Enter]
Sweep range of sizes [n]: [Enter]
Type escape sequence to abort.
Sending 10000, 1500-byte ICMP Echos to 172.16.1.203, timeout is 2
seconds:
!!!!!!!!!!!!!!!!!!!!!!!!!!!!!!!!!!!!!!!!!!!!!!!!!!!!!!!!!!!!!!!!!!!!!!!!
<... output omitted ...>
```

Step 15. Verify the counters on Switch 1 for both interfaces:

```
Switch1# show interface ethernet 1/1 | i packets output
    32 packets output, 2108 bytes, 0 underruns
Switch1# show interface ethernet 1/2 | i packets output
    10002 packets output, 15140188 bytes, 0 underruns
```

The majority of the traffic went over the Ethernet 1/2 port.

Step 16. Clear the interface counters on Switch 1 by using the **clear counters** command:

```
Switch1# clear counters
Clear "show interface" counters on all interfaces [confirm] [Enter]
```

Step 17.   Perform an extended ping from PC 2 to PC 3:

```
PC2# ping
Protocol [ip]: [Enter]
Target IP address: 172.16.1.203
Repeat count [5]: 10000
Datagram size [100]: 1500
Timeout in seconds [2]: [Enter]
Extended commands [n]: [Enter]
Sweep range of sizes [n]: [Enter]
Type escape sequence to abort.
Sending 10000, 1500-byte ICMP Echos to 172.16.1.203, timeout is 2
  seconds:
!!!!!!!!!!!!!!!!!!!!!!!!!!!!!!!!!!!!!!!!!!!!!!!!!!!!!!!!!!!!!!!!!!!!!!!!!!!!
<... output omitted ...>
```

Step 18.   Verify counters on Switch 1 for both interfaces:

```
Switch1# show interface ethernet 1/1 | i packets output
      31 packets output, 2329 bytes, 0 underruns
Switch1# show interface ethernet 1/2 | i packets output
      10004 packets output, 15140597 bytes, 0 underruns
```

Now that the load balancing is based on destination IP, the behavior has changed. Because the only input information for calculation of the hash is destination IP address, it does not matter whether you ping PC 3 from PC 1 or PC 2. In both cases, the hash function will be the same, and traffic will go over the same link (in this example, Ethernet ½).

> **Note**   The default method of load balancing usually works for most scenarios, but you can change it based on the traffic needs in the network.

EtherChannel Guard

The EtherChannel Guard feature is used to detect EtherChannel misconfigurations between the switch and a connected device.

EtherChannel misconfiguration occurs when the channel parameters do not match on both sides of the EtherChannel, resulting in the following message:

```
%PM-SP-4-ERR_DISABLE: channel-misconfig error detected on Po3, putting E1/3 in
err-disable state
```

The EtherChannel Guard feature can be enabled by using the **spanning-tree etherchannel guard misconfig** global configuration command.

However, EtherChannel Guard is enabled by default. To verify whether it is configured, use the **show spanning-tree summary** command, as demonstrated in Example 3-13.

Example 3-13   *Show VTP Status and Show VLAN outputs from SW1 and SW3*

```
Switch1# show spanning-tree summary
Switch is in pvst mode
Root bridge for: VLAN0001
Extended system ID            is enabled
Portfast Default              is disabled
PortFast BPDU Guard Default   is disabled
Portfast BPDU Filter Default  is disabled
Loopguard Default             is disabled
EtherChannel misconfig guard  is enabled
<...output omitted...>
```

Study Tips

- VLAN provides logical grouping of the hosts to restrict the broadcast domain.

- VLANs are usually categorized into local and end-to-end VLANs, and each has its own pros and cons.

- With the help of trunking, VLANS can be easily extended over a single physical link.

- ISL and 802.1Q are two trunking protocols, with dot1Q the industry standard.

- Dot1Q frames insert 4 bytes and recalculate the CRC.

- Native VLAN is not encapsulated in dot1Q trunking, and it is important to have same native VLAN on both sides of the switches.

- VTP is used to distribute VLAN databases. It has multiple versions and modes. VTP works in server, client, and transparent mode.

- Any switch with a higher revision number can overwrite the VLAN database. Insert the new switch with caution and follow the recommended steps.

- EtherChannel is a technology that was originally developed by Cisco as a LAN switch-to-switch technique of grouping several Fast or Gigabit Ethernet ports into one logical channel.

- PagP and LACP are the two main protocols for EtherChannel.

- For EtherChannel, it is highly recommended to use the even number of ports in the channel to have better load balancing.

Summary

In review, a VLAN is a logical grouping of switch ports that connects nodes of nearly any type, regardless of physical location. VLAN segmentation is based on traffic flow patterns. A VLAN is usually defined as an end-to-end VLAN or a local VLAN. An end-to-end VLAN spans the entire switched network, whereas a local VLAN is limited to the switches in the building access and building distribution submodules. The creation of a VLAN implementation plan depends on the business and technical requirements.

Furthermore, a trunk is a Layer 2 point-to-point link between networking devices that can carry the traffic of multiple VLANs. ISL and 802.1Q are the two trunking protocols that connect two switches. The 802.1Q protocol is an open standard protocol also used for VLAN trunking.

VTP is used to distribute and synchronize information about VLANs configured throughout a switched network. VTP pruning helps to stop flooding of unnecessary traffic on trunk links. VTP configuration sometimes needs to be added to small network deployments, whereas VTP transparent mode is usually privileged for larger networks. When configuring VLANs over several switches, ensure that the configuration is compatible throughout switches in the same domain.

To increase bandwidth and provide redundancy, use EtherChannel by aggregating individual, similar links between switches. EtherChannel can be dynamically configured between switches using either the Cisco proprietary PAgP or the IEEE 802.3ad LACP. EtherChannel is configured by assigning interfaces to the EtherChannel bundle and configuring the resulting port channel interface. EtherChannel load balances traffic over all the links in the bundle. The method that is chosen directly impacts the efficiency of this load-balancing mechanism.

Review Questions

Use the questions here to review what you learned in this chapter. The correct answers are found in Appendix A, "Answers to Chapter Review Questions."

1. True or False: It is important to have the same native VLAN on both switch link partners for ISL trunking.

2. True or False: The Cisco Catalyst 6500 supports up to 1024 VLANs in the most recent software releases.

3. True or False: When removing the native VLAN from a trunk port, CDP, PAgP, and DTP, use the lowest-numbered VLAN to send traffic.

4. True or False: In VTP client mode, switches can add and delete VLANs.

5. True or False: Token Ring support is available in VTP Version 1.

Questions 6 through 8 are based on the configuration in Example 3-14.

Example 3-14 *Configuration Example for Questions 6 Through 8*

```
Catalyst6500-IOS# show run interface gigabitEthernet 3/9
Building configuration...
Current configuration : 137 bytes !
interface GigabitEthernet3/9
mtu 9216
no ip address
switchport
switchport access vlan 5
switchport trunk encapsulation dot1q
end
```

6. If the interface in Example 3-14 negotiates trunking, what would be the native VLAN?

   a. VLAN 1

   b. VLAN 5

   c. VLAN 9216

   d. No native VLAN if the port negotiated trunking

7. Under what condition can the interface in Example 3-14 negotiate ISL trunking?

   a. If the port is a member of an EtherChannel.

   b. If the link partner defaults to ISL trunking for negotiated ports.

   c. If the link partner is configured for trunking in the on mode.

   d. The interface cannot negotiate trunking because it is configured statically for 802.1Q trunking.

8. Which statement is true for the configuration of the interface in Example 3-14?

   a. The interface is a member of VLAN 5 and may negotiate to a trunk port.

   b. The interface may negotiate to an ISL trunk with a native VLAN of 5.

   c. The interface may negotiate to an 802.1Q trunk and operate with a native VLAN of 1.

   d. The interface will not negotiate to a trunk port because it is configured in access VLAN 5.

   e. If a host workstation is connected to the interface, it must be configured for trunking.

Questions 9 through 11 are based on the configuration in Example 3-15.

Example 3-15 *Configuration Example for Questions 9 Through 11*

```
svs-san-6509-2# show interfaces gigabitEthernet 3/9 switchport
Name: Gi3/9
Switchport: Enabled
Administrative Mode: dynamic auto
Operational Mode: down
Administrative Trunking Encapsulation: dot1q
Negotiation of Trunking: On
Access Mode VLAN: 1 (default)
Trunking Native Mode VLAN: 2 (VLAN0002)
Voice VLAN: none
Administrative private-vlan host-association: none
Administrative private-vlan mapping: none
Operational private-vlan: none
Trunking VLANs Enabled: ALL
Pruning VLANs Enabled: 2-1001
Capture Mode Disabled
Capture VLANs Allowed: ALL
```

9. What is the trunk native VLAN based on in Example 3-15?

   a. VLAN 1

   b. VLAN 2

   c. VLAN 5

   d. No Native VLAN if the port negotiated trunking

10. Based on Example 3-15, what statement is true if the link partner (peer switch) is configured for the dynamic trunking mode?

    a. The interface cannot negotiate to a trunk port because it is configured for dot1Q encapsulation.

    b. The interface cannot negotiate to a trunk port because the native VLAN and access VLANs are mismatched.

    c. The interface can negotiate to a trunk port if the peer is configured for the dynamic desirable trunking mode.

    d. The interface can negotiate to a trunk port if access VLAN is the same on both sides.

11. What is the interface's access mode VLAN in Example 3-15?

    a. VLAN 1

    b. VLAN 2

    c. VLAN 5

    d. VLAN 1001

12. How does implementing VLANs help improve the overall performance of the network?

    a. By isolating problem employees

    b. By constraining broadcast traffic

    c. By grouping switch ports into logical communities

    d. By forcing the Layer 3 routing process to occur between VLANs

13. What are the advantages of using local VLANs over end-to-end VLANs? (Choose two.)

    a. Eases management

    b. Eliminates the need for Layer 3 devices

    c. Allows for a more deterministic network

    d. Groups users by logical commonality

    e. Keeps users and resources on the same VLAN

14. Which prompt indicates that you are in VLAN configuration mode of Cisco IOS?

    a. Switch#

    b. Switch(vlan)#

    c. Switch(config)#

    d. Switch(config-vlan)#

15. Which switch port mode unconditionally sets the switch port to access mode regardless of any other DTP configurations?

    a. Access

    b. Nonegotiate

    c. Dynamic auto

    d. Dynamic desirable

16. What information is contained in the FCS of an ISL-encapsulated frame?

  a. CRC calculation

  b. Header encapsulation

  c. ASIC implementation

  d. Protocol independence

17. 802.1Q uses an internal tagging mechanism, where a tag is inserted after the _____ field.

  a. Type

  b. SA

  c. Data

  d. CRC

18. Which command correctly configures a port with ISL encapsulation in Cisco IOS?

  a. Switch(config-if)# **switchport mode trunk isl**

  b. Switch(config-if)# **switchport mode encapsulation isl**

  c. Switch(config-if)# **switchport trunk encapsulation isl**

  d. Switch(config-if)# **switchport mode trunk encapsulation isl**

19. Which command correctly sets the native VLAN to VLAN 5?

  a. switchport native vlan 5

  b. switchport trunk native 5

  c. switchport native trunk vlan 5

  d. switchport trunk native vlan 5

20. If the Layer 2 interface mode on one link partner is set to dynamic auto, a trunk will be established if the link partner is configured for which types of interface modes in Cisco IOS? (Choose two.)

  a. Trunk

  b. Access

  c. Nonegotiate

  d. Dynamic auto

  e. Dynamic desirable

21. What is the default VTP mode for a Catalyst switch?

   a. Client

   b. Access

   c. Server

   d. Transparent

22. When is a consistency check performed with VTP Version 2?

   a. When information is read from NVRAM

   b. When the digest on a received VTP message is correct

   c. When new information is obtained from a VTP message

   d. When you enter new information through the CLI or SNMP

23. Which command correctly sets the VTP version to version 1 in Cisco IOS global configuration mode?

   a. vtp v1-mode

   b. vtp v2-mode

   c. no vtp version

   d. no vtp version 2

24. Which of the following are valid VTP Version 1 and 2 modes? (Choose all that apply.)

   a. Primary server mode

   b. Server mode

   c. Client mode

   d. Transparent mode

25. After you complete the VTP configuration, which command should you use to verify your configuration?

   a. show vtp status

   b. show vtp counters

   c. show vtp statistics

   d. show vtp status counters

26. What command might correct a problem with incorrect VTP passwords?

    a. password vtp 0

    b. clear vtp password

    c. clear password vtp

    d. vtp password password_string

27. True or False: The EtherChannel would come up if one side of the EtherChannel mode is set to auto and the other to on.

28. Which of the following solutions are provided by EtherChannel? (Choose two.)

    a. Provide redundancy

    b. Help to overcome bandwidth limitation

    c. Because of EtherChannel, can transmit more than one VLAN over the links between switches

    d. Can limit the broadcast to the local switches

29. Which statement identifies network benefits provided by VLANs?

    a. VLANs allow you to group stations without regard to the physical location of the users.

    b. VLANs help to isolate problem employees.

    c. VLANs reduce the impact of network problems.

    d. VLANs can transmit frames to all ports in all VLANs.

30. Match each command to its explanation.

    a. Switch(config-if)# **switchport voice vlan** *vlan-id*

    b. Switch(config-if)# **switchport mode access**

    c. Switch(config-if)# **switchport access vlan** *vlan-id*

    d. Switch(config-if)# **switchport trunk native vlan** *vlan-id*

    e. Switch(config-if)# **switchport trunk allowed vlan add** *vlan-id*

    f. Switch(config-if)# **switchport mode trunk**

        1. Configures the port to be assigned only to a single VLAN

        2. Configures the port to be assigned to multiple VLANs

        3. Configures a VLAN to be added to trunk port

        4. Configures a native VLAN for the trunk

        5. Configures a port to be a part of voice VLAN

        6. Configures a port to be a part of data VLAN

31. How can you reset VTP revision number on a switch? (Choose two.)

    a. Set the switch to transparent mode and then to server mode.

    b. Set the switch to client mode and then to server mode.

    c. Change the VTP domain name to a nonexistent VTP domain and then back to the original name.

    d. Reload the switch.

32. Which statement about transparent VTP mode is true?

    a. Creates, modifies, and deletes VLANs on all switches in VTP domain

    b. Creates, modifies, and deletes local VLANs only

    c. Does not forward advertisements to other switches in VTP domain

    d. Synchronizes VLAN configurations from other switches in VTP domain

33. What is the correct command for configuring load balancing on an EtherChannel link?

    a. Switch(config)# **channel-group number load-balance** *method*

    b. Switch(config-if)# **channel-group number load-balance** *method*

    c. Switch(config-if)# **port-channel number load-balance** *method*

    d. Switch(config)# **port-channel load-balance** *method*

34. Which of the following EtherChannel modes does not send or receive any negotiation frames?

    a. Passive

    b. Active

    c. On

    d. Desirable auto

Chapter 4

Spanning Tree in Depth

Upon completing this chapter, you will be able to meet these objectives:

■ Data plane techniques to protect the network edge and core, including the different router interface types

■ Spanning Tree Protocol (STP) overview, its operations, and history

■ Implement Rapid Spanning Tree Protocol (RSTP)

■ Describe how and where to configure the following features: PortFast, UplinkFast, BackboneFast, BPDU Guard, BPDU Filter, Root Guard, Loop Guard, Unidirectional Link Detection, and FlexLinks

■ Configure Multiple Spanning Tree (MST)

■ Troubleshooting STP

High availability is a primary goal for enterprise networks that rely heavily on their multilayer switched network to conduct business. One way to ensure high availability is to provide Layer 2 redundancy of devices, modules, and links throughout the network. Network redundancy at Layer 2, however, introduces the potential for bridging loops, where packets loop endlessly between devices, crippling the network. The Spanning Tree Protocol (STP) identifies and prevents such Layer 2 loops.

By default, Cisco switches use PVST+ (Per-VLAN Spanning Tree Protocol Plus). However, it is highly recommended to use either Rapid PVST+ (RPVST+) or MST (Multiple Spanning Tree) wherever possible.

STP provides a number of features. Some are implemented to speed up performance (UplinkFast, BackboneFast, PortFast), and others are configured to increase stability (BPDU Guard, BPDU Filter, Root Guard, Loop Guard). In addition, other mechanisms are not directly related to STP, but can be used to either complement STP operation (UDLD [Unidirectional Link Detection]) or to replace it (FlexLinks). This chapter provides an overview of the spanning-tree protocols, including PVRST+ and MST. This chapter also covers how to configure the protocols and how to configure STP stability mechanisms.

Spanning Tree Protocol Overview

Redundant topology can eliminate the possibility of a single point of failure causing a loss of function for the entire network. Although it has benefits, redundant topology also causes problems, such as loops. STP provides network link redundancy while eliminating potential problems.

A limitation of the traditional STP is the convergence delay after a topology change, so use of RSTP is recommended instead.

Upon completing this section, you will be able to meet these objectives:

- Explain the need for STP
- List different standards of STP
- Describe basic STP operation
- Describe bridge protocol data units
- Explain the root bridge election
- Explain the root port election
- Explain designated port election
- Explain STP port states
- Explain PVST+
- Explain STP topology changes

STP Need

Redundant topology can eliminate single points of failure in the network as shown in Figure 4-1; however, STP blocks certain ports, so there is only one active path to each segment.

STP blocks certain ports, so there is only one active path to each network segment.

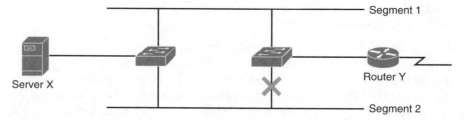

Figure 4-1 *STP Overview*

However, redundant topology can cause some of the following key problems:

■ **Broadcast storms:** Each switch on a redundant network floods broadcast frames endlessly. Switches flood broadcast frames to all ports except the port on which the frame was received. These frames then travel around the loop in all directions.

■ **Multiple frame transmission:** Multiple copies of the same unicast frames may be delivered to destination station, which can cause problems with the receiving protocol. Many protocols expect to receive only a single copy of each transmission. Multiple copies of the same frame can cause unrecoverable errors.

■ **MAC database instability:** This results from copies of the same frame being received on different ports of the switch. A MAC address table maps the source MAC address on a packet received to the interface it was received on. If a loop occurs, the same source MAC address could be seen on multiple interfaces causing instability. Data forwarding can be impaired when the switch consumes the resources that are coping with instability in the MAC address table.

To solve all of these problems, there was a need of loop-avoidance mechanism. STP was developed to address these issues.

STP allows physical path redundancy while preventing the undesirable effects of active loops in the network. STP forces certain ports into a standby state so that they do not listen, forward, or flood data frames. There is only one active path to each network segment.

If there is a problem with connectivity to any of the segments, STP reestablishes connectivity by automatically activating a previously inactive path. STP uses bridge protocol data units (BPDUs) for its operations. BPDUs are messages that STP uses to determine current topology information and how to react if any devices added or removed or changed in the topology. By default they are sent out every 2 seconds on all switch ports. BDPUs are discussed later in detail.

STP Standards

There are several varieties of STP, and STP has been evolving a lot. Following are the key types of STP:

■ STP itself is the original IEEE 802.1D version, which provides a loop-free topology in a network with redundant links. STP was created for a bridged network, so it supports only a single LAN or one VLAN.

■ Common Spanning Tree (CST) assumes one spanning-tree instance for the entire network. Unlike 802.1D, it supports more than one VLAN.

■ PVST and PVST+ are Cisco proprietary protocols that provide a separate spanning-tree instance for each VLAN configured in the network. PVST protocol is obsolete.

- MST maps multiple VLANs into the same spanning-tree instance. MST was defined based on the Cisco prestandard MST. Cisco switches now use the standard implementation.

- RSTP is standard, described in IEEE 802.1w. It is an evolution of STP that provides faster convergence of STP.

- RPVST+ is a Cisco implementation of RSTP that is based on PVST+.

Table 4-1 shows the summary of all the STP types of protocols and their need of resources and effects on convergences when an event happened in the network.

Table 4-1   *STP Standards*

	Standard	Resources Needed	Convergence	
CST	802.1D	Low	Slow	All VLANs
PVST+	Cisco	High	Slow	Per VLAN
RSTP	802.1w	Medium	Fast	All VLANs
RPVST+	Cisco	Very high	Fast	Per VLAN
MST	802.1s	Medium or high	Fast	VLAN list

Spanning-tree varieties that use more than one instance of STP have higher CPU and memory requirements. The CPU and memory requirements are also higher when spanning-tree protocols with faster convergence are used because the algorithm needs to make calculations more frequently.

Note   There is also a Cisco proprietary implementation of 802.1s, which is prestandard.

STP Operations

STP (see Figure 4-2) provides loop resolution by managing the physical path to the given network segment, by performing the following three steps:

1. **Elects one root bridge:** Only one bridge can act as the root bridge. The root bridge is the reference point; all data flows in the network are from the perspective of this switch. All ports on a root bridge are forwarding traffic.

2. **Selects the root port on the nonroot bridge:** One port on each nonroot bridge is the root port. It is the port with the lowest-cost path from the nonroot bridge to the root bridge. By default, STP path cost is calculated from the bandwidth of the link. You can also set STP path cost manually.

3. **Selects the designated port on each segment:** There is one designated port on each segment. It is selected on the bridge with the lowest-cost path to the root bridge.

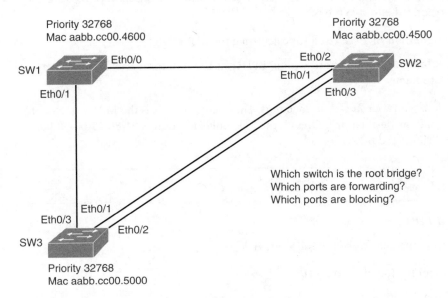

Figure 4-2   *STP Operations*

Ports that are neither root nor designated must be nondesignated. Nondesignated ports are normally in the blocking state to break the loop topology.

There are four port roles in STP, as illustrated in Table 4-2.

Table 4-2   *STP Port Roles*

Port role	Description
Root port	This port exists on nonroot bridges and is the switch port with the best path to the root bridge. Only one root port is allowed per bridge.
Designated port	This port exists on root and nonroot bridges. For root bridges, all switch ports are designated ports. For nonroot bridges, a designated port is the switch port that will receive and forward frames toward the root bridge as needed. Only one designated port is allowed per segment. If multiple switches exist on the same segment, an election process determines the designated switch, and the corresponding switch port begins forwarding frames for the segment.
Nondesignated port	The nondesignated port is a switch port that is not forwarding (blocking) data frames.
Disabled port	The disabled port is a switch port that is shut down.

Bridge Protocol Data Units

STP uses BPDUs to exchange STP information, specifically for root bridge election and for loop identification. By default, BPDUs are sent out every 2 seconds. BPDUs are generally categorized into two types:

- **Configuration BDPUs:** Used for calculating the STP

- **TCN (topology change notification) BPDUs:** Used to inform changes in the network topology

Every switch sends out BPDU on each port. The source address is the MAC address of that port, and the destination address is the STP multicast address 01-80-c2-00-00-00. Figure 4-3 shows the BDPU frame.

Protocol ID	Version	Message Type	Flags	Root Bridge ID	Root Path Cost	Sender Bridge ID	Port ID	Massage Age	Maximum Age	Hello Time	Forward Delay

Figure 4-3   *BPDU*

The BPDU frame consists of the following fields:

- **Protocol ID:** Identifies the STP

- **Version:** Identifies the current version of the protocol

- **Message Type:** Identifies the type of BPDU (configuration or TCN BPDU)

- **Flags:** Used in response to a TCN BPDU

- **Root Bridge ID:** Identifies the bridge ID (BID) of the root bridge

- **Root Path Cost:** Identifies the cost from the transmitting switch to the root

- **Sender Bridge ID:** Identifies the BID of the transmitting switch

- **Port ID:** Identifies the transmitting port

- **Message Age:** Indicates the age of the current BPDU

- **Max Age:** Indicates the timeout value

- **Hello Time:** Identifies the time interval between generations of configuration BPDUs by the root

- **Forward Delay:** Defines the time a switch port must wait in the listening and learning state

Root Bridge Election

To prevent loops in a network, STP uses a reference point: the root bridge. The root bridge is the logical center of the spanning tree topology. All paths that are not needed to reach the root bridge from anywhere in the network are placed in STP blocking mode.

The root bridge is chosen with an election. In STP, each switch has a unique BID that consists of the following, as shown in Figure 4-4:

- Bridge priority (a value between 0 and 65,535, with the default being 32,768)
- MAC address

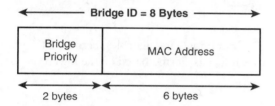

Figure 4-4 *STP Bridge ID*

The root bridge is selected based on the lowest BID. If all switches in the network have the same priority, the switch with the lowest MAC address becomes the root bridge, as illustrated in Figure 4-5.

In the beginning, each switch assumes that it is the root bridge. Each switch sends BPDUs to its neighbors, presenting its BID. At the same time, it receives the BPDUs from all the neighbors. Each time a switch receives a BPDU, it checks its BID against its own. If the received BID is better than its own, then the switch knows it is not the root bridge. Otherwise it keeps its assumption of being the root bridge.

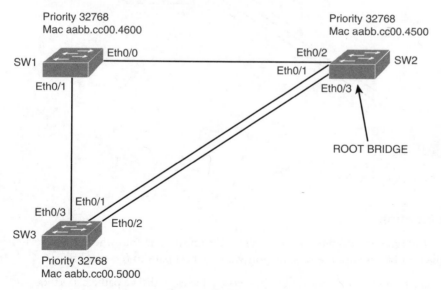

Figure 4-5 *Root Bridge Selection Process*

Eventually the election converges and all switches agree that one of them is the root bridge.

Root bridge election is an ongoing process. So if a new switch appears with a better BID, it will be elected as the new root bridge.

Note   The term *root bridge* comes from the days of when STP was developed. Even though you do not have bridges in your network, this term is still used. The root bridge of your topology might be better called the *root switch*.

The switch with the lowest priority will be the root bridge. In Figure 4-6, because all three switches have the same priority, the root bridge is elected based on the lowest MAC address.

• Port with the lowest cost to the root bridge is called the root port.
• If two ports have the same cost, senders port ID is used to break the tie.

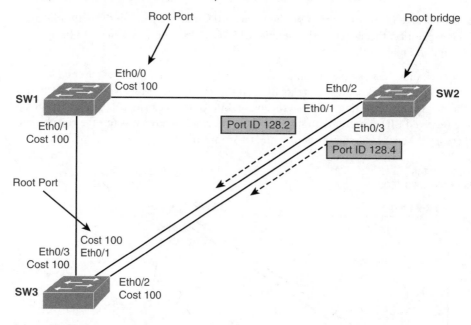

Figure 4-6   *Root Port Election*

Root Port Election

After the root bridge is elected, each nonroot bridge must figure out where it is in relation to the root bridge. Root port is the port with the best path to the root bridge.

To determine root ports on nonroot bridges, cost value is used. The path cost is the cumulative cost of all links to the root bridge. Root port indicates the lowest cost to the root bridge.

As shown in Figure 4-6, SW1 has two paths to the root bridge. Which port will be elected the root port? The path cost through Ethernet 0/1 is cumulative. The cost of link SW1-SW2 is 100, and the cost between SW3 and SW2 is 100; one of these links will be blocked by the STP. So the cost to get to the root bridge through Ethernet 0/1 is 200. SW1's path through Ethernet 0/0 has cost of 100. Because the path through Ethernet 0/0 has a lower cost, Ethernet 0/0 will be elected the root port. If the two ports have the same cost, sender port ID is used to break the tie.

STP cost is calculated from the bandwidth of the link. The administrator can manually change it. However, this is not a common practice.

Table 4-3 shows common cost values of the link. The higher the bandwidth of a link, the lower the cost of transporting data across it.

Table 4-3 *STP Costs and the Link Speeds*

Link	Cost
10 Gbps	1
1 Gbps	4
100 Mbps	19
10 Mbps	100

Note Bandwidth of the EtherChannel is calculated as the sum of all the links that are bundled into the EtherChannel. The cost of the EtherChannel link is calculated based on the summed bandwidth.

When two ports have the same cost, arbitration can be done using the advertised port ID (from the neighboring switch).

In Figure 4-6, SW3 has three paths to the root bridge. Through Ethernet 0/3, the cumulative cost is 200 (links SW3-SW1 and SW1-SW2). Through Ethernet 0/1 and Ethernet 0/2, the cost is the same: 100. Because lower cost is better, one of these two ports will be elected the root port. Port ID is a combination of a port priority, which is 128 by default, and a port number. For example, in Figure 4-6, the port Ethernet 0/1 on Switch 2 will have the port ID 128.1, the port Ethernet 0/3 will have port ID 128.3, and so on. The lowest port ID is always chosen when port ID is the determining factor. Because Ethernet 0/1 receives a lower port ID from SW2 (128.2) than Ethernet 0/2 receives (128.4), Ethernet 0/1 will be elected the root port.

Note Remember that the port ID's selection is based on the port ID of the advertised neighboring switch.

Designated Port Election

After the root bridge and root ports on nonroot bridges have been elected, to prevent the loops STP has to identify which port on the segment will forward the traffic.

Only one of the links on a segment should forward traffic to and from that segment. The designated port, the one forwarding the traffic, is also chosen based on the lowest cost to the root bridge.

On the root bridge, all ports are designated.

If there are two paths with equal cost to the root bridge, STP uses the following criteria for best path determination and consequently for determination of designated and non-designated ports on the segment:

- Lowest root BID
- Lowest root path cost to root bridge
- Lowest sender BID
- Lowest sender port ID

As shown in Figure 4-7, SW2 is the root bridge, so it has all ports designated. To prevent loops, a blocking port for the SW1-SW3 segment has to be determined. Because SW3 and SW1 have the same path cost to the root bridge, 100, the lower BID breaks the tie. SW1 has lower BID than SW3, so the designated port for the segment is Ethernet 0/1 on SW1.

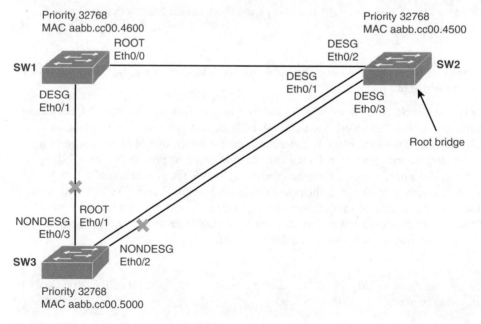

Figure 4-7 *Designated Port Election*

Only one port on a segment should forward traffic. All ports that are not root or designated ports are nondesignated ports. Nondesignated ports go to the blocking state to prevent a loop.

In Figure 4-7, root ports are determined on nonroot bridges. We have just determined which ports are designated. All the other ports are nondesignated. The only two interfaces that are not root or designated ports are Ethernet 0/2 and Ethernet 0/3 on SW3. Both are nondesignated (blocking).

STP Port States

To participate in the spanning-tree process, a switch port must go through several states. A port will start in disabled state, and then, after an administrator enables it, move through various states until it reaches forwarding state (that is, if it is allowed to be forwarding). If not, it will be moved into blocking state. Table 4-4 outlines all the STP states and their functionality as defined further in the list that follows.

Table 4-4   *STP Port States*

STP Port State	Receive BPDUs	Send BPDUs	Learn MAC Addresses	Receive Data	Send Data	Duration of State
Blocking	✓	X	X	X	X	Undefined (if there is a loop)
Listening	✓	✓	X	X	X	Forward delay (15 seconds)
Learning	✓	✓	✓	X	X	Forward delay (15 seconds)
Forwarding	✓	✓	✓	✓	✓	Undefined (as long as there is a loop)
Disabled	X	X	X	X	X	Until administrator enables it

- **Blocking:** In this state, the port ensures that no bridging loops occur. A port in this state cannot receive or transmit data, but it receives BPDUs, so the switch can hear from its neighbor switches and determine the location, and root ID, of the root switch and port roles of each switch. A port in this state is a nondesignated port, and therefore it does not participate in active topology.

- **Listening:** A port is moved from blocking to listening state if there is a possibility to be selected as the root or designated port. The port in this state still cannot send or receive data frames. But it is allowed to send and receive BPDUs, so it is participating in active topology.

- **Learning:** After a period of time (forward delay) in listening state, the port is moved to learning state. The port still sends and receives BPDUs; in addition, it can learn and add new MAC addresses to its table. A port in this state cannot send any data frames.

■ **Forwarding:** After another period of time (forward delay) in learning state, the port is moved to forwarding state. It is considered as part of the active topology. It sends and receives frames and also sends and receives BPDUs.

■ **Disabled:** In this state, a port is administratively shut down. It does not participate in spanning tree, and it does not forward frames.

Per-VLAN STP Plus (PVST+)

Per-VLAN STP Plus (PVST+) is a Cisco implementation of STP that provides a separate spanning-tree instance for each configured VLAN in the network.

Unlike CST, PVST+ runs one spanning-tree instance for each VLAN. This allows you to load balance traffic over redundant links when they are assigned to a different VLAN.

Figure 4-8 shows PVST+ configured. Switch A is configured the root for VLAN 1, and Switch B is configured the root for VLAN 2. The uplink on the left forwards traffic for VLAN 1, and VLAN 1 traffic is blocked on the right uplink. It is the reverse for VLAN 2 traffic. The uplink on the right forwards traffic for VLAN 2, and VLAN 2 traffic is blocked on the left uplink.

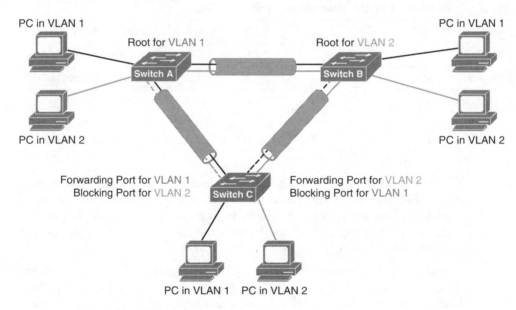

Figure 4-8   *Per-VLAN STP+*

In case of CST, there would be only one root bridge, and one link would forward traffic for both VLANs; the other link would be blocked for all VLANs

Note   PVSTP+ is usually the default STP on Cisco switches.

Spanning-tree operation requires that each switch has a unique BID. To carry BID information, the extended system ID is accommodated. The original 16-bit bridge priority field is split into two fields, resulting in the following components in the BID:

- **Bridge priority:** A 4-bit field used to carry bridge priority. The default priority is 32,768, which is the midrange value. The priority is conveyed in discrete values in increments of 4096.

- **Extended system ID:** A 12-bit field carrying the VLAN ID.

- **MAC address:** A 6-byte field with the MAC address of the switch.

By virtue of the MAC address, a BID is always unique. If no priority has been configured, every switch will have the same default priority, and the election of the root for each VLAN is based on the MAC address. Because this method is random, it is advisable to assign a lower priority to the switch that should serve as the root bridge.

STP Topology Changes

When a switch moves a port into the forwarding state or into blocking state, that means that an STP topology changes.

The switch announces a topology change by sending a TCN BPDU out from the root port. This BPDU does not contain data about the change, but it only informs other switches in the network that the change has occurred.

In Figure 4-9, when the root bridge receives the TCN BPDU, it first sends an acknowledgement BPDU topology change acknowledgment (TCA) to the switch from which it received the TCN. The root bridge then signals the topology change to other switches in the network by changing topology change flag in its BPDU (TC), as shown in Figure 4-9. Switches then shorten their bridge table aging times to the forward delay time.

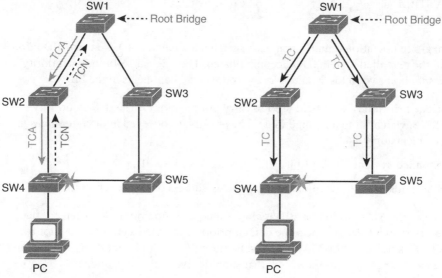

Figure 4-9   *STP Topology Changes*

There are three types of topology change:

■ A **direct topology change** can be detected on an interface. In the figure, SW4 has detected a link failure on one of the interfaces. It then sends out a TCN message on the root port to reach the root bridge. SW1, the root bridge, then announces the topology change to other switches in the network. All switches shorten their bridging table aging time to the forward delay. That way they get new associations of port and MAC address after 15 seconds, not after 300 seconds, which is the default bridging table aging time. The convergence time in that case is two times the forward delay period, so 30 seconds.

■ With an **indirect topology change**, the link status stays up. Something (for example, another device such as firewall) on the link has failed or is filtering traffic, and no data is received on each side of the link. Because there is no link failure, no TCN messages are sent. The topology change is detected because there are no BPDUs from the root bridge. With indirect link failure, the topology does not change immediately, but the STP converges again, thanks to timer mechanisms. The convergence time in that case is longer than with direct topology change, around 50 seconds.

■ **Insignificant topology change** occurs if, for example, a PC connected to SW4 is turned off. An event causes SW4 to send out TCNs. However, because none of the switches had to change port states to reach the root bridge, no actual topology change occurred. The only consequence of shutting down the PC is that all switches will age out entries from the content-addressable memory (CAM) table sooner than normal. This can become a problem if you have a lot of PCs. A lot of PCs going up and down can cause a lot of TCN exchanges. To avoid, you can enable PortFast on end-user ports. If a PortFast-enabled port goes up or down, a TCN is not generated.

Rapid Spanning Tree Protocol

Rapid Spanning Tree Protocol (IEEE 802.1w, also referred to as RSTP) significantly speeds the recalculation of the spanning tree when the network topology changes. RSTP defines the additional port roles of alternate and backup and defines port states as discarding, learning, or forwarding. This section describes the differences between STP (802.1D) and RSTP (802.1w).

The 802.1D STP standard was designed with the understanding that recovering connectivity after an outage within a minute or so gives adequate performance. With the advent of Layer 3 switching in LAN environments, bridging now competes with routed solutions in which protocols such as Open Shortest Path First (OSPF) and Enhanced Interior Gateway Routing Protocol (EIGRP) can provide an alternative path in approximately 1 second.

Cisco enhanced the original 802.1D specification with features such as UplinkFast, BackboneFast, and PortFast to speed up the convergence time of a bridged network. The drawback is that these mechanisms are proprietary and need additional configuration.

Note   UplinkFast, BackboneFast, and PortFast are discussed in more detail in later sections of this chapter.

The IEEE 802.1w standard (RSTP) is an evolution, rather than a revolution, of the 802.1D standard. The 802.1D terminology remains primarily the same, and most parameters are left unchanged. So, users who are familiar with 802.1D can rapidly feel at home when configuring the new protocol. In most cases, RSTP performs better than the Cisco proprietary extensions, with negligible additional configuration. In addition, 802.1w can revert to 802.1D to interoperate with legacy bridges on a per-port basis. Reverting to 802.1D negates the benefits of 802.1w for that particular segment.

RSTP selects one switch as the root of an active spanning-tree-connected topology and assigns port roles to individual ports on the switch, depending on whether the ports are part of the active topology. RSTP provides rapid connectivity following the failure of a switch, switch port, or LAN. A new root port and the designated port of the connecting bridge transition to forwarding through an explicit handshake protocol between them. RSTP enables switch port configuration so that the ports transition to forwarding directly when the switch reinitializes.

On Cisco Catalyst switches, a rapid version of PVST+, called *PVRST+*, is the per-VLAN version of the RSTP implementation. All the current-generation Catalyst switches support PVRST+.

Upon completing this section, you will be able to meet these objectives:

- List and explain RSTP port roles

- Compare RSTP and STP port states

- Explain how STP handles topology changes

- Describe RSTP link types

- Configure and modify STP behavior

- Explain how RSTP handles topology changes

RSTP Port Roles

The port role defines the ultimate purpose of a switch port and the way it handles data frames. With RSTP, port roles differ slightly with STP.

RSTP defines the following port roles. Figure 4-10 illustrates the port roles in a three-switch topology:

- **Root:** The root port is the switch port on every nonroot bridge that is the chosen path to the root bridge. There can be only one root port on every switch. The root port is considered as part of active topology. It forwards, sends, and receives BPDUs (data messages).

- **Designated:** Each switch has at least one switch port as the designated port for the segment. In active topology, the switch with the designated port receives frames on the segment that are destined for the root bridge. There can be only one designated port per segment.

- **Alternate:** The alternate port is a switch port that offers an alternate path toward the root bridge. It assumes a discarding state in an active topology. The alternate port makes a transition to a designated port if the current designated path fails.

- **Disabled:** A disabled port has no role within the operation of spanning tree.

- **Backup:** The backup port is an additional switch port on the designated switch with a redundant link to the shared segment for which the switch is designated. The backup port has the discarding state in active topology.

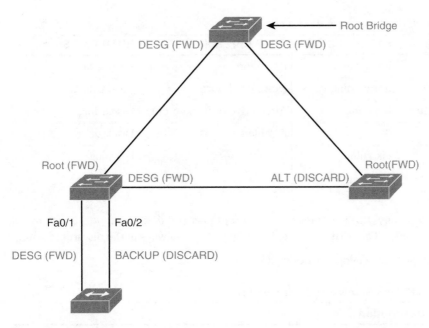

Figure 4-10 *RSTP Port Roles*

There is a difference between STP and RSTP port roles. Instead of STP nondesignated port role, there are now alternate and backup ports.

Additional port roles allow RSTP to define a standby switch port before a failure or topology change. The alternate port moves to the forwarding state if there is a failure on the designated port for the segment.

Note   You will probably not see a backup port role in practice. It is used only when switches are connected to a shared segment. To build shared segments, you need hubs, and these are obsolete.

Comparison of RSTP and STP Port States

The RSTP port states correspond to the three basic operations of a switch port: discarding, learning, and forwarding. There is no listening state as there is with STP. Listening and blocking STP states are replaced with the discarding state. Table 4-5 shows the STP port roles and RSTP port roles.

Table 4-5   *Comparison of STP and RSTP Port States*

STP Port Role	STP Port State	RSTP Port Role	RSTP Port State
Root port	Forwarding	Root port	Forwarding
Designated port	Forwarding	Designated port	Forwarding
Nondesignated port	Blocking	Alternative or backup port	Discarding
Disabled	—	Disabled	Discarding
In transition	Listening	In transition	Learning
	Learning		

In a stable topology, RSTP ensures that every root port and designated port transit to forwarding, while all alternate ports and backup ports are always in the discarding state.

Table 4-6 depicts the characteristics of RSTP port states:

Table 4-6   *RSTP Ports States and Their Characteristics*

Port State	Description
Discarding	This state is seen in both a stable active topology and during topology synchronization and changes. The discarding state prevents the forwarding of data frames, thus "breaking" the continuity of a Layer 2 loop.
Learning	This state is seen in both a stable active topology and during topology synchronization and changes. The learning state accepts data frames to populate the MAC table to limit flooding of unknown unicast frames.
Forwarding	This state is seen only in stable active topologies. The forwarding switch ports determine the topology. Following a topology change, or during synchronization, the forwarding of data frames occurs only after a proposal and agreement process.

A port will accept and process BPDU frames in all port states.

RSTP Topology Changes

For RSTP, a topology change is only when a nonedge port transitions to the forwarding state. This means that a loss of connectivity is not considered as a topology change any more, contrary to STP.

A switch announces a topology change by sending BPDUs with the TC bit set out from all the nonedge designated ports. This way, all the neighbors are informed about the topology change, and so they can correct their bridging tables.

In Figure 4-11, SW4 sends BPDUs out all its ports after it detects a link failure. SW2 then sends the BPDU to all its neighbors, except the one that received the BPDU from SW4, and so on.

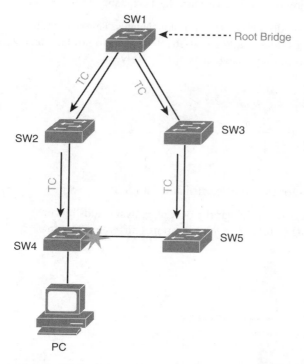

Figure 4-11 *RSTP Topology Changes*

When a switch receives a BPDU with TC bit set from a neighbor, it clears the MAC addresses learned on all its ports except the one that receives the topology change. The switch also receives BPDUs with the TC bit set on all designated ports and the root port.

RSTP no longer uses the specific TCN BPDUs unless a legacy bridge needs to be notified.

With RSTP, the TC propagation is now a one-step process. In fact, the initiator of the topology change floods this information throughout the network, as opposed to 802.1D, where only the root did. This mechanism is much faster than the 802.1D equivalent. There is no need to wait for the root bridge to be notified and then maintain the topology change state for the whole network for <max age plus forward delay> seconds. In just a few seconds, or a small multiple of hello times, most of the entries in the CAM tables of the entire network (VLAN) flush. This approach results in potentially more temporary flooding; however, it clears potential stale information that prevents rapid connectivity restitution.

Why does RSTP not consider link failure a topology change? Loss of connectivity does not provide new paths in topology. If a switch loses the link to a downstream switch, the downstream switch either has an alternate path to the root bridge or it does not. If the downstream switch has no alternate path, no action will be taken to improve convergence. If the downstream switch has an alternate path, the downstream switch will unblock it and consequently generate its own BPDUs with the TC bit set.

Like with STP, PortFast-enabled ports do not create topology changes. This reduces the amount of topology change messages flooding. PortFast-enabled ports do not have associated MAC addresses flushed if a topology change message is received.

Note PortFast is discussed later in this chapter.

RSTP Link Types

Link type provides a categorization for each port participating in RSTP.

The link type can predetermine the active role that the port plays as it stands by for immediate transition to a forwarding state. Figure 4-12 illustrates different link types.

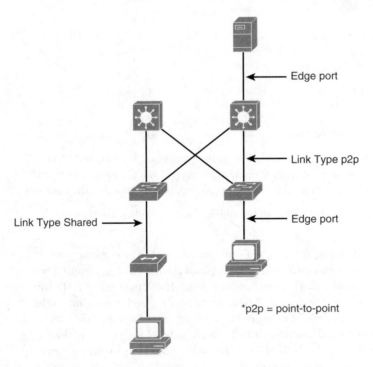

Figure 4-12 *RSTP Link Types*

These parameters differ for edge ports and nonedge ports. Nonedge ports are categorized into the two link types shown in Table 4-7.

Table 4-7 *RSTP Nonedge Ports Link Types*

Link Type	Description
Point to point	A port operating in full-duplex mode. It is assumed that the port is connected to a single switch device at the other end of the link.
Shared	A port operating in half-duplex mode. It is assumed that the port is connected to shared media, where multiple switches might exist.

Link type is automatically determined but can be overwritten with an explicit port configuration.

An edge port is a switch port that is never intended to be connected to another switch device. Edge ports, equivalent of point-to-point links, are candidates for rapid transition to a forwarding state. Before the link type parameter can be considered for expedient port transition, RSTP must determine the port role. The following list highlights the ports types and how they use link type parameters for transition:

- **Root ports:** Root ports do not use the link type parameter. Root ports are able to make a rapid transition to the forwarding state as soon as the port is in the sync state.

- **Alternate and backup ports:** In most cases, alternate and backup ports do not use the link type parameter.

- **Designated ports:** Designated ports make the most use of the link type parameter. Rapid transition to the forwarding state for the designated port occurs only if the link type parameter indicates a point-to-point link.

To verify the port type, issue the **show spanning-tree** command, as shown in Example 4-1.

Example 4-1 *Show Spanning-Tree Status for Link Type*

```
Switch# show spanning tree
<... output omitted ...>


Interface          Role Sts Cost      Prio.Nbr Type
------------------ ---- --- --------- -------- --------------------------------
Et0/0              Desg FWD 100       128.1    Shr
Et0/1              Desg FWD 100       128.2    P2p
Et0/2              Desg FWD 100       128.2    Edge
```

Note   An edge port has only a single host that is connected to it. If an edge port ever receives a BPDU, it immediately loses the edge port status.

Configuring and Modifying STP Behavior

In this section, using the topology shown in Figure 4-13, you learn how to manually configure a root bridge and the path for spanning tree and also observe the difference between the STP and RSTP convergence time.

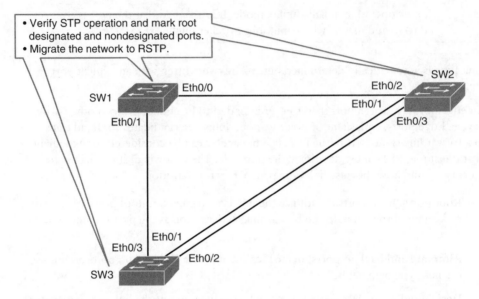

Figure 4-13 *Configuration Topology*

All switches are in VLAN 1.

There are two loops in this topology: SW1-SW2-SW3 and SW2-SW3. Wiring the network in such a way provides redundancy, but Layer 2 loops will occur if STP does not block redundant links. By default, STP is enabled on all the Cisco switches for VLAN 1. To find out which switch is the root switch and the STP port rule for each switch, complete the following steps:

Step 1.   Discover which switch is the root bridge. Issue the **show spanning-tree** command on all three switches. The following example shows the output for all three switches:

```
SW3# show spanning-tree


VLAN0001
  Spanning tree enabled protocol ieee
  Root ID    Priority    32769
             Address     aabb.cc00.4500
             Cost        100
             Port        4 (Ethernet0/3)
             Hello Time   2 sec  Max Age 20 sec  Forward Delay 15 sec


  Bridge ID  Priority    32769   (priority 32768 sys-id-ext 1)
             Address     aabb.cc00.5000
```

```
<... output omitted ...>

SW2# show spanning-tree


VLAN0001
  Spanning tree enabled protocol ieee
  Root ID    Priority    32769
             Address     aabb.cc00.4500
             Cost        100
             Port        3 (Ethernet0/2)
             Hello Time  2 sec  Max Age 20 sec  Forward Delay 15 sec


  Bridge ID  Priority    32769  (priority 32768 sys-id-ext 1)
             Address     aabb.cc00.4600
<... output omitted ...>

SW1# show spanning-tree


VLAN0001
  Spanning tree enabled protocol ieee
  Root ID    Priority    32769
             Address     aabb.cc00.4500
             This bridge is the root
             Hello Time  2 sec  Max Age 20 sec  Forward Delay 15 sec


  Bridge ID  Priority    32769  (priority 32768 sys-id-ext 1)
             Address     aabb.cc00.4500
<... output omitted ...>
```

SW1 is the root bridge. All three switches have the same priority, so the one with the lowest MAC address is elected as the root bridge.

Step 2.   Investigate port roles on all three switches.

Again use the **show spanning-tree** command to look for STP port roles in each switch, as demonstrated here:

```
SW1# show spanning-tree
<... output omitted ...>
Interface           Role Sts Cost      Prio.Nbr Type
------------------- ---- --- --------- -------- --------------------------------
Et0/0               Desg FWD 100       128.1    Shr
Et0/1               Desg FWD 100       128.2    Shr


SW2# show spanning-tree
<... output omitted ...>
Interface           Role Sts Cost      Prio.Nbr Type
------------------- ---- --- --------- -------- --------------------------------
Et0/1               Desg FWD 100       128.2    Shr
Et0/2               Root FWD 100       128.3    Shr
Et0/3               Desg FWD 100       128.4    Shr
```

```
SW3# show spanning-tree
<... output omitted ...>
Interface          Role Sts Cost      Prio.Nbr Type
------------------ ---- --- --------- -------- -------------------------------
Et0/1              Altn BLK 100       128.2    Shr
Et0/2              Altn BLK 100       128.3    Shr
Et0/3              Root FWD 100       128.4    Shr
```

Because SW1 is the root bridge, it has both connected ports in designated (forwarding) state.

Because SW2 and SW3 are not the root bridge, one port must be elected root on each of these two switches. This is the port with the lowest cost to the root bridge. Because SW2 has lower BID than SW3, other than root, all the rest of the ports on SW2 are set to designated. Other than the root port, the rest of the ports on SW3 are nondesignated. Figure 4-14 shows the summary of the spanning-tree topology and the STP port states for the three-switch topology.

Note   Cisco's PVSTP+ uses the term *alternate* for nondesignated port.

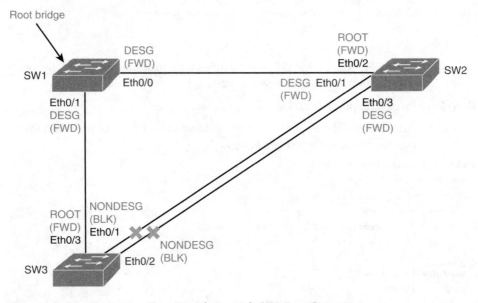

Figure 4-14   *Spanning-Tree Topology with STP Port States*

Changing STP Priority

It is not advised for the network to choose the root bridge by itself. If all switches have default STP priorities, the switch with the lowest MAC address will become the root bridge. The oldest switch will have the lowest MAC address because the lower MAC addresses were factory-assigned first. To manually set the root bridge, you can change a switch's priority.

In Figure 4-14 topology, assume that the access layer switch SW3 becomes the root bridge because it has the oldest MAC address. If SW3 were the root bridge, the link between the distribution layer switches would get blocked. The traffic between SW1 and SW2 would then need to go through SW3, which is not optimal.

Note   It is highly recommended to configure the distribution or core switches to become the root bridge.

The priority can be a value between 0 and 65,535, in increments of 4096. The default value is 32,768.

Note   With PVST, an extended system ID is used for calculating bridge priority. The priority reduces from 16 to 4 bits, because 12 bits represent the VLAN ID. With 4-bit priority, there are 16 total combinations. The increment starts at 4096 and increments another 15 times, until the value is 65,535. This means that you cannot change the priority from 32,768 to 32,789, but you have to add a multiple of 4096. So, for example, the next possible priority value is 36,864.

The better solution is to use **spanning-tree vlan** *vlan-id* **root** {**primary** | **secondary**} command. This command is actually a macro that lowers the switch's priority number for it to become the root bridge.

To configure the switch to become the root bridge for a specified VLAN, use the **primary** keyword. Use the **secondary** keyword to configure a secondary root bridge. This is to prevent the slowest and oldest access layer switch from becoming the root bridge if the primary root bridge fails.

The spanning-tree **root** command calculates the priority by learning the current root priority and lowering the 4096 value to it. For example, if the current root priority is more than 24,576, the local switch sets its priority to 24,576. If the root bridge has priority lower than 24,576, the local switch sets its priority to 4096 less than the one of the current root bridge. Configuring the secondary root bridge sets a priority of 28,672. There is no way for the switch to figure out what is the second best priority in the network. So, setting the secondary priority to 28,672 is just a best guess.

If you issue the **show running-configuration** command, the config shows the switch's priority as a number (not the **primary** or **secondary** keyword).

Note If the priority of the root bridge is set to 0, configuring another switch with the **root primary** command will yield no results. The command will fail because it cannot make a local switch priority for 4096 lower than that of the root bridge.

To make the SW2 the root bridge, you configure the following:

```
SW2(config)# spanning-tree vlan 1 root primary
```

Example 4-2 verifies that SW2 is now the root bridge for VLAN 1.

Example 4-2 *Verifying the Root Bridge*

```
SW2# show spanning-tree


VLAN0001
  Spanning tree enabled protocol ieee
  Root ID    Priority    24577
             Address     aabb.cc00.4600
             This bridge is the root
             Hello Time   2 sec  Max Age 20 sec  Forward Delay 15 sec

  Bridge ID  Priority    28673  (priority 28672 sys-id-ext 1)
             Address     aabb.cc00.4600
             Hello Time   2 sec  Max Age 20 sec  Forward Delay 15 sec
             Aging Time  15  sec


Interface          Role Sts Cost      Prio.Nbr Type
------------------ ---- --- --------- -------- --------------------------------
Et0/1              Desg FWD 100       128.2    Shr
Et0/2              Desg FWD 100       128.3    Shr
Et0/3              Desg FWD 100       128.4    Shr
```

Observe the changed port roles on SW1 and SW3.

Because SW2 is the root bridge, all its ports will be in a designated (forwarding) state. SW1 and SW3 have changed port roles according to the change of the root bridge. Example 4-3 shows the STP port roles of SW1 and SW3.

Example 4-3 *Verification of STP Port Roles for SW1 and SW3*

```
SW1# show spanning-tree
<... output omitted ...>
Interface          Role Sts Cost      Prio.Nbr Type
------------------ ---- --- --------- -------- --------------------------------
Et0/0              Root FWD 100       128.1    Shr
Et0/1              Desg FWD 100       128.2    Shr
```

```
SW3# show spanning-tree
<... output omitted ...>
Interface          Role Sts Cost     Prio.Nbr Type
------------------ ---- --- --------- -------- --------------------------------
Et0/1              Root FWD 100       128.2    Shr
Et0/2              Altn BLK 100       128.3    Shr
Et0/3              Altn BLK 100       128.4    Shr
```

Figure 4-15 shows the port roles after you configure SW2 as the root bridge.

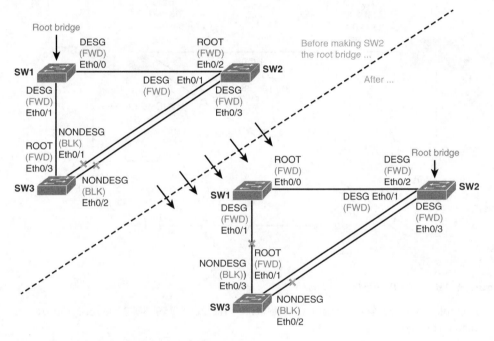

Figure 4-15   *Before and After Changing SW2 to Root*

STP Path Manipulation

For port role determination, the cost value is used. If all ports have the same cost, the sender's port ID breaks the tie. To control active port selection, change the cost of the interface or sender's interface port ID.

You can modify port cost by using the **spanning-tree vlan** *vlan-list* **cost** *cost-value* command. The cost value can be between 1 and 65,535.

The port ID consists of a port priority and a port number. The port number is fixed, because it is based only on its hardware location, but you can change port ID by configuring the port priority.

You can modify the port priority by using the **spanning-tree vlan** *vlan-list* **port-priority** *port-priority* command. The value of port priority can be between 0 and 255; the default is 128. A lower port priority means a more preferred path to the root bridge.

As shown in Figure 4-16, Ethernet 0/1 and Ethernet 0/2 have the same interface STP cost. Ethernet 0/1 is forwarding because its sender's port ID (128.2) is lower than that of Ethernet 0/2 (128.4). One way that you could make SW3's Ethernet 0/2 forwarding is to lower the port cost on Ethernet 0/2. Another way to make SW3's Ethernet 0/2 forwarding is to lower the sender's port priority. In this case, this is Ethernet 0/3 on SW2.

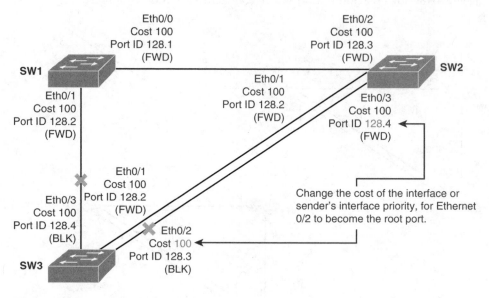

Figure 4-16   *STP Path Manipulation*

Example 4-4 shows the configuration to make Ethernet 0/2 on SW3 the root port by changing its cost.

Right now, Ethernet 0/1 is the root port on SW because of the lower port priority. Ethernet 0/2 has a port priority of 128.3, and Ethernet 0/1 has a port priority of 128.2. Because only the cost is changed, the port priority will not be observed. STP checks port priority only when costs are equal. Figure 4-17 shows before and after effects of manipulating the STP port cost.

Example 4-4   *Configuration to Change the STP Port Cost*

```
SW3(config)# interface Ethernet 0/2
SW3(config-if)# spanning-tree vlan 1 cost 16
```

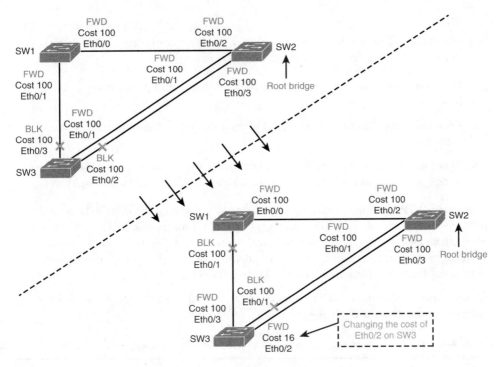

Figure 4-17 *STP Path Manipulation Before and After*

Again, investigate STP port roles on SW1 and SW3 by using the **show spanning-tree** command, as shown in Example 4-5. Because interface Ethernet 0/2 now has a lower cost, it is assigned as the root port as compared to its original state. STP reconsiders a new path, so new port roles are assigned on SW1 and SW3. Because SW2 is the root bridge, it will have all ports as designated (forwarding). Example 4-5 shows the port roles after manually configuring root port on SW3.

Example 4-5 *Verifying the STP Port States After Port Cost Changes*

```
SW1# show spanning-tree
<... output omitted ...>
Interface           Role Sts Cost       Prio.Nbr Type
------------------- ---- --- ---------- -------- --------------------------------

Et0/0               Root FWD 100        128.1    Shr
Et0/1               Altn BLK 100        128.2    Shr


SW3# show spanning-tree
<... output omitted ...>
Interface           Role Sts Cost       Prio.Nbr Type
------------------- ---- --- ---------- -------- --------------------------------

Et0/1               Altn BLK 100        128.2    Shr
Et0/2               Root FWD 16         128.3    Shr
Et0/3               Desg FWD 100        128.4    Shr
```

STP Timers

STP uses three different timers to ensure proper loop-free convergence. The three key STP timers and their default values are as follows:

- **Hello time:** The time between each BPDU that is sent on a port. Equals 2 seconds, by default.

- **Forward delay:** The time that is spent in the listening and learning state. Equals 15 seconds, by default.

- **Max (maximum) age:** Controls the maximum length of time that passes before a bridge port saves its configuration BPDU information. Equals 20 seconds, by default.

Turn on the STP topology events debugging on SW3 as shown in Figure 4-17 after the port cost changes to observe STP convergence (that is, how much time does STP need to establish a new path after a link failure in real time). Example 4-10 shows the debug of a spanning-tree event to measure the time to take to move the port into forwarding mode. Shut down the forwarding uplink on SW3 (Ethernet 0/2).

Observe how much it takes STP to notice the failure and make the redundant link forwarding, as shown in Example 4-6.

Example 4-6   *Debug a Spanning-Tree Event to Measure the Convergences of Link Shut*

```
SW3# debug spanning-tree events

SW3(config)# interface Ethernet 0/2
SW3(config-if)# shutdown

*Nov  8 07:52:45.237: STP: VLAN0001 new root port Et0/1, cost 100
*Nov  8 07:52:45.237: STP: VLAN0001 Et0/1 -> listening
*Nov  8 07:52:45.237: STP[1]: Generating TC trap for port Ethernet0/2
SW3(config-if)#
*Nov  8 07:52:47.243: %LINK-5-CHANGED: Interface Ethernet0/2, changed state to
  administratively down
SW3(config-if)#
*Nov  8 07:52:47.243: STP: VLAN0001 sent Topology Change Notice on Et0/1
*Nov  8 07:52:48.245: %LINEPROTO-5-UPDOWN: Line protocol on Interfac Ethernet0/2,
  changed state to down
SW3(config-if)#
*Nov  8 07:53:00.243: STP: VLAN0001 Et0/1 -> learning
SW3(config-if)#
*Nov  8 07:53:04.160: STP: VLAN0001 sent Topology Change Notice on Et0/1
*Nov  8 07:53:04.160: STP[1]: Generating TC trap for port Ethernet0/3
*Nov  8 07:53:04.160: STP: VLAN0001 Et0/3 -> blocking
SW3(config-if)#
*Nov  8 07:53:15.247: STP[1]: Generating TC trap for port Ethernet0/1
*Nov  8 07:53:15.247: STP: VLAN0001 Et0/1 -> forwarding
```

The transition between port states takes from 30 to 50 seconds, depending on the topology change. This can be adjusted with STP timers. STP hello time can be tuned between 1 and 10 seconds, forward delay between 4 and 30 seconds, and maximum age between 6 and 40 seconds.

Note However, the timer values should never be changed without consideration. When changing the timers, you should apply changes only on the root bridge. The root bridge will then propagate the timer values to other switches.

Note Normally, you do not change the STP timers; you would instead use RSTP.

To manually configure timers, use the **spanning-tree** [**vlan** *vlan-id*] {**hello-time** | **forward-time** | **max-age**} *seconds* command. To verify configured STP timers, issue **show spanning-tree vlan** *vlan-id* command. Example 4-7 shows the convergence time to turn the interface Ethernet 0/2 on SW3 back on. To see how topology changes after a failed interface comes back up, take a look at how STP port roles get redefined after the failed interface comes back up.

Example 4-7 *STP Port Roles After Unshutting Ethernet 0/2*

```
SW3(config)# interface Ethernet 0/2
SW3(config-if)# no shutdown

SW1# show spanning-tree
<... output omitted ...>
Interface          Role Sts Cost      Prio.Nbr Type
------------------ ---- --- --------- -------- --------------------------------
Et0/0              Root FWD 100       128.1    Shr
Et0/1              Altn BLK 100       128.2    Shr

SW3# show spanning-tree
<... output omitted ...>
Interface          Role Sts Cost      Prio.Nbr Type
------------------ ---- --- --------- -------- --------------------------------
Et0/1              Altn BLK 100       128.2    Shr
Et0/2              Root FWD 16        128.3    Shr
Et0/3              Desg FWD 100       128.4    Shr
```

Port roles are again the same as they were before shutting down the interface. The port roles on SW2 have not changed, because it is the root bridge, and all ports are designated.

Note   After you bring Ethernet 0/2 on SW3 back up, it will take around 30 seconds for STP to make ports either forwarding or blocking.

Observe the convergence effects after enabling RSTP on all switches. Example 4-8 shows how to configure all the switches with RSTP.

Example 4-8   *Changing the STP Mode to RSTP*

```
SW1(config)# spanning-tree mode rapid-pvst

SW2(config)# spanning-tree mode rapid-pvst

SW3(config)# spanning-tree mode rapid-pvst
```

Note   If all but one switch in the network is running RSTP, the interfaces that lead to legacy STP switches will automatically fall back to non-RSTP. Cisco switches fall back to PVST+. You can check that all the switches have RSTP configured by observing the convergence time.

Verify that the RSTP is enabled on all three switches. Example 4-9 depicts the **show** command to verify the mode of STP.

Example 4-9   *Verify the STP Mode After Changing to RSTP*

```
SW1# show spanning-tree

VLAN0001
  Spanning tree enabled protocol rstp
  <... output omitted ...>

SW2# show spanning-tree

VLAN0001
  Spanning tree enabled protocol rstp
  <... output omitted ...>

SW3# show spanning-tree

VLAN0001
  Spanning tree enabled protocol rstp
  <... output omitted ...>
```

Now, again shut down interface Ethernet 0/2 on SW3 to trigger topology changes to measure the convergence time of port states. How much time will it take spanning tree to converge now that you have enabled the rapid version? Example 4-10 shows the debugs of spanning tree to measure the time it takes to move to forwarding state after enabling RSTP.

Example 4-10 *Debug STP for Link Shut After Enabling RSTP*

```
SW3(config)# interface Ethernet 0/2
SW3(config-if)# shutdown

Observe the convergence time of RSTP.
*Nov  8 08:17:33.415: RSTP(1): transmitting a proposal on Et0/3
*Nov  8 08:17:33.510: RSTP(1): updt roles, root port Et0/2 going down
*Nov  8 08:17:33.510: RSTP(1): Et0/1 is now root port
*Nov  8 08:17:33.510: RSTP(1): syncing port Et0/3
*Nov  8 08:17:33.514: STP[1]: Generating TC trap for port Ethernet0/1
*Nov  8 08:17:33.514: RSTP(1): transmitting a proposal on Et0/3
*Nov  8 08:17:33.519: RSTP(1): updt roles, received superior bpdu on Et0/3
*Nov  8 08:17:33.519: RSTP(1): Et0/3 is now alternate
```

The convergence time for RSTP is much shorter than for STP. The entire convergence happens at the speed of BPDU transmission. That can be less than 1 second.

Implementing STP Stability Mechanisms

STP is a mature protocol, benefiting from years of development and production deployment. However, STP makes assumptions about the quality of the network, and the protocol can fail. Those failures are generally high-profile failures because of the extent to which they impact the network. STP is designed to never open a loop, even temporarily, during its operation. However, like any protocol, it is based on some assumptions that might not be valid in the network. To help STP converge faster and for the protocol behavior to match your network infrastructure, several features are available to filter the way that BPDUs are sent or received, and to alter the way the network should react in case of an unexpected network topology change.

The Cisco Spanning Tree Protocol Toolkit provides tools to better manage STP. The key features of the Cisco STP Toolkit that improve STP performance are as follows:

- **UplinkFast:** Enables fast uplink failover on access switch

- **BackboneFast:** Enables fast convergence in distribution or core layer when STP change occurs

- **PortFast:** Configures access port to transition directly to forwarding state

The key features of the Cisco STP Toolkit that ensure STP stability are as follows:

- **BPDU Guard:** Disables the PortFast-enabled port if a BPDU is received
- **BPDU Filter:** Suppresses BPDUs on ports
- **Root Guard:** Prevents external switches from becoming roots
- **Loop Guard:** Prevents an alternate port from becoming the designated port if no BPDUs are received

PortFast, UplinkFast, and BackboneFast improve convergence times of non-RSTP. Other tools provide stability and protect the network from STP failures if used properly.

UplinkFast and BackboneFast are mechanisms that can be enabled only with non-RSTP. Both of these two mechanisms are integrated into RSTP versions. Therefore, you do not need to enable them.

Upon completing this section, you will be able to meet these objectives:

- List and briefly explain Cisco STP Toolkit
- Describe UplinkFast
- Configure BackboneFast
- Describe how to configure PortFast
- Describe how to configure BPDU Guard
- Describe how to configure BPDU Filter
- Describe how to configure Root Guard
- Describe the problem with unidirectional links
- Describe Loop Guard
- Configure Loop Guard
- Verify Loop Guard configuration
- Describe how UDLD detects a unidirectional link and what action does it take
- Configure UDLD
- Compare UDLD to Loop Guard
- Describe the recommended practice for the UDLD implementation
- Describe the recommended practice for the implementation of STP stability mechanisms
- Describe how to configure FlexLinks

Use UplinkFast

If forwarding uplink fails, it will take 30 to 50 seconds for the other uplink to take over. UplinkFast is a Cisco proprietary solution that greatly reduces convergence time.

The UplinkFast feature is based on the definition of an uplink group. On a given switch, the uplink group consists of the root port and all the ports that provide an alternate connection to the root bridge. If the root port fails, which means if the primary uplink fails, a port with the next lowest cost from the uplink group is selected to immediately replace it.

To accelerate the recovery time, the access layer switch will start announcing all MAC addresses as source addresses in dummy multicast frames that are sent upstream through the new forwarding port. The total time to recover the primary link failure will normally be less than 1 second.

In Figure 4-18, if ASW's Ethernet 0/1 (root port) fails, Ethernet 0/2 will become active immediately if ASW has UplinkFast enabled.

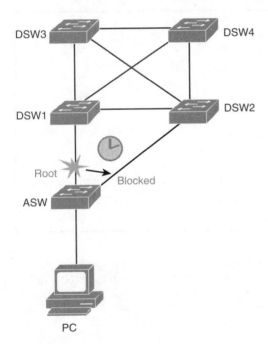

Figure 4-18 *UplinkFast*

UplinkFast works only when the switch has blocked ports. The feature is usually designed for an access switch that has redundant blocked uplinks. UplinkFast is enabled for the entire switch and cannot be enabled for individual VLANs.

Note   UplinkFast is a Cisco proprietary feature.

To enable UplinkFast, use the following command:

```
ASW(config)# spanning-tree uplinkfast
```

> **Note**   By default, UplinkFast is disabled.

Only enable UplinkFast on access layer switches with redundant uplinks. If you enable a transit switch for UplinkFast, you risk an occurrence of an STP loop. A transit switch is a switch that connects to both the root bridge and another switch. In the figure, DSW1 is an example of a transit switch if DSW3 is the root bridge. The only acceptable use of UplinkFast in Figure 4-18 is on ASW.

To verify the current status of STP UplinkFast, use the command shown in Example 4-11.

Example 4-11   *Verify UplinkFast Configuration*

```
ASW# show spanning-tree uplinkfast
UplinkFast is enabled


Station update rate set to 150 packets/sec.


UplinkFast statistics
-----------------------
Number of transitions via uplinkFast (all VLANs)          : 2
Number of proxy multicast addresses transmitted (all VLANs) : 0


Name                    Interface List
------------------      -----------------------------------
VLAN0001                Et0/1(fwd), Et0/2
```

> **Note**   With RSTP, the UplinkFast mechanism is already integrated into the protocol in a standards-based way.

Use BackboneFast

In the network backbone, core, or distribution layer, BackboneFast can be used to shorten convergence times of non-RSTP. When an indirect link failure occurs, BackboneFast checks whether an alternative path exists to the root bridge. Indirect failure is when a link that is not directly connected to a switch fails.

As shown in Figure 4-19, DSW3 is the root bridge, and DSW2 is the one blocking DSW3's alternate path to DSW1. When DSW1's root port fails, DSW1 declares itself the root bridge and starts sending BPDUs to all switches it is connected to (in this case, only DSW2). These BPDUs are inferior. When a switch receives an inferior BPDU on a blocked port, it runs a procedure to validate that it still has an active path to the currently known root bridge.

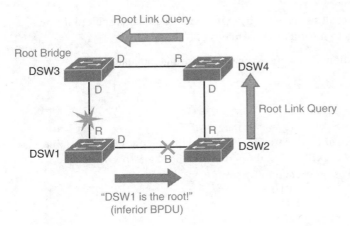

Figure 4-19 *BackboneFast*

Normally a switch must wait for the maximum age timer to expire before responding to the inferior BPDUs. However BackboneFast searches for an alternative path:

If the inferior BPDU arrives on a port that is blocked, the switch assumes that the root port and all other blocked ports are an alternative path.

If the inferior BPDU arrives on a port that is root, the switch assumes all blocked are an alternate path. If no ports are blocked, the switch assumes that it lost connectivity with the root bridge and considers itself as the root bridge.

In the example, an inferior BPDU is received on a blocked port. DSW2 assumes that the root port (connects to DSW4) is an alternate path to the root bridge.

After the switch identifies potential alternative ports, it starts sending RLQs (request link queries). By sending these queries, it finds out whether upstream switches have a path to the root bridge.

When a switch, which is either the root bridge or has a connection to the root bridge, receives an RLQ, the switch sends back an RLQ reply. Otherwise, an RLQ gets forwarded until it gets to a switch that is the root bridge or has a connection to the root bridge.

If exchange of RLQ messages results in validation that the root bridge (DSW3) is still accessible, the switch (DSW2) starts sending existing root bridge information to the bridge that lost connectivity through its root port (DSW1). If this validation fails, DSW2 can start the root bridge election process. In either of these cases, if validation is successful or not, maximum age time is shortened.

To configure BackboneFast, use the following command:

```
DSW1(config)# spanning-tree backbonefast
```

> **Note**   By default, BackboneFast is disabled.

Configure BackboneFast on all switches in the network, because it is required if you want to use RLQ messages to inform other switches of STP stability.

To verify the current BackboneFast state, issue the following command:

```
DSW1# show spanning-tree backbonefast
BackboneFast is enabled
```

> **Note**   BackboneFast was implemented into RSTP. RSTP implementation differs a bit from BackboneFast. Whereas BackboneFast relies on RLQ messages to validate the current root bridge, RSTP relies on cached information.

Use PortFast

An end-user PC connects to access layer switches. When the PC is turned on, STP will have to go through all the states: blocking, listening, learning, and eventually forwarding. With the default STP timers, this transition takes about 30 seconds (15 seconds for listening to learning, and 15 seconds from learning to forwarding). The PC cannot transmit or receive data before the switch transitions the port to forwarding state. How can this affect the user PC? The PC might run into trouble with acquiring of DHCP addresses in its first try, and therefore it might take quite some time for the PC to become operational.

When PortFast is enabled, the port transitions immediately from blocking to forwarding, as shown in Figure 4-20. As mentioned before, PortFast is enabled on access layer switches where the hosts are connected.

An additional benefit of using PortFast is that TCN BPDUs are not sent when a switch port in PortFast mode goes up or down. In a large network, PCs might go up and down, and that can mean a lot of TCNs if your access ports are not configured with PortFast.

By default, PortFast is disabled on all switch ports. You can configure PortFast in two ways: per port and globally. If you configure PortFast globally (that is, a conditional configuration), all ports that are configured as access ports automatically become PortFast enabled, and the port will immediately transition to forwarding (unless they receive a BPDU). If a port does receive a BPDU, that port will go into blocking mode. If you configure PortFast per port, in some implementations that can be an unconditional configuration. The port will be PortFast enabled even if it receives BPDUs. Example 4-12 shows the PortFast configuration.

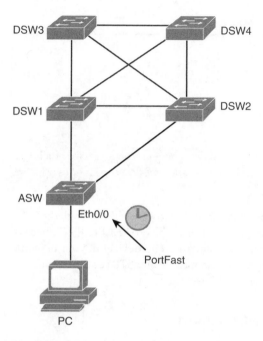

Figure 4-20 *STP PortFast*

Example 4-12 *PortFast Configuration*

```
ASW(config-if)# spanning-tree portfast
! Enables PortFast on per-port basis
ASW(config)# spanning-tree portfast default
! Enables PortFast on ALL switch ports that are defined as access
ASW# show spanning-tree interface ethernet 0/0 portfast
! Displays current state of PortFast
```

Note   Never use the PortFast feature on switch ports that connect to other switches, hubs, or routers. These connections can cause physical loops, and spanning tree must go through the full initialization procedure in these situations. A spanning-tree loop can bring your network down. If you turn on PortFast for a port that is part of a physical loop, there can be a window of time when packets are continuously forwarded (and can even multiply) in such a way that the network cannot recover.

You can also enable PortFast on trunk ports. This is useful if you have a trunk enabled for a host such as a server that needs multiple VLANs. To enable a port for PortFast on an interface that connects to such a server, use the interface configuration commands shown in Example 4-13.

Example 4-13 *PortFast Configuration for a Trunk*

```
ASW(config-if)# spanning-tree portfast trunk
! To display the current status of PortFast, use the following command:
ASW# show spanning-tree interface ethernet 0/0 portfast
VLAN0001          enabled
```

Note You must only configure PortFast on interfaces that connect to end devices such as PCs and servers. Otherwise, you risk creating a loop and bringing down your network.

With RSTP, PortFast is enabled with the same commands. However, these single-host ports are called *edge ports*. But why would you want to enable PortFast in RSTP, because convergence times are much shorter? If you have numerous end devices in your network, and they are going up and down all the time, that can mean many STP recalculations. Defining the edge ports reduces the number of STP recalculations.

Securing PortFast Interface with BPDU Guard

Even though PortFast is enabled, the interface will listen for BPDUs. If a BPDU is received, the port will be moved into a blocking state. However, a loop can be detected only in a finite amount of time; some time is needed to move a port into a blocked state.

BPDU Guard protects the integrity of ports that are PortFast enabled. If any BPDU is received on a PortFast-enabled port, that port is put into err-disabled state. That means the port is shut down and must be manually reenabled or automatically recovered through the error-disabled timeout function.

You will receive the following command-line interface (CLI) notification if a switch is connected to a port that has BPDU Guard enabled:

```
%SPANTREE-2-BLOCK_BPDUGUARD: Received BPDU on port Et0/0 with BPDU Guard enabled.
Disabling port.
%PM-4-ERR_DISABLE: bpduguard error detected on Et0/0, putting Et0/0 in err-disable
state
```

Note It is highly recommended to always enable BPDU Guard on all PortFast-enabled ports! This will prevent adding a switch to a switch port that is dedicated to an end device.

BPDU Guard does not prevent all loop occurrences. A hub or some unmanaged switches do not send BPDUs; therefore, BPDU Guard will not be able to detect them. If a hub or a switch connects to two locations in a network, you might end up with a loop in your network.

By default, BPDU Guard is disabled on all switch ports. As with PortFast, you can configure BPDU Guard in two ways, globally and per port, as shown in Example 4-14.

Example 4-14 *BPDU Guard Configuration*

```
ASW(config-if)# spanning-tree bpduguard enable
! Configures BPDU Guard on a port
ASW(config)# spanning-tree portfast bpduguard default
! Configures BPDU Guard on all switch ports that have PortFast enabled
ASW# show spanning-tree summary totals
! Verifies BPDU Guard configuration
```

Note   Global configuration is conditional: If the port is not PortFast enabled, BPDU Guard will not be activated.

Disabling STP with BPDU Filter

BPDUs are sent on all ports, even if they are PortFast enabled. You should always run STP to prevent loops. However, in special cases, you need to prevent BPDUs from being sent out. You can achieve that by using BPDU Filter.

Configuring BPDU Filter so that all configuration BPDUs received on a port are dropped can be useful for service provider environments, where a service provider provides Layer 2 Ethernet access for customers. Ideally, the service provider does not want to share any spanning-tree information with customers, because such sharing might jeopardize the stability of the service provider's internal spanning-tree topology. By configuring PortFast and BPDU Filter on each customer access port, the service provider will not send any configuration BPDUs to customers and will ignore any configuration BPDUs sent from customers, as shown in Figure 4-21.

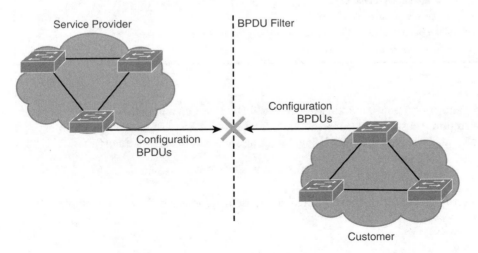

Figure 4-21 *BPDU Filters with STP*

This kind of configuration sometimes appears in companies where there are multiple administrators. A similar situation occurs as with the service provider example. This is a bad implementation practice.

BPDU Filter behaves differently if applied globally or on a per-port basis.

When enabled globally, BPDU Filter has these attributes:

- It affects all operational PortFast ports on switches that do not have BPDU Filter configured on the individual ports.

- If BPDUs are detected, the port loses its PortFast status, BPDU Filter is disabled, and the STP sends and receives BPDUs on the port as it would with any other STP port on the switch.

- Upon startup, the port transmits ten BPDUs. If this port receives any BPDUs during that time, PortFast and PortFast BPDU Filter are disabled.

When enabled on an individual port, BPDU Filter has these attributes:

- It ignores all BPDUs received.

- It sends no BPDUs.

Example 4-15 shows how to configure the BPDU Filter globally and per port.

Example 4-15   *BPDU Filter Configuration Commands*

```
Switch(config-if)# spanning-tree bpdufilter enable
! Enables BPDU Filter on a specific switch port
Switch(config)# spanning-tree portfast bpdufilter default
! Enables BPDU Filter on all switch ports that are PortFast-enabled
Switch# show spanning-tree totals
! Verifies global BPDU Filter configuration
Switch# show spanning-tree interface Ethernet 0/0 detail
! Verifies BPDU Filter configuration on a specific port
```

Note   An explicit configuration of PortFast BPDU Filter on a port that is not connected to a host station can result in bridging loops. The port ignores any incoming BPDUs and changes to the forwarding state. This does not occur when PortFast BPDU Filter is enabled globally.

To verify global BPDU Filter configuration, use the command shown in Example 4-16.

Example 4-16 *Verify BPDU Filter Configuration*

```
Switch# show spanning-tree summary totals
Switch is in rapid-pvst mode
Root bridge for: none
Extended system ID          is enabled
Portfast Default            is disabled
PortFast BPDU Guard Default is disabled
Portfast BPDU Filter Default is enabled
Loopguard Default           is disabled
<... output omitted ...>
```

To verify BPDU Filter configuration on a specific port, use the command shown in Example 4-17.

Example 4-17 *Verify BPDU Filter Configuration on a Specific Port*

```
Switch# show spanning-tree interface ethernet 0/0 detail
 Port 1 (Ethernet0/0) of VLAN0001 is designated forwarding
   Port path cost 100, Port priority 128, Port Identifier 128.1.
   Designated root has priority 28673, address aabb.cc00.0300
   Designated bridge has priority 32769, address aabb.cc00.0200
   Designated port id is 128.1, designated path cost 100
   Timers: message age 0, forward delay 0, hold 0
   Number of transitions to forwarding state: 1
   Link type is shared by default
   Bpdu filter is enabled
   Loop guard is enabled on the port
   BPDU: sent 6732, received 0
```

Note   If you configure BPDU Guard and BPDU Filter on a switch, only BPDU Filter will be active. BPDU Filter is an older mechanism than BPDU Guard. Never implement BPDU Guard and BPDU Filter on the same interface.

Use Root Guard

Root Guard is useful in avoiding Layer 2 loops during network anomalies. The Root Guard feature forces an interface to become a designated port to prevent surrounding switches from becoming a root switch. In other words, Root Guard provides a way to enforce the root bridge placement in the network. Catalyst switches force Root Guard-enabled ports to be designated ports. If the bridge receives superior STP BPDUs on a Root Guard-enabled port, the port moves to a root-inconsistent STP state (effectively equal to a listening state), and the switch does not forward traffic out of that port. As a result, this feature effectively enforces the position of the root bridge.

Figure 4-22 shows a sample topology to illustrate the Root Guard feature. Switches A and B comprise the core of the network, and Switch A is the root bridge for a VLAN. Switch C is an access layer switch. The link between Switch B and Switch C is blocking on the Switch C side. Figure 4-22 shows the flow of STP BPDUs with arrows.

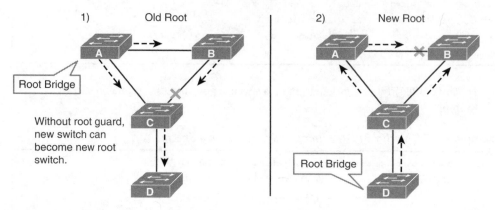

Figure 4-22   *Network With and Without Root Guard*

In Figure 4-22, when Switch D is connected to Switch C, it begins to participate in STP. If the priority of Switch D is 0 or any value lower than that of the current root bridge, Switch D becomes the root bridge for that VLAN based on normal STP guidelines. In this specific scenario, however, having Switch D as the root causes the Gigabit Ethernet link that is connecting the two core switches to block, thus causing all the data in that particular VLAN to flow via a 100-Mbps link across the access layer. If there is more data flowing between the core switches in that VLAN than this link may accommodate, packet loss can occur, causing performance issues or network connectivity problems. An even worse scenario might occur if Switch D is unstable and causes frequent reconvergence of the root bridge.

The Root Guard feature can protect against such issues. After the Root Guard feature is enabled on a port, the switch does not enable that port to become an STP root port. The port remains as an STP-designated port. In addition, if a better BPDU is received on the port, Root Guard disables (err-disables) the port instead of processing the BPDU. If an unauthorized device starts sending BPDUs with a better BID, the normal STP process elects the new switch as the root switch. By disabling the port, the network topology is protected.

The current design recommendation is to enable Root Guard on all access ports so that a root bridge is not established through these ports. Figure 4-22 shows Root Guard enabled on Switches A, B, and C on the following ports:

- **Switch A (Distribution/Core):** Any access port

- **Switch B (Distribution/Core):** Any access port

- **Switch C (Access):** Any access port including the port connecting to Switch D

In this configuration, Switch C blocks the port connecting to Switch D when it receives a better (superior) BPDU. The port transitions to a special STP state (root-inconsistent), which is effectively the same as the listening state. No traffic passes through the port in root-inconsistent state.

When Switch D stops sending superior BPDUs, the port unblocks again and goes through regular STP transition of listening and learning, and eventually to the forwarding state. Recovery is automatic; no intervention is required.

In addition, Catalyst switches log the following message when a Root Guard-enabled port receives a superior BPDU:

```
%SPANTREE-2-ROOTGUARDBLOCK: Port 1/1 tried to become non-designated in VLAN 77.
Moved to root-inconsistent state
```

To enable Root Guard on a Layer 2 access port to force it to become a designated port, or to disable Root Guard, use the following interface-level command on Cisco IOS-based Catalyst switches:

```
[no] spanning-tree guard root
```

Example 4-18 illustrates a user enabling the Root Guard feature on Fast Ethernet interface 5/8 and verifying the configuration.

Example 4-18 *Configuring and Verifying Root Guard on Cisco IOS-Based Catalyst Switches*

```
Switch# configure terminal
Enter configuration commands, one per line. End with CNTL/Z.
Switch(config)# interface FastEthernet 5/8
Switch(config-if)# spanning-tree guard root
Switch(config-if)# end
Switch# show running-config interface FastEthernet 5/8
Building configuration... Current configuration: 67 bytes ! interface
   FastEthernet5/8 switchport mode access spanning-tree guard root end !
```

Example 4-19 shows how to determine whether any interfaces are in root-inconsistent state.

Example 4-19 *Displaying Root-Inconsistent Interfaces on Cisco IOS–Based Catalyst Switches*

```
Switch# show spanning-tree inconsistentports
Name Interface Inconsistency
VLAN0001      FastEthernet3/1        Port Type Inconsistent
VLAN0001      FastEthernet3/2        Port Type Inconsistent
VLAN1002      FastEthernet3/1        Port Type Inconsistent
VLAN1002      FastEthernet3/2        Port Type Inconsistent
```

Loop Guard Overview

The STP Loop Guard feature provides additional protection against Layer 2 loops. A Layer 2 loop is created when an STP blocking port in a redundant topology erroneously transitions to the forwarding state. This usually happens because one of the ports of a physically redundant topology (not necessarily the STP blocking port) no longer receives STP BPDUs. In its operation, STP relies on continuous reception or transmission of BPDUs based on the port role. The designated port transmits BPDUs, and the nondesignated port receives BPDUs.

When one of the ports in a physically redundant topology no longer receives BPDUs, the STP conceives that the topology is loop free. Eventually, the blocking port from the alternate or backup port becomes designated and moves to a forwarding state. This situation creates a loop.

The Loop Guard feature makes additional checks. If BPDUs are not received on a nondesignated port, and Loop Guard is enabled, that port is moved into the STP loop-inconsistent blocking state, instead of the listening/learning/forwarding state. Without the Loop Guard feature, the port assumes the designated port role. The port moves to the STP forwarding state and creates a loop, as shown in Figure 4-23.

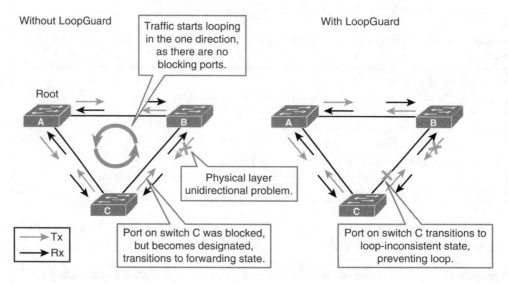

Figure 4-23   *Loop Guard Benefits*

When the Loop Guard blocks an inconsistent port, this message is logged:

```
%SPANTREE-2-LOOPGUARD_BLOCK: LoopGuard blocking port FastEthernet0/24 o VLAN0050.
```

Once the BPDU is received on a port in a loop-inconsistent STP state, the port transitions into another STP state. According to the received BPDU, this means that the recovery is automatic and intervention is not necessary. After recovery, this message is logged:

```
%SPANTREE-2-LOOPGUARD_UNBLOCK: LoopGuard unblocking port FastEthernet0/24
VLAN0050.
```

In Figure 4-24, Switch A is the root. Switch C does not receive BPDUs from Switch B because of the unidirectional link failure on the link between Switch B and Switch C. Without Loop Guard, the STP blocking port on Switch C transitions to the STP listening state when the maximum age timer expires, and then it transitions to the forwarding state in two times the forward delay time. This situation creates a loop. With Loop Guard enabled, the blocking port on Switch C transitions into STP loop-inconsistent state when the maximum age timer expires. A port in STP loop-inconsistent state does not pass user traffic, so a loop is not created. The loop-inconsistent state is effectively equal to blocking state.

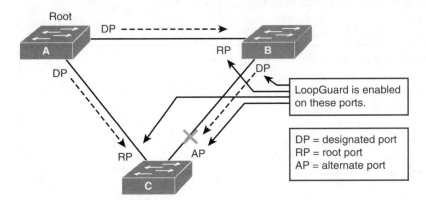

Figure 4-24 *Loop Guard Placement*

The Loop Guard feature is enabled on a per-port basis. However, as long as it blocks the port on the STP level, Loop Guard blocks inconsistent ports on a per-VLAN basis (because of PVSTP). That is, if BPDUs are not received on the trunk port for only one particular VLAN, only that VLAN is blocked (moved to loop-inconsistent STP state). For the same reason, if the Loop Guard feature is enabled on an EtherChannel interface, the entire channel is blocked for a particular VLAN, not just one link (because EtherChannel is regarded as one logical port from the STP point of view).

The Root Guard is mutually exclusive with the Loop Guard. The Root Guard is used on designated ports, and it does not allow the port to become nondesignated. The Loop Guard works on nondesignated ports and does not allow the port to become designated through the expiration of maximum age. The Root Guard cannot be enabled on the same port as the Loop Guard, as shown in Example 4-21. When the Loop Guard is configured on the port, it disables the Root Guard configured on the same port.

By default, Loop Guard is disabled. You can configure Loop Guard globally or on a port-per-port basis.

If you enable Loop Guard globally, then effectively, it is enabled on all point-to-point links. The point-to-point link is detected by the duplex status of the link. If duplex is full, the link is considered point to point. It is still possible to configure, or override, global settings on a per-port basis. Example 4-20 shows the commands needed to configure the Loop Guard on a per-port basis and globally.

Example 4-20   *Loop Guard Commands for Configuration*

```
Switch(config)# interface Ethernet 0/0
Switch(config-if)# spanning-tree guard loop
! Enables Loop Guard on a per-interface basis
Switch(config)# spanning-tree loopguard default
! Enables Loop Guard globally on all point-to-point links
```

To verify the Loop Guard configuration, use the **show spanning-tree interface** and **show spanning-tree summary** commands, as shown in Example 4-21.

Example 4-21   *Loop Guard Verification*

```
Switch# show spanning-tree interface ethernet 0/0 detail
<...output omitted...>
   Bpdu filter is enabled
   Loop guard is enabled on the port
   BPDU: send 6732, received 0
! Shows if Loop Guard is configured for a specific interface


Switch# show spanning-tree summary
Switch is in rapid-pvst mode
Root bridge for: none
Extended system ID              is enabled
Portfast Default                is disabled
PortFast BPDU Guard Default     is disabled
Portfast BPDU Filter Default    is enabled
Loopguard Default               is enabled
EtherChannel misconfig guard    is enabled
<...output omitted...>
! Shows if Loop Guard is configured globally
```

Use UDLD

With bidirectional links, traffic flows in both directions. If for some reason one direction of traffic flow fails, that results in a unidirectional link. A unidirectional link occurs when traffic is transmitted between neighbors in one direction only. Unidirectional links can cause spanning-tree topology loops. Unidirectional Link Detection (UDLD) enables devices to detect when a unidirectional link exists and also to shut down the affected interface. UDLD is useful on a fiber port to prevent network issues resulting in miswiring at the patch panel causing the link to be in up/up status but the BPDUs are lost. Assume you have the three switches network and transmit circuitry in gigabit interface converter (GBIC), or SPF module failed, as shown in Figure 4-25.

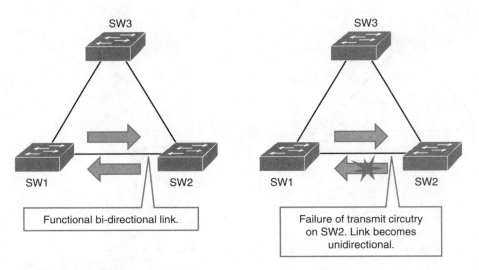

Figure 4-25 *The Need for UDLD*

In Figure 4-26, SW1 has a port that is connected to SW2 and blocked by STP. Because SW1 is no longer receiving BPDUs from SW2, SW1 will proceed to unblock the port.

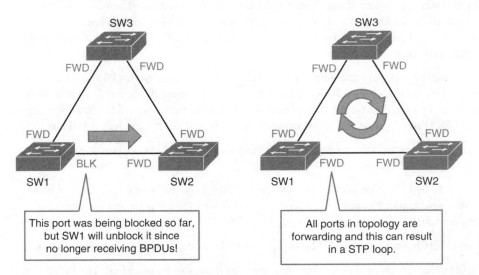

Figure 4-26 *L2 Loop Due to Bad SFP/GBIC*

The final result will be that all ports in the topology are forwarding. The result is a Layer 2 loop. UDLD is a Cisco proprietary protocol that detects unidirectional links and prevents Layer 2 loops from occurring, as shown in Figure 4-27.

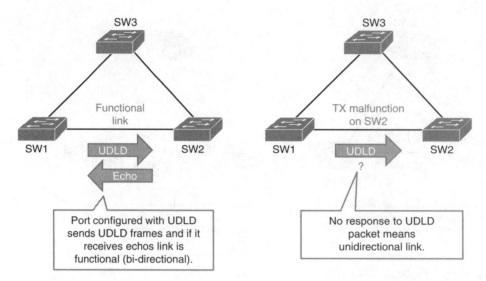

Figure 4-27   *UDLD Overview*

UDLD is a Layer 2 protocol that works with the Layer 1 mechanisms to determine the physical status of a link. If one fiber strand in a pair is disconnected, autonegotiation will not allow the link to become active or stay up. If both fiber strands are operant from a Layer 1 perspective, UDLD determines whether traffic is flowing bidirectionally between the correct neighbors.

The switch periodically transmits UDLD packets on an interface with UDLD enabled. If the packets are not echoed back within a specific time frame, the link is flagged as unidirectional, and the interface is error-disabled. Devices on both ends of the link must support UDLD for the protocol to successfully identify and disable unidirectional links.

Both UDLD peers discover each other by exchanging special frames that are sent to well-known MAC address 01:00:0C:CC:CC:CC.

Although the UDLD protocol falls outside of STP, UDLD has numerous benefits that make it essential in a Layer 2 network. The function of UDLD is to prevent one-way communication between adjacent devices.

In an EtherChannel bundle, UDLD will error-disable only the physical link that has failed.

UDLD messages are sent at regular intervals. This timer can be modified. The default setting varies between platforms. The typical value is 15 seconds.

UDLD is a Cisco proprietary protocol that is also defined in RFC 5171.

After UDLD detects a unidirectional link, it can take two courses of action, depending on configured mode. UDLD has two modes:

- **Normal mode:** When a unidirectional link is detected, the port is allowed to continue its operation. UDLD just marks the port as having an undetermined state. A syslog message is generated.

■ **Aggressive mode:** When a unidirectional link is detected, the switch tries to reestablish the link. It sends one message a second, for 8 seconds. If none of these messages is sent back, the port is placed in error-disabled state.

As with other commands, like PortFast, you can enable UDLD on a per-port basis or globally. It is supported only at the fiber ports. Example 4-22 shows the UDLD configuration.

Example 4-22 *UDLD Commands Configuration*

```
Switch(config)# udld {enable | aggressive}
! Enables UDLD globally on all fiber-optic interfaces
Switch(config-if)# udld port [aggressive]
! Enables UDLD on an individual interface
Switch# show udld
! Displays UDLD status of interface
Switch# udld reset
! Resets all interfaces that were shut down by UDLD
```

For normal mode, use the **enable** keyword. For aggressive mode, use the **aggressive** keyword.

Table 4-8 depicts the default status for the UDLD on a global and an interface basis.

Table 4-8 *UDLD Feature and Its Default Status*

Feature	Default Status
UDLD global enable state	Globally disabled.
UDLD per-interface enable state for fiber-optic media	Enabled on all Ethernet fiber-optic interfaces.
UDLD per-interface enable state for twisted-pair (copper) media	Disabled on all Ethernet 10 or 100 and 1000BASE-TX interfaces.

To display the UDLD status for the specified interface or for all interfaces, use the **show udld** [*interface slot/number*] privileged EXEC command.

Use the **udld reset** command to reset all the interfaces that were shut down by UDLD. You can achieve the same thing by first shutting down the interface and then bringing it back up.

Loop Guard and UDLD functionality overlap, partly in the sense that both protect against STP failures that are caused by unidirectional links. However, these two features differ in functionality and how they approach the problem. Table 4-9 shows the key difference between Loop Guard and UDLD.

Table 4-9   *Comparing Loop Guard with UDLD*

Functionality	Loop Guard	UDLD
Action granularity	Per-VLAN	Per-port
Protection against STP failures that are caused by unidirectional links	Yes, when enabled on all potentially nondesignated ports in redundant topology	Yes, when enabled on all links in redundant topology
Protection against STP failures that are caused by problem in software, resulting in designated switch not sending BPDU	Yes	No
Protection against miswiring	No	Yes

UDLD provides no protection against STP failures that are caused by software and that result in the designated switch not sending BPDUs. However, this type of failure is less common than problems caused by a hardware failure.

On an EtherChannel bundle, UDLD will disable individual failed links. The channel itself remains functional if other links are available. Loop Guard will put the entire channel into a loop-inconsistent state if any physical link in the bundle fails.

Loop Guard does not work on shared links or on a link that has been unidirectional since its initial setup. Enabling both UDLD and Loop Guard provides the highest level of protection.

UDLD Recommended Practices

UDLD supports both fiber-optic and copper Ethernet cables that are connected to LAN ports. Figure 4-28 highlights the key recommendation for UDLD:

- Typically, it is deployed on any fiber-optic interconnection.

- Use UDLD aggressive mode for best protection.

- Turn on in global configuration to avoid operational errors and misses.

A recommended practice is to enable UDLD aggressive mode in all environments where fiber-optic interconnections are used.

Enable UDLD in global mode that will enable UDLD on every individual fiber-optic interface.

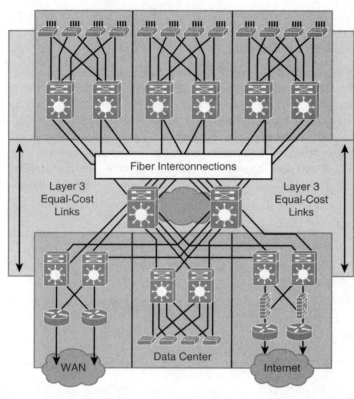

- Typically, it is deployed on any fiber-optic interconnection.

- Use UDLD aggressive mode for best protection.

- Turn on in global configuration to avoid operational errors and misses.

Figure 4-28 *UDLD Recommended Practices*

Use FlexLinks

FlexLinks is a Layer 2 availability feature that provides an alternative solution to STP and allows users to turn off STP and still provide basic link redundancy. FlexLinks can coexist with spanning tree turned on in the distribution layer switches; however, the distribution layer is unaware of the FlexLinks feature. This enhancement enables a convergence time of less than 50 milliseconds. In addition, this convergence time remains consistent regardless of the number of VLANs or MAC addresses configured on switch uplink ports. FlexLinks are Cisco proprietary.

In summary, FlexLinks are a pair of a Layer 2 interfaces, where one interface is configured to act as a backup to the other. FlexLinks are typically configured in service provider or enterprise networks where customers do not want to run STP. FlexLinks provide link-level redundancy that is an alternative to STP. STP is automatically disabled on FlexLinks interfaces.

To configure the FlexLinks feature, you configure one Layer 2 interface as the standby link for the link that you want to be primary. With FlexLinks configured for a pair of interfaces, only one of the interfaces is in the linkup state and is forwarding traffic. If the primary link shuts down, the standby link starts forwarding traffic. When the inactive link comes back up, it goes into standby mode.

In Figure 4-29, ports Fast Ethernet 0/1 and Fast Ethernet 0/2 on Switch A are connected to uplink Switches B and C. Because they are configured as FlexLinks, only one of the interfaces is forwarding traffic; the other one is in standby mode. If Fast Ethernet 0/1 is the active link, it begins forwarding traffic between port Ethernet 0/1 and Switch B; the link between Fast Ethernet 0/2 (the backup link) and Switch C is not forwarding traffic. If port Fast Ethernet 0/1 goes down, port Fast Ethernet 0/2 comes up and starts forwarding traffic to Switch C. When port Ethernet 0/1 comes back up, it goes into standby mode and does not forward traffic; port Fast Ethernet 0/2 continues to forward traffic.

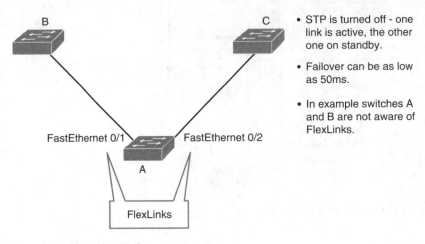

Figure 4-29 *FlexLinks*

After the primary link comes back up, it will not take over forwarding of traffic. Preemption is not enabled for FlexLink by default; it needs to be configured.

If a primary (forwarding) link goes down, a trap notifies the network management stations. If the standby link goes down, a trap notifies the users.

When a primary link fails, the feature takes the following actions:

Step 1.   Detects the failure.

Step 2.   Moves any dynamic unicast MAC addresses that are learned on the primary link to the standby link.

Step 3.   Moves the standby link to a forwarding state.

Step 4.   Transmits dummy multicast packets over the new active interface. The dummy multicast packet format is as follows:

■ **Destination:** 01:00:0c:cd:cd:cd

■ **Source:** MAC address of the hosts or ports on the newly active FlexLinks port

In Figure 4-30, ports Fast Ethernet 0/1 and Fast Ethernet 0/2 on Switch A are connected to Switches B and D through a FlexLinks pair. Fast Ethernet 0/1 is forwarding traffic, and Fast Ethernet 0/2 is in the blocking state. Traffic from the PC to the server is forwarded from Fast Ethernet 0/1 to Fast Ethernet 0/3. The MAC address of the PC has been learned on Port 3 of Switch C. Traffic from the server to the PC is forwarded from Port 3 to Port 1.

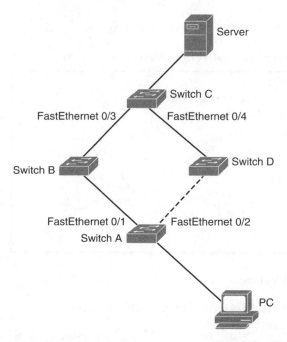

Figure 4-30 *FlexLinks Active Link Failure Mechanism*

If Fast Ethernet 0/1 shuts down, Fast Ethernet 0/2 starts forwarding traffic. If there is no traffic from the PC to the server after failover to Fast Ethernet 0/2, Switch C does not learn the MAC address of the PC on Fast Ethernet 0/4, and because of that, Switch C keeps forwarding traffic from the server to the PC out of Fast Ethernet 0/3. There is traffic loss from the server to the PC because Fast Ethernet 0/1 is down. To alleviate this problem, the feature sends out a dummy multicast packet with the source MAC address of the PC over Fast Ethernet 0/2. Switch C learns the PC MAC address on Fast Ethernet 0/4 and starts forwarding traffic from the server to the PC out of Fast Ethernet 0/4. One dummy multicast packet is sent out for every MAC address.

Note   Example 4.23 shows a simple configuration of an access layer switch. However, you can configure FlexLinks even on much more complex switch networks. You must take special care to avoid creating a loop in the topology. None of the converged states can have a topology loop. Configuring FlexLinks outside of access layer switches can be very complex.

Example 4-23 shows the FlexLinks sample configuration and how to verify.

Example 4-23   *FlexLinks Sample Configuration and Verification Commands*

```
Switch(config)# interface FastEthernet0/1
Switch(config-if)# switchport backup interface FastEthernet0/2
! Configures an interface with a backup interface


Switch# show interface switchport backup
Switch Backup Interface Pairs:
Active Interface Backup Interface State
---------------------------------------------------------
FastEthernet0/1 FastEthernet0/2 Active Up/Backup Standby
! Displays all FlexLinks configured on the switch and the state of each active and
  backup interface (up or standby mode)
```

Follow these guidelines to configure FlexLinks:

- You can configure only one FlexLinks backup link for any active link, and it must be a different interface from the active one.

- An interface can belong to only one FlexLinks pair. An interface can be a backup link for only one active link. An active link cannot belong to another FlexLinks pair.

- Neither of the links can be a port that belongs to an EtherChannel. However, you can configure two port channels (EtherChannel logical interfaces) as FlexLinks, and you can configure a port channel and a physical interface as FlexLinks, with either the port channel or the physical interface as the active link.

- A backup link does not have to be the same type (Fast Ethernet, Gigabit Ethernet, or port channel) as the active link. However, you should configure both FlexLinks with similar characteristics so that there are no loops or changes in behavior if the standby link begins to forward traffic.

- STP is disabled on FlexLinks ports. A FlexLinks port does not participate in STP, even if the VLANs that are present on the port are configured for STP. When STP is not enabled, be sure that there are no loops in the configured topology.

- It is a pair of Layer 2 interfaces, either switch ports or port channels, that are configured to act as a backup to another Layer 2 interface. The feature provides an alternative solution to the STP, and it allows users to turn off STP and still provide basic link redundancy. An active/standby link pair is defined on a common access switch.

- FlexLinks is configured at the interface level with the command **switchport backup interface** *interface-slot/number*.

- To verify FlexLinks configuration, use **show interface switchport backup** command.

STP Stability Mechanisms Recommendations

There are many arguments in favor of using large Layer 2 domains in a corporate network. There are also good reasons why you should avoid Layer 2 in the network. The traditional way of doing transparent bridging requires the computation of a spanning tree for the data plane. *Spanning* means that there will be connectivity between any two devices that have at least one path physically available between them in the network. *Tree* means that the active topology will use a subset of the links physically available so that there is a single path between any two devices. (For example, there is no loop in the network.) Note that this requirement is related to the way frames are forwarded by bridges, not to the STP that is just a control protocol in charge of building such a tree. This behavior can result in a single copy being delivered to all the nodes in the network without any duplicate frames. This approach has the following two main drawbacks:

- **Networkwide failure domain:** A single source can send traffic that is propagated to all the links in the network. If an error condition occurs and the active topology includes a loop, because Ethernet frames do not include a Time-To-Live (TTL) field, traffic might circle around endlessly, resulting in networkwide flooding and link saturation.

- **No multipathing:** Because the forwarding paradigm requires the active topology to be a tree, only one path between any two nodes is used. That means that if there are *n* redundant paths between two devices, all but one will be simply ignored. Note that the introduction of a per-VLAN tree allows working around this constraint to a certain extent.

To limit the impact of such limitations, the general recommendation is to use Layer 3 connectivity at the distribution or core layer of the network, keeping Layer 2 for the access layer, as shown in Figure 4-31. Using Layer 3 between the distribution and core layer allows multipathing (up to 16 paths) using Equal-Cost Multipathing (ECMP) without dependency of STP and is strongly preferred unless there is a need to extend Layer 2 across a data center pod (distribution block). ECMP refers to the situation in which a router has multiple equal-cost paths to a prefix, and thus load balances traffic over each path. Newer technologies, such as Catalyst 6500 Virtual Switching System or Nexus 7000 virtual Port Channel (vPC), enable multipathing at Layer 2.

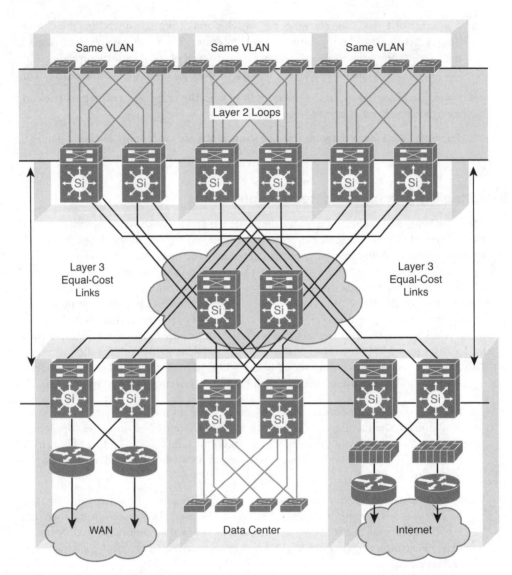

Figure 4-31   *Avoiding Spanning Layer 2 Domain in an Enterprise Network*

In modern networks, a 50-second convergence time is usually not acceptable. For this reason, RSTP is widely preferred over legacy 802.1D implementations. In networks where a large number of VLANs are configured over many switches, it might be necessary to group STP instances with MST. Most of the time, the same VLAN would not be configured over many switches. VLANs would be local to a floor, thus spanning across a limited number of switches. In this configuration, RSTP provides the best efficiency.

RSTP is far superior to 802.1D STP and even PVST+ from a convergence perspective. It greatly improves the restoration times for any VLAN that requires a topology convergence due to linkup, and it also greatly improves the convergence time over BackboneFast for any indirect link failures.

Note   If a network includes other vendor switches, isolate the different STP domains with Layer 3 routing to avoid STP compatibility issues.

Even if the recommended design does not depend on STP to resolve link or node failure events, STP is required to protect against user-side loops. A loop can be introduced on the user-facing access layer ports in many ways. Wiring mistakes, misconfigured end stations, or malicious users can create a loop. STP is required to ensure a loop-free topology and to protect the rest of the network from problems created in the access layer.

Note   Some security personnel have recommended disabling STP at the network edge. This practice is not recommended because the risk of lost connectivity without STP is far greater than any STP information that might be revealed.

Spanning tree should be used and its topology controlled by root bridge manual designation. Once the tree is created, use the STP Toolkit to enhance the overall mechanism performances and reduce the time lost during topology changes.

To configure a VLAN instance to become the root bridge, enter the **spanning-tree vlan** *vlan-ID* **root** command to modify the bridge priority from the default value (32768) to a significantly lower value. Manually placing the primary and secondary bridges along with enabling STP Toolkit options enables you to support a deterministic configuration where you know which ports should be forwarding and which ports should be blocking.

The Cisco RSTP implementation is far superior to 802.1D STP and even to PVST+ from a convergence perspective. It greatly improves the restoration times for any VLAN that requires a topology convergence due to linkup, and it also greatly improves the convergence time over BackboneFast for any indirect link failures and UplinkFast for any uplink failures. Figure 4-32 illustrates recommended placements for STP Toolkit features.

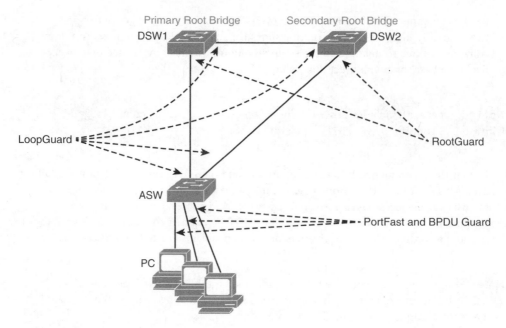

Figure 4-32   *STP Best Practice Recommendation*

Following are the recommended practices for using STP stability mechanisms:

- **PortFast:** Apply to all end-user ports. To secure PortFast-enabled ports, always combine PortFast with BPDU Guard.

- **Root Guard:** Apply to all ports where root is never expected.

- **Loop Guard:** Apply to all ports that are or can become nondesignated.

- **UDLD:** The UDLD protocol enables devices to monitor the physical configuration of the cables and detect when a unidirectional link exists. When a unidirectional link is detected, UDLD shuts down the affected LAN port. UDLD is often configured on port linking switches.

Depending on the security requirements of an organization, the port security feature can be used to restrict the ingress traffic of a port by limiting the MAC addresses that are allowed to send traffic into the port.

The use of Root Guard and Loop Guard is mutually exclusive.

Note   Examples where you will need to implement BPDU Filters are rare. Under no circumstances should you use BPDU Filter and BPDU Guard on the same interface.

Configuring Multiple Spanning Tree Protocol

Multiple Spanning Tree (MST) extends the IEEE 802.1w RST algorithm to multiple spanning trees. The main purpose of MST is to reduce the total number of spanning-tree instances to match the physical topology of the network and thus reduce the CPU cycles of a switch. PVRST+ runs STP instances for each VLAN and does not take into consideration the physical topology that might not require many different STP topologies. MST, in contrast, uses a minimum number of STP instances to match the number of physical topologies present.

The 802.1Q and PVST+ represent two extremes of STP operation. 802.1Q has only a single instance for all VLANs in the network. If your network is running 1000 VLANs, only 1 instance runs for all 1000 VLANs. With PVST+, one instance is used for each active VLAN in the network. If your network has 1000 VLANs, there will be 1000 independent instances of STP running.

MST is a concept of mapping one or more VLANs to a single STP instance.

Upon completing this section, you will be able to meet these objectives:

- Describe when and why to use MST
- Describe MST regions
- Describe STP instances with MST
- Describe the extended system ID for MST
- Configure and Verify MST
- Configure MST path cost
- MST protocol migration
- Configure MST port priority
- Describe recommended practices when migrating a network to MST
- Describe the MST recommended practices
- Troubleshoot SPT

Introducing MST

The main purpose of MST is to reduce the total number of spanning-tree instances to match the physical topology of the network. Reducing the total number of spanning-tree instances will reduce the CPU loading of a switch. The number of instances of spanning tree is reduced to the number of links (that is, active paths) that are available.

Figure 4-33 shows a common network design, featuring an access switch, A, connected to two building distribution submodule switches, D1 and D2. In this setup, there are 1000 VLANs, and the network administrator typically seeks to achieve load balancing on the access switch uplinks based on even or odd VLANs (or any other scheme deemed appropriate).

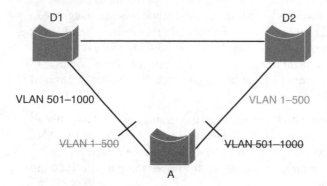

Figure 4-33 *VLAN Load Balancing*

Figure 4-33 illustrates two links and 1000 VLANs. The 1000 VLANs map to two MST instances. Rather than maintaining 1000 spanning trees, each switch needs to maintain only two spanning trees, reducing the need for switch resources. This concept of two MST instances for the topology, as shown in Figure 4-33, extends to 4096 VLANs. MST converges faster than PVRST+ and is backward compatible with 802.1D STP, 802.1w (RSTP), and the Cisco PVST+ architecture.

MST allows for the building of multiple spanning trees over trunks by grouping and associating VLANs to spanning-tree instances. Each instance may have a topology that is independent of other spanning-tree instances. This architecture provides multiple forwarding paths for data traffic and enables load balancing. A failure in one forwarding path does not affect other instances with different forwarding paths; hence, this architecture improves network fault tolerance.

In large networks, using different VLANs and a different spanning-tree topology enables better administration of the network and use of the redundant paths available. An MST spanning-tree instance might exist only on bridges that have compatible VLAN instance assignments. Configuring a set of bridges with the same MST configuration information allows them to participate in a specific set of spanning-tree instances. The term *MST region* refers to the set of interconnected bridges that have the same MST configuration.

Implementation of MST is not required if the enterprise campus model is being employed because the number of active VLAN instances, and hence the STP instances would be small and stable due to the design.

In the scenario described in Figure 4-34, only two different final logical topologies exist and therefore require only two spanning-tree instances. There is no need to run 1000 instances if, as shown in Figure 4-34, half of the 1000 VLANs map to a different spanning-tree instance.

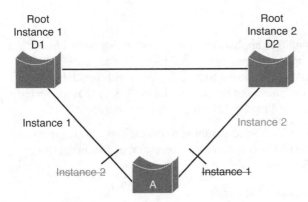

Figure 4-34 *MST*

In a network running MST, as depicted in Figure 4-34, the following is true:

- The desired load-balancing scheme is still possible because half the VLANs follow one separate instance.

- The switch utilization is low because it has to handle only two instances.

- From a technical standpoint, MST is the best solution for the scenario presented in Figure 4-34. Because MST is a newer protocol, however, the following issues could arise:

  - The protocol is more complex than the usual spanning tree and therefore requires additional training of the operation staff.

  - Interaction with legacy bridges is sometimes challenging.

MST enables you to build multiple spanning trees over trunks by grouping VLANs and associating them with spanning-tree instances. Each instance can have a topology independent of other spanning-tree instances. This architecture provides multiple active forwarding paths for data traffic and enables load balancing.

Network fault tolerance is improved over Common Spanning Tree (CST) because a failure in one instance (forwarding path) does not necessarily affect other instances. This VLAN-to-MST grouping must be consistent across all bridges within an MST region.

In large networks, you can more easily administer the network and use redundant paths by locating different VLAN and spanning-tree assignments in different parts of the network. A spanning-tree instance can exist only on bridges that have compatible VLAN instance assignments.

You must configure a set of bridges with the same MST configuration information, which allows them to participate in a specific set of spanning-tree instances. Interconnected bridges that have the same MST configuration are referred to as an *MST region*. Bridges with different MST configurations or legacy bridges running 802.1D are considered separate MST regions.

MST Regions

MST differs from the other spanning-tree implementations in combining some but not necessarily all VLANs into logical spanning-tree instances. This difference raises the problem of determining which VLAN is supposed to be associated with which instance. VLAN-to-instance association is communicated by tagging the BPDUs so that the receiving device can identify the instances and the VLANs to which they apply.

To provide this logical assignment of VLANs to spanning trees, each switch that is running MST in the network has a single MST configuration consisting of following three attributes, as shown in Figure 4-35:

- An alphanumeric configuration name (32 bytes)

- A configuration revision number (2 bytes)

- A 4096-element table that associates each of the potential 4096 VLANs supported on the chassis with a given instance

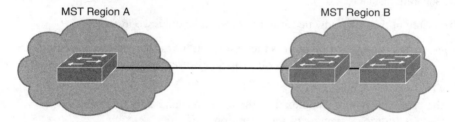

Figure 4-35   *MST Regions*

To be part of a common MST region, a group of switches must share the same configuration attributes. It is the responsibility of the network administrator to propagate the configuration properly throughout the region. Currently, this step is possible only with the CLI or through SNMP. Other methods can be implemented in the future because the IEEE specification does not explicitly mention how to accomplish this task.

To ensure a consistent VLAN-to-instance mapping, it is necessary for the protocol to be able to identify the boundaries of the regions exactly. For that purpose, the characteristics of the region are included in BPDUs. The exact VLAN-to-instance mapping is not propagated in the BPDU because the switches need to know only whether they are in the same region as a neighbor.

Therefore, only a digest of the VLAN-to-instance mapping table is sent, along with the revision number and the name. After a switch receives a BPDU, it extracts the digest (a numeric value derived from the VLAN-to-instance mapping table through a mathematical function) and compares it with its own computed digest. If the digests differ, the mapping must be different, so the port on which the BPDU was received is at the boundary of a region.

In generic terms, a port is at the boundary of a region if the designated bridge on its segment is in a different region or if it receives legacy 802.1D BPDUs.

The configuration revision number gives you a method of tracking changes that are made to the MST region. It does not automatically increase each time that you make changes to the MST configuration. Each time that you make a change, you should increase the revision number by one.

STP Instances with MST

MST does not send BPDUs for every active STP instance separately. A special instance (instance 0) is designed to carry all STP-related information. BPDUs carry all the usual STP information, in addition to configuration name, revision number, and hash value that is calculated over VLAN-to-instance mapping tables. If hash values do not match, an MST misconfiguration exists between the two switches.

MST supports a number of instances. Instance 0 is the internal spanning tree (IST).

Figure 4-36 shows how different MST instances (MSTIs) exist within a single MST region. MSTI1 and MSTI2 are mapped to different VLANs. Their topologies converge differently because root bridges are configured differently. Within the MST region, there are three independent STP instances: MSTI0 (IST), MSTI1, and MSTI2.

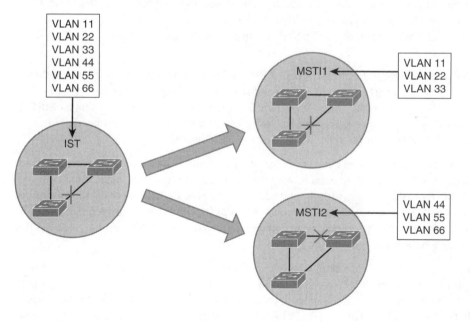

Figure 4-36 *STP Instances with MST*

In Figure 4-36, on the left, all six VLAN instances initially belong to MSTI0. This is the default behavior. Then make the half of VLAN instances (11, 22, and 33) mapped to MSTI1, and the other half (44, 55, and 66) mapped to MSTI2. If different root bridges are configured for MSTI1 and MSTI2, their topologies will converge differently. By having different Layer 2 topologies between MST instances, links are more evenly utilized.

Within a topology where multiple variations of STP are used, Common Spanning Tree (CST) topology considers an MST region as a single black box. CST maintains a loop-free topology with the links that connect the regions to each other and to switches that are not running MST, as shown in Figure 4-37.

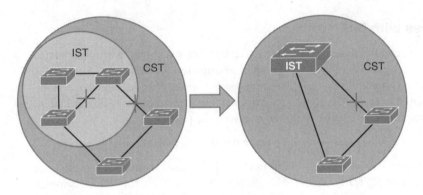

Figure 4-37   *STP Instances with MST*

Within the MST region, the IST instance maintains a loop-free topology. IST presents the whole MST region as a single virtual bridge to the outside STP. BPDUs between the MST's STP instance and the CST's STP instance are exchanged over the native VLAN, as if a single CST were used.

MST is compatible with other flavors of STP. In Figure 4-37, on the left, there are three switches running within an MST region and two switches that are not running MST. Figure 4-37, on the right, shows how the IST provides a loop-free path within an MST region. The IST instance makes the whole region look like one single bridge that interacts with BPDUs with the switches outside the MST region.

The MSTIs are simple RSTP instances that only exist inside a region. These instances run the RSTP automatically by default, without any extra configuration work. Unlike the IST, MSTIs never interact with the outside of the region. Remember that MST runs only one spanning tree outside of the region; so except for the IST instance, regular instances inside of the region have no outside counterpart. In addition, MSTIs do not send BPDUs outside a region, only the IST does.

By default, all VLANs are mapped to the IST instance. This represents the case of classic IEEE RSTP with all VLANs sharing the same spanning tree. You must explicitly map them to other instances. Recommended practice is to map VLAN instances other than MSTI0. Leave MSTI0 for mapping VLANs that connect to switches that are not running MST. Every MSTI assigns its own priorities to the switches and uses its own link costs to come up with a private logical topology, separate from the IST. MST does not send the MST's information in separate BPDUs. MSTI information is carried in the IST's BPDU.

This information is carried in so-called M-Record fields (one for every active MSTI, as shown in Figure 4-38).

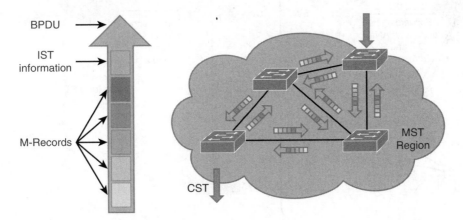

Figure 4-38 *IST BDPBU with M-Records*

Extended System ID for MST

As with PVST, the 12-bit Extended System ID field is used in MST. In MST, this field carries the MST instance number. Figure 4-39 shows the MST frame.

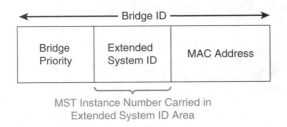

Figure 4-39 *Extended System ID for MST*

Configuring and Verifying MST

In this section, you will learn how to configure multiple spanning tree protocol.

Figure 4-40 on the left represents STP configuration at the beginning of this lab. All three switches are configured with PVST+ and four user-created VLANs: 2, 3, 4, and 5. SW1 is configured as the root bridge for VLANs 2 and 3. SW2 is configured as the root bridge for VLANs 4 and 5. This configuration distributes forwarding of traffic between the SW3-SW1 and SW3-SW2 uplinks.

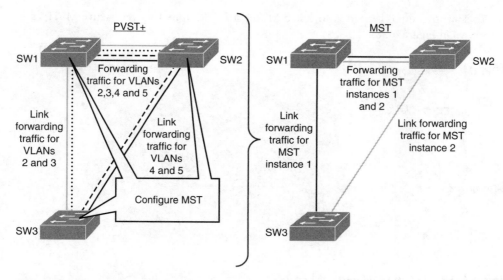

Figure 4-40 *MST Configuration Topology*

Figure 4-40 on the right shows the STP configuration that you will perform in this section. VLANs 2 and 3 are mapped into MST instance 1. VLANs 4 and 5 are mapped into MST instance 2.

Follow the following steps to configure the MST in the topology shown in Figure 4-41. Investigate spanning-tree instances on SW3. Example 4-24 shows the summary of current SPT configuration before moving to MST.

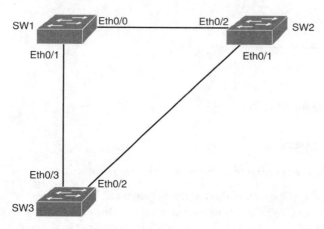

Figure 4-41 *MST Configuration Topology Detail*

Example 4-24 *Verifying Current STP State*

```
SW3# show spanning-tree summary
Switch is in pvst mode
Root bridge for: none
<... output omitted ...>
Name       Blocking Listening Learning Forwarding STP Active
---------- -------- --------- -------- ---------- ----------
VLAN0001   1        0         19       0          20
VLAN0002   1        0         2        0          3
VLAN0003   1        0         2        0          3
VLAN0004   1        0         2        0          3
VLAN0005   1        0         2        0          3
---------- -------- --------- -------- ---------- ----------
5 vlans    5        0         27       0          32
```

An STP instance is created for each VLAN with PVST+. Five VLANs translate into five STP instances.

SW1 and SW2 also run the same number of running STP instances as SW3.

Configure all three switches to be a part of the same MST region, CCNP, and have the same revision, 1. Example 4-25 shows the configuration of MST with the CCNP region.

Example 4-25 *Configuring MST with the CCNP Region on SW1, SW2, and SW3*

```
SW1(config)# spanning-tree mst configuration
SW1(config-mst)# name CCNP
SW1(config-mst)# revision 1

SW2(config)# spanning-tree mst configuration
SW2(config-mst)# name CCNP
SW2(config-mst)# revision 1

SW3(config)# spanning-tree mst configuration
SW3(config-mst)# name CCNP
SW3(config-mst)# revision 1
```

Now all three switches belong to the same MST region.

On all three switches, map VLANs 2 and 3 to MST instance 1. Map VLANs 4 and 5 to MST instance 2, as shown in Example 4-26.

Example 4-26   *MST Instance 1 and 2 Configuration on SW1, SW2, and SW3*

```
SW1(config)# spanning-tree mst configuration
SW1(config-mst)# instance 1 vlan 2,3
SW1(config-mst)# instance 2 vlan 4,5
SW1(config-mst)# end

SW2(config)# spanning-tree mst configuration
SW2(config-mst)# instance 1 vlan 2,3
SW2(config-mst)# instance 2 vlan 4,5
SW2(config-mst)# end

SW3(config)# spanning-tree mst configuration
SW3(config-mst)# instance 1 vlan 2,3
SW3(config-mst)# instance 2 vlan 4,5
SW3(config-mst)# end
```

At this point, MST is configured with three instances. VLANs 2 and 3 belong to instance 1. VLANs 4 and 5 belong to instance 2. All other VLANs between 1 and 4094, that are not in instances 1 or 2, belong to instance 0.

Note   Using the **end** or **exit** command will apply configuration. If you want to abort the change use the **abort** keyword.

Configure SW1 as primary root bridge for MST instance 1 and secondary root for instance 2, as illustrated in Example 4-27.

Example 4-27   *SPT Root Bridge Configuration for SW1*

```
SW1(config)# spanning-tree mst 1 root primary
SW1(config)# spanning-tree mst 2 root secondary
```

Note   In this example, you have changed the MST switch priority using **spanning-tree mst** *instance-id* **root {primary | secondary}**. This command is actually a macro that sets the switch's MST priority, which is a number. If you issue a **show running-config**, you will see switch priority as a number, not the primary or secondary keyword.

Alternatively you can change the switch's bridge priority directly by using the **spanning-tree mst** *instance-id* **priority** *priority* command.

Configure SW2 as secondary root bridge for MST instance 1 and primary root for instance 2, as shown in Example 4-28.

Example 4-28 *SPT Root Bridge Configuration for SW2*

```
SW2(config)# spanning-tree mst 1 root secondary
SW2(config)# spanning-tree mst 2 root primary

Change STP mode to MST on all three switches as shown in example 4-29.
Example 4-29 Changing the SPT mode to MST
SW1(config)# spanning-tree mode mst

SW2(config)# spanning-tree mode mst

SW3(config)# spanning-tree mode mst
```

Note Changing STP mode to MST before doing the actual VLAN-to-instance mappings is not advisable. Every change in the mapping will result in recalculation of the STP tree.

Note A switch cannot run MST and PVST+ at the same time. If you issue **show spanning-tree** on either of the three switches, you will notice that MSTP is now the enabled protocol.

Again, investigate spanning-tree instances on SW3, as shown in Example 4-29.

Example 4-29 *Verifying Spanning-Tree Configuration for MST*

```
SW3# show spanning-tree summary
Switch is in mst mode (IEEE Standard)
<... output omitted ...>


Name       Blocking Listening Learning Forwarding STP Active
---------- -------- --------- -------- ---------- ----------
MST0          0        0         0         24         24
MST1          0        0         0         4          4
MST2          0        0         0         4          4
---------- -------- --------- -------- ---------- ----------
3 msts        0        0         0         32         32
```

MST runs three instances: the default MSTI0 and the two you configured (MSTI1 and MSTI2).

Investigate MST configuration on SW3, as shown in Example 4-30.

Figure 4-30   *Verifying the MST Configuration*

```
SW3(config)# spanning-tree mst configuration
SW3(config-mst)# show current
Current MST configuration
Name        [CCNP]
Revision  1      Instances configured 3


Instance  Vlans mapped
--------  ------------------------------------------------------------------
0         1,6-4094
1         2-3
2         4-5
          ------------------------------------------------------------------
```

Note   VLANs 2 and 3 are mapped to MSTI1 . VLANs 4 and 5 are mapped to MSTI2.
All other VLANs are mapped to MSTI0 or IST.

Note   To verify currently applied MST configuration, use **show current** under MST
configuration mode. To verify pending MST configuration, use **show pending** under
MST configuration mode. When you type **exit** or **end**, pending configuration will
become current. So, **show current** and **show pending** will produce the same outputs.

Verify the MST message digest on all three switches, as shown in Example 4-31.

Example 4-31   *Verifying MST Digest on All Three Switches*

```
SW1# show spanning-tree mst configuration digest
Name        [CCNP]
Revision  1      Instances configured 3
Digest          0x47CAC1CE872FFD89640049F4CC87BCB2
Pre-std Digest  0x6E07725683888804D99F3D3BE25CA594

SW2# show spanning-tree mst configuration digest
Name        [CCNP]
Revision  1      Instances configured 3
Digest          0x47CAC1CE872FFD89640049F4CC87BCB2
Pre-std Digest  0x6E07725683888804D99F3D3BE25CA594

SW3# show spanning-tree mst configuration digest
```

```
Name        [CCNP]
Revision  1      Instances configured 3
Digest           0x47CAC1CE872FFD89640049F4CC87BCB2
Pre-std Digest   0x6E07725683888804D99F3D3BE25CA594
```

Note Because MST configuration is identical on all three switches in a region, the digest matches. A mismatch in digest would indicate that the VLAN lists do not match between switches. Note that digest may be different in your case. It only matters that the digest is the same on all three switches.

The Pre-std Digest refers to Cisco's legacy prestandard implementation of MST. Cisco developed a proprietary version of MST before MST was released called *MISTP*, which has similar principles as MST.

On SW3 verify MSTI1 and MSTI2 mappings and Layer 2 convergence, as shown in Example 4-32.

Example 4-32 *Verifying MST Instances Mappings*

```
SW3# show spanning-tree mst 1


##### MST1     vlans mapped:    2-3
<... output omitted ..>
Et0/2             Altn BLK 2000000    128.3     Shr
Et0/3             Root FWD 2000000    128.4     Shr
<... output omitted ..>


SW3# show spanning-tree mst 2


##### MST2     vlans mapped:    4-5
<... output omitted ..>
Et0/2             Root FWD 2000000    128.3     Shr
Et0/3             Altn BLK 2000000    128.4     Shr
<... output omitted ..>
```

MST instances 1 and 2 have two distinct Layer 2 topologies. Instance 1 uses uplink toward SW1 as the active link and blocks uplink toward SW2. Instance 2 uses uplink toward SW2 as the active link and blocks uplink toward SW1, as shown in Figure 4-42.

You can use **show spanning-tree mst 1** to verify that SW1 is the root bridge for instance 1. Also, you can use **show spanning-tree mst 2** on SW2 to verify that SW2 is the root bridge for instance 2.

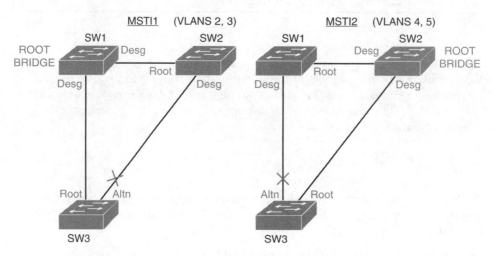

Figure 4-42 *Topology for Each MST Instance*

Configuring MST Path Cost

Path cost functions the same as with other STPs, except with MST port costs are configured per instance.

MST, like any other STP, uses the sequence of four criteria to choose the best path:

■ Lowest BID

■ Lowest root path cost

■ Lowest sender BID

■ Lowest sender port ID

You can assign lower-cost values to interfaces that you want selected first and higher-cost values that you want selected last. If all interfaces have the same cost value, the MST puts the interface with the lowest sender port ID in the forwarding state and blocks the other interfaces. Example 4-33 shows the configuration sample of how to change the cost and how to verify the change.

Example 4-33 *MST Path Cost*

```
Switch(config)# interface Ethernet 0/2
Switch(config-if)# spanning-tree mst 1 cost 1000000
! Sets the MST cost of the interface to 1000000
```

```
SW3# show spanning-tree mst
<... output omitted ..>
Interface          Role   Sts  Cost    Prio.Nbr   Type
------------------ ----   ---- ------- ---------  -----
Et0/2              Altn   BLK  1000000 128.3      Shr
Et0/3              Root   FWD  2000000 128.4      Shr
Et1/0              Desg   FWD  2000000 128.5      Shr
Et1/1              Desg   FWD  2000000 128.6      Shr
! Verify MST path cost configuration
```

Configuring MST Port Priority

Port priority functions the same as with other STPs, except with MST port priorities are configured per instance.

MST, like any other STP, uses the sequence of four criteria to choose the best path:

- Lowest BID

- Lowest root path cost

- Lowest sender BID

- Lowest sender port ID

You can assign higher sender's priority values (lower numeric values) to interfaces that you want selected first and lower sender's priority values (higher numeric values) that you want selected last. If all sender's interfaces have the same priority value, the MST puts the interface with the lowest sender port ID in the forwarding state and blocks the other interfaces. Example 4-34 shows the sample of configuration to configure the port priority in MST and how to verify it.

Example 4-34 *MST Port Priority Example*

```
Switch(config)# interface Ethernet 0/2
Switch(config-if)# spanning-tree mst 1 port-priority 32
! Sets the MST port priority for given MST interface

SW3# show spanning-tree mst
<... output omitted ..>
Interface          Role   Sts  Cost    Prio.Nbr   Type
------------------ ----   ---- ------- ---------  -----
Et0/2              Altn   BLK  1000000 32.3       Shr
Et0/3              Root   FWD  2000000 128.4      Shr
Et1/0              Desg   FWD  2000000 128.5      Shr
Et1/1              Desg   FWD  2000000 128.6      Shr
! Verify port ID settings that are sent
```

MST Protocol Migration

Following are some of the guidelines for MST protocol migration:

■ The first step in the migration to 802.1s is to properly identify point-to-point and edge ports. Ensure that all switch-to-switch links on which a rapid transition is desired are full duplex. Edge ports are defined through the PortFast feature.

■ Carefully decide how many instances are needed in the switched network, and keep in mind that an instance translates to a logical topology.

■ Decide what VLANs to map onto those instances, and carefully select a root and a backup root for each instance.

■ Choose a configuration name and a revision number that will be common to all switches in the network. Cisco recommends that you place as many switches as possible into a single region; it is not advantageous to segment a network into separate regions.

■ Avoid mapping any VLANs onto instance 0.

■ Migrate the core first. Change the STP type to MST, and work your way down to the access switches.

■ MST can interact with legacy bridges running PVST+ on a per-port basis, so it is not a problem to mix both types of bridges if interactions are clearly understood. Always try to keep the root of the CST and IST inside the region. If you interact with a PVST+ bridge through a trunk, ensure that the MST bridge is the root for all VLANs allowed on that trunk.

Note   When you enable MST, it also enables RSTP. The spanning-tree UplinkFast and BackboneFast features are PVST+ features, and are disabled when you enable MST because those features are built in to RSTP, and MST relies on RSTP. Within the migration, you can remove those commands in IOS.

■ The configuration of the features such as the PortFast, BPDU Guard, BPDUF Filter, Root Guard, and Loop Guard are also applicable in MST mode. The usage of these features is the same as in PVST+ mode. If you have already enabled these features in the PVST+ mode, it remains active after the migration to MST mode.

Note   Do not use Loop Guard in combination with BPDU Guard. If BPDU Guard and BPDU Filter are enabled at the same time, only BPDU Filter is active.

MST Recommended Practices

You may run across some issues because MST instances do not map one-to-one with VLANs.

PVST+ not allowing a VLAN on a trunk link would also disable STP on that link. With MST, every instance is running on every link in the region. If you disallow a VLAN on a trunk link, you might end up with connectivity issues.

Part 1 of Figure 4-43 shows a network where VLANs are manually pruned on trunks. Because pruning is not consistent with MST configuration, VLAN 10's traffic is blocked between Switch 1 and Switch 2.

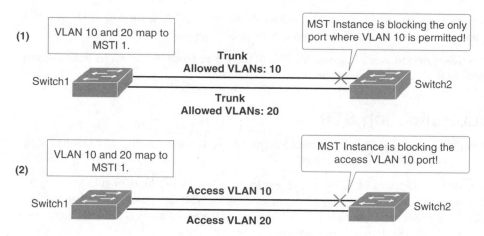

Figure 4-43   *MST Recommended Practices*

You would have the same problem if you configure one of the two links as access. For example, one link as access VLAN 10 and the other link as access VLAN 20, as part 2 of Figure 4-43 shows. These two access VLANs use the same STP instance.

It is recommended that you do not run MST on access ports and that you do not manually prune VLANs from trunks.

Figure 4-44 shows Switch 1 and Switch 2 connected with access ports each located in different VLANs. VLAN 10 and VLAN 20 are mapped to different instances. VLAN 10 is mapped to instance 0, and VLAN 20 is mapped to instance 1.

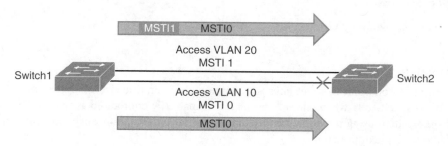

Figure 4-44   *MST Recommended Practice for IST Instances*

With this configuration, no VLAN 10 traffic will be able to pass between the switches. How is that possible with no apparent loop?

This issue is explained by the fact that MST information is conveyed with only one BPDU (IST BPDU), regardless of the number of internal instances. Individual instances do not send individual BPDUs. When Switch 1 and Switch 2 exchange STP information for VLAN 20, the switches send an IST BPDU for instance 1 because that is where VLAN 20 is mapped. However, because it is an IST BPDU, this BPDU also contains information for instance 0. This means that the IST instance is active on all ports inside an MST region, whether these ports carry VLANs mapped to the IST instance or not.

Switch 2 receives two BPDUs, for instance 0 from Switch 1 (one on each port). Switch 2 then needs to block one of the two ports to prevent a loop.

The solution is to avoid mapping VLANs to the IST instance or to convert links to trunks and allow all VLANs to pass through.

Troubleshooting STP

Bridging loops generally characterize STP problems. Troubleshooting STP involves identifying and preventing such loops.

The primary function of STP is to prevent loops created by redundant links in bridged networks. STP operates at Layer 2 of the OSI model. STP fails in specific cases, such as hardware or software anomalies. Troubleshooting these situations is typically difficult depending on the design of the network.

Potential STP Problems

The following subsections highlight common network conditions that lead to STP problems:

- Duplex mismatch

- Unidirectional link failure

- Frame corruption

- Resource errors

- PortFast configuration error

Duplex Mismatch

Duplex mismatch on point-to-point links is a common configuration error. Duplex mismatch occurs specifically when one side of the link is manually configured as full duplex and the other side is using the default configuration for autonegotiation. Such a configuration leads to duplex mismatch.

The worst-case scenario for a duplex mismatch is when a bridge that is sending BPDUs is configured for half duplex on a link while its peer is configured for full duplex. In Figure 4-45, the duplex mismatch on the link between Switch A and Switch B could potentially lead to a bridging loop. Because Switch B is configured for full duplex, it starts forwarding frames even if Switch A is already using the link. This is a problem for Switch A, which detects a collision and runs the backoff algorithm before attempting another transmission of its frame. If there is enough traffic from Switch B to Switch A, every packet (including the BPDUs) sent by Switch A is deferred or has a collision and is subsequently dropped. From an STP point of view, because Switch B no longer receives BPDUs from Switch A, it assumes that the root bridge is no longer present. Consequently, Switch B moves its port to Switch C into the forwarding state, creating a Layer 2 loop.

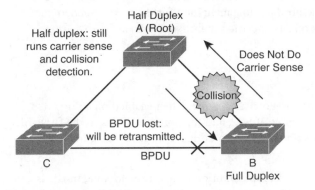

Figure 4-45   *Duplex Mismatch*

Unidirectional Link Failure

A unidirectional link is a frequent cause for a bridging loop. An undetected failure on a fiber link or a problem with a transceiver usually causes unidirectional links. With STP enabled to provide redundancy, any condition that results in a link maintaining a physical link connected status on both link partners but operating in a one-way communication state is detrimental to network stability because it could lead to bridging loops and routing black holes.

To resolve this problem, configure aggressive mode UDLD to detect incorrect cabling or unidirectional links and automatically put the affected port in err-disabled state. The general recommended practice is to use aggressive mode UDLD on all point-to-point interfaces in any multilayer switched network.

Frame Corruption

Frame corruption is another cause for STP failure. If an interface is experiencing a high rate of physical errors, the result may be lost BPDUs, which may lead to an interface in the blocking state moving to the forwarding state. However, this case is rare because STP default parameters are conservative. The blocking port needs to miss consecutive BPDUs for 50 seconds before transitioning to the forwarding state. In addition, any single BPDU that is successfully received by the switch breaks the loop. This case is more common for nondefault STP parameters and aggressive STP timer values. Frame corruption is generally a result of a duplex mismatch, bad cable, or incorrect cable length.

Resource Errors

Even on high-end switches that perform most of their switching functions in hardware with specialized application-specific integrated circuits (ASICs), STP is performed by the CPU (software based). Therefore, if the CPU of the bridge is overutilized for any reason, it might lack the resources to send out BPDUs. STP is generally not a processor-intensive application and has priority over other processes; therefore, a resource problem is unlikely to arise. However, you need to exercise caution when multiple VLANs in PVST+ mode exist. Consult the product documentation for the recommended number of VLANs and STP instances on any specific Catalyst switch to avoid exhausting resources.

PortFast Configuration Errors

As discussed earlier in this chapter, the PortFast feature, when enabled on a port, bypasses the listening and learning states of STP, and the port transitions to the forwarding mode on linkup. The fast transition can lead to bridging loops if configured on incorrect ports.

The problem with this type of transient loop condition is that if the looping traffic is intensive, the bridge might have trouble successfully sending the BPDU that stops the loop. The BPDU Guard prevents this type of event from occurring.

Study Tips

- STP allows physical path redundancy, while preventing the effect of loops.

- If you don't manually set the root bridge, the oldest and thus slowest switch might become the root bridge, slowing down the whole network.

- RPVST+ has faster convergences time because of its immediate transition to the forwarding state in the most common scenario. It is highly recommended to always configure RSTP if possible.

- If not all the switches have the RSTP configured, interfaces that lead to legacy STP switches will fall back to non-RSTP.

- UplinkFast and BackboneFast make non-RSTP converges faster. No need to enable with RSTP.

- BPDU Guard protects the operations of STP on PortFast-configured ports.

- Modify STP switches' priority and implement Root Guard. It prevents unwanted switches in your network from becoming the root bridge.

- Loop Guard detects and disables an interface with Layer 2 unidirectional connectivity, protecting the network from anomalous STP conditions.

- UDLD and FlexLinks are not STP mechanisms. UDLD helps STP detect unidirectional links, and FlexLinks can be used as an alternative to STP.

- MST allows you to map multiple VLANs to single spanning-tree instances.

- With MST, use trunks and do not prune VLANs from trunks.

- MST instance 0 is the only one that communicates to other regions and non-MST switches.

Summary

STP is a fundamental protocol to prevent Layer 2 loops and at the same time provide redundancy in the network. This chapter covered the basic operation and configuration of RSTP and MST. Enhancements now enable STP to converge more quickly and run more efficiently.

RSTP provides faster convergence than 802.1D when topology changes occur. RSTP enables several additional port roles to increase the overall mechanism's efficiency.

show spanning-tree is the main family of commands used to verify RSTP operations.

MST reduces the encumbrance of PVRST+ by allowing a single instance of spanning tree to run for multiple VLANs.

The Cisco STP enhancements provide robustness and resiliency to the protocol. These enhancements add availability to the multilayer switched network. These enhancements not only isolate bridging loops but also prevent bridging loops from occurring.

To protect STP operations, several features are available that control the way BPDUs are sent and received:

- BPDU Guard protects the operation of STP on PortFast-configured ports.

- BPDU Filter is a variant that prevents BPDUs from being sent and received while leaving the port in forwarding state.

- Root Guard prevents root switch being elected via BPDUs received on a Root Guard-configured port.

- Loop Guard detects and disables an interface with Layer 2 unidirectional connectivity, protecting the network from anomalous STP conditions.

- UDLD detects and disables an interface with unidirectional connectivity, protecting the network from anomalous STP conditions.

  In most implementations, the STP Toolkit should be used in combination with additional features, such as FlexLinks.

STP troubleshooting is achieved with careful planning and documentation before the problem and following a set of logical troubleshooting steps to identify and correct the problem. The troubleshooting exercise needs to be completed by documenting findings and making appropriate changes to the planning document.

Review Questions

Use the questions here to review what you learned in this module. The correct answers are found in Appendix A, "Answers to Chapter Review Questions."

1. Which command enables RSTP on a switch?

   a. spanning-tree mode rapid-pvst

   b. no spanning-tree mode pvst

   c. spanning tree mode rstp

   d. rapid spanning-tree enable

2. When a switch running RSTP receives an 802.1D BPDU, what happens?

   a. The switch disables RSTP.

   b. The switch begins to use 802.1D rules on that port.

   c. BPDU is discarded.

   d. 802.1D BPDU is translated into 802.1w BPDU and processed.

3. Which of the following is an STP port state but not an RSTP port state?

   a. Forwarding

   b. Learning

   c. Listening

   d. Discarding

4. Why is it important to protect the placement of the root bridge?

   a. To prevent Layer 2 loops

   b. To keep Layer 2 topology predictable in such a way that traffic flows are always efficient

   c. To prevent from two switches to become root bridges

   d. To prevent Layer 3 loops

5. Can PortFast be configured on a trunk link?

   a. No, PortFast is disabled by the command **switchport mode trunk**.

   b. Yes, enabling PortFast globally applies PortFast to all ports, including trunks.

   c. Yes, it can be configured on a port-to-port basis, but with caution, because loops may occur.

   d. No, the **portfast** keyword is available only with the **switchport mode access** command.

6. Which two statements are true of Loop Guard?

   a. It allows a blocked port in a physically redundant topology to stop receiving BPDUs.

   b. It provides additional protection against Layer 2 STP loops.

   c. It moves ports into the STP loop-inconsistent state, if BPDUs are not received on a nondesignated port.

   d. It enables the blocking port to move to the forwarding state.

7. Which standard describes Multiple Spanning Tree protocol?

   a. 802.1s

   b. 802.1D

   c. 802.1w

   d. 802.1Q

8. Which two features apply to MST?

   a. It groups a set of instances to a single VLAN.

   b. It can group a set of VLANs to a single spanning-tree instance.

   c. A failure in one instance can cause a failure in another instance.

   d. The total number of spanning-tree instances should match the number of redundant switch paths.

9. How are VLANs mapped to instances by default with MST?

   a. All VLANs are mapped to MST instance 0.

   b. All VLANs are mapped to MST instance 1.

   c. Each VLAN is mapped to its own instance.

   d. All VLANs are unmapped.

Chapter 5

Inter-VLAN Routing

Upon completing this chapter, you will be able to implement inter-VLAN routing in a campus network. This ability includes being able to meet these objectives:

■ Given an enterprise network, design, implement, and verify inter-VLAN routing using an external router or a multilayer switch, using either switch virtual interfaces or routed interfaces

■ Understand Layer 3 EtherChannel and its configuration

■ Understand DHCP operation and its implementation and verification in a given enterprise network

Network topologies generally associate VLANs with individual networks or subnetworks, as discussed in Chapter 3, "Campus Network Architecture." However, network devices in different VLANs cannot communicate with each other without a Layer 3 switch or a router to forward traffic between the VLANs. The initial VLAN design recommends that each VLAN is associated with a different subnet as a best practice; therefore, inter-VLAN routing is required to route traffic between VLANs. Cisco provides several solutions to enable inter-VLAN routing. Many Catalyst switches have integrated Layer 3 routing capabilities using hardware switching to achieve line-rate performance. In addition, several families of switches use Layer 3 modules to provide inter-VLAN routing.

This chapter discusses the advantages and disadvantages of different methods of inter-VLAN routing. In addition, it covers Layer 3 EtherChannel configuration and basic routing concepts. This chapter also discusses how to configure and implement Dynamic Host Configuration Protocol (DHCP).

Describing Inter-VLAN Routing

Following the recommendation from campus design, the distribution and collapsed core switches always have many VLANs terminating to these switches. Switches at the distribution layer, or in a collapsed core, will almost certainly have multiple VLANs connected to them. A switch with multiple VLANs requires a means of passing Layer 3 traffic to communicate between those VLANs.

This section describes the process and the various methods of routing traffic from VLAN to VLAN. A router that is external to the Layer 2 switch hosting the VLANs can perform inter-VLAN routing. In addition, a Cisco Catalyst multilayer switch can be used to perform both intra-VLAN frame forwarding and inter-VLAN routing.

This section focuses on how to perform inter-VLAN packet transfer using an external router and a multilayer switch. These sections focus on the following topics:

- Introduction to inter-VLAN routing

- Inter-VLAN routing using an external router

- Inter-VLAN routing with switch virtual interfaces

- Routing with routed ports

- Configuring inter-VLAN routing using SVI and routed ports

- Troubleshooting inter-VLAN routing

Introduction to Inter-VLAN Routing

Because VLANs isolate traffic to a defined broadcast domain and subnet, network devices in different VLANs cannot communicate with each other natively. As shown in Figure 5-1, the devices in different VLANs cannot communicate without a Layer 3 device. The devices in each VLAN can communicate to the network devices in another VLAN only through a Layer 3 routing device, referred to as an *inter-VLAN router* (see Figure 5-2). Cisco recommends the implementation of routing in the distribution or core switches of the multilayer-switched network to terminate local VLANs. This helps to isolate network problems and prevent them from affecting the campus backbone. In addition, packet manipulation and control of the traffic across VLANs is simplified by routing in the distribution layer instead of in the core layer.

The following devices can provide inter-VLAN routing (see Figure 5-2):

- Any Layer 3 multilayer Catalyst switch

- Any external router with an interface that supports trunking (router-on-a-stick)

- Any external router or group of routers with a separate interface in each VLAN

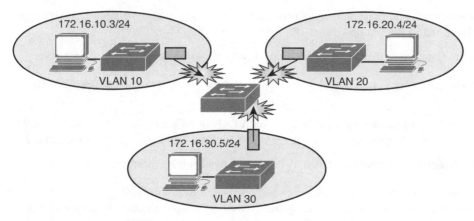

Figure 5-1   *VLAN Isolation*

Note   Adding an external router with an individual interface in each VLAN is a nonscalable solution, especially when you have between 20 and 50 VLANs in the network. Also, adding an external router for inter-VLAN routing on trunk interfaces does not scale beyond 50 VLANs. This chapter discusses only using Layer 3 switches and external routers with trunk interfaces (router-on-a-stick) to route VLANs. Furthermore, Cisco IOS routers support trunking in specific Cisco IOS Software feature sets, such as the IP Plus feature set. Refer to the documentation at Cisco.com for software requirements before deploying inter-VLAN routing on Cisco IOS routers.

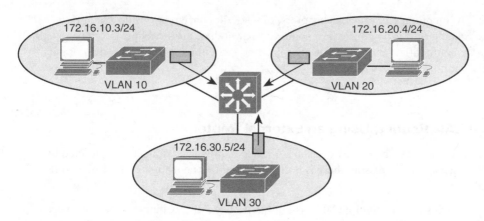

Figure 5-2   *Inter-VLAN Routing*

Router-on-a-stick is simple to implement because routers are usually available in every network, but most enterprise networks use multilayer switches to achieve high packet-processing rates using hardware switching. In addition, Layer 3 switches usually have packet-switching throughputs in the millions of packets per second (pps), whereas traditional general-purpose routers provide packet switching in the range of 100,000 pps to more than 1 million pps.

All the Catalyst multilayer switches support three different types of Layer 3 interfaces:

- **Routed port:** A pure Layer 3 interface similar to a routed port on a Cisco IOS router.

- **Switch virtual interface (SVI):** A virtual VLAN interface for inter-VLAN routing. In other words, switch virtual interfaces (SVIs) are the virtual routed VLAN interfaces.

- **Bridge virtual interface (BVI):** A Layer 3 virtual bridging interface.

Because of high-performance switches such as the Catalyst 6500 and Catalyst 4500, almost every function, from spanning tree to routing, is done through hardware switching using features such as MLS and Cisco Express Forwarding (CEF)-based mutilayer switching (MLS), both of which are discussed in detail in later sections of this chapter.

All Layer 3 Cisco Catalyst switches support routing protocols, but several models of Catalyst switches require enhanced software for specific routing protocol features.

Catalyst switches use different default settings for interfaces. For example, all members of the Catalyst 3550 and 4500 families of switches use Layer 2 interfaces by default, whereas members of the Catalyst 6500 family of switches running Cisco IOS use Layer 3 interfaces by default. Recall that default interface configurations do not appear in the running or startup configuration. As a result, depending on which Catalyst family of switches is used, the **switchport** or **no switchport** command might be present in the running-config or startup-config files.

Note   As mentioned in previous chapters, the default configurations do not appear in the running or startup config. For some Cisco switches, the **switchport** command is the default configuration, and for others the **no switchport** command is the default configuration.

Inter-VLAN Routing Using an External Router

A VLAN defines a broadcast domain. At Layer 3, broadcast domains are defined by IP subnets. For this reason, there is normally a one-to-one mapping of VLANs to IP subnets.

If a switch supports multiple VLANs but has no Layer 3 capability to route packets between those VLANs, the switch must be connected to an external device with Layer 3 capability. That device is normally a router, although it could be a multilayer switch. The most efficient way to perform this setup is to provide a single trunk link between the Layer 2 switch and the router. The trunk link carries the traffic of multiple VLANs. The traffic between VLANs is routed by the Layer 3 device: the router.

Figure 5-3 shows a configuration where the router is connected to a core switch using a single 802.1Q trunk link that carries VLAN 10 and 20. This configuration is commonly referred to as *router-on-a-stick*. The router can receive packets on one VLAN and forward them to another VLAN. In the example, PC1 can send packets (via an external router) to PC2, which is in a different VLAN.

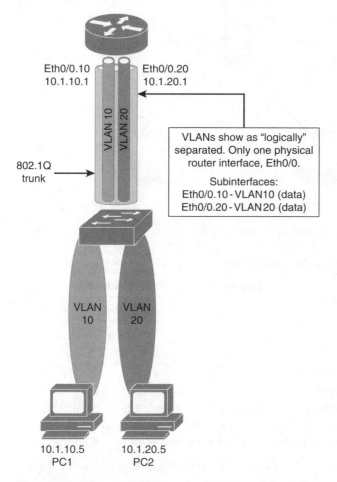

Figure 5-3 *Inter-VLAN Routing Using an External Router*

To support 802.1Q trunking, you must subdivide the physical router interface into multiple, logical, addressable interfaces, one per VLAN. The resulting logical interfaces are called *subinterfaces*.

Configuring Inter-VLAN Routing Using an External Router

Figure 5-4 shows an example of how to configure inter-VLAN routing using an external router, also known as *router-on-a-stick*.

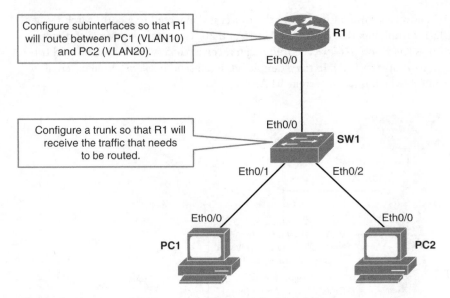

Configure subinterfaces so that R1 will route between PC1 (VLAN10) and PC2 (VLAN20).

Configure a trunk so that R1 will receive the traffic that needs to be routed.

Figure 5-4   *Inter-VLAN Routing Using an External Router*

Table 5-1 shows the parameters used in the configurations.

Table 5-1   *Device Information for the Configuration*

Device	Interface	Neighbor	IP Address
PC1	Eth0/0	SW1	10.0.10.100
PC2	Eth0/0	SW1	10.0.20.100

Routing with an External Router

In the configuration example shown in Figure 5-4, PC1 is part of VLAN 10 and will be communicating with the PC2 in VLAN 20 via an external router using subinterfaces. Complete the following steps for both configuration and verification:

Step 1.   On R1's Ethernet 0/0, configure a subinterface for routing of VLAN 10 traffic.

The router that provides inter-VLAN routing must be configured with subinterfaces. There must be one subinterface for each VLAN:

```
R1(config)# interface ethernet 0/0.10
R1(config-subif)# encapsulation dot1q 10
R1(config-subif)# ip address 10.0.10.1 255.255.255.0
```

A trunk on a router is configured using subinterfaces. Each subinterface on the physical link of the router must have the same trunk encapsulation protocol. That protocol must match the encapsulation type that is configured on the switch side of the link. Normally, 802.1Q encapsulation is used.

To configure 802.1Q encapsulation on a subinterface, use the **encapsulation dot1q** *vlan-id* subinterface command.

The subinterface number does not have to match the encapsulation VLAN number. However, it is a good practice to do so because it makes it easier to manage the configuration.

The IP address on the subinterface is used as the default gateway IP address for clients in that VLAN.

Step 2.   On R1's Ethernet 0/0, configure a subinterface for routing of VLAN 20 traffic:

```
R1(config)# interface ethernet 0/0.20
R1(config-subif)# encapsulation dot1q 20
R1(config-subif)# ip address 10.0.20.1 255.255.255.0
```

Step 3.   On R1's Ethernet 0/0, configure a subinterface for routing of all untagged traffic.

Configure a subinterface for native VLAN. By default this is VLAN 1:

```
R1(config)# interface ethernet 0/0.1
R1(config-subif)# encapsulation dot1q 1 native
R1(config-subif)# ip address 10.0.1.1 255.255.255.0
```

Note   The other option to configure routing of untagged traffic is to configure a physical interface with the native VLAN IP address. The disadvantage of that configuration is that when you do not want the untagged traffic to be routed, you shut down the physical interface, but that also shuts down all the subinterfaces on that interface.

Step 4.   On R1, verify that all the configured subinterfaces are up:

```
R1# show ip interface brief
Interface          IP-Address    OK? Method Status                 Protocol
Ethernet0/0        unassigned    YES NVRAM  up                     up
Ethernet0/0.1      10.0.1.1      YES manual up                     up
Ethernet0/0.10     10.0.10.1     YES manual up                     up
Ethernet0/0.20     10.0.20.1     YES manual up                     up
Ethernet0/1        unassigned    YES NVRAM  administratively down  down
Ethernet0/2        unassigned    YES NVRAM  administratively down  down
Ethernet0/3        unassigned    YES NVRAM  administratively down  down
```

Step 5.   Configure SW1's Ethernet 0/0 as a trunk port. Allow only VLAN 1, 10, and 20 traffic.

The link between SW1 and R1 must be configured as a trunk, to carry traffic from all the configured VLANs. The trunk has already been configured on R1. Configure the trunk on the SW1 side as well.

It is recommended practice that you only configure a static trunk link and only allow traffic from VLANs that are in use:

```
SW1(config)# interface ethernet 0/0
SW1(config-if)# switchport trunk encapsulation dot1q
SW1(config-if)# switchport mode trunk
SW1(config-if)# switchport trunk allowed vlan 1,10,20
```

Step 6.   On SW1, verify that the SW1-R1 link is carrying traffic for user VLANs 10 and 20 and the native VLAN.

Issue the **show interface** *interface* **switchport** command and verify that the SW1's interface that is connected to R1 has VLANs 10 and 20 allowed:

```
SW1# show interfaces ethernet0/0 switchport
Name: Et0/0
Switchport: Enabled
Administrative Mode: trunk
Operational Mode: trunk
Administrative Trunking Encapsulation: dot1q
Operational Trunking Encapsulation: dot1q
Negotiation of Trunking: On
Access Mode VLAN: 1 (default)
Trunking Native Mode VLAN: 1 (default)
<... output omitted ...>
Trunking VLANs Enabled: 1,10,20
Pruning VLANs Enabled: 2-1001
```

Also notice that the configured (default) native VLAN is VLAN 1.

Step 7.   Use the **traceroute** command to verify the traffic flow between PC1 and PC2:

```
PC1# traceroute 10.0.20.100
Type escape sequence to abort.
Tracing the route to 10.0.20.100
VRF info: (vrf in name/id, vrf out name/id)
  1 10.0.10.1 0 msec 0 msec 1 msec
  2 10.0.20.100 0 msec 1 msec *
External Router: Advantages and Disadvantages
```

External Routers: Advantages Disadvantages

The following are advantages of external router usage:

- An external router works with any switch because Layer 3 services are not required on the switch. Many switches do not contain Layer 3 forwarding capability, especially switches that are used at the access layer of a hierarchical network. If you are using local VLANs, none of the switches at the access layer will have Layer 3 forwarding ability. Depending on the network design, it is possible that there are no switches in the network with Layer 3 forwarding capability.

- The implementation is simple. Only one switch port and one router interface require configuration. If the switch allows all VLANs to cross the trunk (the default), you need to use only a few commands to configure the switch.

- The router provides communication between VLANs. If the network design includes only Layer 2 switches, the design and also the process for troubleshooting traffic flow become very simple because there is only one place in the network where VLANs interconnect.

The following are disadvantages of external router usage:

- The router is a single point of failure.

- A single traffic path may become congested. With a router-on-a-stick model, the trunk link is limited by the speed of the router interface being shared across all trunked VLANs. Depending on the size of the network, the amount of inter-VLAN traffic, and the speed of the router interface, congestion could result from this design.

- Latency may be introduced as frames leave and reenter the switch chassis multiple times and as the router makes software-based routing decisions. Any time that traffic must flow between devices, latency is introduced. In addition, routers make routing decisions in software, which always incur a greater latency penalty than switching with hardware.

Because the usage of an external router has physical limitations such as link congestions, latency and speed, it is not recommended to use it in large deployments. You normally implement an external router in small networks or branch offices of small to medium-size businesses, because there is no need to upgrade to a high-performing, more expensive device that is a multilayer switch.

Note   Except some models of Catalyst 2960 series switches, all the switches support integrated inter-VLAN routing.

Inter-VLAN Routing Using Switch Virtual Interfaces

In the early days of switched networks, switching was fast (often at hardware speed), and routing was slow (routing had to be processed in software). This prompted network designers to extend the switched part of the network as much as possible. Access, distribution, and core layers were often partly configured to communicate at Layer 2. This architecture is referred to as *switched*, as shown in Figure 5-5. This topology created loop issues. To solve these issues, spanning-tree technologies were used to prevent loops while still enabling flexibility and redundancy in interswitch connections.

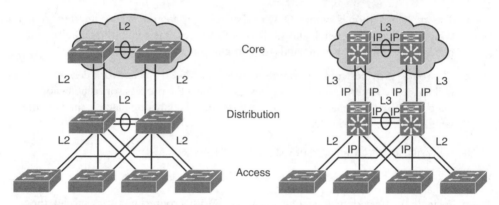

Figure 5-5   *Routed Versus Switched Campus Architecture*

As network technologies evolved, routing became faster and cheaper. Today, routing can be performed at hardware speed. One consequence of this evolution is that routing can be brought down to the core and the distribution layers without impacting network performance. Because many users are in separate VLANs, and because each VLAN is usually a separate subnet, it is logical to configure the distribution switches as Layer 3 gateways for the users of each access switch VLAN. This implies that each distribution switch must have IP addresses matching each access switch VLAN. This architecture is referred to as *routed*, as shown in Figure 5-5.

As shown in Figure 5-5, the link between Core and Distribution is L3 routed ports instead of L2 switchport. Because dynamic routing protocols can dynamically adapt to any change in the network topology, this new topology also eliminates Layer 2 loops. Between access and distribution switches, where Layer 2 connections remain, FlexLink technology can be used to activate only one link at a time or Layer 2 EtherChannel can be used, thus removing the risk of loops and the need for spanning tree.

Note   FlexLink is discussed in detail in Chapter 4 "Spanning Tree in Depth."

An SVI is a virtual interface configured within a multilayer switch, as compared to external router configuration, where the trunk is needed, as shown in Figure 5-6. An SVI can be created for any VLAN that exists on the switch, as illustrated in Figure 5-6. Only one VLAN associates with one SVI. An SVI is "virtual" in that there is no physical port dedicated to the interface, yet it can perform the same functions for the VLAN as a router interface would and can be configured in much the same way as a router interface (IP address, inbound/outbound access control lists [ACLs], and so on). The SVI for the VLAN provides Layer 3 processing for packets to or from all switch ports associated with that VLAN.

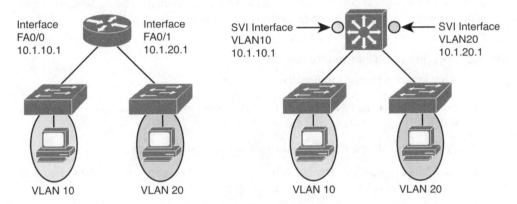

Figure 5-6 *SVI Versus External Router*

By default, an SVI is created for the default VLAN (VLAN1) to permit remote switch administration. Additional SVIs must be explicitly created. SVIs are created the first time the VLAN interface configuration mode is entered for a particular VLAN (for instance, when the command **interface vlan ##** is entered). The VLAN number used corresponds to the VLAN tag associated with data frames on an 802.1Q encapsulated trunk or to the VLAN ID (VID) configured for an access port. For instance, if creating an SVI as a gateway for VLAN 10, name the SVI interface VLAN 10. Configure and assign an IP address to each VLAN SVI that is to route traffic off of and on to a VLAN.

Whenever the SVI is created, make sure that particular VLAN is present in the VLAN database manually or learned via VTP. As shown in Figure 5-6, the switch should have VLAN 10 and VLAN 20 present in the VLAN database; otherwise, the SVI interface will stay down.

The following are some of the reasons to configure SVI:

■ To provide a gateway for a VLAN so that traffic can be routed into or out of that VLAN

■ To provide fallback bridging if it is required for nonroutable protocols

Note   If you use fallback bridging, non-IP packets can be forwarded across the routed interfaces. This book focuses only on inter-VLAN routing, so only IP connectivity is discussed.

- To provide Layer 3 IP connectivity to the switch

- To support routing protocol and bridging configurations

A BVI is a Layer 3 virtual interface that acts like a normal SVI to route packets. This is a legacy method where Layer 2 is bridged across Layer 3 interfaces. Bridging creates a single instance of spanning tree in multiple VLANs. It complicates spanning tree and the behavior of other protocols. In turn, this makes troubleshooting difficult. Bridging across routed domains is not recommended in today's networks.

SVI: Advantages and Disadvantages

The following are some of the advantages of SVI:

- It is much faster than router-on-a-stick because everything is hardware switched and routed.

- No need for external links from the switch to the router for routing.

- Not limited to one link. Layer 2 EtherChannels can be used between the switches to get more bandwidth.

- Latency is much lower because it does not need to leave the switch.

The following are some of the disadvantages:

- It needs a Layer 3 switch to perform inter-VLAN routing, which is more expensive (for example, Catalyst 3500 series).

Routing with Routed Ports

A routed port is a physical port that acts similarly to a port on a traditional router with Layer 3 addresses configured. Unlike an access port, a routed port is not associated with a particular VLAN. A routed port behaves like a regular router interface. Also, because Layer 2 functionality has been removed, Layer 2 protocols, such as Spanning Tree Protocol (STP) and VLAN Trunking Protocol (VTP), do not function on a routed interface. However, protocols such as Link Aggregation Control Protocol (LACP), which can be used to build either Layer 2 or Layer 3 EtherChannel bundles, would still function at Layer 3.

Note   Routed interfaces do not support subinterfaces as with Cisco IOS routers.

Routed ports are used for point-to-point links; connecting WAN routers and connecting security devices are examples of the use of routed ports. In the campus switched network, routed ports are mostly configured between switches in the campus backbone and building distribution switches if Layer 3 routing is applied in the distribution layer.

Figure 5-7 illustrates an example of routed ports for point-to-point links in a campus switched network.

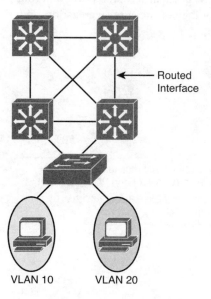

Figure 5-7   *Inter-VLAN Routing with Routed Ports*

To configure routed ports, make sure to configure the respective interface as a Layer 3 interface using the **no switchport** interface command if the default configurations of the interfaces are Layer 2 interfaces, as with the Catalyst 3560 family of switches. In addition, assign an IP address and other Layer 3 parameters as necessary. After assigning the IP address, make certain that IP routing is globally enabled and that applicable routing protocols are configured.

The number of routed ports and SVIs that can be configured on a switch is not limited by software. However, the interrelationship between these interfaces and other features configured on the switch may overload the CPU because of hardware limitations, so a network engineer should fully consider these limits before configuring these features on numerous interfaces.

Routed Ports: Advantages

Following are some of the advantages of routed ports:

- A multilayer switch can have SVI and routed ports in a single switch. How is this an advantage of a routed port?

- Multilayer switches forward either Layer 2 or Layer 3 traffic in hardware, so it helps to do routing faster.

Configuring Inter-VLAN Routing Using SVI and Routed Ports

This section will discuss not only how to configure SVIs but also routed ports, and routing on a multilayer switch. Figure 5-8 shows the topology of the core, aggregation, and access layer models.

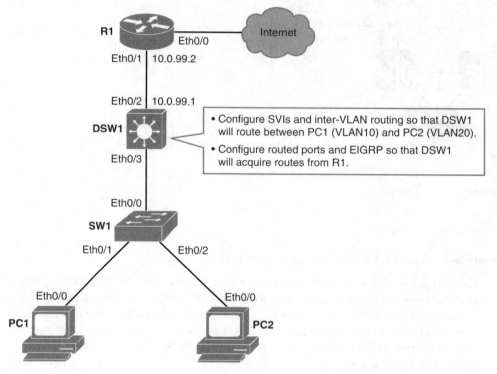

Figure 5-8   *Topology for Inter-VLAN Routing Using SVI and Routed Ports*

As shown in Figure 5-8, SW1's ports are configured to have PC1 in VLAN 10 and PC2 in VLAN 20. The link between SW1 and DSW1 is configured as a trunk link. PCs 1 and 2 are configured with IP addresses. R1 is configured with IP addresses and EIGRP.

There is no connectivity between PC1 and PC2, so configure DSW1 to route between PC1 and PC2 and also configure DSW1's uplink to exchange routes with R1. Table 5-2 lists the IP addresses that are used for the configuration example.

Table 5-2   *Parameters Used in Configuration*

Device	Interface	IP Address
PC1	Ethernet 0/0	10.0.10.100/24
PC2	Ethernet 0/0	10.0.20.100/24
DSW1	VLAN 10	10.0.10.1/24
DSW1	VLAN 20	10.0.20.1/24

Device	Interface	IP Address
DSW1	Ethernet 0/2	10.0.99.1/24
R1	Ethernet 0/1	10.0.99.2/24
R1	Ethernet 0/0	209.165.201.2/30
Server on the Internet	N/A	209.165.201.1

Routing on a Multilayer Switch

Perform the following steps to configure PC1 and PC2 to communicate using SVI and also to verify the configuration:

Step 1.   On DSW1, create VLANs 10 and 20:

```
DSW1(config)# vlan 10
DSW1(config-vlan)# vlan 20
```

If a VLAN that is to be routed by an SVI interface does not already exist on the multilayer switch, you must create it.

In this example VLANs 10 and 20 were already preconfigured on DSW1 and verified with the **show vlan** command. However, these VLANs will not be present on a new device, and if you forget to configure them, the switch will not be able to perform inter-VLAN routing.

Step 2.   On DSW1, enable IPv4 routing:

```
DSW1(config)# ip routing
```

Multilayer switches might or might not have IP routing enabled by default. For the switch to route between SVIs, you need to enable IPv4 routing.

Note   In this lab, IP routing was already enabled, but this is something someone can easily forget to turn on.

Step 3.   On DSW1, configure SVI for VLAN 10 with IP address 10.0.10.1/24.

PC1 is in VLAN 10 and already configured with default gateway of 10.0.10.1 (an IP address that will now be configured on DSW1):

```
DSW1(config)# interface vlan 10
DSW1(config-if)# ip address 10.0.10.1 255.255.255.0
DSW1(config-if)# no shutdown
```

Create an SVI interface for each VLAN that is to be routed within the multilayer switch.

SVI needs to be enabled using the **no shutdown** command. Otherwise, it will stay in "administratively shutdown" state.

Step 4.   On DSW1, configure SVI for VLAN 20 with IP address 10.0.20.1/24.

PC2 is in VLAN 20 and already configured with default gateway of 10.0.20.1 (an IP address that will now be configured on DSW1):

```
DSW1(config)# interface vlan 20
DSW1(config-if)# ip address 10.0.20.1 255.255.255.0
DSW1(config-if)# no shutdown
```

Step 5.   On DSW1, verify IP interface configuration for VLANs 10 and 20:

```
DSW1# show ip interface brief
<... output omitted ...>
Vlan10              10.0.10.1        YES manual up                    up
Vlan20              10.0.20.1        YES manual up                    up
```

For SVIs to be fully operational, they need to have the correct IP address configured and be in up/up state.

Step 6.   Use traceroute to test connectivity between PC1 to PC2:

```
PC1# traceroute 10.0.20.100
Type escape sequence to abort.
Tracing the route to 10.0.20.100
VRF info: (vrf in name/id, vrf out name/id)
  1 10.0.10.1 1001 msec 1 msec 0 msec
  2  *  *
    10.0.20.100 1 msec
```

You should be able to ping from PC1 to PC2. Traffic from PC1 goes through SW1 to DSW1's SVI for VLAN 10, gets routed to DSW1's SVI for VLAN 20 and then goes through SW1 to PC 2, as shown in Figure 5-9. The reverse path is the same.

Step 7.   On DSW1, turn the interface that connects to R1 (Ethernet 0/0) into a routed interface. Configure it with IP 10.0.99.1/24.

The link between DSW1 and R1 should be a Layer 3 link. R1's interface is already configured with an IP address:

```
DSW1(config)# interface ethernet 0/2
DSW1(config-if)# no switchport
*Nov 28 15:03:55.138: %LINK-3-UPDOWN: Interface Ethernet0/2, changed
state to up
*Nov 28 15:03:56.142: %LINEPROTO-5-UPDOWN: Line protocol on Interface
Ethernet0/2, changed state to up
DSW1(config-if)# ip address 10.0.99.1 255.255.255.0
```

When the interface is configured with the **no switchport** command, it turns it from Layer 2 to Layer 3 interface.

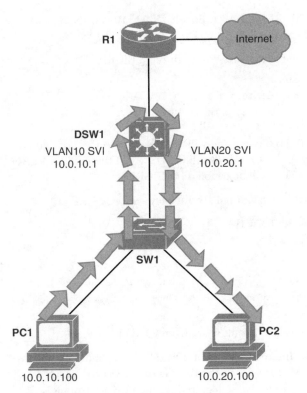

Figure 5-9 *Path for Traffic Forwarding Using SVI*

Note   When you issue the no switchport command, the interface will be shut down and then brought back up. Once the interface is configured with Layer 3 mode, it will delete all Layer 2 configuration on the interface.

Step 8.   On DSW1, verify the routed port IP interface configuration:

```
DSW1# show ip interface brief
Interface          IP-Address     OK? Method Status          Protocol
Ethernet0/0        unassigned     YES unset  up              up
Ethernet0/1        unassigned     YES unset  up              up
Ethernet0/2        10.0.99.1      YES manual up              up
<... output omitted ...>
```

DSW1's routed interface has an IP address configured and is in up/up state. It functions like a port on a router.

Step 9.   On DSW1, configure EIGRP with AS 1. Enable VLAN 10, VLAN 20, and Ethernet 0/2 interfaces for EIGRP.

R1 is already configured to exchange routes through EIGRP:

```
DSW1(config)# router eigrp 1
DSW1(config-router)# network 10.0.0.0
*Nov 28 15:12:22.448: %DUAL-5-NBRCHANGE: EIGRP-IPv4 1: Neighbor
10.0.99.2 (Ethernet0/2) is up: new adjacency
```

Issuing the **network 10.0.0.0** command will enable all interfaces configured with an IP address within the 10.0.0.0/8 subnet. DSW1's Ethernet 0/2, VLAN 10, and VLAN 20 interfaces will be enabled for EIGRP.

Notice that DSW1 established an EIGRP adjacency with R1.

Step 10.   Verify the routing table on DSW1:

```
DSW1# show ip route
<... output omitted ...>
D*EX  0.0.0.0/0 [170/307200] via 10.0.99.2, 00:07:13, Ethernet0/2
      10.0.0.0/8 is variably subnetted, 6 subnets, 2 masks
<... output omitted ...>
```

Notice that DSW1 acquired a default route from R1 via EIGRP.

A ping from PC1 to the Internet address of 209.165.201.1 should be successful. PC1 has its default gateway set to the IP of DSW1's SVI for VLAN 10, and DSW1 has a default route that it acquired through EIGRP from R1.

Using the SVI autostate exclude Command

The SVI interface is brought up when one Layer 2 port in the VLAN has had time to converge (transition from STP listening-learning state to forwarding state). The default action when a VLAN has multiple ports is that the SVI goes down when all ports in the VLAN go down. This action prevents features such as routing protocols from using the VLAN interface as if it were fully operational and minimizes other problems, such as routing black holes.

You can use the SVI **autostate exclude** command to configure a port so that it is not included in the SVI line-state up-and-down calculation. One example is the use of a network analyzer, where the traffic capture is being made without the device being an active participant in the VLAN that is assigned to the interface.

When enabled on a port, **autostate exclude** applies to all VLANs that are enabled on that port. You would therefore need to carefully consider the implications of activating this feature on a trunk link.

Configuring a Layer 2 switch port for **autostate exclude** requires two steps:

Step 1.   Select the interface for configuration:

```
Switch(config)# interface interface slot/number
```

Step 2.   Exclude the access port or trunk in defining the status of an SVI (up or down):

```
Switch(config-if)# switchport autostate exclude
```

This command would commonly be used for ports that are used for monitoring, for instance, so that a monitoring port did not cause the SVI to remain in the up state when no other ports are active in the VLAN.

The line state of an SVI is in the up state when all of these are true:

■ The VLAN exists and is active in the VLAN database on the switch.

■ The VLAN interface exists and is not administratively down.

■ At least one Layer 2 (access or trunk) port exists, has a link in the up state on this VLAN, and is in the spanning-tree forwarding state on the VLAN.

To use **switchport autostate** on the switch interface, use the following commands.

```
Switch(config)#interface fastethernet 0/1
Switch(config-if)#switchport autostate exclude
```

SVI **autostate exclude** will remove a port from line-state up-and-down calculation.

Note   In some IOS releases (for example, 12.4T), you can use the **no autostate** VLAN interface command. This disables the SVI autostate and makes the SVI interface permanently active.

SVI Configuration Checklist

Before implementing inter-VLAN routing on a multilayer switch, it is important to plan the right steps that are necessary to make it successful. Planning, which includes logically organizing the necessary steps and providing checkpoints and verification, can help you reduce the risk of problems during the installation:

■ Identify which VLANs require a Layer 3 gateway.

■ Create a VLAN on a multilayer switch if it does not already exist.

■ Create an SVI interface for each VLAN.

■ Configure the SVI interface with an IP address.

■ Enable the SVI interface.

- Enable IP routing on the multilayer switch.

- Determine whether a dynamic routing protocol is needed.

- Configure a dynamic routing protocol if needed.

- Identify any switch ports that require autostate exclude.

- Configure autostate exclude on identified switch ports.

The first step is to identify the VLANs that require a Layer 3 gateway within the multilayer switch. It is possible that not all VLANs will need to reach other VLANs within the enterprise. For example, a company may have a VLAN in use in an R&D laboratory. The network designer has determined that this VLAN should not have connectivity with other VLANs in the enterprise or to the Internet. However, the R&D VLAN is not a local VLAN but spans the switch fabric, due to the presence of an R&D server in the data center, so it cannot simply prune it from the trunk between the multilayer switch and the R&D lab switch. One way of ensuring the desired segregation might be to configure such a VLAN without a Layer 3 gateway.

If a VLAN needs to be routed, create an SVI interface for each VLAN to be routed within the multilayer switch. Assuming that the enterprise uses only IP as a routed protocol, configure each SVI interface with an appropriate IP address and mask. At that point, just enable the SVI interface using the **no shutdown** interface command.

In that case, you must enable the routing function on the multilayer switch. Routing is usually not enabled by default. You can also configure the multilayer switch to exchange routes via a dynamic routing protocol. Dynamic routing protocols are discussed later in this chapter.

Depending on the size of the network and the design that you provide, it might be necessary for the multilayer switch to exchange dynamic routing protocol updates with one or more other routing devices in the network. You must determine whether this need exists, and if so, configure an appropriate dynamic routing protocol on the multilayer switch. The choice of protocol may be specified by the network designer, or the choice may be left to you.

- Finally, after carefully considering the network structure, you may decide to exclude certain switch ports from contributing to the SVI line-state up-and-down calculation. You would configure any such switch ports by using the **autostate exclude** interface configuration command.

Troubleshooting Inter-VLAN Problems

To troubleshoot inter-VLAN routing issues, the following are some checkpoint implementations:

- Correct VLANs on switches and trunks.

- Correct routes.

- Correct primary and secondary root bridges.

- Correct IP address and subnet masks.

Table 5-3 lists the common problems that can be seen during Inter-VLAN routing configuration.

Table 5-3 *Common Inter-VLAN Routing Problems*

Problem	Possible Cause
Missing VLAN	VLAN might not be defined across all the switches. VLAN might not be enabled on the trunk ports. Ports might not be in the right VLANs.
Layer 3 interface mis-configuration	Virtual interface might have the wrong IP address or subnet mask. Virtual interface might not be up. Virtual interface number might not match with the VLAN number. Routing has to be enabled to route frames between VLAN. Routing might not be enabled.
Routing protocol mis-configuration	Every interface or network needs to be added in the routing protocol. The new interface might not be added to the routing protocol. Routing protocol configuration is needed only if VLAN subnets need to communicate to the other routers, as previously mentioned in this chapter.
Host misconfiguration	Host might not have the right IP address or subnet mask. Each host has to have the default gateway that is the SVI or Layer 3 interface to communicate with other networks and VLAN. Host might not be configured with the default gateway.

Note You need to know on a particular VLAN that the IP addresses should be taken from the range used for the subnet/VLAN and that the mask should match; otherwise, the host and SVI—even though in the same VLAN—might not be able to communicate because they are in different networks.

To plan how to troubleshoot the inter-VLAN problems, you need to first understand the implementation and design layout of the topology before starting the troubleshooting. The following subsection discusses the example of a troubleshooting plan.

Example of a Troubleshooting Plan

The XYZ company is adding a new floor to the current network, and based on this, the current requirements are to make sure that the users on the new floor five can communicate with users on other floors. The current issue is that users on floor five cannot communicate with users on the other floors. Following is the example of the implementation plan to install a new VLAN for their use and make sure it is routing to other VLANs.

Your implementation plan lists the following steps:

Step 1.   Create a new VLAN 500 on the fifth floor switch and on the distribution switches. Name it **Accounting_dept**.

Step 2.   Identify the ports needed for the users and switches. Set the **switchport access VLAN** command to 500 and make sure the trunk is configured using the configuration mentioned in Chapter 2, "Network Design Fundamentals," between the switches and the VLAN 500 is allowed on the trunk.

Step 3.   Create an SVI interface on the distribution switches and make sure the IP address is assigned.

Step 4.   Verify connectivity. The troubleshooting plan might look like this:

1. If a new VLAN has been created:

   Was the VLAN created on all the switches?

   If VTP is configured, make sure that VLANs are defined on the VTP server and are getting propagated across all the domains.

   Verify with a **show vlan** command.

2. Make sure that ports are in the right VLAN and that trunking is working as expected:

   Did all access ports get the command **switchport access VLAN 500** added?

   Were there any other ports that should have been added? If so, make those changes.

   Were these ports previously used? If so, make sure there are no extra commands enabled on these ports that can cause conflicts. If not, is the port enabled?

   Are the access ports set to switchport access and not trunks? If not, issue the command **switchport mode access**.

   Are the trunk ports set to trunk mode, and manually prune all the VLANs.

   Is manual pruning of VLANs a possibility? If so, make sure that the trunks necessary to carry this VLAN traffic have the VLAN in the allowed statements.

3. If SVI interfaces are created:

   Is the VLAN virtual interface already created with the correct IP address and subnet mask?

   Is it enabled?

Is the routing enabled?

Is this SVI added in the routing protocol?

4. Verify connectivity.

Are all the links between the different switches on the path enabling this VLAN to be transported?

Are all the links between switches in trunk mode?

Is this VLAN allowed on all trunks?

Is spanning tree blocking one of those links?

Are the ports enabled?

Does the host have the right default gateway assigned?

Also make sure the default route or some routing protocol is enabled if it needs to talk to other routers.

Layer 2 Versus Layer 3 EtherChannel

As discussed in Chapter 2, use the EtherChannel technology to bundle ports of the same type for better bandwidth. On a Layer 2 switch, EtherChannel is used to aggregate access ports or trunks. EtherChannel links are used to connect to several switches, and pairs of ports are used to create EtherChannel bundles. Because each EtherChannel link is detected as one logical connection, both ports of each are in forwarding mode and hash the traffic across all links.

On Layer 3 switches, switched ports can be converted to routed ports. These ports do not perform switching at Layer 2 anymore, but become Layer 3 ports that are similar to those that are found on router platforms. EtherChannel links can also be created on Layer 3 links. On the left part of Figure 5-10, Layer 3 switches must connect through an aggregated link. Two physical ports on each side are converted to routed ports and are then aggregated into a Layer 3 EtherChannel link. Also, Figure 5-10 shows the typical Layer 2 EtherChannel between access layer to the Aggregation switches. Layer 2 EtherChannel bundles access or trunk ports between other devices and Layer 3 EtherChannel bundles routed ports between switches.

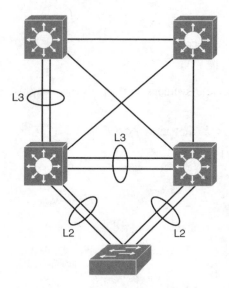

Figure 5-10 *Layer 2 Versus Layer 3 EtherChannel*

On a multilayer switch, you can configure Layer 2 or Layer 3 EtherChannels, depending on what type of devices that will be connected, and depending on their position in the network. Here again, this configuration supposes that ports on both sides are configured the same way: as switch ports (access or trunk) or as routed ports. The bottom switch is Layer 2 only; it is probably an access switch. Layer 2 EtherChannel is configured. At the distribution layer or the core layer, where Layer 3 links are recommended, Layer 3 EtherChannels are configured.

Layer 3 EtherChannel Configuration

To configure and verify a Layer 3 EtherChannel interface, follow these steps:

Step 1.   Create a virtual Layer 2 interface:

```
Switch(config)# interface port-channel 1
```

Step 2.   Change interface to Layer 3 and enable the use of the **ip address** command:

```
Switch(config-if)# no switchport
```

Step 3.   Assign an IP address to the port channel interface because this will now be a Layer 3 interface:

```
Switch(config-if)# ip address 172.32.52.10 255.255.255.0
```

Step 4.   Navigate to the interface that is to be associated with the EtherChannel bundle. This example shows navigation to a range of interfaces with the port channel. Individual interfaces can be used also:

```
Switch(config)# interface range fastethernet 5/4 - 5
```

Step 5.   Remove the independent Layer 2 and Layer 3 functionality of the port so that the port can function as part of a group:

```
Switch(config-if-range)# no switchport
Switch(config-if-range)# channel-protocol pagp
```

This step is very important. On a Layer 3 switch, interfaces are, by default, in Layer 2 mode. If you set the port channel interface to a Layer 2 mode, and if the physical ports are in Layer 3 mode, the EtherChannel will not form. Optionally, you can specify the channel protocol.

Step 6.   Assign all of the physical interfaces in the range to the EtherChannel group:

```
Switch(config-if-range)# channel-group 1 mode desirable
```

Figure 5-11 shows a configuration example of two switches using a Layer 3 EtherChannel bundle. The left switch has created a virtual interface with an IP address, and the physical interfaces are assigned to the matching channel group number. The same is true with the right switch. Again, the interfaces do not need to have the same number as any of the partner switches.

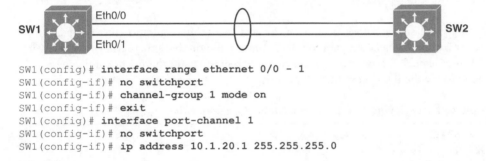

```
SW1(config)# interface range ethernet 0/0 - 1
SW1(config-if)# no switchport
SW1(config-if)# channel-group 1 mode on
SW1(config-if)# exit
SW1(config)# interface port-channel 1
SW1(config-if)# no switchport
SW1(config-if)# ip address 10.1.20.1 255.255.255.0
```

Figure 5-11   *Configuration Example for Layer3 EtherChannel*

For example, Ethernet 0/1 does not need to connect to Ethernet 0/1 on the other side of the link. The port channel number does not need to match between the switches on the opposite side of the link.

The following are the guidelines for configuration for EtherChannel:

■ **Speed and duplex:** Configure all interfaces in an EtherChannel to operate at the same speed and in the same duplex mode.

■ **Interface mode:** Because the port channel interface is a routed port, the **no switchport** command was applied to it. The physical interfaces are, by default, switched, which is a mode that is incompatible with a router port. The **no switchport** command was applied also to the physical ports, to make their mode compatible with the EtherChannel interface mode.

Note   In some IOS releases, you can only statically configure Layer 3 EtherChannel using Link Aggregation Control Protocol (LACP) or Port Aggregation Protocol (PAgP) because the negotiation protocol might result in nonfunctional link.

- **Verifying the EtherChannel configuration:** After EtherChannel is configured, use the following commands to verify and troubleshoot EtherChannel:

```
show interface port-channel channel-group-number
show etherChannel channel-group-number summary
show spanning-tree vlan vlan-number detail
```

Note   This chapter discusses only the configuration for Layer 3 port channel. The concepts of EtherChannel and Layer 2 EtherChannel configuration is discussed in detail in Chapter 3.

Example 5-1 shows the verification of the port channel configuration that is similar to Layer 2 port channel configuration. The output tells you that EtherChannel 1 is a Layer 3 EtherChannel (R flag). You can see that Ethernet 0/0 and Ethernet 0/1 are indeed bundled by the P flag next to each of them.

Example 5-1   *Verifying Layer 3 Port Channel Configuration*

```
SW1# show etherchannel summary
Flags:  D - down         P - bundled in port-channel
        I - stand-alone s - suspended
        H - Hot-standby (LACP only)
        R - Layer3       S - Layer2
        U - in use       f - failed to allocate aggregator

        M - not in use, minimum links not met
        u - unsuitable for bundling
        w - waiting to be aggregated
        d - default port


Number of channel-groups in use: 1
Number of aggregators:           1

Group  Port-channel  Protocol    Ports
------+-------------+-----------+------------
1      Po1(RU)          -        Et0/0(P)   Et0/1(P)
```

Ports Ethernet 0/0 and Ethernet 0/1 will now behave as one "virtual" physical interface. For example, if you issue **show ip route**, routes will be seen as accessible through port channel 1 and not Ethernet 0/1 or Ethernet 0/0.

Verifying Routing Protocols

To verify whether the routing protocol is working as expected, use the **show ip route** and **show ip protocol** commands. Figure 5-12 shows the configuration of small topology as a reference to help understand the command's output. It shows how to enable EIGRP as the routing protocol and how to advertise local networks into the routing protocol.

On a Layer 3 switch, just like on a router, use the **show ip route** command to display which Layer 3 routes are known to the local multilayer switch, as shown in Example 5-2. Each route type is identified by a code D, for example, which means that routes are learned via Enhanced Interior Gateway Routing Protocol (EIGRP). In Example 5-2, the 10.1.10.0/24 subnet is directly connected (which can be identified with the letter *C* at the left of the route); the other routes are known via EIGRP (which can be identified with the letter *D* at the left of the route).

Both 10.1.2.0/24 and 10.1.3.0/24 subnets are learned via 10.1.10.10. Their administrative distance is 90, and the cost to each of these networks is 28416. The link to 10.1.10.10 goes through the VLAN 10 interface. Notice that VLAN 10 here is the name of the SVI, the Layer 3 interface, through which the networks are reachable.

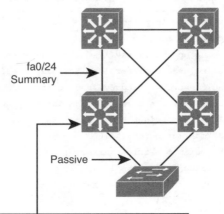

```
sw(config)# ip routing
sw(config)# router eigrp 100
sw(config-router)# no auto-summary
sw(config-router)# network 10.0.0.0
sw(config-router)# passive-interface default
sw(config-router)# no passive-interface fa0/24
sw(config)# interface f0/24
sw(config-if)# description Uplink
sw(config-if)# ip summary-address eigrp 100 10.1.0.0 255.255.240.0
```

Figure 5-12 *Routing Protocol Configuration*

Example 5-2 *show ip route Command*

```
switch# show ip route
Codes: C - connected, S - static, R - RIP, M - mobile, B - BGP
D - EIGRP, EX - EIGRP external, O - OSPF,
IA - OSPF inter area
N1 - OSPF NSSA external type 1,
N2 - OSPF NSSA external type 2
E1 - OSPF external type 1, E2 - OSPF external type 2
i - IS-IS, su - IS-IS summary, L1 - IS-IS level-1,
L2 - IS-IS level-2
ia - IS-IS inter area, * - candidate default,
U - per-user static route
o - ODR, P - periodic downloaded static route Gateway of last resort is not set
10.0.0.0/8 is variably subnetted, 13 subnets, 2 masks
D 10.1.3.0/24 [90/28416] via 10.1.10.10, 08:09:49, Vlan10
D 10.1.2.0/24 [90/28416] via 10.1.10.10, 08:09:49, Vlan10
C 10.1.10.0/24 is directly connected, Vlan10
```

The **show ip protocol** command shows information about the routing protocols that are enabled on the switch or router, as shown in Example 5-3.

Example 5-3 *show ip protocol Command*

```
Switch# show ip protocol
Routing Protocol is "eigrp 1"
Outgoing update filter list for all interfaces is not set
Incoming update filter list for all interfaces is not set
Default networks flagged in outgoing updates
Default networks accepted from incoming updates
EIGRP metric weight K1=1, K2=0, K3=1, K4=0, K5=0
EIGRP maximum hopcount 100
EIGRP maximum metric variance 1
Redistributing: eigrp 1
Automatic network summarization is in effect
Maximum path: 4
Routing for Networks:
10.0.0.0
Passive Interface(s): Vlan1 Vlan11
Routing Information Sources:
Gateway           Distance    Last Update
10.100.117.202    90          20:25:10
10.100.113.201    90          20:25:10
Distance: internal 90 external 170
```

Implementing DHCP

Dynamic Host Configuration Protocol (DHCP) is a network protocol that enables network administrators to manage and automate IP configuration assignment. Without DHCP, administrators must manually assign and configure IP addresses, subnet masks, default gateways, and so on, which can, in larger environments, become an excessive administrative problem, especially if devices are moved from one internal network to another.

In an enterprise environment, a DHCP server is usually a dedicated device; whereas in smaller deployments or some branch offices, it can be configured on a Cisco Catalyst switch or a Cisco router.

This section covers the following topics:

- Explain the idea behind DHCP

- Configure a DHCP server

- Configure manual DHCP bindings

- Configure a DHCP relay

- Configure DHCP options

DHCP Overview

As defined in RFC 2131, DHCP provides configuration parameters to Internet hosts. DHCP consists of two components: a protocol for delivering host-specific configuration parameters from a DHCP server to a host, and a mechanism for allocating network addresses to hosts. DHCP is built on a client/server model in which designated DHCP server hosts allocate network addresses and deliver configuration parameters to dynamically configured hosts, as shown in Figure 5-13. Clients in access VLANs need DHCP services, and not only external servers but also routers can be used for DHCP services. By default, Cisco multilayer switches running Cisco IOS Software include DHCP server and relay agent software.

Distribution multilayer switches often act as Layer 3 gateways for clients connecting to the access switches on various VLANs. Therefore, the DHCP service can be provided directly by the distribution switches, as shown in Figure 5-14. Alternatively, DHCP services can be concentrated in an external, dedicated DHCP server, as also reflected in Figure 5-14. In that case, distribution switches need to redirect the incoming clients' DHCP requests to the external DHCP server.

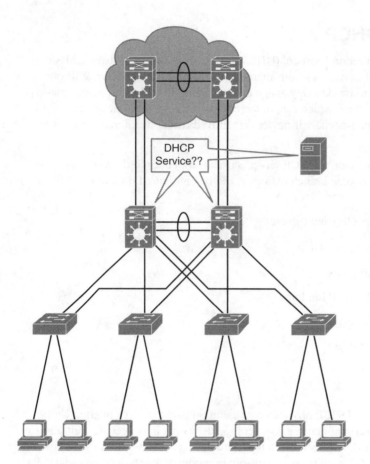

Figure 5-13   *DHCP Overview*

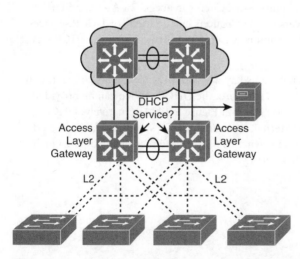

Figure 5-14   *DHCP Implementation in Campus Enviroment*

Configuring DHCP in Multilayer Switched Network

This section provides the configuration steps for the DHCP configuration using the topology layout mentioned in Figure 5-15. In addition, it configures a manual binding for one of the DHCP clients.

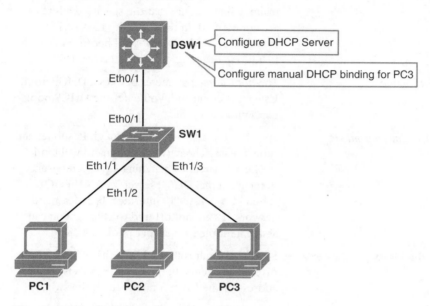

Figure 5-15   *Topology for DHCP Configuration*

Table 5-5 shows the devices information that will be needed for configuration.

Table 5-5   *Device Information*

Device	Interface	IP Address
DSW1	VLAN 1	10.0.1.1/24
DSW1	VLAN 10	10.0.10.1/24

Step 1.   Access DSW1. Configure a DHCP server for VLAN 10 devices. Only after the switch has a Layer 3 address, which is preconfigured in this example, can you configure a DHCP server on the switch. The switch acting as a DHCP server will intercept broadcast packets from client machines within a VLAN:

```
DSW1(config)# ip dhcp excluded-address 10.0.10.1
DSW1(config)# ip dhcp pool VLAN10POOL
DSW1(config-dhcp)# network 10.0.10.0 255.255.255.0
DSW1(config-dhcp)# default-router 10.0.10.1
DSW1(config-dhcp)# lease 2
```

Table 5-6 describes the commands used for this step.

Table 5-6 *Step 1 Commands*

Command	Description
ip dhcp excluded-address *start-ip end-ip*	If there are addresses within the IP subnet that should not be offered to DHCP clients, this command will make sure that the specified addresses are not offered. In the example, 10.0.10.1 was excluded from the DHCP pool because this is the IP address of the Layer 3 interface on DSW1.
ip dhcp pool *pool-name*	The *pool-name* parameter defines a DHCP pool. Using this command, you enter the DHCP pool configuration mode.
network *ip-address subnet-mask*	Specifies the address range through IP subnet and subnet mask. The network command will bind the DHCP server to matching Layer 3 interface. In the example, DHCP server VLAN10POOL is bound to VLAN 10 interface. Broadcast and network IPs are not offered to clients. You can assign multiple subnets per pool.
default-router ip-address [*ip-address2*] [*ip-address3*] ...	Sets the default router address that will be offered to clients. In the example, this is the IP address of the Layer 3 interface on the switch.
lease {infinite | {days [hours [minutes]]}}	Sets IP address lease duration. By default, the IP address is leased to a client for 1 day. In the example, it is set to 2 days.

Step 2. On DSW1 verify the configured DHCP pool using the **show ip dhcp pool** command:

```
DSW1# show ip dhcp pool
Pool VLAN10POOL :
 Utilization mark (high/low)    : 100 / 0
 Subnet size (first/next)       : 0 / 0
 Total addresses                : 254
 Leased addresses               : 0
 Excluded addresses             : 1
 Pending event                  : none
 1 subnet is currently in the pool :
 Current index     IP address range                        Leased/Excluded/Total
 10.0.10.1         10.0.10.1        - 10.0.10.254   0    / 1     / 254
```

Notice that no addresses are leased to the clients right now. Excluded IP addresses are not part of the **show ip dhcp pool** output.

Step 3.   Enable DHCP packet debugging on DSW1:

```
DSW1# debug ip dhcp server packet
DHCP server packet debugging is on.
```

Step 4.   Configure PC1 interface Ethernet 0/0 to acquire an IP address via DHCP and observe command-line interface (CLI) output on DSW1. The port on SW1 to which PC1 is connected to is already assigned to VLAN 10, so PC1 will get an IP from VLAN 10 subnet:

```
PC1(config)# interface ethernet 0/0
PC1(config-if)# ip address dhcp
PC1(config-if)# no shutdown
```

As soon as you enable the interface on PC1, it will send a broadcast, requesting an IP:

```
DSW1#
*Oct  3 11:21:52.364: %SYS-5-CONFIG_I: Configured from console by console
DSW1#
*Oct  3 11:23:09.256: DHCPD: Reload workspace interface Vlan10 tableid 0.
*Oct  3 11:23:09.256: DHCPD: tableid for 10.0.10.1 on Vlan10 is 0
*Oct  3 11:23:09.256: DHCPD: client's VPN is .
*Oct  3 11:23:09.256: DHCPD: using received relay info.
*Oct  3 11:23:09.256: DHCPD: DHCPDISCOVER received from client 0063.6973.636f.2d
61.6162.622e.6363.3030.2e34.3830.302d.4574.302f.30 on interface Vlan10.
*Oct  3 11:23:09.256: DHCPD: using received relay info.
DSW1#
*Oct  3 11:23:11.264: DHCPD: Sending DHCPOFFER to client 0063.6973.636f.2d61.616
2.622e.6363.3030.2e34.3830.302d.4574.302f.30 (10.0.10.2).
*Oct  3 11:23:11.264: DHCPD: no option 125
*Oct  3 11:23:11.264: DHCPD: broadcasting BOOTREPLY to client aabb.cc00.4800.
*Oct  3 11:23:11.265: DHCPD: Reload workspace interface Vlan10 tableid 0.
*Oct  3 11:23:11.265: DHCPD: tableid for 10.0.10.1 on Vlan10 is 0
*Oct  3 11:23:11.265: DHCPD: client's VPN is .
*Oct  3 11:23:11.265: DHCPD: DHCPREQUEST received from client 0063.6973.636f.2d6
1.6162.622e.6363.3030.2e34.3830.302d.4574.302f.30.
DSW1#
*Oct  3 11:23:11.265: DHCPD: Sending DHCPACK to client 0063.6973.636f.2d61.6162.
622e.6363.3030.2e34.3830.302d.4574.302f.30 (10.0.10.2).
*Oct  3 11:23:11.265: DHCPD: no option 125
*Oct  3 11:23:11.265: DHCPD: broadcasting BOOTREPLY to client aabb.cc00.4800.
DSW1#
```

The preceding debug shows you the whole DHCP negotiation process, which is also shown in Figure 5-16.

In the DHCP process, the client sends a DHCPDISCOVER broadcast message to locate a Cisco IOS DHCP server. A DHCP server offers configuration parameters to the client in a DHCPOFFER unicast message. Typical configuration parameters are an IP address, a domain name, and a lease for the IP address.

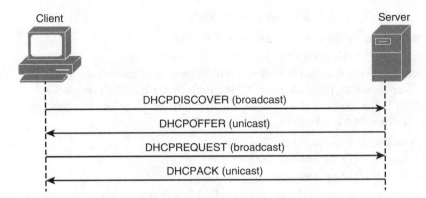

Figure 5-16 *DHCP Discovery Process*

A DHCP client may receive offers from multiple DHCP servers and can accept any one of the offers; however, the client usually accepts the first offer that it receives. In addition, the offer from the DHCP server is not a guarantee that the IP address will be allocated to the client; however, the server usually reserves the address until the client has had a chance to formally request the address.

The client returns a formal request for the offered IP address to the DHCP server in a DHCPREQUEST broadcast message. The DHCP server confirms that the IP address has been allocated to the client by returning a DHCPACK unicast message to the client.

In addition to these four messages, the following DHCP messages are displayed with debug output:

- **DHCPDECLINE:** Message sent from the client to the server that the address is already in use.

- **DHCPNAK:** The server sends a refusal to the client for request for configuration.

- **DHCPRELEASE:** Client tells a server that it is giving up a lease.

- **DHCPINFORM:** A client already has an IP address but is requesting other configuration parameters that the DHCP server is configured to deliver such as DNS address.

Step 5.   Configure PC2 and PC3 to obtain IP address through DHCP:

```
PC2(config)# interface ethernet 0/0
PC2(config-if)# ip address dhcp
PC2(config-if)# no shutdown

PC3(config)# interface ethernet 0/0
PC3(config-if)# ip address dhcp
PC3(config-if)# no shutdown
```

Step 6.   On DSW1 investigate the DHCP binding table:

```
DSW1# show ip dhcp binding
Bindings from all pools not associated with VRF:
IP address          Client-ID/              Lease expiration      Type
                    Hardware address/
                    User name
10.0.10.2           0063.6973.636f.2d61.    Oct 05 2013 03:23 AM     Automatic
                    6162.622e.6363.3030.
                    2e34.3830.302d.4574.
                    302f.30
10.0.10.3           0063.6973.636f.2d61.    Oct 05 2013 04:04 AM     Automatic
                    6162.622e.6363.3030.
                    2e34.6130.302d.4574.
                    302f.30
10.0.10.4           0063.6973.636f.2d61.    Oct 05 2013 04:04 AM     Automatic
                    6162.622e.6363.3030.
                    2e34.3930.302d.4574.
                    302f.30
```

Notice that the DHCP server leased three IP addresses.

You could also verify that the three clients acquired IP addresses by issuing the **show ip interface brief** command on each client.

Note   Sometimes a manually assigned IP address is preferred. For example, it is beneficial for the servers to have an IP address that does not change.

Because you are using DHCP and with that assigning all IP addresses from a central point, it would be nice if you could also assign a specific address to a specific device. And you can do that with DHCP as well.

Step 7.   Find out PC3's client identifier.

When a Cisco router sends a DHCP Discover message, it will include a client identifier to uniquely identify the device. You can use this value to configure a static binding:

```
DSW1# show ip dhcp binding 10.0.10.4
IP address          Client-ID/              Lease expiration      Type
                    Hardware address/
                    User name
10.0.10.4           0063.6973.636f.2d61.    Oct 05 2013 10:07 AM Automatic
                    6162.622e.6363.3030.
                    2e30.3630.302d.4574.
                    302f.30
```

If you do not like this long client identifier, you can also assign PC3 to use the MAC address as the client identifier. You can do so by using the **ip address dhcp client-id ethernet 0/0** command.

Step 8.   On DSW1 clear IP DHCP binding table.

If you already have a binding for a client and you want to manually set its IP address you have to clear the DHCP binding table:

```
DSW1(config)# clear ip dhcp binding 10.0.10.4
```

You could also delete all automatic address bindings. Because you will manually set only the PC3's IP address, you only need to delete PC3's current IP address from the binding table.

Step 9.   On DSW1 assign IP address of 10.0.10.200 to PC3.

You might have examples where it is needed for a client to have the same IP address all the time because of some application requirements:

```
DSW1(config)# ip dhcp pool CLIENT3
DSW1(dhcp-config)# host 10.0.10.200 255.255.255.0
DSW1(dhcp-config)# client-identifier
0063.6973.636f.2d61.6162.622e.6363.3030.2e30.3630.302d.4574.302f.30
```

To configure a manual binding, create a host pool first, and then specify the IP address of the client and client identifier. Only a client with the specified client identifier will be assigned this IP address.

At this moment, Client 3 will not acquire the specified IP address. Client 3 will only request an IP address after its lease expires or if it requests a renewal.

Note   Some devices, usually running Linux, do not send client identifiers with DHCP messages. In these cases, you can bind an IP address to a device using the client's MAC address. Instead of using the **client-identifier** *number* command use the **hardware-address** *MAC-address* **command.**

Step 10.   Force PC3 to request a new lease from the DHCP server:

```
PC3(config)# interface ethernet 0/0
PC3(config-if)# shutdown
PC3(config-if)# no shutdown
*Oct  3 18:25:17.680: %DHCP-6-ADDRESS_ASSIGN: Interface Ethernet0/0
assigned DHCP address 10.0.10.200, mask 255.255.255.0, hostname PC3
```

A notification is raised when client acquires address 10.0.10.200—the IP address which it was bound to by using the **client-identifier** *identifier* command.

Configuring a DHCP Relay

As you know, DHCP is a client/server application, in which the DHCP client, usually a desktop computer, contacts a DHCP server for configuration parameters using a broadcast request. Today's enterprise multilayer switched networks use centralized DHCP server services with other centralized services like Network Time Protocol (NTP) and monitoring tools. Because broadcast is not forwarded across the VLAN boundaries, to forward the DHCP broadcast, the router needs to use the DHCP relay agent feature, as shown in Figure 5-17, where a switch is configured with the DHCP relay agent using the **IP helper-address** command to forward the broadcast traffic in the directed unicast to the server.

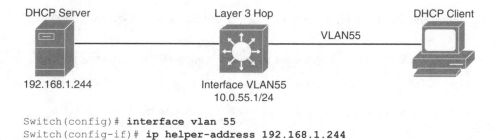

```
Switch(config)# interface vlan 55
Switch(config-if)# ip helper-address 192.168.1.244
```

Figure 5-17   *DHCP Service and Client Configuration*

As illustrated in Figure 5-17, a client that resides in VLAN 55 needs to have the following two configurations to forward the DHCP broadcast to the centralized server 192.168.1.244:

- The multilayer switch must have a Layer 3 IP address that will receive the client DHCP request that is 10.0.55.1/24, as shown in Figure 5-17. This address may be a routed port or an SVI.

- The **ip helper-address** command must be configured on the multilayer switch Layer 3 interface.

With the DHCP relay address, when the switch receives a DHCP request in the form of a broadcast message from a client, the switch forwards this request, as a unicast message, to the IP address that is specified in the **ip helper-address** command. With this feature, the switch relays the dialog between the DHCP client and the DHCP server. When the switch receives the packets, it makes sure that it assigns an IP address only from the range of the subnet in which the client resides.

The **ip helper-address** command not only forwards DHCP UDP packets but also forwards TFTP, DNS, time, NetBIOS, name server, and BOOTP packets by default.

Configuring DHCP Options

Advanced configuration parameters and other control information are carried in tagged data items, also known as DHCP options.

Use DHCP options to "expand" the basic DHCP commands. For example, the **lease** command is one of the basic commands that is used to set the duration of lease validity. With DHCP options, it can modify the behavior of leasing out IP addresses. For example, just change the lease renewal time by using the **dhcp-renewal-time** option.

Using options, you can configure clients with additional information that cannot be passed down to the clients through basic configuration. The following are some of the commonly used options.

- **Option 43:** Vendor-encapsulated option that enables vendors to have their own list of options on the server. For example, you can use it to tell a lightweight access point where the Wireless LAN Controller (WLC) is.

- **Option 69:** SMTP server, if you want to specify available SMTP servers to the client.

- **Option 70:** POP3 server, if you want to specify available POP3 servers to the client.

- **Option 150:** TFTP server that enables your phones to access a list of TFTP servers.

Example 5-4 shows how to pass the TFTP server information to the Clients using the DHCP options.

Example 5-4   *Configuration of TFTP Server Using the DHCP Options*

```
Switch(config)# ip dhcp pool TELEPROFILES
Switch(dhcp-config)# options 150.10.10.1
```

For more information on DHCP options, visit http://www.cisco.com/en/US/docs/net_mgmt/network_registrar/6.1.1/user/guide/UserApB.html#wp1004238.

Study Tips

- Inter-VLAN routing can be done via external router or multiplayer switches.

- To use the inter-VLAN routing, the most efficient method is to use SVI on multi-layer switches.

- You can use the SVI **autostate exclude** command to configure a port so that it is not included in the SVI line-state up-and-down calculation.

- Layer 2 EtherChannel uses access layer or trunk ports to bundle the interfaces, whereas Layer 3 EtherChannel uses routed ports for bundling.

- Routing needs to be enabled explicitly on some routers for routing across VLANs or other networks.

- Router can be used as the DHCP server for the client IP request. Configuration examples are provided only to allow certain ranges of IP but also to exclude the certain ranges.

- To request the IP address when the servers boots up, DHCP uses DHCPDISCOVER broadcast messages to request the IP address. DHCP server responds with DHCPOFFER Unicast message.

- Using DHCP relay with the **ip helper-address** command, a client can extend its DHCP request across the VLANs.

- With DHCP services options, you can provide clients with TFTP and critical server information (for example, in the case of IP phone, TFTP server information).

Summary

This chapter discussed in detail Layer 3 routing and its implementation, including coverage of inter-VLAN routing and router-on-a-stick, and DHCP services. This chapter can be summarized as follows:

- Inter-VLAN routing provides communication between the devices in different VLANs. Recall that a VLAN is a single broadcast domain, and the devices within a VLAN cannot communicate beyond VLAN boundaries unless through a Layer 3 device. Multilayer switches support two types of Layer 3 interfaces: routed ports and SVIs (VLAN interfaces).

- Routed ports are point-to-point connections such as those that interconnect the building distribution submodules and the campus backbone submodules when using Layer 3 in the distribution layer.

- SVIs are VLAN interfaces that route traffic between VLANs and VLAN group ports. In multilayer switched networks with Layer 3 in the distribution layer and Layer 2 in the access layer, SVIs can route traffic from VLANs on the access layer switches.

- Using router-on-a-stick is an alternative and legacy method of implementing inter-VLAN routing for low-throughput and latency-tolerant applications.

- On multilayer switches, Layer 3 links can be aggregated using Layer 3 EtherChannels.

- When a Layer 3 interface is configured, routing can be enabled.

- DHCP server function can be configured on the Cisco switches and routers.

- If the network uses a centralized DHCP server, a DHCP relay agent feature can be configured on the switches by using the **ip helper-address** command.

Review Questions

Use the questions here to review what you learned in this chapter. The correct answers are found in Appendix A, "Answers to Chapter Review Questions."

1. True or False: An SVI is a physical Layer 3 interface, whereas a routed port is a virtual Layer 3 interface.

2. True or False: Multilayer switches generally outperform routers of multiple Ethernet interfaces.

3. True or False: A router can forward DHCP requests across VLAN or IP subnet boundaries by using the DHCP relay agent feature.

Questions 4 and 5 are based on the configuration in Example 5-5.

Example 5-5 *Configuration for Questions 4 and 5*

```
switch# show run interface vlan 10
Building configuration...
Current configuration : 60 bytes ! interface Vlan10
ip address 10.1.1.1 255.255.255.0
no ip proxy-arp end
switch# show run int vlan 20
Building configuration...
Current configuration : 60 bytes ! interface Vlan20
ip address 10.2.1.1 255.255.255.0 no ip proxy-arp end
```

4. Based on Example 5-5, can the hosts that reside in VLAN 20 communicate with hosts on VLAN 10 if their default gateway is set to 10.2.1.1?

   a. Yes, if the hosts on VLAN 10 have their default gateway set to 10.1.1.1.

   b. No, the default gateway of the hosts that reside in VLAN 20 should be set to 10.1.1.1.

   c. Yes, but there is no need to define default gateways.

   d. No, because the routing protocol or static routes are not defined.

5. Based on Example 5-5, if the hosts that reside on VLAN 10 have their default gateway defined as 10.1.1.1 and ICMP can ping 10.2.1.1 but not a host that resides in VLAN 20, what could be a possible reason?

   a. Hosts on VLAN 10 are not configured with the correct default gateway.

   b. Hosts on VLAN 20 are not configured with the correct default gateway.

   c. The routing protocol or static routes are not defined on the Layer 3 switch.

   d. VLAN 20 is not defined in the switch database.

6. When performing router-on-a-stick inter-VLAN routing, a router interface is subdivided into what?

    a. VLAN subinterfaces

    b. 802.1Q subinterfaces

    c. Layer 3 subinterfaces

    d. EtherChannel subinterfaces

7. Which two commands should be used to configure a router and switch to identify VLAN 10 as the native VLAN on an 802.1Q trunk link? (Choose two.)

    a. encapsulation dot1q vlan 10 native

    b. encapsulation dot1q 10 native

    c. encapsulation dot1q native vlan 10

    d. switchport trunk dot1q native vlan 10

    e. switchport mode trunk dot1q vlan 10 native

    f. switchport trunk native vlan 10

8. Place the following five items in the proper order of processing.

    a. If necessary, an input router ACL check is performed.

    b. The Layer 2 and Layer 3 header are rewritten.

    c. The Layer 2 forwarding engine forwards the frame.

    d. The Layer 2 engine performs the input VLAN ACL lookup.

    e. The destination IP address is compared against the Layer 3 forwarding table for the longest match.

9. Which of the following are *not* reasons for configuring an SVI? (Choose two.)

    a. To provide fallback bridging if it is required for nonroutable protocols

    b. To provide Layer 3 IP connectivity to the switch

    c. To provide failover if the primary SVI for a VLAN fails

    d. To provide a gateway for a VLAN so that traffic can be routed into or out of that VLAN

    e. To provide connectivity to an external router for inter-VLAN routing

10. On which of the following ports would a network engineer be most likely to use the **autostate exclude** command?

    a. An 802.1Q trunk port connected to an external router

    b. A monitoring port connected to an intrusion prevention sensor

    c. The secondary SVI for a VLAN

    d. A routed interface on a multilayer switch

    e. All of these answers are correct

11. When must the command **ip routing** be used when configuring SVIs on a multilayer switch?

    a. When an SVI is being used to provide IP connectivity to the switch itself for a given VLAN.

    b. When the SVI is being configured as part of a Layer 2 EtherChannel bundle.

    c. When EIGRP is not being used as a routing protocol.

    d. When an SVI is being used to provide Layer 3 IP forwarding services to its assigned VLAN.

    e. Never; IP routing is enabled by default on a multilayer switch.

12. How is a port on a multilayer switch configured as a routed port?

    a. By configuring an IP address and subnet mask on the port

    b. By using the command **switchport mode routed**

    c. By removing the Layer 2 switching capability of the switch port

    d. By using the command **no switchport mode**

13. What command is used on Cisco IOS switches to change the interface from a Layer 3 interface to a Layer 2 interface?

    a. switchport mode access

    b. ip routing

    c. switchport

    d. switchport mode trunk

14. Which Cisco IOS command enables IP routing on a Catalyst switch?

    a. ip routing

    b. interface *vlan-id*

    c. ip address *n.n.n.n mask*

    d. router *ip-routing-protocol*

15. What is the function of a DHCP relay agent?

16. Which of the following UDP protocols are forwarded in addition to DHCP when a Layer 3 interface is configured with the **ip helper-address** command? (Choose all that apply.)

    a. Mobile IP

    b. DNS

    c. Time

    d. FTP

17. Which of the following arrangements can be considered "router-on-a-stick"?

    a. One switch, two VLANs, one connection to a router.

    b. One switch, two VLANs, two connections to a router.

    c. Two switches, two VLANs, two connections to a router.

    d. All of these answers are correct.

18. Which two statements are typical characteristics of VLAN arrangements? (Choose two.)

    a. A new switch has no VLANs configured.

    b. Connectivity between VLANs requires a Layer 3 device.

    c. Each VLAN usually uses a separate address space.

    d. VLANs cannot span multiple switches.

19. How do you configure a trunk on a router's interface that will have connections to more than one VLAN?

    a. Use subinterfaces on a physical interface, for each VLAN.

    b. Use the **switchport mode trunk** command.

    c. You do not need to explicitly configure a trunk on an interface.

    d. Use the **no switchport** command.

20. You have configured a switch to perform Layer 3 routing via an SVI and have assigned that interface to VLAN 20. To check the status of the SVI, you issue the **show interfaces vlan 20** command. You see from the output display that the interface is in an up/up state. Among others, what must be true in an SVI configuration to bring the VLAN and line protocol up?

   a. The port must be physically connected to another Layer 3 device.

   b. At least one port in VLAN 20 must be active.

   c. Because this is a virtual interface, the operational status will always be in an up/up state.

   d. All of these answers are correct.

21. While configuring SVIs on a multilayer switch, when must you use the **ip routing** command?

   a. When using an SVI to provide IP connectivity to the switch itself for a given VLAN.

   b. When configuring the SVI as part of a Layer 2 EtherChannel bundle.

   c. When using an SVI to provide Layer 3 IP forwarding services to its assigned VLAN.

   d. Never, because IP routing is enabled by default on a multilayer switch.

22. True or False: In Layer 3 EtherChannel two links were bundled. On each of the two switches, there are two IP addresses configured.

Chapter 6

First-Hop Redundancy

Upon completing this chapter, you will be able to do the following:

- Overview of FHRP and HSRP

- Configure and verify VRRP

- Configure and verify GLBP

Hosts and servers in a subnet need a gateway to reach devices that are not in the same subnet. Because gateways perform a key role in operations of all devices, their availability is paramount. Providing redundant gateways is one solution to ensure that they operate in a way that provides redundancy and load balancing, and so they need to be configured for first-hop redundancy protocol. A first-hop redundancy protocol (FHRP) is a networking protocol that is designed to protect the default gateway by allowing two or more routers or Layer 3 switches to provide backup for that address. If one first-hop device fails, the backup router takes over the address, by default, within a few seconds.

Hot Standby Router Protocol (HSRP), Virtual Router Redundancy Protocol (VRRP), and Gateway Load Balancing Protocol (GLBP) are three first-hop redundancy protocols. All three protocols have versions that support first-hop redundancy, not only in IPv4 environments but also IPv6. However, not all platforms and their IOS versions support all three protocols for both IPv4 and IPv6.

Overview of FHRP and HSRP

A network with high availability provides alternative means by which all infrastructure paths and key servers can be accessed at all times. To provide default gateway redundancy to network hosts, HSRP is one of the most commonly deployed protocols. HSRP optimization provides immediate or link-specific failover and a recovery mechanism.

This section covers the following topics:

- The need for first-hop redundancy protocols

- HSRP overview

- HSRP state transitions

- Aligning HSRP with STP topology

- Configuring and tuning HSRP

- Load sharing with HSRP

- Options HSRP has for tracking

- Configuring HSRP interface tracking

- Configuring object tracking in combination with HSRP

- Configuring HSRP authentication

- Tuning HSRP timers

- The differences between HSRP Versions 1 and 2

The Need for First-Hop Redundancy

As illustrated in Figure 6-1, both router A and router B are connected to the 10.1.10.0/24 network and are advertising it with the routing protocol. All the packets that are destined to the 10.1.10.0/24 network are routed to router A. Should router A become unavailable, the routing protocol will dynamically converge, and packets will be routed to router B without modifying the gateway.

Workstations in the 10.1.10.0/24 subnet, as shown in Figure 6-1, however, like most workstations, servers, printers, and other network hosts, do not support dynamic routing protocols. Whenever a network host wants to communicate with a host that is located in a different subnet, packets must be relayed through a Layer 3 device (router or Layer 3 switch). Packets that are destined to another subnet are sent to a Layer 3 device by either Proxy Address Resolution Protocol (ARP) or default gateway setting.

With the Proxy ARP technique, a Layer 3 device offers its own MAC address in response to an ARP query to a MAC address that exists outside the source subnet, thus accepting all subsequent packets destined to that address, routing them to another subnet. The Proxy ARP technique has no fallback mechanisms, and the introduction of multiple routers that use this technique in the same subnet will cause issues such as MAC flapping.

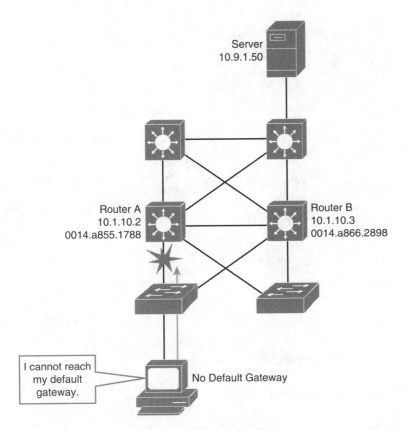

Figure 6-1 *The Need for First-Hop Redundancy*

Network hosts are configured with a single default gateway IP address. All packets destined to another subnet are sent to the default gateway IP address, which does not change when network topology changes occur. If the router whose IP address serves as the default gateway to the network host fails, a network host will be unable to send packets to another subnet, effectively disconnecting it from the rest of the network. Even if a redundant router exists that could serve as a default gateway for that subnet, there is no dynamic method by which these devices can determine the address of a new default gateway.

With first-hop router redundancy, a set of routers or Layer 3 switches work together to present the illusion of a single virtual router to the hosts on the LAN. By sharing an IP address and a MAC (Layer 2) address, two or more routers can act as a single "virtual" router, as shown in Figure 6-2.

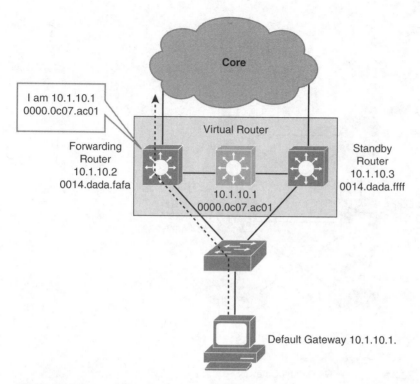

Figure 6-2 *First-Hop Redundancy Process Overview*

HSRP Overview

The default gateway for the workstations on a specific IP subnet is the virtual IP of the protocol. When frames are to be sent from the workstation to the default gateway, the workstation uses ARP to resolve the MAC address that is associated with the IP address of the default gateway. The ARP resolution will return the MAC address of the virtual router. Frames that are sent to the MAC address of the virtual router can then be physically processed by an active router that is part of that virtual router group.

A protocol is used to identify two or more routers as devices that are responsible for processing the frames that are sent to the MAC or IP address of a single virtual router. Host devices send traffic to the address of the virtual router, which is then picked up and routed by an active physical router. The physical router that forwards this traffic is transparent to the network hosts.

The redundancy protocol provides the mechanism for determining which router should take the active role in forwarding traffic and determining when that role must be taken over by a standby router. The transition from one forwarding router to another is transparent to the network hosts.

When the forwarding router or a link to it fails, as shown in Figure 6-3,

- The standby router stops seeing hello messages from the forwarding router.

- The standby router assumes the role of the forwarding router.

- As the new forwarding router assumes both the IP and MAC addresses of the virtual router, the end stations see no disruption in service.

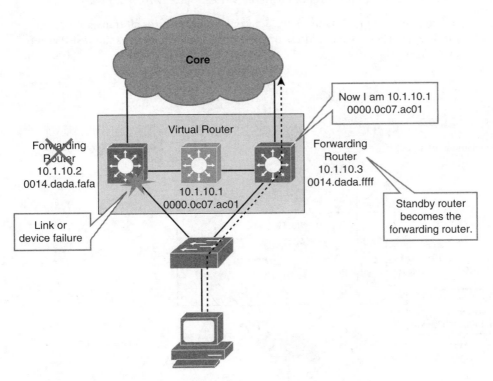

Figure 6-3 *Active HSRP Router Link Failure*

HSRP active and standby routers send hello messages to multicast address 224.0.0.2 (all routers) for Version 1, or 224.0.0.102 for Version 2, using User Datagram Protocol (UDP) port 1985. Hello messages are used to communicate between routers in the HSRP group. All the routers in the HSRP group need to be L2 adjacent so that hello packets can be exchanged.

All the routers in an HSRP group have specific roles and interact in specific manners:

- **Virtual router:** An IP and MAC address pair that end devices have configured as their default gateway. The active router processes all packets and frames sent to the virtual router address. The virtual router processes no physical frames. There is one virtual router in an HSRP group.

- **Active router:** Within an HSRP group, one router is elected to be the active router. The active router physically forwards packets sent to the MAC address of the virtual router. There is one active router in an HSRP group.

  The active router responds to traffic for the virtual router. If an end station sends a packet to the virtual router MAC address, the active router receives and processes that packet. If an end station sends an ARP request with the virtual router IP address, the active router replies with the virtual router MAC address.

  In Figure 6-4, router A assumes the active role and forwards all frames addressed to the assigned HSRP MAC address of 0000.0c07.acxx, where xx is the HSRP group identifier.

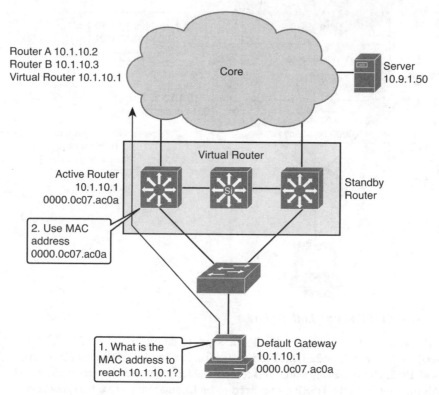

Figure 6-4   *HSRP Active Router Operation*

- **Standby router:** Listens for periodic hello messages. When the active router fails, the other HSRP routers stop seeing hello messages from the active router. The standby router then assumes the role of the active router. There is one standby router in an HSRP group.

- **Other routers:** There can be more than two routers in an HSRP group, but only one active and one standby router is possible. The other routers remain in the initial state, and if both the active and standby routers fail, all routers in the group contend for the active and standby router roles.

HSRP State Transition

A router in an HSRP group can be in one of these states: initial, listen, speak, standby, or active. When a router exists in one of these states, it performs the actions required for that state. Not all HSRP routers in the group will transition through all states. For example, if there are three routers in the HSRP group, the router that is not the standby or active router will remain in the listen state.

Table 6-1 describes the different HSRP states.

Table 6-1 *HSRP States*

State	Definition
Initial	The beginning state. The initial state indicates that HSRP does not run. This state is entered via a configuration change or when an interface first comes up.
Listen	The router knows the virtual IP address, but the router is neither the active router nor the standby router. It listens for hello messages from those routers.
Speak	The router sends periodic hello messages and actively participates in the election of the active or standby router. A router cannot enter speak state unless the router has the virtual IP address.
Standby	The router is a candidate to become the next active router and sends periodic hello messages. With the exclusion of transient conditions, there is, at most, one router in the group in standby state.
Active	The router currently forwards packets that are sent to the group virtual MAC address. The router sends periodic hello messages. With the exclusion of transient conditions, there must be, at the most, one router in the active state in the group.

All routers begin in the initial state. This is the starting state, and it indicates that HSRP is not running. This state is entered via configuration change, such as when HSRP is disabled on an interface, or when an HSRP-enabled interface is first brought up (for instance, when the **no shutdown** command is issued).

The purpose of the listen state is to determine whether there are any active or standby routers already present in the group. In the speak state, the routers are actively participating in the election of the active router, standby router, or both.

Each router uses three timers for the HSRP hello messages. When a timer expires, the router transitions to a new HSRP state.

In the example shown in Figure 6-5, router A starts. Because it is the first router in the subnet that is configured for standby group 1, it transits through the listen and speak states, and then becomes the active router. Router B starts after router A. While router B is in the listen state, router A is already assuming the standby and then the active role. Because there is an active router already present, router B assumes the standby role.

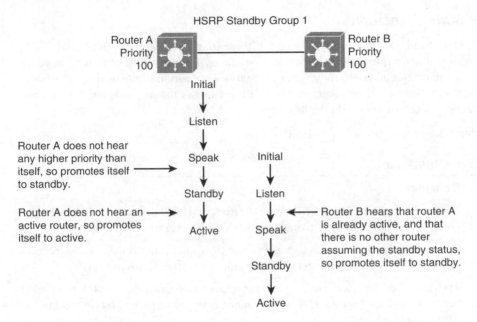

Figure 6-5   *HSRP State Transition*

When two routers participate in an election process, a priority can be configured to determine which router should become active. Without specific priority configuration, each router has a default priority of 100, and the router with the highest IP address is elected as the active router.

Regardless of other router priorities or IP addresses, an active router will stay active by default. A new election will occur only if the active router is removed. When the standby router is removed, a new election is made to replace the standby router. This behavior can change with the preempt option.

Aligning HSRP with STP Topology

Spanning Tree Protocol (STP) is running between the Layer 3 and Layer 2 switches. In a redundant spanning-tree topology, some links are blocked. The spanning-tree topology has no awareness of the HSRP configuration. No automatic relationship exists between the HSRP active router election process and the spanning-tree root bridge election process.

As shown in Figure 6-6, VLAN traffic destined for the core is sent to SW1, because it is an STP root bridge, and the STP blocks the other links. However, SW2 is an active HSRP gateway, so traffic needs to be forwarded to SW2 before being routed to the core network. The traffic path is thus suboptimal, with traffic passing more devices than needed. So, it is important that the configured active router should be the same as STP root bridge. Otherwise, a blocked uplink causes traffic to take a less-than-optimal path.

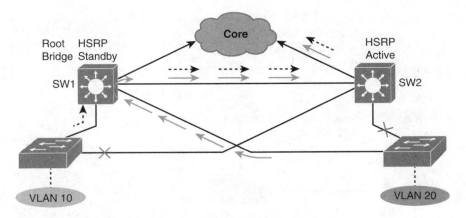

Figure 6-6 *HSRP and STP Root Placement*

It is a good practice to configure the same Layer 3 switch to be both the spanning-tree root and the HSRP active router for a single VLAN. This approach ensures that the Layer 2 forwarding path leads directly to the Layer 3 device that is the HSRP active gateway, thus achieving maximum efficiency.

Configuring and Tuning HSRP

In this section, HSRP, which is an example of an FHRP, can be configured on Layer 3 switches and routers. Figure 6-7 illustrates the HSRP topology that is used for configuration, and Figure 6-8 illustrates the detail design with IP addresses of the topology.

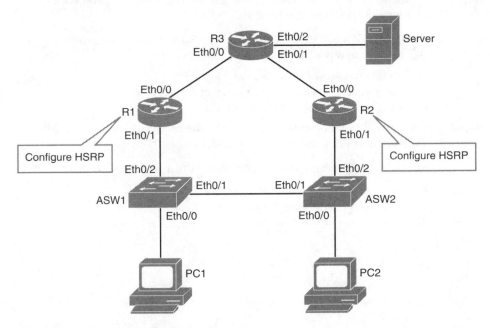

Figure 6-7 *HSRP Configuration Topology*

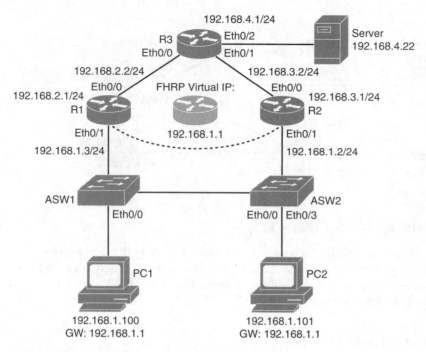

192.168.4.1/24
R3   Eth0/2
Eth0/0   Eth0/1

Server
192.168.4.22

192.168.2.2/24
Eth0/0   FHRP Virtual IP:
192.168.2.1/24
R1

192.168.3.2/24
Eth0/0
192.168.3.1/24
R2

Eth0/1
192.168.1.3/24   192.168.1.1

Eth0/1
192.168.1.2/24

ASW1   ASW2
Eth0/0   Eth0/0 Eth0/3

PC1
192.168.1.100
GW: 192.168.1.1

PC2
192.168.1.101
GW: 192.168.1.1

Figure 6-8   *Detailed Topology with IP addresses*

To configure and tune HSRP, follow these steps:

Step 1.   Configure R1's Ethernet 0/1 (LAN-facing interface) with 192.168.1.3/24 IP address and HSRP standby IP of 192.168.1.1.

The IP of 192.168.1.1 is HSRP's virtual IP address that is also configured as the default gateway IP address on PC 1 and PC 2:

```
R1(config)# interface ethernet 0/1
R1(config-if)# ip address 192.168.1.3 255.255.255.0
R1(config-if)# standby 1 ip 192.168.1.1
```

Step 2.   Configure R2's Ethernet 0/1 (LAN-facing interface) with 192.168.1.2/24 IP address and HSRP standby IP of 192.168.1.1.

Both R1 and R2 must have the same HSRP virtual IP address configured:

```
R2(config)# interface ethernet 0/1
R2(config-if)# ip address 192.168.1.2 255.255.255.0
R2(config-if)# standby 1 ip 192.168.1.1
```

Note   An HSRP group is a set of HSRP devices emulating a virtual router. You have assigned both routers a common HSRP group: group 1. If you leave out the group number, it will be set to default group 0. With HSRP Version 1, a group number can be any integer between 0 and 255. If you are configuring HSRP on a multilayer switch, it is a good practice to configure the HSRP group number equal to the VLAN number. HSRP group numbers are significant to all the routers that provide gateway redundancy. For example, HSRP group 1 on interface VLAN 22 is independent from HSRP group 1 on interface VLAN 33.

The Internet Control Message Protocol (ICMP) allows a router to redirect an end station to send packets for a particular destination to another router on the same subnet (that is, if the first router knows that the other router has a better path to that particular destination). As was the case for default gateways, if the router to which an end station has been redirected for a particular destination fails, the end station's packets to that destination were not delivered. In standard HSRP, this is exactly what happens. For this reason, we recommend disabling ICMP redirects if HSRP is turned on.

Step 3.   On R1, verify the ARP table:

```
R1# show ip arp
Protocol   Address        Age (min)   Hardware Addr   Type   Interface
Internet   192.168.1.1          -     0000.0c07.ac01  ARPA   Ethernet0/1
Internet   192.168.1.2          -     aabb.cc01.ba10  ARPA   Ethernet0/1
Internet   192.168.1.3         50     aabb.cc01.bb10  ARPA   Ethernet0/1
Internet   192.168.2.1          -     aabb.cc01.ba00  ARPA   Ethernet0/0
Internet   192.168.2.2         51     aabb.cc01.bc00  ARPA   Ethernet0/0
```

The IP address and the corresponding MAC address of the virtual router are maintained in the ARP table of the active router in an HSRP group.

The HSRP MAC address is in the following format: 0000.0c07.acXX, where XX is the HSRP group number. Clients use this MAC address to forward data.

Forwarding Through the Active Router

All the routers in an HSRP group have specific roles and interact in specific ways.

The virtual router is simply an IP and MAC address pair that end devices have configured as their default gateway. The active router will process all packets and frames that are sent to the virtual router address. The virtual router processes no physical frames.

Within an HSRP group, one router is elected to be the active router, as illustrated in Figure 6-9. The active router responds to traffic for the virtual router. If an end station sends a packet to the virtual router MAC address, the active router receives and processes that packet. If an end station sends an ARP request with the virtual router IP address, the active router replies with the virtual router MAC address. In this example, R1 assumes the active role and forwards all frames that are addressed to the well-known MAC address of 0000.0c07.acXX, where XX is the HSRP group identifier.

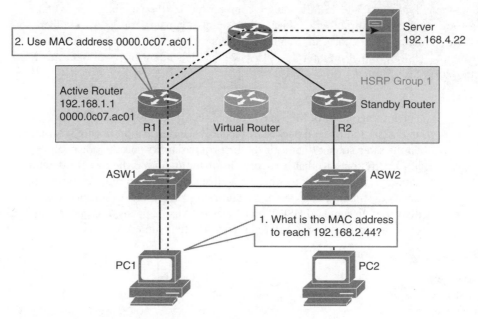

Figure 6-9 *Forwarding Through the Active Router*

Configure R2's HSRP group 1 with priority of 110:

```
R2(config)# interface ethernet 0/1
R2(config-if)# standby 1 priority 110
```

HSRP priority is a parameter that enables you to choose the active router between HSRP-enabled devices in a group. Priority is a value between 0 and 255. The default value is 100. The device with the highest priority will become active.

If HSRP group priorities are the same, the device with the highest IP address will become active, as shown in Figure 6-10. In this example that is R2.

Setting priority is wise for deterministic reasons. It is always good to know how your network will behave under normal conditions rather than guess. Knowing that R2 is the active gateway for VLAN 1 clients enables you to write up good documentation.

However, now that you have changed R2's priority to 110, it will not automatically become the active router because preemption is not enabled by default. Preemption is the ability of an HSRP-enabled device to trigger the re-election process.

Configure R1's and R2's Ethernet 0/1 HSRP group 1 interfaces with preemption:

```
R1(config)# interface ethernet 0/1
R1(config-if)# standby 1 preempt
R2(config)# interface ethernet 0/1
R2(config-if)# standby 1 preempt
```

Notice that after HSRP preemption is enabled, R1 will change its state to standby, and R2 will change its state to active.

On R1 and R2, verify HSRP status:

```
R1# show standby
Ethernet0/1 - Group 1
  State is Standby
    10 state changes, last state change 00:14:15
  Virtual IP address is 192.168.1.1
  Active virtual MAC address is 0000.0c07.ac01
    Local virtual MAC address is 0000.0c07.ac01 (v1 default)
  Hello time 3 sec, hold time 10 sec
    Next hello sent in 1.152 secs
  Preemption enabled
  Active router is 192.168.1.2, priority 110 (expires in 9.744 sec)
  Standby router is local
  Priority 100 (default 100)
  Group name is "hsrp-Et0/1-1" (default)


R2# show standby brief
                     P indicates configured to preempt.
                     |
Interface   Grp  Pri P State   Active       Standby        Virtual IP
Et0/1       1    110 P Active  local        192.168.1.3    192.168.1.1
```

R1 is the standby router, and R2 is the active router. The output of **show standby** can be condensed using the **brief** keyword.

Enable a continuous ping from PC 1 to the server at 192.168.2.44:

```
PC1# ping 192.168.4.22 repeat 10000000
Type escape sequence to abort.
Sending 1000000, 100-byte ICMP Echos to 192.168.4.22, timeout is 2 seconds:
!!!!!!!!!!!!!!!!!!!!!!!!!!!!!!!!!!!!!!!!!!!!!!!!!!!!!!!!!!!!!!!!!!!!!!!!!!!
<... output omitted ...>
```

Right now traffic flows from PC 1 through ASW1, ASW2, R2, R3, to the server, and back, as indicated in Figure 6-10. This is because R2 is the active router.

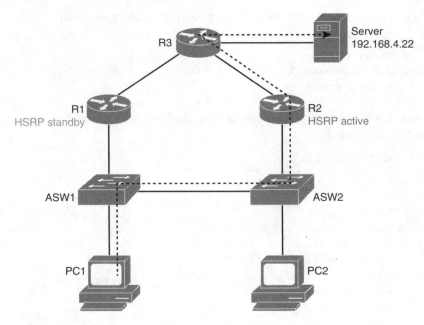

Figure 6-10   *Forwarding Through R2 as the Active Router*

To simulate R2's failure, shut down its Ethernet 0/1 interface, as shown in Figure 6-11.

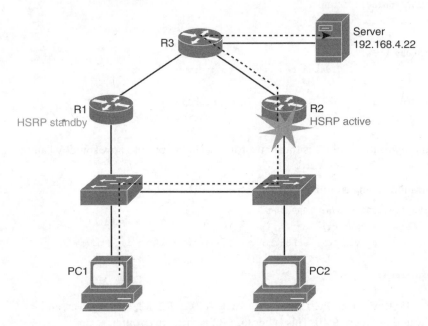

Figure 6-11   *Router R2 Failure Scenario*

A few attempts might get lost on your continuous ping from PC 1 to the server, but the
switchover from R2 to R1 should be quick and seamless for PC 1:

```
R2(config)# interface ethernet 0/1
R2(config-if)# shutdown
```

On R1 and R2, investigate the HSRP status, as shown in Figure 6-12.

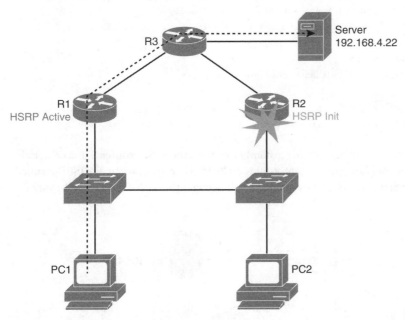

Figure 6-12   *HSRP States after R2 Failure*

```
R1# show standby brief
                      P indicates configured to preempt.
                      |
Interface   Grp  Pri P State   Active      Standby       Virtual IP
Et0/1       1    100 P Active  local       unknown       192.168.1.1


R2# show standby brief
                      P indicates configured to preempt.
                      |
Interface   Grp  Pri P State   Active      Standby       Virtual IP
Et0/1       1    110 P Init    unknown     unknown       192.168.1.1
```

R1 has taken over as the active router and R2 is stuck in the Init state. The Init state
indicates that R1 and R2 are not recognizing each other as HSRP peers. This is logical
because they have lost direct connectivity over LAN interfaces.

On R2, bring up the Ethernet 0/1 interface:

```
R2(config)# interface ethernet 0/1
R2(config-if)# no shutdown
```

Will R2 become the active or the standby router? Observe the behavior in Figure 6-13. Investigate the HSRP status on R1 and R2:

```
R1# show standby brief
                     P indicates configured to preempt.
                     |
Interface  Grp  Pri P State   Active        Standby        Virtual IP
Et0/1       1   100 P Standby 192.168.1.2   local          192.168.1.1

R2# show standby brief
                     P indicates configured to preempt.
                     |
Interface  Grp  Pri P State   Active        Standby        Virtual IP
Et0/1       1   100   Active  local         192.168.1.3    192.168.1.1
```

After R2 is available again, it almost instantly becomes the active router. R1 is on standby again. This is only because preemption is enabled. Therefore, when an HSRP-enabled device with higher priority comes online, it will become the active device, as shown in Figure 6-13.

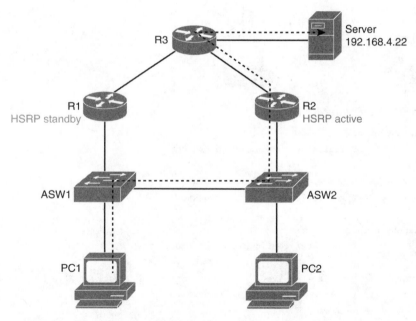

Figure 6-13 *HSRP States After R2 Recover*

With preemption disabled, which is the default behavior, R2 would not regain active status after coming back online.

If you would perform a traceroute from PC 1 to the server, you would see that R2 answers with its "real" interface address (192.168.1.2), not the virtual HSRP address

(192.168.1.1). This is really helpful if you want to verify through which first-hop device traffic is going.

Load Sharing with HSRP

In Figure 6-14, two HSRP-enabled Layer 2 switches participate in two separate VLANs, using IEEE 802.1Q trunks. If you leave the default HSRP priority values, a single Layer 2 switch will likely become an active gateway for both VLANs, effectively utilizing only one uplink toward the core of the network.

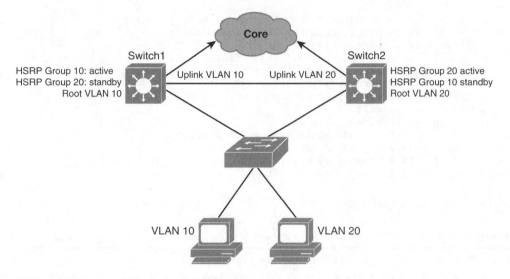

Figure 6-14   *Load Sharing with HSRP*

To use both paths toward the core network, configure HSRP with Multigroup HSRP (MHSRP). Group 10 is configured for VLAN 10. Group 20 is configured for VLAN 20. For group 10, Switch 1 is configured with higher priority to become the active gateway, and Switch 2 becomes the standby gateway. For group 20, Switch 2 is configured with higher priority to become the active gateway, and Switch 1 becomes the standby router. Now both uplinks toward the core are used, one with VLAN 10 and one with VLAN 20 traffic. Also make sure that the spanning-tree root for the VLANs are on the same switch as the active HSRP gateway for that VLAN.

Note   MHSRP load sharing can also be configured in a flat network (that is, when all end devices belong to the same VLAN). Two or more HSRP groups with different virtual IPs can be configured per single interface, serving different clients in a single VLAN.

As shown in Figure 6-15, Switch 1 has two HSRP groups configured for two VLANs and corresponding STP root configuration. Switch 1 is the active router for HSRP group 10 and the standby router for group 20. Example 6-1 shows the sample configuration of Switch 1 where it is root and has active HSRP for VLAN 10.

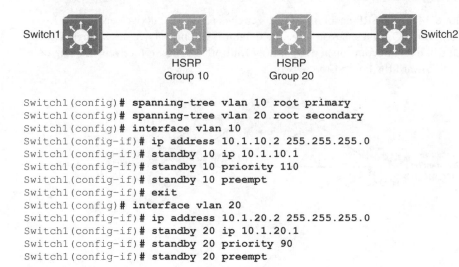

```
Switch1(config)# spanning-tree vlan 10 root primary
Switch1(config)# spanning-tree vlan 20 root secondary
Switch1(config)# interface vlan 10
Switch1(config-if)# ip address 10.1.10.2 255.255.255.0
Switch1(config-if)# standby 10 ip 10.1.10.1
Switch1(config-if)# standby 10 priority 110
Switch1(config-if)# standby 10 preempt
Switch1(config-if)# exit
Switch1(config)# interface vlan 20
Switch1(config-if)# ip address 10.1.20.2 255.255.255.0
Switch1(config-if)# standby 20 ip 10.1.20.1
Switch1(config-if)# standby 20 priority 90
Switch1(config-if)# standby 20 preempt
```

Figure 6-15   *Switch MHSRP*

Example 6-1   *MHSRP Configuration for Switch1*

```
Switch1(config)# spanning-tree vlan 10 root primary
Switch1(config)# spanning-tree vlan 20 root secondary
Switch1(config)# interface vlan 10
Switch1(config-if)# ip address 10.1.10.3 255.255.255.0
Switch1(config-if)# standby 10 ip 10.1.10.1
Switch1(config-if)# standby 10 priority 110
Switch1(config-if)# standby preempt
Switch1(config-if)# exit
Switch1(config-if)# interface vlan 20
Switch1(config-if)# ip address 10.1.20.3 255.255.255.0
Switch1(config-if)# standby 20 ip 10.1.20.1
Switch1(config-if)# standby 20 priority 90
```

Switch 2 has two HSRP groups configured for two VLANs, as shown in Figure 6-16 and corresponding STP root configuration. Switch 2 is the active router for HSRP group 20 and standby router for group 10, as shown in Example 6-2.

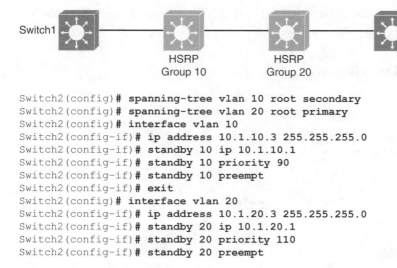

```
Switch2(config)# spanning-tree vlan 10 root secondary
Switch2(config)# spanning-tree vlan 20 root primary
Switch2(config)# interface vlan 10
Switch2(config-if)# ip address 10.1.10.3 255.255.255.0
Switch2(config-if)# standby 10 ip 10.1.10.1
Switch2(config-if)# standby 10 priority 90
Switch2(config-if)# standby 10 preempt
Switch2(config-if)# exit
Switch2(config)# interface vlan 20
Switch2(config-if)# ip address 10.1.20.3 255.255.255.0
Switch2(config-if)# standby 20 ip 10.1.20.1
Switch2(config-if)# standby 20 priority 110
Switch2(config-if)# standby 20 preempt
```

Figure 6-16   *MHSRP Configuration for Switch 2*

Example 6-2   *MHSRP Configuration for Switch2*

```
Switch2(config)# spanning-tree vlan 10 root secondary
Switch2(config)# spanning-tree vlan 20 root primary
Switch2(config)# interface vlan 10
Switch2(config-if)# ip address 10.1.10.3 255.255.255.0
Switch2(config-if)# standby 10 ip 10.1.10.1
Switch2(config-if)# standby 10 priority 90
Switch2(config-if)# exit
Switch2(config-if)# interface vlan 20
Switch2(config-if)# ip address 10.1.20.3 255.255.255.0
Switch2(config-if)# standby 20 ip 10.1.20.1
Switch2(config-if)# standby 20 priority 110
Switch2(configif)# standby 20 preempt
```

The Need for Interface Tracking with HSRP

HSRP can track interfaces or objects and decrement priority if an interface or object
fails. Interface tracking enables the priority of a standby group router to be automatically adjusted, based on the availability of the router interfaces. When a tracked interface
becomes unavailable, the HSRP priority of the router is decreased. When properly configured, the HSRP tracking feature ensures that a router with an unavailable key interface
will relinquish the active router role.

When the conditions that are defined by the object are fulfilled, the router priority
remains the same. As soon as the verification that is defined by the object fails, the

router priority is decremented. The amount of decrease can be configured. The default value is 10.

HSRP Interface Tracking

HSRP has a built-in mechanism for detecting link failures and starting the HSRP reelection process.

As illustrated in Figure 6-17, R1 and R2 are configured with HSRP. R2 is configured to be the active default gateway, and R1 will take over if R2 or R2's HSRP-enabled interface fails.

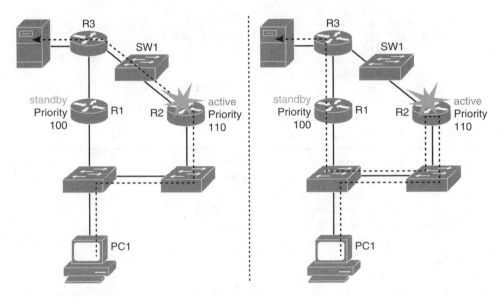

Figure 6-17   *HSRP with No Interface Tracking Feature*

What happens if the R2's uplink fails? The uplink interface is not an HSRP-enabled interface, so its failure does not affect HSRP. R2 is still the active default gateway. All the traffic from PC 1 to the server now has to go through R2, and then gets routed to R1 and forwarded to the server, resulting in an inefficient traffic path.

HSRP provides a solution to the presented problem: HSRP interface tracking. Interface tracking allows you to specify another interface on the router for the HSRP process to monitor to alter the HSRP priority for a given group. If the specified interface's line protocol goes down, the HSRP priority of this router is reduced, allowing another HSRP router with higher priority to become active. Preemption must be enabled.

Let's look at the same scenario as before. R2's uplink interface fails shown in Figure 6-18, but this time HSRP, by virtue of HSRP interface tracking, detects this failure, and R2's HSRP priority is decreased by 20. With preemption enabled, R1 will then take over as the active HSRP peer, as it has a higher priority.

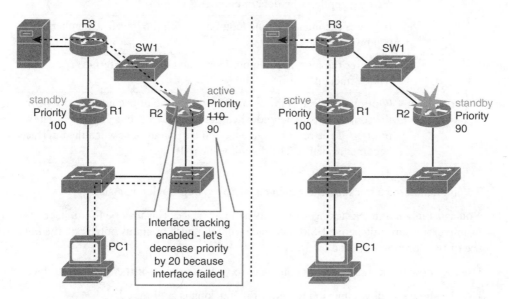

Figure 6-18 *HSRP with Interface Tracking On*

Traffic path is now optimal. Traffic from PC 1 to the server goes directly through R1.

The following shows the configuration of router 2 from Figure 6-18. Note that **standby 10 track Ethernet 0/1 20** lowers the priority 20 points, as soon as interface Ethernet 0/1 goes down. Also, it is highly recommended to have the preempt feature enabled so that as soon as the interface Eth0/1 is back, the interface tries to become the active again:

```
R2(config)# interface ethernet 0/1
R2(config-if)# ip address 192.168.10.2
R2(config-if)# standby 10 ip 192.168.10.1
R2(config-if)# standby 10 priority 110
R2(config-if)# standby 10 preempt
R2(config-if)# standby 10 track ethernet1/1 20
```

Table 6-2 shows the HSRP tracking configuration arguments.

Table 6-2 *HSRP Tracking Configuration Arguments.*

Variable	Description
group-number	(Optional) Indicates the group number on the interface to which the tracking applies. The default number is 0.
type	Indicates the interface type (combined with the interface number) that will be tracked.
number	Indicates the interface number (combined with the interface type) that will be tracked.
interface-priority	(Optional) Indicates the amount by which the hot standby priority for the router is decremented when the interface becomes disabled. The priority of the router is incremented by this amount when the interface becomes available. The default value is 10.

To disable interface tracking, enter the **no standby group track** command.

You can apply multiple tracking statements to an interface. This may be useful if, for example, the currently active HSRP interface will relinquish its status only upon the failure of two (or more) tracked interfaces.

Use the **show track** *track-number* command to verify the state of the tracked interface.

Use the **show standby** command to verify that tracking is configured.

HSRP and Object Tracking

In certain scenarios, HSRP interface tracking cannot provide the optimal path or provide solutions even if the uplink ports are down, as shown in Figure 6-19, where R1 and R2 are configured with HSRP. R2 is configured to be the active default gateway, and R1 will take over if R2 or R2's HSRP-enabled interface fails. The HSRP native interface tracking mechanism can concede elections if R1's or R2's uplink interface fails, provided we also configured preemption.

Let's look at the switch between R3 and R2. What happens if the switch's R3-facing interface fails? In this case, if R2 has a statically configured default route pointing upward, it will not figure out that there was a change in topology. Dynamic routing protocol will bypass the failure but at a cost of a suboptimal traffic path. In both cases, HSRP on R2 will not detect a change, and R2 will still be the active router.

By using HSRP native interface tracking, you can monitor the state of R2-SW1 link and trigger the reelection process of the HSRP active router. But how do you tell R2 to trigger the election process if R3-SW1 link is down? This is where HSRP's ability to use object tracking and reaction to changes comes in action, as illustrated in Figure 6-20.

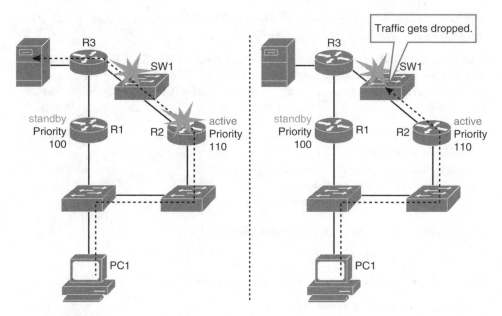

Figure 6-19 *HSRP and Object Tracking Scenario*

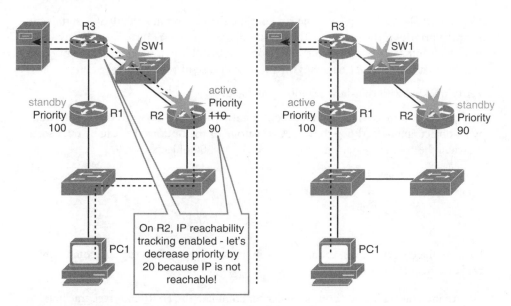

Figure 6-20 *HSRP and Object Tracking (Continued)*

R3 can be reached from R2 only if the link is operational. In this case, define an IP service level agreement (SLA) reachability test on R2, and then create an object to track this IP SLA test. Tell the HSRP process to track the created object. When R2 loses connectivity to R3's SW1-facing interface, the HSRP priority of R2 will be decreased by a specified amount. With preemption configured, R2 will lose its active status to R1. R1 will then be the active default gateway for PC 1.

Configure an IP SLA test that will track the reachability of R3's SW1-facing interface first, as shown in the following configuration steps, where an ICMP echo ping to the next-hop router is the criteria for tracking. It also specifies the frequency of test execution. Remember to schedule the test to start.

First, define an IP SLA ICMP echo test:

```
R2(config)# ip sla 10
R2(config-ip-sla)# icmp-echo 192.168.3.2
R2(config-ip-sla-echo)# frequency 5
R2(config-ip-sla-echo)# ip sla schedule 10 life forever start-time now
```

Then create an object and track the IP SLA instance:

```
R2(config)# track 100 ip sla 10
```

Then configure HSRP to track an object and decrement priority if the test fails:

```
R2(config)# interface ethernet 0/1
R2(config-if)# standby 1 track 100 decrement 20
```

After the IP SLA test is up and running, configure HSRP to track the IP SLA and decrement the priority if the test fails. The default decrease is 10. You can specify any value between 0 and 255. As shown in the previous configuration, it decrements the priority to 20 so that the other R1 becomes the primary in case of ping failure.

Verify tracking with the **show standby** command.

Tracked objects are defined in global configuration with the keyword **track**, followed by an object number. Although IP SLA is just one of the options that can be tracked, as shown in the following syntax, you can track up to 500 objects:

```
Switch(congi)#track 1 ?
  interface      Select an interface to track
  ip             IP protocol
  list           Group objects in a list
```

Tracked objects offer a vast group of possibilities. A few options that are commonly available include the following

- **An interface:** This performs a similar function like the HSRP interface tracking mechanism, but with advanced features. This tracking object can not only verify the interface status (line protocol) but also whether IP routing is enabled, whether an IP address is configured on the interface, and whether the interface state is up, before reporting to the tracking client that the interface is up.

- **IP route:** A tracked IP-route object is considered up and reachable when a routing table entry exists for the route and the route is accessible. To provide a common interface to tracking clients, route metric values are normalized to the range of 0 to 255, where 0 is connected and 255 is inaccessible. You can track route reachability, or even metric values, to determine best-path values to the target network. The tracking process uses a per-protocol configurable resolution value to convert the real metric to the scaled metric. The metric value that is communicated to clients is always such that a lower metric value is better than a higher metric value.

■ **IP SLA:** This special case allows you to track advanced parameters such as IP reachability, delay, or jitter.

■ **A list of objects:** You can track several objects and interrelate their results to determine whether one or several of them should trigger the "success" or "fail" condition.

Configuring HSRP Authentication

HSRP authentication prevents rogue Layer 3 devices on the network from joining the HSRP group. A rogue device may claim the active role and can prevent the hosts from communicating with the rest of the network, creating a denial-of-service (DoS) attack. A rogue router could also forward all traffic and capture traffic from the hosts, achieving a man-in-the-middle attack.

HSRP provides the following two types of authentication:

■ Plain text

■ Message digest 5 (MD5) algorithm

To configure plain-text authentication, use the following interface configuration command on HSRP peers:

```
Switch(config-if)# standby group authentication string
```

With plain-text authentication, a message that matches the key configured on an HSRP peer is accepted. The maximum length of a key string is eight characters. Clear-text messages can easily be intercepted, so avoid plain-text authentication if MD5-type authentication is available.

To configure MD5 authentication, use the following interface configuration command on HSRP peers:

```
Switch(config-if)# standby group authentication md5 key-string [0 | 7] string
```

Using an MD5 key, a hash is computed on a portion of each HSRP message. The hash is sent along with the HSRP message. When a peer receives the message and a hash, it performs hashing on the received message. If the received hash and the newly computed hash match, the message is accepted. It is difficult to reverse the hash value itself, and hash keys itself are never exchanged. MD5 authentication is preferred.

By default, the key string is given as plain text. After you enter the key string, it will get encrypted and stored into the running configuration. You can copy and paste an encrypted key string value into this command by preceding the string with the 7 keyword. However, keep in mind that this type of encryption is weak. Alternatively, you can define MD5 strings as keys on a key chain. This is a more flexible method because you can define multiple keys with different validity times.

To configure MD5 authentication using key chains, use the following command sequence:

```
Switch(config)# key chain chain-name
Switch(config-keychain)# key key-number
Switch(config-keychain-key)# key-string [0 | 7] string
Switch(config-keychain-key)# exit
Switch(config)# interface interface-slot/number
Switch(config-if)# standby group authentication md5 key-chain chain-name
```

Tuning HSRP Timers

A hello message contains the priority of the router, the hello time, and hold-time parameter values. The hello timer parameter value indicates the interval between the hello messages that the router sends. The hold-time parameter value indicates how long the current hello message is considered valid. The standby timer includes an **msec** parameter to allow for subsecond failovers. Lowering the hello timer results in increased traffic for hello messages and should be used with caution.

If an active router sends a hello message, the receiving routers consider the hello message to be valid for one hold-time period. The hold-time value should be at least three times the value of the hello time. The hold-time value must be greater than the value of the hello time. You can adjust the HSRP timers to tune the performance of HSRP on distribution devices, thereby increasing their resilience and reliability in routing packets off the local VLAN.

By default, the HSRP hello time is 3 seconds, and the hold time is 10 seconds, which means that the failover time could be as much as 10 seconds for clients to start communicating with the new default gateway. In some cases, this interval may be excessive for application support. The hello-time and the hold-time parameters are configurable. To configure the time between the hello messages and the time before other group routers declare the active or standby router to be nonfunctioning, enter this command in the interface configuration mode:

```
Switch(config-if)# standby group-number timers [msec] hellotime [msec] holdtime
standby [group-number] timers [msec] hellotime [msec] holdtime
```

The hello interval is specified in seconds unless the **msec** keyword is used. This is an integer from 1 through 255. The default is 3 seconds. The dead interval, also specified in seconds, is a time before the active or standby router is declared to be down. This is an integer from 1 through 255, unless the **msec** keyword is used. The default is 10 seconds. The hello and the dead timer intervals must be identical for all the devices within the HSRP group. To reinstate the default standby-timer values, enter the **no standby group timers** command.

Ideally, to achieve fast convergence, these timers should be configured to be as low as possible. Within milliseconds after the active router fails, the standby router can detect the failure, expire the hold-time interval, and assume the active role.

Note   Decreasing the HSRP timers will enable you to detect a first-hop failure faster. However, shorter HSRP timers mean more HSRP hello packets, which in turn means more overhead traffic.

Nevertheless, timer configuration should also take into account other parameters relevant to the network convergence. For example, both HSRP routers may be running a dynamic routing protocol. The routing protocol probably has no awareness of the HSRP configuration, and sees both routers as individual hops toward other subnets. If HSRP failover occurs before the dynamic routing protocol converges, suboptimal routing information may still exist. In a worst-case scenario, the dynamic routing protocol continues seeing the failed router as the best next hop to other networks, and packets are lost. When configuring HSRP timers, make sure that they harmoniously match the other timers that can influence which path is chosen to carry packets in your network.

Preemption is an important feature of HSRP that allows the primary router to resume the active role when it comes back online after a failure or a maintenance event. Preemption is a desired behavior as it forces a predictable routing path for the VLAN traffic during normal operations. It also ensures that the Layer 3 forwarding path for a VLAN parallels the Layer 2 STP forwarding path whenever possible.

When a preempting device is rebooted, HSRP preemption communication should not begin until the distribution switch has established full connectivity to the rest of the network. This situation allows the routing protocol convergence to occur more quickly, after the preferred router is in an active state.

To accomplish this, measure the system boot time and set the HSRP preemption delay to a value that is about 50 percent greater than device's boot time. This value ensures that the primary distribution switch establishes full connectivity to the network before the HSRP communication occurs. For example, if the boot time for the distribution device is 150 seconds, the preempt delay should be set to 225 seconds (see Example 6-3).

Example 6-3   *Configuring HSRP Timers*

```
switch(config)# interface vlan 10
switch(config-if)# ip address 10.1.1.2 255.255.255.0
switch(config-if)# standby 10 ip 10.1.1.1
switch(config-if)# standby 10 priority 110
switch(config-if)# standby 10 preempt
switch(config-if)# standby 10 timers msec 200 msec 750
switch(config-if)# standby 10 preempt delay minimum 225
```

HSRP Versions

There are two HSRP versions available on most Cisco routers and Layer 3 switches: HSRPv1 and HSRPv2.

Version 1 is a default version on Cisco IOS devices. HSRPv2 is supported in Cisco IOS Release 12.2(46)SE and later. HSRPv2 allows group numbers up to 4095, thus allowing you to use VLAN number as the group number.

HSRP Version 2 must be enabled on an interface before HSRP IPv6 can be configured.

HSRP Version 2 will not interoperate with HSRP Version 1. All devices in an HSRP group must have the same version configured; otherwise, the hello messages are not understood. An interface cannot operate both Version 1 and Version 2 because they are mutually exclusive.

The MAC address of the virtual router and the multicast address for the hello messages are different with Version 2. HSRPv2 uses the new IP multicast address 224.0.0.102 to send the hello packets instead of the multicast address of 224.0.0.2, which is used by Version 1. This new address allows Cisco Group Multicast Protocol processing to be enabled at the same time as HSRP.

HSRPv2 has a different packet format. It includes a 6-byte identifier field that is used to uniquely identify the sender of the message by its interface MAC address, making troubleshooting easier.

To enable HSRP Version 2, enable the following configuration:

```
Switch(config-if) standby hsrp-number version 2
```

Note   For additional information, see http://www.cisco.com/c/en/us/support/docs/ip/hot-standby-router-protocol-hsrp/9234-hsrpguidetoc.html.

Configuring Layer 3 Redundancy with VRRP

The Virtual Router Redundancy Protocol (VRRP) is a first-hop redundancy protocol and serves as a standard-based alternative to Cisco proprietary HSRP.

Upon completing this section, you will be able to do the following:

- Describe the idea behind VRRP

- Configure and verify VRRP

- Describe the differences between HSRP and VRRP

- Describe tracking options with VRRP

- Configure VRRP interface object tracking

About VRRP

VRRP is an open standard alternative to HSRP. VRRP is similar to HSRP, both in operation and configuration. The VRRP master is analogous to the HSRP active gateway, and the VRRP backup is analogous to the HSRP standby gateway. A VRRP group has one master device and one or multiple backup devices. A device with the highest priority is the elected master. Priority can be a number between 0 and 255. Priority value 0 has a special meaning; it indicates that the current master has stopped participating in VRRP. This setting is used to trigger backup devices to quickly transition to master without having to wait for the current master to time out.

VRRP differs from HSRP in that it allows you to use an address of one of the physical VRRP group members as a virtual IP address. In this case, the device with the used physical address is a VRRP master whenever it is available.

The master is the only device that sends advertisements (analogous to HSRP hellos). Advertisements are sent to the 224.0.0.18 multicast address, protocol number 112. The default advertisement interval is 1 second. The default hold time is 3 seconds. HSRP, in comparison, has the default hello timer set to 3 seconds and the hold timer to 10 seconds.

Although VRRP as per RFC 3768 does not support millisecond timers, Cisco devices allow you to configure millisecond timers. You need to manually configure the millisecond timer values on both the master and the backup devices. Use the millisecond timers only where absolutely necessary and with careful consideration and testing. Millisecond values work only under favorable circumstances, and you must be aware that the use of the millisecond timer values restricts VRRP operation to Cisco devices only.

When you use millisecond values, the master advertisement value that is displayed by the **show vrrp** command output on the backup routers is always 1 second, even though the actual value may differ.

In Figure 6-21, Layer 3 switches A, B, and C are configured as VRRP virtual routers and are members of the same VRRP group. Because Switch A has the highest priority, it is elected as the master for this VRRP group; end-user devices will use it as their default gateway. Layer 3 switches B and C function as virtual router backups. If the master fails, the device with the highest configured priority will become the master and provide uninterrupted service for the LAN hosts. When Switch A recovers and preemption is enabled, Switch A becomes the master again. Contrary to HSRP, preemption is enabled by default with VRRP.

Like with HSRP, load sharing is also available with VRRP. Multiple virtual router groups can be configured. For instance, you could configure clients 3 and 4 to use a different default gateway than clients 1 and 2 use. Then you would configure the three Layer 3 switches with another VRRP group and designate Switch B to be the master VRRP device for the second group. Table 6-3 depicts the differences between HSRP and VRRP.

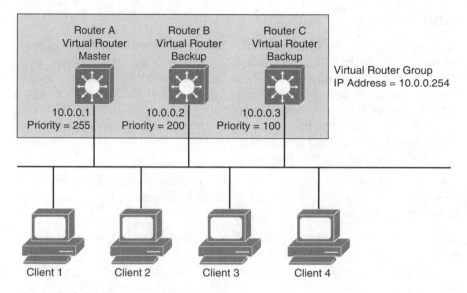

Figure 6-21   *VRRP Overview*

Table 6-3   *HSRP and VRRP Differences*

HSRP	VRRP
Cisco proprietary.	Industry standard.
1 active, 1 standby, several candidates.	1 master, several backups.
Virtual IP is different from real IP addresses.	Virtual IP address can be the same as the real IP address of one of the group members.
Uses 224.0.0.2.	Uses 224.0.0.18.
Can track interfaces or objects.	Can track only objects.
Default timers: hello 3 sec; hold time 10 sec.	Default timers: hello 1 sec; hold time 3 sec.
Authentication supported.	Authentication no longer in RFC, but still supported in Cisco IOS.

Configuring VRRP and Spotting the Differences from HSRP

In this configuration section, you learn how to configure VRRP and the differences between VRRP and HSRP. Figure 6-22 shows the topology for the VRRP configuration.

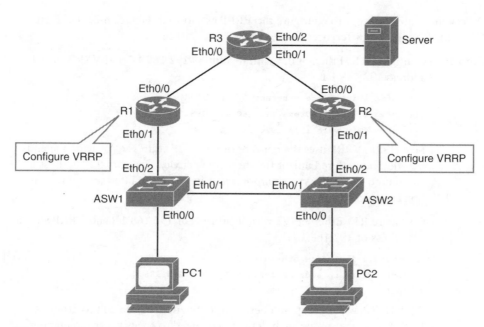

Figure 6-22 *VRRP Configuration Topology*

Figure 6-23 illustrates the IP address scheme that is used for the VRRP configuration.

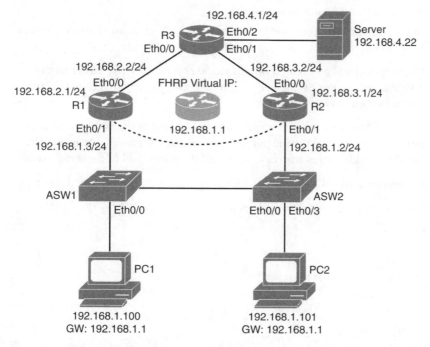

Figure 6-23 *IP Addressing for the VRRP Configuration*

Follow the following steps to configure the VRRP as shown in Figures 6-22 and Figure 6-23 and also spot the differences between HSRP and VRRP:

Step 1.   Configure R1's Ethernet 0/1 with IP address 192.168.1.3 and VRRP virtual IP address 192.168.1.1:

```
R1(config)# interface ethernet 0/1
R1(config-if)# ip address 192.168.1.3 255.255.255.0
R1(config-if)# vrrp 1 ip 192.168.1.1
```

Like HSRP, VRRP uses the concept of virtual IP address to provide the end-user devices with redundant first-hop connectivity. The virtual IP address is configured using the **vrrp** *group-number* **ip** *virtual-ip* interface configuration command.

Configure R2's Ethernet 0/1 with IP address of 192.168.1.2 and VRRP virtual IP address of 192.168.1.1:

```
R2(config)# interface ethernet 0/1
R2(config-if)# ip address 192.168.1.2 255.255.255.0
R2(config-if)# vrrp 1 ip 192.168.1.1
```

With HSRP, when group number is not defined, it will default to group 0. With VRRP, there is no such default. You need to specify a group number, which can be anything between 1 and 255.

Step 2.   Configure R2's Ethernet 0/1 with VRRP priority of 110:

```
R2(config-if)# vrrp 1 priority 110
```

In the routers' command-line interfaces (CLIs), notice that one of the devices transitioned to master state and the other to backup state.

Higher priority is configured on a device that should be the master of the VRRP group. In this example, configure R2 with priority of 110. R1 is left with a default priority of 100.

However, if one of the router's IP addresses is used as the virtual IP address, priorities are ignored for the purpose of electing the master. The router that has the IP address that matches the virtual IP address will become the master.

VRRP has preemption enabled by default. HSRP has preemption disabled by default.

On VRRP-enabled devices, verify the VRRP status:

```
R1# show vrrp
Ethernet0/1 - Group 1
  State is Backup
  Virtual IP address is 192.168.1.1
  Virtual MAC address is 0000.5e00.0101
  Advertisement interval is 1.000 sec
  Preemption enabled
  Priority is 100
  Master Router is 192.168.1.2, priority is 110
```

```
Master Advertisement interval is 1.000 sec
Master Down interval is 3.609 sec (expires in 3.049 sec)
```

In the output of R1, notice the MAC address of the virtual router. The MAC address has the following form: 0000.5e00.01XX, where XX is the two-digit hexadecimal group number:

```
R2# show vrrp brief
Interface        Grp Pri Time  Own Pre State   Master addr     Group addr
Et0/1            1   110 3570      Y   Master  192.168.1.2     192.168.1.1
```

To verify VRRP status, use the **show vrrp** command. If appended with **brief**, it provides the more condensed view.

VRRP and Authentication

The VRRP standard that was defined in RFC 2338 used plain-text and MD5 authentication, which was later revoked in RFC 3768 and RFC 5798m. However, Cisco IOS devices still support authentication mechanisms. Cisco's implementation follows RFC 2338 and provide the Cisco IOS commands to configure the VRRP authentication.

According to RFC 5798, operational experience and further analysis determined that VRRP authentication did not provide sufficient security to overcome the vulnerability of misconfigured secrets, causing multiple masters to be elected. Due to the nature of VRRP, even if VRRP messages are cryptographically protected, it does not prevent hostile nodes from behaving as if they are the VRRP master, creating multiple masters. Authentication of VRRP messages could have prevented a hostile node from causing all properly functioning routers from going into backup state. However, having multiple masters can cause as much disruption as no routers, which authentication cannot prevent. Also, even if a hostile node could not disrupt VRRP, it can disrupt ARP and create the same effect as having all routers go in backup state.

Independent of any authentication type, VRRP includes a mechanism (setting TTL = 255, checking on receipt) that protects against VRRP packets being injected from another remote network. This limits most vulnerabilities to local attacks.

With Cisco IOS devices, the default VRRP authentication is plain text. MD5 authentication can be configured by specifying a key string or, as with HSRP, referencing a key chain.

Configure MD5 authentication for VRRP on R1's Ethernet 0/1 interface:

```
R1(config)# interface ethernet 0/1
R1(config-if)# vrrp 1 authentication md5 key-string MyVRRP
```

In the CLI output of R1, notice the "bad authentication" message. R1 is currently configured with the MD5 authentication, whereas R2 has no VRRP authentication configured. As a consequence, routers do not consider each other as members of the same group. If you verify VRRP status on both devices, you will see that both consider themselves the master for VRRP group 1:

```
%VRRP-4-BADAUTHTYPE: Bad authentication from 192.168.1.2, group 1, type 0,
expected 254.
```

Configure MD5 authentication for VRRP on R2's Ethernet 0/1 interface:

```
R2(config)# interface ethernet 0/1
R2(config-if)# vrrp 1 authentication md5 key-string MyVRRP
```

Notice that now that you have configured matching MD5 VRRP authentications, you got a message in CLI of R1 saying that it is transitioning to backup:

```
%VRRP-6-STATECHANGE: Et0/1 Grp 1 state Master -> Backup
```

Tracking and VRRP

Without configured tracking, the VRRP master will only lose its status if a VRRP-enabled interface fails or if the VRRP router itself fails. While VRRP does not have a native interface tracking mechanism, it does have the ability to track objects.

Object tracking is an independent process that manages creating, monitoring, and removing tracked objects, such as the state of the line protocol of an interface. Clients such as HSRP or VRRP register their interest with specific tracked objects and act when the state of an object changes. Each tracked object is identified by a unique number that is specified on the tracking CLI. Client processes such as VRRP use this number to track a specific object. The tracking process periodically polls the tracked objects and notes any change of value. The changes in the tracked object are communicated to interested client processes, either immediately or after a specified delay. The object values are reported as either up or down. The priority of a device can change dynamically if it has been configured for object tracking and the object that is being tracked goes down.

Examples of objects that can be tracked are the line protocol state of an interface or the reachability of an IP route. If the specified object goes down, the VRRP priority is reduced. The VRRP router with the higher priority can now become the virtual router master if it has the preemption enabled.

Note   Objects that can be tracked depend on the IOS version and platform that you are using. Some common objects are interfaces, IP service level agreement (SLA), and IP routes.

As shown in Figure 6-24's topology, R2 is currently the VRRP master, and R1 is backup.

If R2's uplink fails, it will not lose its master status. PC1 will not lose connectivity to the server, provided that routing is properly configured. However, the path between PC 1 and the server will be suboptimal. Traffic from PC 1 will first go to R2 as default gateway, only to be rerouted to R1 and only then to the server.

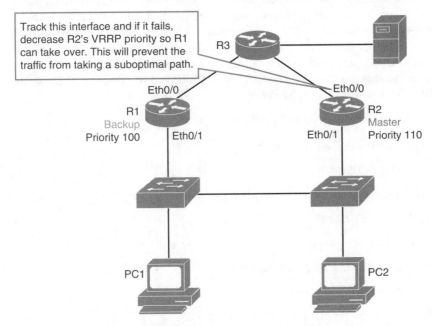

Figure 6-24 *VRRP Interface Tracking Configuration*

With HSRP, the solution to this problem was the implementation of HSRP interface tracking or implementation of object tracking. With VRRP, only the latter is possible, because it does not have a native interface tracking mechanism.

The following steps show an example of VRRP object tracking. Tracked object 1 is created and observes the line protocol status of R2's Ethernet 0/0. VRRP group 1 is told to track that object and decrease the router's VRRP priority by 20 should the uplink fail. As with HSRP, the default priority decrement is 10.

Create a tracked object, where the status of the uplink interface is tracked:

```
R2(config)#track 1 interface ethernet 0/0 line-protocol
```

Configure VRRP to track previously created object and decrease VRRP priority by 20 should the uplink fail:

```
R2(config)#interface ethernet 0/1
R2(config-if)#vrrp 1 track 1 decrement 20
```

Note For additional information, see http://www.cisco.com/c/en/us/td/docs/ios-xml/ios/ipapp_fhrp/configuration/12-4/fhp-12-4-book/fhp-vrrp.html.

Configuring Layer 3 Redundancy with GLBP

Gateway Load Balancing Protocol (GLBP), similarly to HSRP and VRRP, provides automatic router backup for IP hosts configured with a single default gateway on the LAN. Multiple first-hop routers on the LAN are combined to offer a single virtual first-hop IP address while sharing the IP packet forwarding load. Other routers on the LAN may act as redundant GLBP routers that will become active if any of the existing forwarding routers fail. So, the major difference between HSRP/VRRP and GLBP is that with the latter all GLBP routers forward traffic by default.

Upon completing this section, you will be able to do the following:

- Describe the basic idea behind GLBP

- Compare GLBP to HSRP

- Describe the possible states of GLBP virtual gateway and virtual forwarder

- Configure and verify GLBP

- Understand GLBP operations

- List and describe GLBP load-balancing options

- Secure GLBP using authentication

- Describe GLBP behavior in VLANs with running STP

- Describe the system of weights and decrements in GLBP

Introducing GLBP

GLBP shares some concepts with VRRP and HSRP, but the terminology differs, and its behavior is more dynamic and robust.

Although HSRP and VRRP provide gateway resiliency with redundant members of the FHRP group, the redundant member upstream bandwidth is not used while the device is not active. Only the active router within the group forwards the traffic for the virtual MAC. HSRP and VRRP can accomplish load sharing by manually specifying multiple groups and assigning multiple default gateways. That, however, introduces overhead in the form of additional configuration as well as supporting services, such as Dynamic Host Configuration Protocol (DHCP). In addition, because of the manual assignment of the default gateway to the end hosts, load sharing is rarely equally balanced among all participating gateways.

GLBP is a Cisco proprietary solution that allows for automatic selection and simultaneous use of multiple available gateways, in addition to automatic failover between those gateways. Multiple routers share the load of packets that, from a client's perspective, are sent to a single default gateway address.

GLBP can use resources without the administrative burden of configuring multiple groups and managing multiple default gateway configurations, as is required with HSRP and VRRP. There is also no need to configure a specific gateway address on an individual host. All hosts can use the same default gateway.

GLBP divides a function that is performed by the HSRP and VRRP routers into two roles: a gateway and a forwarder:

- **GLBP AVG (active virtual gateway):** Members of a GLBP group elect one gateway to be the AVG for that group. Other group members provide a backup for the AVG when the AVG becomes unavailable; these will be in standby state. The AVG assigns a virtual MAC address to each member of the GLBP group. The AVG listens to the ARP requests for the default gateway IP and replies with a MAC address of one of the GLBP group members, thus load sharing traffic among all the group members.

- **GLBP AVF (active virtual forwarder):** Each gateway assumes responsibility for forwarding packets that are sent to the virtual MAC address that is assigned to that gateway by the AVG. These gateways are known as AVFs. There can be up to four forwarders within a GLBP group. All other devices will be secondary forwarders, serving as backup if the current AVF fails. Forwarders that are forwarding traffic for a specific virtual MAC are in the active state and are called AVFs. Forwarders that are serving as backups are in the listen state.

Comparing GLPB to HSRP

HSRP and GLBP are Cisco proprietary protocols. VRRP is an industry standard protocol.

With HSRP, one virtual router is active and one is serving as a backup in standby mode and not forwarding traffic. GLBP has two different roles, gateway and forwarder, each with its own states. Virtual gateway shares its states with HSRP. There is one active and one standby virtual gateway; all other gateways are in the listen state. Per GLBP group, there can be up to four active forwarders (one per virtual MAC). All others are in the listen state.

GLBP members communicate with each other through hello messages that are sent by default every 3 seconds to the multicast address 224.0.0.102, UDP port 3222 (source and destination).

Table 6-4 highlights the key difference between HSRP and GLBP.

Table 6-4 *GLBP Versus HRSP*

HSRP	GLBP
Cisco proprietary, 1994.	Cisco proprietary, 2005.
1 active, 1 standby, several candidates.	Active virtual gateway (AVG): 1 active, 1 standby, several candidates.
	Active virtual forwarder (AVF): Multiple active, several candidates.

HSRP	GLBP
Virtual IP is different from real IP addresses.	Virtual IP is different from IPs on interfaces.
Uses 224.0.0.2 v1, 224.0.0.102 UDP port 1985.	Uses 224.0.0.102 UDP port 3222.
Can track interfaces or objects.	Can track only objects.
Default timers: hello 3 sec; hold time 10 sec.	Default timers: hello 3 sec; hold time 10 sec.
Authentication supported.	Authentication supported.

The routers participating in GLBP monitor each other's presence to assume the role of AVG if it fails. Monitoring is done by exchanging hello messages. These are, as with HSRP, by default sent every 3 seconds. If hello messages are not received from a GLBP peer within a "hold time," that peer is presumed to have failed. The default hold time is 10 seconds. The GLBP timers can be adjusted with the **glbp group timers [msec] hellotime [msec] holdtime glbp** *group* **timers [msec]** *hellotime* **[msec]** *holdtime* command. Timer values are given in seconds unless preceded by the **msec** keyword.

GLBP, using concepts of virtual gateway and virtual forwarder, separates the functions of protocol and traffic forwarding. Each AVF has a MAC address that is assigned to it by the AVG. With HSRP, there is only one MAC address per each HSRP group.

GLBP does not have a native interface tracking mechanism like HSRP does. Like VRRP, you can only configure object tracking. Because interface tracking is one of the options within object tracking, native interface tracking is not really missed.

Both GLBP and HSRP support two types of authentication: plain text and MD5. Out of the two, MD5 is recommended to secure GLBP group from unauthorized devices joining.

GLBP States

GLBP states of virtual gateway and virtual forwarder are slightly different, as shown in Table 6-5.

Table 6-5 *GLBP States*

State	Virtual Gateway	Virtual Forwarder
Disabled	✓	✓
Initial	✓	✓
Listen	✓	✓
Speak	✓	X
Standby	✓	X
Active	✓	✓

Following are the possible virtual gateway states:

- **Disabled:** The virtual IP address has not been configured or learned, but there is some GLBP configuration.

- **Initial:** The virtual IP address has been configured or learned, but configuration is not complete. The interface must be operational on Layer 3 and configured to route IP.

- **Listen:** The virtual gateway is receiving hello packets. It is ready to change to speak state if the active or standby virtual gateway becomes unavailable.

- **Speak:** The virtual gateway is trying to become the active or standby virtual gateway.

- **Standby:** This gateway is next in line to be the active virtual gateway.

- **Active:** This gateway is the AVG, and is responsible for responding to ARP requests for the virtual IP address.

The following are the possible virtual forwarder states:

- **Disabled:** The virtual MAC address has not been assigned or learned. The disabled virtual forwarder will be deleted shortly. This state is transitory only.

- **Initial:** The virtual MAC address is known but configuration of virtual forwarder is not complete. The interface must be operational on Layer 3 and configured to route IP.

- **Listen:** This virtual forwarder is receiving hello packets and is ready to change to the active state if the active virtual forwarder becomes unavailable.

- **Active:** This gateway is the AVF, and is responsible for forwarding packets sent to the virtual forwarder's MAC address.

Configuring and Verifying GLBP

This section covers the topology shown in Figure 6-25 and shows how to configure the GLBP and how to verify its configuration.

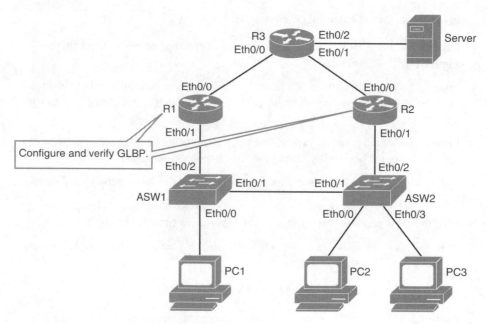

Figure 6-25   *GLBP Configuration Topology*

Figure 6-26 shows the IP addressing scheme for this exercise.

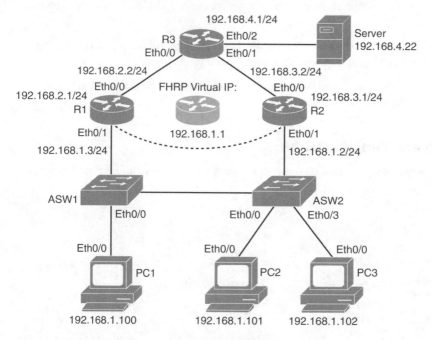

Figure 6-26   *IP Addresses Used in GLBP Configuration*

Follow these steps to configure the GLBP:

Step 1.   Configure Layer 3 redundancy with GLBP.

Configure R1's Ethernet 0/1 with IP address of 192.168.1.3 and GLBP virtual IP address of 192.168.1.1:

```
R1(config)# interface ethernet 0/1
R1(config-if)# ip address 192.168.1.3 255.255.255.0
R1(config-if)# glbp 1 ip 192.168.1.1
```

Note   The basic configuration of GLBP is very similar to those of HSRP and VRRP. To configure a GLBP group, use **glbp** *group-number* **ip** *virtual-ip-address* command, where the GLBP group is a number between 0 and 1023.

Step 2.   Configure R2's Ethernet 0/1 with IP address of 192.168.1.2 and GLBP virtual IP address of 192.168.1.1:

```
R2(config)# interface ethernet 0/1
R2(config-if)# ip address 192.168.1.2 255.255.255.0
R2(config-if)# glbp 1 ip 192.168.1.1
```

With GLBP, you do not actually need to specify the virtual IP address on non-AVG routers. You can leave it empty and the device will learn the virtual IP address from the AVG.

PC 1, PC 2, and PC 3 are already configured to use the 192.168.1.1 IP address as their default gateway. At this point, you should have a functional first-hop redundancy already working. However, much more can be done with GLBP to fine-tune its behavior.

Step 3.   Configure R1's Ethernet 0/1 with GLBP priority of 110 and enable preemption for both GLBP routers:

```
R1(config)# interface ethernet 0/1
R1(config-if)# glbp 1 priority 110
R1(config-if)# glbp 1 preempt
```

```
R2(config)# interface ethernet 0/1
R2(config-if)# glbp 1 preempt
```

Note   GLBP priority is a number between 1 and 255. The default value is 100. The GLBP-enabled device with the highest priority value is elected the AVG. If priorities of all routers are tied, the device with the highest IP address becomes the AVG.

Like with HSRP, but unlike with VRRP, GLBP has preemption disabled by default. So, by default, another router cannot take over an active role until the current active router fails. You need to explicitly enable this feature.

Step 4.   On R1, verify the status of GLBP:

```
R1# show glbp
Ethernet0/1 - Group 1
  State is Active
    1 state change, last state change 00:15:11
  Virtual IP address is 192.168.1.1
  Hello time 3 sec, hold time 10 sec
    Next hello sent in 2.240 secs
  Redirect time 600 sec, forwarder timeout 14400 sec
  Preemption enabled, min delay 0 sec
  Active is local
  Standby is 192.168.1.2, priority 100 (expires in 9.184 sec)
  Priority 110 (configured)
  Weighting 100 (default 100), thresholds: lower 1, upper 100
  Load balancing: round-robin
Group members:
    aabb.cc00.3510 (192.168.1.3) local
    aabb.cc00.3610 (192.168.1.2)
  There are 2 forwarders (1 active)
  Forwarder 1
    State is Active
      1 state change, last state change 00:14:59
    MAC address is 0007.b400.0101 (default)
    Owner ID is aabb.cc00.0910
    Redirection enabled
    Preemption enabled, min delay 30 sec
    Active is local, weighting 100
  Forwarder 2
    State is Listen
    MAC address is 0007.b400.0102 (learnt)
    Owner ID is aabb.cc00.0a10
    Redirection enabled, 599.200 sec remaining (maximum 600 sec)
    Time to live: 14399.200 sec (maximum 14400 sec)
    Preemption enabled, min delay 30 sec
    Active is 192.168.1.2 (primary), weighting 100 (expires in 11.072 sec)
```

The first part of the output refers to the status of the AVG. Notice that GLBP group 1 is configured under R1's Ethernet 0/1, and that R1 has the role of the AVG for group 1. The virtual router IP address is 192.168.1.1, and preemption is enabled. R1 sees a standby router at 192.168.1.2 (on R2). If R1 fails, R2 will assume the role of AVG of the GLBP group. The priority of virtual router on R1 is 110.

The rest of the output shows the status of virtual forwarders. In this example, there are two forwarders (1 and 2), and the AVG (R1) assigns virtual MAC addresses to them.

Step 5.   On R2, verify the status of GLBP:

```
R2# show glbp
Ethernet0/1 - Group 1
  State is Standby
    1 state change, last state change 00:14:39
  Virtual IP address is 192.168.1.1 (learnt)
  Hello time 3 sec, hold time 10 sec
    Next hello sent in 0.416 secs
  Redirect time 600 sec, forwarder timeout 14400 sec
  Preemption enabled, min delay 0 sec
  Active is 192.168.1.3, priority 110 (expires in 9.312 sec)
  Standby is local
  Priority 100 (default)
  Weighting 100 (default 100), thresholds: lower 1, upper 100
  Load balancing: round-robin
  Group members:
    aabb.cc00.3510 (192.168.1.3)
    aabb.cc00.3610 (192.168.1.2) local
  There are 2 forwarders (1 active)
  Forwarder 1
    State is Listen
    MAC address is 0007.b400.0101 (learnt)
    Owner ID is aabb.cc00.0910
    Time to live: 14398.560 sec (maximum 14400 sec)
    Preemption enabled, min delay 30 sec
    Active is 192.168.1.3 (primary), weighting 100 (expires in 9.376 sec)
  Forwarder 2
    State is Active
      1 state change, last state change 00:14:46
    MAC address is 0007.b400.0102 (default)
    Owner ID is aabb.cc00.0a10
    Preemption enabled, min delay 30 sec
    Active is local, weighting 100
```

The virtual MAC addresses of GLBP are in the form of 0007.b4XX.XXYY. XXXX is a 16-bit value that represents six 0 bits, followed by a 10-bit GLBP group number. YY is an 8-bit value, and it represents the virtual forwarder number. The AVG assigned forwarder 1 virtual MAC address of 0007. b400.0101 and forwarder 2 virtual MAC address of 0007.b400.0102, as shown in Figure 6-27.

Notice that R2's virtual router is in active state for forwarder 2. This means that it is actively forwarding traffic for clients that send traffic to the MAC address of forwarder 2. R2 is in listen state for forwarder 1. This means that R1's virtual router is the one forwarding traffic from clients that send traffic to the MAC address of forwarder 1. R2, with its forwarder 1 listen state, is serving as backup.

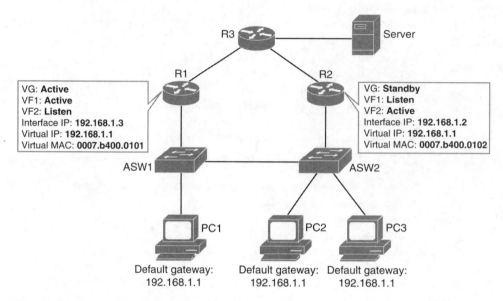

Figure 6-27 *GLBP Final Configuration*

Step 6. From PC 1, trace the path that packets take to the server at 192.168.4.22 and then verify PC 1's ARP table:

```
PC1# traceroute 192.168.4.22
Type escape sequence to abort.
Tracing the route to 192.168.4.22
VRF info: (vrf in name/id, vrf out name/id)
  1 192.168.1.3 1 msec 1 msec 0 msec
  2 192.168.2.2 2 msec 1 msec 0 msec
  3 192.168.4.22 0 msec 0 msec *
PC1# show arp
Protocol  Address         Age (min)  Hardware Addr   Type   Interface
Internet  192.168.1.1            5   0007.b400.0101  ARPA   Ethernet0/0
Internet  192.168.1.100          -   aabb.cc00.0200  ARPA   Ethernet0/0
```

You can see from the output that PC 1 has its default gateway configured to 192.168.1.1 and that the MAC address it associates with this IP is that of the device that is active for AVF1. Because R1 is the AVF 1, PC 1's traffic goes through R1.

Step 7.   From PC 2, trace the path that packets take to the server at 192.168.4.22 and then verify PC 2's ARP table:

```
PC2# traceroute 192.168.4.22
Type escape sequence to abort.
Tracing the route to 192.168.4.22
VRF info: (vrf in name/id, vrf out name/id)
  1 192.168.1.2 0 msec 0 msec 1 msec
  2 192.168.3.2 0 msec 0 msec 0 msec
  3 192.168.4.22 0 msec 1 msec *
PC2# show arp
Protocol  Address          Age (min)  Hardware Addr   Type   Interface
Internet  192.168.1.1              4  0007.b400.0102  ARPA   Ethernet0/0
Internet  192.168.1.101            -  aabb.cc00.0300  ARPA   Ethernet0/0
```

You can see from the output that PC 2 has its default gateway configured to 192.168.1.1 and that the MAC address it associates with this IP is that of the device that is active for VF2. Because R2 is the AVF 2, PC 2's traffic goes through R2.

Step 8.   From PC 3, trace the path that packets take to the server at 192.168.4.22, and then verify PC 3's ARP table:

```
PC3# traceroute 192.168.4.22
Type escape sequence to abort.
Tracing the route to 192.168.4.22
VRF info: (vrf in name/id, vrf out name/id)
  1 192.168.1.3 1005 msec 0 msec 0 msec
  2 192.168.2.2 0 msec 1 msec 0 msec
  3 192.168.4.22 1 msec 1 msec *
PC3# show arp
Protocol  Address          Age (min)  Hardware Addr   Type   Interface
Internet  192.168.1.1              2  0007.b400.0101  ARPA   Ethernet0/0
Internet  192.168.1.102            -  aabb.cc00.1800  ARPA   Ethernet0/0
```

You can see from the output that PC 3 has its default gateway configured to 192.168.1.1 and that the MAC address it associates with this IP is that of the device that is active for VF1. Because R1 is the AVF 1, PC 3's traffic goes through R1.

After the GLBP group is established, all PCs will send ARP requests. The ARP request is a broadcast as shown in Figure 6-28.

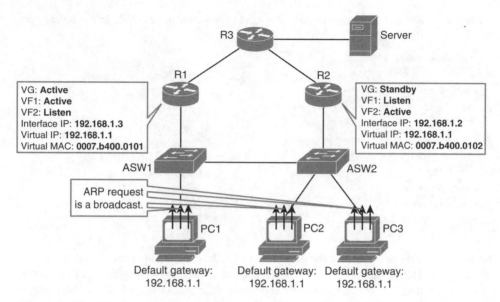

Figure 6-28 *GLBP Operations: ARP Broadcast*

The AVG, in this instance a role assigned to R1, responds to ARP requests by using the configured load-balancing method. By default, the load-balancing method is round-robin. So, PC 1 received ARP 0007.b400.0101, PC 2 received ARP 0007.b400.0102, and PC 3 received ARP 0007.b400.0101. MAC address 0007.b400.0101 is a virtual MAC address of the AVF 1, and 0007.b400.0102 is a virtual MAC address of the AVF 2, as shown in Figure 6-29.

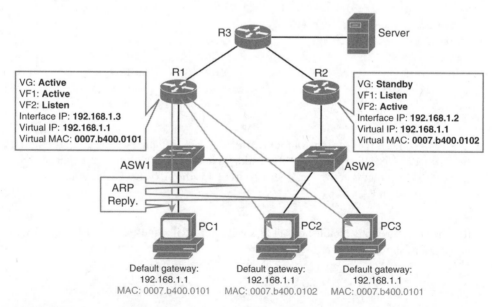

Figure 6-29 *GLBP Operations: Virtual MAC Address Assignment*

So, even though all PCs have the same configured default gateway, devices will send data to different first hops. PC 1 and PC 3 will send data to the AVF 1 (in this case, R1). PC2 will send data to AVF 2 (in this case, R2), as shown in Figure 6-30.

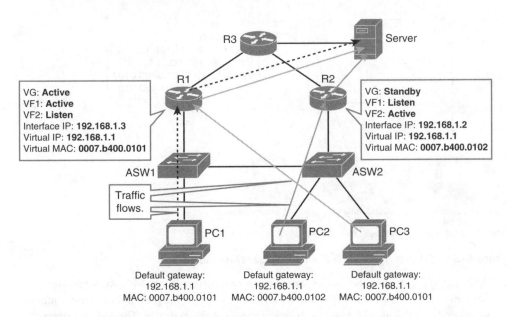

Figure 6-30 *GLBP Operations: Traffic Path for Each PC*

Now, simulate the failure on R1 by shutting down the Ethernet 0/0 and Ethernet 0/1:

```
R1(config)# interface range ethernet 0/0, ethernet 0/1
R1(config-if-range)# shutdown
```

On R2, investigate GLBP status:

```
R2# show glbp brief
Interface   Grp  Fwd  Pri  State   Address          Active router     Standby router
Et0/1       1    -    100  Active  192.168.1.1      local             unknown
Et0/1       1    1    -    Active  0007.b400.0101   local             -
Et0/1       1    2    -    Active  0007.b400.0102   local             -
```

Notice that R2 is now the AVG for group 1. Because R2 is the only functional GLBP-enabled device of group 1, it is also elected to be AVF 1 and AVF 2. R2 will now forward traffic for all clients (PC 1, PC 2, and PC 3), as shown in Figure 6-31.

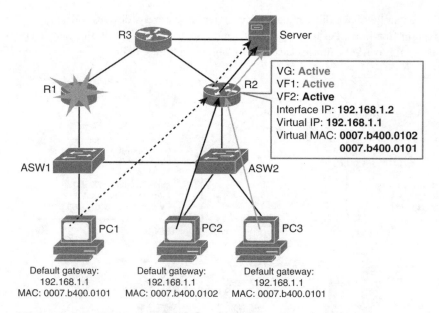

Figure 6-31 *GLBP Operations: Failed R1 New Data Path*

Although the virtual router at this moment has two different virtual MAC addresses to support function for two AVFs, it does not make sense to keep them both for a longer time period. AVG maintains two different timers for this purpose. The redirect timer is used to determine when the AVG will stop using the old virtual MAC address in ARP replies. The AVF that uses an old virtual MAC address continues to act as a gateway for any client that tries to use it. When the timeout timer expires, the old MAC address of the virtual router and the virtual forwarder are flushed from all GLBP peers. AVG assumes that old AVF will not return to service, so the resource (virtual MAC address) is reclaimed. Clients using an old MAC address must refresh the entry to obtain a new virtual MAC address. By default, the redirect timer is 10 minutes, and the timeout timer is 4 hours.

GLBP Load-Balancing Options

The AVG within the GLBP group is the one that ensures that traffic will be load balanced between the end devices and their first hop. AVG hands out virtual MAC addresses to clients in a deterministic fashion. Each virtual MAC address belongs to one AVF and is assigned to AVF by the AVG. Up to four MAC addresses (that is, four AVFs) can be used in a GLBP group.

GLBP supports the following operational modes for load balancing traffic across multiple default routers that are servicing the same default gateway IP address:

■ **Weighted load-balancing algorithm:** The amount of load that is directed to a router depends on the weighting value that is advertised by that router.

■ **Host-dependent load-balancing algorithm:** A host is guaranteed the use of the same virtual MAC address as long as that virtual MAC address is participating in the GLBP group.

■ **Round-robin load-balancing algorithm:** As clients send ARP requests to resolve the MAC address of the default gateway, the reply to each client contains the MAC address of the next possible router in a round-robin fashion. The MAC addresses of all routers take turns being included in address resolution replies for the default gateway IP address.

To configure the load-balancing option, use the following command:

```
Switch(config-if)# glbp group load-balancing [round-robin|
weighted| host-dependent]
```

GLBP automatically manages the virtual MAC address assignment, determines who handles the forwarding, and ensures that each station has a forwarding path in the event of failures to gateways or tracked interfaces. If failures occur, the load-balancing ratio is adjusted among the remaining AVFs so that resources are used in the most efficient way.

GLBP Authentication

MD5 authentication provides greater security than the alternative plain-text authentication scheme and protects against spoofing software. MD5 authentication allows each GLBP group member to use a secret key to generate a keyed MD5 hash that is part of the outgoing packet. A keyed hash of an incoming packet is generated, and if the hash within the incoming packet does not match the generated hash, the packet is ignored.

The key for the MD5 hash can either be given directly in the configuration using a key string or supplied indirectly through a key chain. The key string cannot exceed 100 characters in length. The following example demonstrates the configuration for GLBP authentication:

```
Router(config)# interface Ethernet0/1
Router(config-if)# ip address 10.0.0.1 255.255.255.0
Router(config-if)# glbp 1 authentication md5 key-string d00b4r987654321a
Router(config-if)# glbp 1 ip 10.0.0.10
```

This same configuration must be applied on all other GLBP peers.

GLBP and STP

With some switching topologies, the operation of STP results in inefficient traffic paths. In such cases, implementation of HSRP might be preferred over GLBP because it is easier to understand, whereas GLBP provides no advantages.

Topologies with layer 2 loops (such as the one on Figure 6-32, where distribution Layer 3 switches are interconnected) run STP, which blocks some of the access-distribution links. The end hosts now only have a direct connection with SW1.

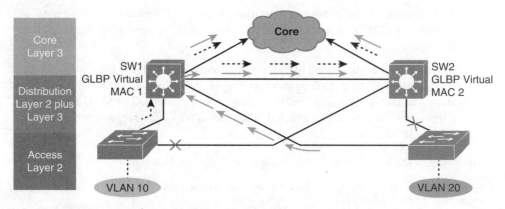

Figure 6-32   *GLBP and STP*

With GLBP configured, SW1 serves as an AVF for some of the end hosts, routing traffic toward the core, while the other half of the traffic is forwarded to SW2, which serves as the other AVF. While distribution-core links are now load balanced, half of the traffic is taking a suboptimal route, passing through both SW1 and SW2, before being routed to the core.

In environments with STP and multiple VLANs, GLBP's load sharing might not be of value, and the configuration of a multigroup HSRP aligned with STP topology may be preferred.

Tracking and GLBP

Changing weight affects the AVF election and the load-balancing algorithm. Both values can be manipulated with object tracking.

In the example shown in Figure 6-33, GLBP gateway S1 is the AVG of GLBP group. This means that S1 is the one that assigns MAC addresses to AVFs of the group, and it is also the one that answers to ARP replies of clients. Both gateways, S1 and S2, are AVFs. S1 is an active forwarder 1, and S2 is an active forwarder 2. All PCs are configured with the same virtual IP address for their default gateway. The AVG will assign virtual MAC addresses to the PCs through ARP replies. About half of PCs will have the virtual MAC address of AVF1 (these PCs will have traffic forwarded through S1) and the other half will have the virtual MAC address of AVF2 (these PCs will have traffic forwarded through S2).

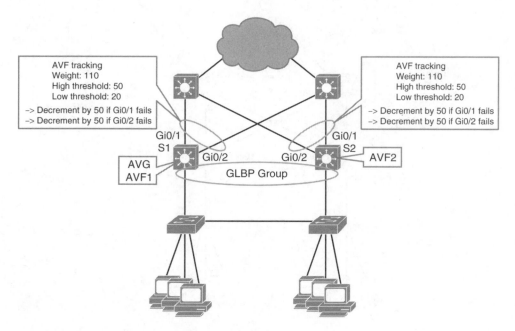

Figure 6-33   *GLBP and Object Tracking Scenario*

GLBP uses a weighting scheme to determine the forwarding capacity of each router in the GLBP group. The weighting that is assigned to a router in the GLBP group can be used to determine whether it will forward packets and, if so, the proportion of hosts in the LAN for which it will forward packets. Thresholds can be set to disable forwarding when the weighting for a GLBP group falls below a certain value, and when it rises above another threshold, forwarding is automatically reenabled.

The GLBP group weighting can be automatically adjusted by tracking the state of an interface within the router. If a tracked interface goes down, the GLBP group weighting is reduced by a specified value. Different interfaces can be tracked to decrement the GLBP weighting by varying amounts.

By default, the GLBP virtual forwarder preemptive scheme is enabled with a delay of 30 seconds. A backup virtual forwarder can become the AVF if the current AVF weighting falls below the low weighting threshold for 30 seconds. To disable the GLBP forwarder preemptive scheme, use the **no glbp forwarder preempt** command or change the delay by using the **glbp forwarder preempt delay minimum** command.

So, let's look at S1 for a moment, as shown in Figure 6-34. It has configured weighting of 110. If S1's Gi0/1 fails, its weighting will be lowered by 50 to 60. At this point, S1 is still the AVF1 because its weight did not go under the lower threshold of 20. If Gi0/2 also fails, the weight of GLBP groups gets decreased to 10. Now, S1's GLBP group has a weight under the configured lower threshold, and so S1 loses its AVF1 role. S2 is now active for forwarders 1 and 2. All PCs will now use S2 to forward traffic.

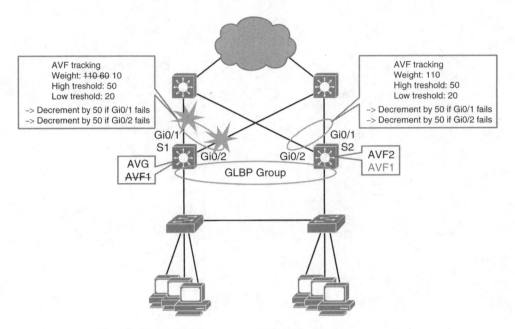

Figure 6-34 *GLBP Tracking Detects Interface Failure*

When either of S1's uplinks comes back up, the weight of S1's virtual router gets incremented by 50. Because the weight went from 10 to 60, it breached the configured high threshold of 50. This means S1 is eligible to become AVF1 again.

How does the weight value influence the traffic flows through S1 or S2? If load balancing for the GLBP group is configured as weighted, traffic distribution should look like what is shown in Table 6-6.

Table 6-6 *GLBP Weighing Option Under Failures*

Number of Active Uplinks on S1	Number of Active Uplinks on S2	Traffic Through S1
2	2	50% (110:110)
2	1	65% (110:60)
2	0	100% (S2 not eligible to forward)
0	2	0% (S1 not eligible to forward)
1	2	35% (60:110)
1	1	50% (110:110)
1	0	100% (S2 not eligible to forward)
0	1	0% (S1 not eligible to forward)
0	0	0% (none eligible for forwarding)

Traffic percentage calculations in the table are approximations, based on the assumption that all end devices produce the same amount of traffic. The more end devices in a GLBP group, the closer real traffic patterns get to those numbers.

If load balancing is configured as round-robin, then, as long as both S1 and S2 are eligible to forward, traffic will be about 50:50 between both first hops.

Configuring tracking through "weighting" does not have an effect on the election of AVG. S1, in this example, will be the AVG as long it has connectivity to S2. Because the only role of AVG is to assign MAC addresses to AVFs and clients, uplink failures do not affect AVG's performance.

To configure tracking, you first need to configure a tracked object. The available tracking options depend on the platform and the software version you are using. Some common examples are interface status, IP SLA, and IP route.

The second part of configuration is to configure the weight of the virtual router and its lower and upper thresholds.

The third part of configuration is to tell GLBP to track the object that is configured. The default decrement is 10.

Figure 6-35 displays the sample configuration for the object tracking for GLBP for S1's downlink (see Example 6-4). Similar configuration applies for S2's downlink.

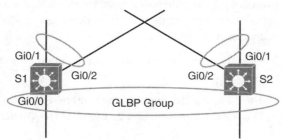

```
s1(config)# track 1 interface GigabitEthernet0/1 line-protocol
s1(config)# track 2 interface GigabitEthernet0/2 line-protocol
s1(config-track)# interface GigabitEthernet0/0
s1(config-if)# ip address 192.168.1.2 255.255.255.0
s1(config-if)# glbp 1 ip 192.168.1.1
s1(config-if)# glbp 1 priority 110
s1(config-if)# glbp 1 preempt
s1(config-if)# glbp 1 weighting 110 lower 20 upper 50
s1(config-if)# glbp 1 weighting track 1 decrement 50
s1(config-if)# glbp 1 weighting track 2 decrement 50
```

Figure 6-35 *GLBP Object Tracking Sample Configuration*

Example 6-4   *GLBP Object Tracking Sample Configuration*

```
S1(config)# track 1 interface GigabitEthernet0/1 line-protocol
S1(config)# track 2 interface GigabitEthernet0/2 line-protocol
S1(config-track)# interface GigabitEthernet 0/0
S1(config-if)# ip address 192.168.1.2 255.255.255.0
S1(config-if)# glbp 1 ip 192.168.1.1
S1(config-if) # glbp 1 priority 110
S1(config-if)# glbp 1 preempt
S1(config-if)# glbp 1 weighing 110 lower 20 upper 50
S1(config-if)# glbp 1 weighing track 1 decrement 50
S1(config-if)# glbp 1 weighing  track 2 decrement 50
```

Note   For additional information, see http://www.cisco.com/c/en/us/td/docs/ios-xml/ios/ipapp_fhrp/configuration/15-mt/fhp-15-mt-book/fhp-glbp.html.

Study Tips

- The redundancy protocol provides the mechanism for determining which router should take the active role in forwarding traffic and determining when that role must be taken over by a standby router.

- HSRP is a Cisco proprietary protocol, whereas VRRP is an industry standard for virtual routing gateways.

- HSRP Version 1 and Version 2 active and standby routers send hello messages to multicast address 224.0.0.2 for Version 1 and 224.0.0.102 for Version 2 on UDP port 1985.

- It is important that the configured active router should be the same as the STP root bridge.

- HSRP and VRRP use the VLAN load-balancing mechanism for load balancing.

- With the new RFC, only the Cisco implementation of VRRP supports VRRP authentication.

- GLBP, by default, provides the virtual gateway and load balancing via multiple virtual MAC addresses.

- Review all the configuration examples and troubleshooting steps for better understanding and for exam preparation.

Summary

HSRP operates with one router acting as active and the other backup router as a standby router. The active, standby, and other HSRP routers use a virtual IP address for redundancy to hosts. If the active router fails, the standby router becomes the active router and takes responsibility of the destination MAC and IP of the virtual IP address. In this manner, HSRP failover is transparent to the host. Routers running HSRP can be configured for preemption such that if a higher-priority HSRP peer comes online, the higher-priority router takes over the active router role. Otherwise, the latest active router remains the active router when new HSRP peers come online.

VRRP is similar to HSRP except that VRRP is an industry standard, whereas HSRP is a Cisco proprietary protocol. GLBP is another Cisco feature in which multiple routers not only act as backup default gateway routers but also share the load in forwarding traffic, unlike HSRP and VRRP, where only the active router forwards traffic. Note that HSPR and VRRP can be distributed across VLANs, achieving load balancing using VLANs.

GLBP provides router redundancy and out-of-the-box gateway load balancing by using the single virtual IP address like HSRP but multiple virtual MAC addresses for each forwarder, unlike HSRP and VRRP. Members of a GLBP group elect one gateway to be the active virtual gateway (AVG) for that group. The main function of AVG is to provide the virtual MAC to each forwarder and answer clients' ARP replies with virtual MAC addresses. Each gateway assumes responsibility for forwarding packets sent to the virtual MAC address assigned to it by the AVG. These gateways are known as active virtual forwarders (AVFs) for their virtual MAC address. You can have up to five active forwarders per GLBP group.

References

For additional information, refer to the following

- HSRP Features and Functionality: http://www.cisco.com/c/en/us/support/docs/ip/hot-standby-router-protocol-hsrp/9234-hsrpguidetoc.html

- Configuring VRRP: http://www.cisco.com/c/en/us/td/docs/ios-xml/ios/ipapp_fhrp/configuration/12-4/fhp-12-4-book/fhp-vrrp.html

- GLBP Configuration Guide: http://www.cisco.com/c/en/us/td/docs/ios-xml/ios/ipapp_fhrp/configuration/15-mt/fhp-15-mt-book/fhp-glbp.html

Review Questions

Use the questions here to review what you learned in this chapter. The correct answers are found in Appendix A, "Answers to Chapter Review Questions."

1. Which command enables HSRP on a Cisco IOS device?

   a. `standby virtual ip 10.1.1.1`

   b. `standby ip 10.1.1.1 group 1`

   c. `hsrp 1 ip 10.1.1.1`

   d. `standby 1 ip 10.1.1.1`

2. Which HSRP group uses the MAC address 0000.0c07.ac01?

   a. Group 0

   b. Group 7

   c. Group 11

   d. Group 1

3. If you have four routers enabled for the same HSRP group, how many of them will be in standby state?

   a. 0

   b. 1

   c. 2

   d. All, except the active router

4. Which VRRP group uses the MAC address 0000.5e00.01ff?

   a. Group 0

   b. Group 1

   c. Group 255

   d. Group 94

5. What is the primary difference between VRRP and HSRP?

   a. HSRP is a standard protocol, whereas VRRP is Cisco proprietary.

   b. VRRP is a standard protocol, whereas HSRP is Cisco proprietary.

   c. HSRP is configured at the global level, whereas VRRP is configured at the interface level.

   d. VRRP offers Layer 2 first-hop redundancy, whereas HSRP offers Layer 3 first-hop redundancy.

6. Which IP address should a client PC use as its default gateway if you have the following configuration on a multilayer switch?

```
interface ethernet 0/1
no switchport
ip address 192.168.199.3 255.255.255.0
vrrp 1 ip address 192.168.199.2
```

    a. 192.168.199.1

    b. 192.168.199.2

    c. 192.168.199.3

    d. Any of the above

7. By default, which MAC address will be sent to the next client that is asking for the GLBP virtual gateway?

    a. 0007.a400.0102

    b. Next virtual MAC in sequence

    c. Virtual MAC of the least-used router

    d. Virtual MAC address of HSRP

8. At a maximum, how many active virtual forwarders can be there within a GLBP group?

    a. 1

    b. 2

    c. 4

    d. 8

9. Which of the following best describes the GLBP *standby* virtual gateway state?

    a. The virtual IP address has not been configured or learned, but there is some GLBP configuration.

    b. The virtual IP address has been configured or learned, but configuration is not complete. The interface must be operational on Layer 3 and configured to route IP.

    c. The virtual gateway is receiving hello packets. It is ready to change to speak state if the active or standby virtual gateway becomes unavailable.

    d. The virtual gateway is trying to become the active or standby virtual gateway.

    e. This gateway is next in line to be the active virtual gateway.

Chapter 7

Network Management

This chapter covers the following topics related to network management and mobility:

- AAA

- Identity-based networking

- 802.1X

- NTP, SNTP, and PTP

- SNMPv3

This chapter covers both mobility and the following critical network management features of any campus network: AAA, NTP, SNMP, and 802.1X. These features ensure proper manageability, control, access, time synchronicity, and event alerts. Although these features are labeled as best practices, they are essentially configuration requirements for any campus network.

AAA

Authentication, authorization, and accounting (AAA, pronounced "triple A") represents an architectural framework through which the network access control policy is enforced on the networking device. The three main functions of the model, configurable in a consistent manner, are as follows:

- **Authentication:** Authentication is the process of identifying a user before that user is allowed access to a protected resource. A user presents valid credentials, which are then compared with security information in a user database. In addition, authentication may offer other services depending on the security protocol selected, such as an additional challenge and response, messaging support, or encryption.

- **Authorization:** After the user gains access to the network, authorization is performed. Authorization allows you to control the level of access users have. For example, via authorization, you can define which privileged EXEC commands are available to the user, or you may control remote access (allowing the user to use protocols such as Point-to-Point Protocol [PPP] or Serial Line Internet Protocol [SLIP]). User capabilities are defined by a set of attribute-value (AV) pairs, which are associated with the user or the user's group. These pairs may be stored locally on the device or on centralized TACACS+/RADIUS server(s).

  When a user tries to perform some specific function, such as configuring an IP address on an interface, the AAA engine on the device queries the authorization server for that specific attribute and user. Based on the reply from the server (that is, the value of the user's attribute in question), the user is then allowed or not allowed to perform that specific function.

- **Accounting:** Accounting is performed after authentication. Accounting enables you to collect information about the user activity and resource consumption. You can log user logins, commands executed by the user, session durations, bytes transferred, and so on. The network device sends this information in the form of attribute-value pairs to the accounting server. Therefore, user activity information from all devices in your network is located in one central place. This information may be leveraged for billing, auditing, and reporting purposes.

Authentication can be valid without authorization and accounting. Authorization and accounting, however, cannot be performed without the authentication.

Although AAA requires additional configuration overhead, there is a tremendous advantage to using AAA. In today's campus networks, AAA is required. The value AAA brings to the network is summarized as follows:

- **Increased flexibility and control of access configuration:** Although Cisco IOS offers possibilities to configure local usernames and passwords, line passwords, and enable secrets without the use of AAA, these methods do not offer a satisfactory level of flexibility and control. AAA offers additional authorization flexibility on a per-command or per-interface level, which is unavailable with local credentials.

- **Scalability:** Storing usernames and passwords in a local database on a device may be an appropriate solution for a small network with a small number of users. As the network grows, managing a large number of users on multiple devices becomes highly impractical and error-prone, with a lot of administrative burden. Outdated credentials or lack of credentials leads to a usage of a single username by a number of network administrators, which results in the inability to track activities back to a single user. The AAA model is the only solution that scales well.

- **Standardized authentication methods:** AAA supports the RADIUS protocol, which is an industry open standard. This ensures interoperability and allows flexibility because you can mix and match different vendors. For example, you can have your network built with Cisco equipment and have a AAA server from another vendor, or you can even build your own custom AAA server based on RADIUS.

■ **Multiple backup systems:** You may specify multiple servers when configuring authentication options on the method list, combining them in a server group. In case of a server failure, the AAA engine on the device will continue to query the next server from the server group.

Authentication Options

Generally speaking, authentication is based on something the user knows (username and password), something the user has (digital certificate issued by certification authority), or something the user is (biometrical scanners which can identify him by his fingerprint or eye retina).

Whichever method is used, the information provided by the user is compared with the information stored in the authentication database. If a match exists, the user is then granted access to the network. The authentication database may be stored either locally on a network device or on a centralized server. In any campus network, databases must be stored on centralized servers; otherwise, local databases become too cumbersome to manage.

Nevertheless, the AAA model on Cisco IOS allows you to configure both local and remote authentication. Configuration is done with the **aaa authentication** command. With this command, the first configuration step is to specify a service type for the authentication. A service type might be a login for command-line interface (CLI) login authentication (**console**, **telnet**, **ssh**, and so on), **ppp** for PPP connections, and so on.

You must also specify a method list. You can specify a default method list with the **default** keyword. The default method list applies to any interface, line, or service if a more specific named method list is not defined. It is typically used in smaller/medium environments where there is a single shared AAA infrastructure. In addition, named method lists can be specified. When defined, a named method list must be explicitly applied to an interface, line, or service. The explicitly applied list to an interface over-rides the default method list. Ultimately, you will define named method lists according to your needs. However, it is recommended to be consistent and keep it simple by lever-aging common lists across multiple interfaces.

You also need to specify a single authentication method or a list of authentication methods. Multiple authentication methods are available, such as local for local database authentication or group to configure groups of remote RADIUS or TACACS+ servers. When multiple authentication methods are configured, additional methods of authen-tication are used only if the previous method returns an error, not if it fails. To specify that the authentication should succeed even if all methods return an error, configure the **none** option as the final method in the command line. Usage of the **none** authentication method is discouraged in production environments because it allows access without suc-cessful authentication.

It is best practice to have multiple methods of authentication in case the primary authentication is down or unreachable. If the primary is down and no backup authentication method exists, you cannot access the network device in question.

The next subsection covers RADIUS and TACACS+. Later subsections provide a few examples of the commands mentioned in this subsection.

RADIUS and TACACS+ Overview

RADIUS and TACACS+ are AAA protocols. Both use the client/server model, as shown in Figure 7-1. As shown in Step 1 of Figure 7-1, a user or machine sends a request to a networking device such as a router that acts as a network access server when running AAA. The network access server then communicates (2, 3) with the server exchanging RADIUS or TACACS+ messages. If authentication is successful, the user is granted (4) an access to a protected resource (5), such as a device CLI, network, and so on. Cisco implements the AAA server functionality in the Cisco Secure Access Control Server (ACS) and Identity Services Engine (ISE), for example.

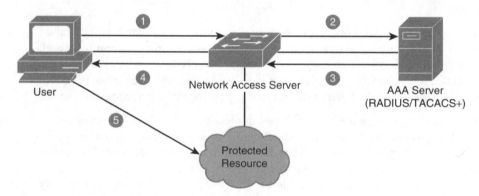

Figure 7-1   *RADIUS and TACACS+ Overview*

RADIUS is a fully open standard protocol developed by Livingston Enterprises. It is described in RFCs 2865 (authentication and authorization) and 2866 (accounting). RADIUS uses UDP port 1812 for the authentication and authorization, and thus combines authentication and authorization into one service. For the accounting service, RADIUS uses UDP port 1813. Communication between the network access server (NAS) and RADIUS server is not completely secure; only the password portion of the RADIUS packet header is encrypted.

TACACS+ is a Cisco proprietary protocol not compatible with the older versions such as TACACS or XTACACS, which are now deprecated. TACACS+ also allows for greater modularity, by the total separation of all three AAA functions. In addition, TACACS+ uses TCP port 49, and thus reliability is ensured by the transport protocol itself. In terms of security, the entire TACACS+ packet is encrypted, so communication between NAS and the TACACS+ server is completely secure. Table 7-1 summarizes the differences between RADIUS and TACACS+.

Table 7-1 *TACACS+ Versus RADIUS*

Feature	RADIUS	TACACS+
Developer	Livingston Enterprise (now industry standard)	Cisco (proprietary)
Transport protocol	UDP ports 1812 and 1813	TCP port 49
AAA support	Combines authentication and authorization and separates accounting	Uses the AAA model and separates all three services
Challenge response	One-way, unidirectional (single challenge response)	Two-way, bidirectional (multiple challenge responses)
Security	Encrypts only the password in the packet	Encrypts the entire packet body

RADIUS Authentication Process

As illustrated in Figure 7-2, the RADIUS authentication process between the NAS and RADIUS server starts when a client sends a login request in the form of an Access-Request packet. This packet contains a username, encrypted password, the NAS IP address, and the NAS port number.

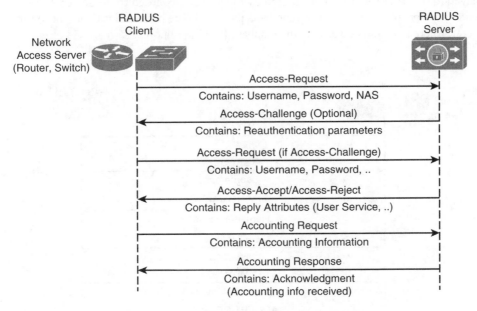

Figure 7-2 *RADIUS Authentication Process*

When the RADIUS server receives the query, it first compares the shared secret key sent in the request packet with the value configured on the server. When shared secrets are not identical, the server silently drops the packet. This ensures that only authorized clients can communicate with the server. If shared secrets are identical, the packet is further processed, comparing the username and password inside the packet with those found in the database.

If a match is found, the server returns an Access-Accept packet with a list of attributes to be used with this session in the form of AV pairs (IP address, access control list [ACL] for NAS). If a match is not found, however, the RADIUS server returns an Access-Reject packet. It is important to notice that authentication and authorization phases are combined in a single Access-Request packet, unlike TACACS+.

During the authentication and authorization phase, an optional Access-Challenge message may be requested by the RADIUS server with the purpose of collecting additional data (PIN, token card, and so on), further verifying the client's identity.

Moreover, the accounting phase is realized separately after the authentication and authorization phases, using Accounting-Request and Accounting-Response messages.

TACACS+ Authentication Process

As shown in Figure 7-3, TACACS+ communication between the NAS and the TACACS+ server starts with a TCP communication, unlike RADIUS (which uses UDP). Next, the NAS contacts the TACACS+ server to obtain a username prompt, which is then displayed to the user. The username entered by the user is forwarded to the server. The server prompts the user again, this time for a password. The password is then sent to the server, where it is validated against the database (local or remote).

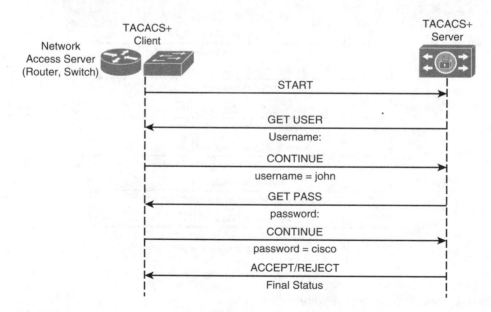

TACACS+ Authentication Communication

Figure 7-3 *TACACS+ Authentication Process*

If a match is found, the TACACS+ server sends an ACCEPT message to the client, and the authorization phase may begin (if configured on the NAS). If a match is not found, however, the server responds with a REJECT message, and any further access is denied.

Recall from earlier discussions that TACACS+ separates all its functions.

Configuring AAA

To enable AAA, the first step is to configure the **aaa new-model** command in global configuration mode. This step essentially enables AAA capability. In addition, until this command is enabled, all other AAA commands are hidden.

As discussed earlier, AAA supports a variety of authentication options. For example, you can use external authentication servers such as RADIUS or TACACS+, or you may specify a local database. Despite these options, it is best practice to configure a local username, to serve as a backup, should all external servers fail. Example 7-1 shows a sample local username and password configuration using the local **username** *user-secret* **password** command.

Example 7-1   *Username and Password Configuration Example*

```
Switch(config)# username User123 secret Secretpwd
```

> **Note**   The **aaa new-model** command immediately applies local authentication to all lines and interfaces (except console line con 0). To avoid being locked out of the router, it is a best practice to define a local username and password before starting the AAA configuration.

To use the local database for authentication, you must specify the **local** keyword in the **aaa authentication** command. To use the local database only as a backup option, specify the **local** keyword at the very end of the authentication methods list in the **aaa authentication** command. Later examples demonstrate these configurations.

Configuring RADIUS for Console and vty Access

The first step in configuring AAA with RADIUS is to specify and configure the RADIUS servers. The following commands illustrate a RADIUS server configuration:

```
Switch(config)# radius server configuration-name
Switch(config-radius-server)# address ipv4 hostname [auth-port integer] [acct-port integer]
Switch(config-radius-server)# key string
```

Configuration-name is just a text identifier for the server in question. In the subconfiguration, the DNS hostname or the IP address is specified. Specification of a custom port number for the UDP communication is optional and rarely used for the case of leveraging nondefault ports. Note that the port numbers for authentication and accounting are different. The **key** string specifies the authentication and encryption key used between the access device and RADIUS server. This value must match on both devices.

The next step is to add the RADIUS server to a server group. You can add multiple RADIUS servers to a group, as long as they were previously defined using the **radius server** command. The following commands configure the RADIUS server group:

```
Switch(config)# aaa group server radius group-name
Switch(config-sg-radius)# server name configuration-name
```

Example 7-2 shows commands to configure a RADIUS server with the IP address 172.16.1.1 using key cisco456 as a part of the group Mygroup2.

Example 7-2 *RADIUS Configuration Example*

```
Switch(config)# radius server myRadius
Switch(config-radius-server)# address ipv4 172.16.1.1
Switch(config-radius-server)# key cisco456
Switch(config)# aaa group server radius Mygroup2
Switch(config-sg-radius)# server name myRadius
```

To configure a login authentication using a named method list radius_list, server group Mygroup2 as primary authentication option, and a local user database as a backup, use the following command:

```
Switch(config)# aaa authentication login radius_list group Mygroup2 local
```

The final step is to apply this method list to the vty0 line. Example 7-3 illustrates this configuration.

Example 7-3 *Apply RADIUS Method List to vty Example*

```
Switch(config)# line vty 0
Switch(config-line)# login authentication radius_list
```

Configuring TACACS+ for Console and vty Access

TACACS+ AAA configuration is nearly identical to RADIUS configuration. As with RADIUS, the first step is to configure the TACACS+ servers using the following commands:

```
Switch(config)# tacacs server configuration-name
Switch(config-server-tacacs)# address ipv4 hostname
Switch(config-server-tacacs)# port integer
Switch(config-server-tacacs)# key string
```

The *configuration-name* is just a text identifier for the server in question. In the subconfiguration, the DNS hostname or the IP address of the server is specified. Specification of a custom port number for the UDP communication is optional and used in the case of leveraging nondefault ports. The **key** string specifies the authentication and encryption key used between the access device and TACACS+ server. This value must match on both devices.

The next step is to add the TACACS+ server to a server group. You can add multiple TACACS+ servers to a group, as long as they were previously defined using the **tacacs server** command. The following commands configure the TACACS+ server group:

```
Switch(config)# aaa group server tacacs+ group-name
Switch(config-sg-tacacs+)# server name configuration-name
```

Example 7-4 shows how to configure a TACACS+ server with the IP address 192.168.1.1 using a shared secret key cisco123 as a part of the server group Mygroup1.

Example 7-4 *TACACS+ Configuration Example*

```
Switch(config)# tacacs server myTacacs
Switch(config-server-tacacs)# address ipv4 192.168.1.1
Switch(config-server-tacacs)# key cisco123
Switch(config)# aaa group server tacacs+ Mygroup1
Switch(config-sg-tacacs+)# server name myTacacs
```

Example 7-5 shows how to configure a default login authentication and EXEC authorization with the server group Mygroup1 as a primary authentication option and a local user database as a backup.

Example 7-5 *TACACS+ Method List Configuration Example*

```
Switch(config)# aaa authentication login default group Mygroup1 local
Switch(config)# aaa authorization exec default group Mygroup1 local
```

Note that the default method list is automatically applied to all interfaces except those that have a named method list explicitly defined.

AAA Authorization

As mentioned earlier, AAA authorization goes beyond authentication to control what actions, commands, and so on a user is allowed to perform. Authorization has the same rules and configuration principles as authentication. Therefore, to configure authorization, complete the following steps:

Step 1.   Define a named list of authorization methods.

Step 2.   Apply that list to one or more interfaces (except for the default method list).

Step 3.   The first listed method is used. If it fails to respond, the second one is used, and so on until all listed methods are exhausted. Once the method list is exhausted, a failure message is logged.

For example, review the configuration command from Example 7-6.

Example 7-6   *Sample RADIUS AAA Configuration*

```
aaa authentication login default group radius local
```

Based on Example 7-6, all users who log in to the network device must be authorized using RADIUS or the local database if the RADIUS server is not functioning, before any actions can be processed.

For authorization, the AAA server leverages specific attributes for users or groups of users. Formally, Cisco devices refer to these values as RADIUS attribute-value (AV) pairs. The nomenclature of AV pairs is commonly used.

For example, if the specific user who logs in to the device is to be granted enable mode access directly, the shell:priv-lvl=15 Cisco AV pair must be configured on the AAA server. This privilege level will allow the user to enter enable mode commands.

Note that specifics about Cisco AV pairs and RADIUS server configuration are beyond the scope of CCNP. You can find details about Cisco AV pairs on Cisco.com. As a review, the following commands configure AAA authorization:

```
Switch(config)# aaa authorization authorization-type list-name method-list
Switch(config)# line line-type line-number
Switch(config)# authorization {arap | commands level | exec | reverse-access}
list-name
```

AAA Accounting

The AAA accounting feature enables you to track the services that users are accessing and the amount of network resources that they are consuming.

AAA accounting has the same rules and configuration steps as authentication and authorization:

Step 1.   You must first define a named list of accounting methods.

Step 2.   Apply that list to one or more interfaces (except for the default method list).

Step 3.   The first listed method is used; if it fails to respond, the second one is used, and so on.

Step 4.   The first listed method is used; if it fails to respond, the second one is used, and so on.

As a review, the following commands configure AAA authorization and apply it to an interface:

```
Switch(config)# aaa accounting accounting-type list-name {start-stop | stop-only
| none} method-list
Switch(config)# interface interface-type interface-number
Switch(config-if)# ppp accounting list-name
```

Note   For more information on the other types of authorization, refer to the following information on Cisco.com: http://www.cisco.com/univercd/cc/td/doc/product/software/ios122/122cgcr/fsecur_c/fsaaa/index.htm.

Limitations of TACACS+ and RADIUS

As with any protocol or feature, there are limitations and caveats as well as advantages and disadvantages of one over the other. For example, RADIUS may not be the optimal choice in the following situations:

- **Device-to-device situations:** RADIUS does not offer two-way authentication. It works strictly in a client/server mode, where authentication may be started only from the client side and where the server always authenticates the client. If you have two devices that need to mutually authenticate each other, RADIUS is not an appropriate solution.

- **Networks using multiple service:** RADIUS generally binds a user to a single service model. An Access-Request RADIUS packet contains information about a type of session you want to use. Two session types may be initiated: character mode (used for the Telnet service) and PPP mode (used for PPP). In character mode, your session will typically terminate on a device for the administrative purposes (for example, to access the CLI). In PPP mode, your session will terminate on a NAS, but your goal is to access network resources behind the NAS. A single RADIUS server cannot bind a user simultaneously to character and PPP mode.

Conversely, TACACS+ may not be the optimal choice in the following situations:

- **Multivendor environment:** TACACS+ is a Cisco proprietary protocol developed as a completely new version of the older TACACS protocol. Some vendors may not support it even though Cisco has published TACACS+ specification in a form of a draft RFC.

- **When speed of response from the AAA services is of concern:** TACACS+ uses TCP as a transport protocol mechanism. TCP is a connection-oriented protocol, which means that a connection between two endpoints has to be established before the data can start to flow. On legacy devices, this mechanism may have higher latency, and TACACS+ might not be the best option if you need fast response from the AAA services. When using current-generation network devices and AAA servers, this is not an issue.

Now that AAA has been covered, the next subsection discusses identity-based networking, which leverages AAA.

Identity-Based Networking

Identity-based networking is a concept that unites several features to include authentication, access control, mobility, and user policy components with the aim to provide and restrict users with the network services that they are entitled to. This feature was chosen for inclusion in this chapter over Chapter 10, "Campus Network Security," because of its relevance to authentication and access control.

Traditional LAN security depends on physical security of the network ports. For example, for a user to gain access to the accounting VLAN, a user must walk into an accounting department and plug his laptop into an Ethernet port assigned to that VLAN. With user mobility as one of the core requirements of modern enterprise networks, especially with mobile devices, physical or location dependency for security or authentication purposes is no longer practical, nor does it provide enough security.

From a switch perspective, identity-based networking allows you to verify users once they connect to a switch port. Identity-based networking authenticates users and places them in a specific VLAN based on their identity. Should any users fail to pass the authentication process, that user's access can be rejected, or he might simply be put in a guest VLAN. Figure 7-4 highlights identity-based networking. Details of the protocols listed in the figure are explained later in this chapter.

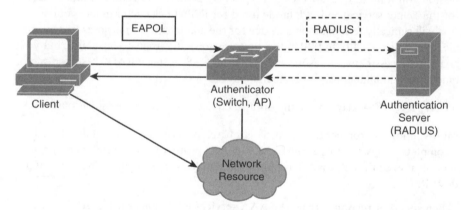

Figure 7-4   *Identity-Based Networking*

The IEEE 802.1X standard allows for implementation of identity-based networking for both physical and wireless connections on switches. The IEEE 802.1X feature support is found on all current-generation Catalyst switches.

IEEE 802.1X Port-Based Authentication Overview

The IEEE 802.1X standard defines a client/server-based access control and authentication protocol that prevents unauthorized clients from connecting to a LAN through switch ports unless they are properly authenticated. As part of the authentication process, the authentication server authenticates each client connected to a switch port before any services offered by the switch or the LAN are made available. Figure 7-5 illustrates this behavior.

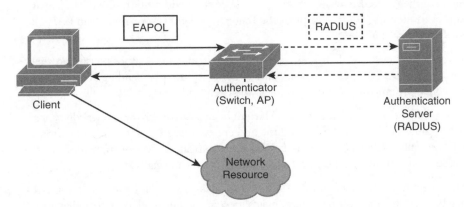

Figure 7-5 *IEEE 802.1X Port-Based Authentication Overview*

Until the client is authenticated, 802.1X access control allows only EAPOL, Cisco Discovery Protocol (CDP), and Spanning Tree Protocol (STP) traffic to pass through the port to which the client is connected. After authentication is successful, normal traffic can pass through the respective port.

Following a typical client/server model, the following definitions apply to 802.1X:

- **Client:** Usually a workstation or laptop with 802.1X-compliant client software. Most modern operating systems include native 802.1X support. The client may start the authentication process by requesting access to the LAN and switch services. The client is also referred to as a *supplicant* in 802.1X terminology.

- **Authenticator:** Usually an edge switch or wireless access point (AP), the authenticator controls the physical access to the network based on the authentication status of the client. The switch acts as an intermediary (proxy) between the client and the authentication server, requesting identity information from the client, verifying that information with the authentication server, and relaying a response to the client. Authenticator includes a RADIUS client, which is responsible for encapsulation and decapsulation of Extensible Authentication Protocol (EAP) frames and interaction with the authentication server. In the campus network, Cisco Catalyst switches are the authenticator for 802.1X.

- **Authentication server:** A server that performs the actual authentication of the client. The authentication server validates the identity of the client and notifies the authenticator whether the client is authorized to access LAN and switch services. Because the authenticator acts as a proxy, the authentication service is transparent to the client. Currently, a RADIUS server with EAP extensions is the only supported authentication server.

Both switch and the client can initiate authentication. The switch initiates authentication when the link state changes from down to up or periodically as long as the port remains up and unauthenticated. The switch sends an EAP-request/identity frame to the client to request its identity. Upon receipt of the frame, the client responds with an EAP-response/identity frame.

However, if EAP-request/identity is sent while the client is in the boot phase, the client does not receive it. The client can than initiate authentication by sending an EAPOL-start frame, which prompts the switch to request the client's identity.

When the client supplies its identity, the switch begins its role as the intermediary, passing EAP frames between the client and the authentication server until authentication succeeds or fails. When a client is successfully authenticated, the port transitions to the authorized state, allowing all traffic for the client to flow normally.

When a client logs off, it sends an EAPOL-logoff message, causing the switch port to change back to the unauthorized state. In addition, if the link state of a port changes from up to down, the port returns to the unauthorized state. Figure 7-6 reviews these steps pictorially.

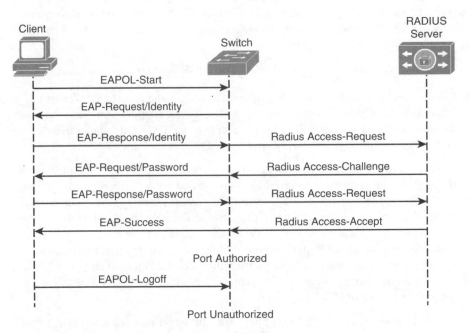

Figure 7-6   *IEEE 802.1X Port-Based Authentication Overview II*

IEEE 802.1X Configuration Checklist

IEEE 802.1X is simple, but does require AAA configuration. To enable 802.1X globally on a switch, use the **dot1x system-auth-control** command. To enable 802.1X authentication on a specific port after 802.1X is globally enabled, use the **dot1x port-control**

auto interface command. An 802.1X authentication method list is required, as well, which you configure by using the **aaa authentication dot1x** command.

Example 7-7 illustrates the configuration for enabling 802.1X on an interface port. Many of the commands listed were discussed in the subsection on AAA. Keep in mind that additional configuration is required on the RADIUS for authentication and mobility to ensure the connected device is authenticated and placed in the correct VLAN.

Example 7-7 *802.1X Configuration Example*

```
Switch(config)# aaa new-model
Switch(config)# radius server host 172.16.1.1 key cisco456
Switch(config)# aaa group server radius Mygroup3
Switch(config-sg-radius)# server 172.16.1.1
Switch(config)# aaa authentication dot1x default group Mygroup3
Switch(config)# dot1x system-auth-control
Switch(config)# interface GigabitEthernet0/2
Switch(config-if)# dot1x port-control auto
```

Note   You will not be able to issue **dot1x** commands on the interface if it is not set to switchport mode access prior. The default state of switch ports varies between switches, but it is not commonly set to the access mode.

This subsection covered only 802.1 briefly. You can find more detail about 802.1X found on Cisco.com. As one example, for more information on configuring 802.1X, refer to http://www.cisco.com/en/US/docs/switches/lan/catalyst3750x_3560x/software/release/15.0_1_se/configuration/guide/sw8021x.html.

Network Time Protocols

Internet Protocol (IP)-based networks are quickly evolving from the traditional best effort delivery model to a model where performance and reliability need to be quantified and, in many cases, guaranteed with service level agreements (SLAs). The need for greater insight into network characteristics has led to significant research efforts being targeted at defining metrics and measurement capabilities to characterize network behavior. The foundation of many metric methodologies is the measurement of time.

Keeping consistent time across network devices in your network will help ensure that you can properly read log messages and other information critical to troubleshooting.

The Need for Accurate Time

The need for accurate time is increasing year by year. Coordinating events, marking logs, and kicking-off scripts all run based on a system clock. The accuracy of the system is getting more important as networks become faster and faster. What was measured in seconds is now measured in milliseconds. Therefore, in today's network, coordination of system clocks and their accuracy is increasing in importance.

From a network device perspective, the system clock runs from the moment the system starts and keeps track of the current date and time. The system clock can be set from a number of sources and, in turn, can be used to distribute the current time through various mechanisms to other systems.

The system clock keeps track of time internally based on Coordinated Universal Time (UTC). All Cisco devices support local time zone configurations and daylight savings time adjustments such that the time is displayed correctly relative to the devices locality.

The system clock also keeps track of whether learned time is authoritative. If it is not authoritative, the time is available only for display purposes and cannot be redistributed. *Authoritative* refers to the trustworthiness of the source. Nonauthoritative sources do not guarantee accurate time.

From a best practice perspective, it is recommended to set clocks on all network devices to UTC regardless of their location, and then configure the time zone to display the local time if desired. In this manner, global operations can fall back to UTC time for relative time.

One example of the need for accurate time is for public key infrastructure that is based on X.509 certificates. These certificates are valid for a specific period. Consider, for example, that a certificate's validity with a granting authority expired on February 10, 2015. However, because of the user's system inaccuracy, the end user device may still consider it valid.

As another example, accurate time is also essential for logging events in your network, such as syslog. Accurately time-synchronizing network devices aids in troubleshooting root cause events in the network.

Configuring the System Clock Manually

The command **show clock** illustrates the Cisco devices current time. The **show clock detail** command shows the time in addition to the source of the clock information such as user configuration. The command **clock set** allows you to manually set the clock in UTC. Example 7-8 illustrates these basic **clock** commands.

Example 7-8 *Basic clock Commands*

```
Switch# show clock
10:10:03.979 UTC Thu Feb 22 2001
! Shows what the device thinks is the current time
```

```
Switch# clock set 12:13:00 10 January 2015
! Manual system clock reconfiguration
Switch# show clock detail
12:13:03.487 UTC Sat Jan 10 2015
Time source is user configuration
! Verification of how system clock has changed. Adding the detail keyword will tell
  you what was the source of clock configuration
```

To configure the time zone, use the **clock timezone** *zone hours-offset* [*minutes-offset*] global configuration command. The time zone can be set in hours and optional minutes from UTC.

To configure automatic switching to summer time (daylight savings time), use one of the following formats of the **clock summer-time** command:

clock summer-time *zone* **recurring** [*week day month hh:mm week day month hh:mm* [*offset*]]

clock summer-time *zone* **date** *date month year hh:mm date month year hh:mm* [*offset*]

clock summer-time *zone* **date** *month date year hh:mm month date year hh:mm* [*offset*]

Example 7-9 illustrates time zone settings.

Example 7-9 *Setting Time Zones and Summer Time*

```
Switch(config)# clock timezone EDT -5
Switch(config)# clock summer-time EDT recurring
! Changes timezone and enables daylight savings time. In this example, EDT is used.
Switch# show clock detail
07:44:12.370 EDT Sat Jan 10 2015
Time source is user configuration
Summer time starts 02:00:00 EDT Sun Mar 8 2015
Summer time ends 02:00:00 EDT Sun Nov 1 2015
! Verifies how clock settings now reflect local time
```

Table 7-2 describes how to use the parameters of the **clock** commands found on Cisco Catalyst switches. This table should be used as a reference.

Table 7-2 *Cisco Catalyst Clock Summer-Time Commands*

Parameter	Description
zone	Name of the time zone (for example, PDT) to be displayed when summer time is in effect
recurring	Indicates that summer time should start and end on the corresponding specified days every year
date	Indicates that summer time should start on the first specific date that is listed in the command and end on the second specific date in the command

Parameter	Description
week	(Optional) Week of the month (1 to 5 or last).
day	(Optional) Day of the week (Sunday, Monday, and so on)
date	Date of the month (1 to 31)
month	(Optional) Month (January, February, and so on)
year	Year (1993 to 2035)
bb:mm	(Optional) Time (military format) in hours and minutes
offset	(Optional) Number of minutes to add during summer time (default = 60)

Continuing the summer-time discussion, summer time is disabled by default. If the **clock summer-time** *zone* **recurring** command is specified without parameters, the summer-time rules default to United States rules. The default of the offset argument is 60.

A number of Cisco devices contain a battery-powered calendar system that tracks the date and time across system restarts and power outages. This calendar system is always used to initialize the system clock when the system is restarted. It can also be considered as an authoritative source of time and redistributed through NTP (Network Time Protocol) if no other source is available.

Furthermore, if NTP is running, the calendar can be periodically updated from NTP, compensating for the inherent drift in the calendar time. When a router with a system calendar is initialized, the system clock is set based on the time in its internal battery-powered calendar. On models without a calendar, the system clock is set to a predetermined time constant. The term *calendar* on a Cisco router or switch often refers to a hardware clock.

To configure the hardware clock on a Cisco Catalyst switch, use the **calendar set** *bb:mm:ss <1-31> month year* command.

Note In the absence of NTP or other reliable time source, make sure that whenever you are manually setting the clock, you update the calendar with it to ensure continuity when the device restarts.

Manually setting the clocks of any network device is neither accurate nor scalable. The best practice is to use Network Time Protocol (NTP), Simple NTP (SNTP), or Precision Time Protocol (PTP); PTP is discussed later in this chapter. Leveraging NTP across a network to propagate NTP is covered in the following subsections.

Network Time Protocol Overview

NTP is designed to synchronize the time throughout an entire network infrastructure, including servers, switches, routers, host machines, wireless access points, uninterruptible power supply (UPS), and so on. NTP leverages UDP port 123 for both the source and destination by default.

Specifically, NTP synchronizes timekeeping efforts among a set of distributed time servers and clients. Multiple masters (primary servers) may exist, but there is no requirement for an election protocol, which simplifies use of the protocol. Figure 7-7 illustrates a sample NTP setup where the NTP is sourcing time from an atomic clock, Global Positioning System (GPS), or other accurate time source and sending NTP info out on the network to synchronize devices.

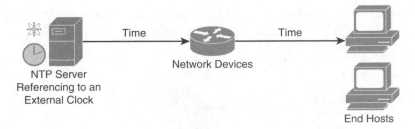

Figure 7-7 *NTP Example*

An NTP network usually gets its reference time from an authoritative time source, such as a radio clock, GPS, or an atomic clock attached to an NTP time server somewhere in the network. NTP then distributes this time across the network. An NTP client makes a transaction with its server somewhere within polling interval of between 64 and 1024 seconds. Depending on network conditions, the time between polling intervals may dynamically change. Generally, longer responses between the NTP servers and clients will result in longer polling intervals.

Moreover, if an NTP server is deemed to have a large dispersion (time difference between local client clock and reference clock), the client will also increase its polling interval. This polling interval cannot be adjusted on Cisco routers and switches.

The NTP associations are usually statically configured. Each network device is given the IP address of other network devices with which it should form associations. Accurate timekeeping is made possible by exchanging NTP messages between each pair of machines with an association. However, in a LAN environment, NTP can be configured to use IP broadcast messages instead. This alternative reduces configuration complexity because each machine can be configured to send or receive broadcast messages. However, the accuracy of timekeeping is marginally reduced because the information flow is one-way only.

To keep accuracy of time, NTP uses the concept of a stratum to describe how many NTP hops away a machine is from an authoritative time source. For example, a stratum 1 time server has a stratum 0 device that is directly attached to it for accurate time synchronization. It then sends its time to a stratum 2 time server through NTP, and so on. A machine running NTP automatically chooses the machine with the lowest stratum number that it is configured to communicate with using NTP as its time source. This strategy effectively builds a self-organizing tree of NTP speakers. NTP performs well over the nondeterministic path lengths of packet-switched networks because it makes robust estimates of the following three key variables in the relationship between a client and a time server:

- Network delay

- Dispersion of time packet exchanges (a measure of maximum clock error between the two hosts)

- Clock offset (the correction applied to a client's clock to synchronize it)

Clock synchronization at the 10-millisecond level over long distance WANs (124.27 miles [2000 km]), and at the 1-millisecond level for LANs, is routinely achieved.

Figure 7-8 illustrates the stratum concept.

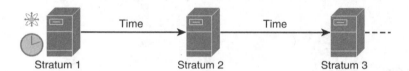

Figure 7-8   *NTP: Stratum*

In addition, NTP avoids in two ways synchronizing to a machine whose time may not be accurate. First, NTP never synchronizes to a machine that is not synchronized itself. Second, NTP compares the time that is reported by several machines and will not synchronize to a machine whose time differs significantly from the others, even if its stratum is lower. These mechanisms may seem simple, but they are effective in most networks at achieving millisecond accuracy of clocks. You can increase the effectiveness of NTP modes of operation via manual configuration, as discussed in the following section.

NTP Modes

NTP can operate in one of four different modes that provide you additional flexibility of managing NTP roles of devices. A device may take on more than one role at a time. These roles are as follows:

- **Server:** Provides accurate time information to clients on the network.

- **Client:** Synchronizes its time to an NTP server. This mode is most suited for file server and workstation clients that are not required to provide any form of time synchronization to other local clients. It can also provide accurate time to other devices.

- **Peers:** Peers only exchange time synchronization information.

- **Broadcast/multicast:** Special "push" mode of NTP server where the local LAN is flooded with updates; used only when time accuracy is not an issue.

With Cisco network devices, server and client modes are usually combined together. Therefore, a Cisco network device that is an NTP client can also act as an NTP server to another Cisco network device. This combination client/server operation is the most common configuration.

To configure a Cisco network device as an NTP client, you simply configure an NTP server address by using the **ntp server** *ip-addr* command and specifying the DNS name or address.

To configure a Cisco network device as an NTP server requires no special configuration because peer devices are configured to communicate directly. Therefore, NTP server mode requires no prior configuration.

In this common client/server model, a client sends an NTP message to one or more servers and processes the replies as received. The server interchanges addresses and ports, overwrites certain fields in the message, recalculates the checksum, and returns the message immediately. Information included in the NTP message allows the client to determine the server time with respect to local time and adjust the local clock accordingly. In addition, the message includes information to calculate the expected timekeeping accuracy and reliability, as well as select the best server. Note that in Cisco terminology, *NTP server mode* generally refers to this client/server model for NTP.

Peer mode is also commonly known as *symmetric mode*. It is intended for configurations where a group of low-stratum peers operate as mutual backups for each other. Each peer operates with one or more primary reference sources, such as a radio clock, or a subset of reliable secondary servers. If one of the peers loses all the reference sources or simply ceases operation, the other peers automatically reconfigure so that time values can flow from the surviving peers to all the others in the clique. In some contexts, this is described as a *push-pull operation*, in that the peer either pulls or pushes the time and values depending on the particular configuration. Symmetric modes are most often used between two or more servers operating as a mutually redundant group. In these modes, the servers in the group members arrange the synchronization paths for maximum performance, depending on network jitter and propagation delay. If one or more of the group members fail, the remaining members automatically reconfigure as required.

Where the requirements in accuracy and reliability are modest, clients can be configured to use broadcast/multicast modes. Normally, these modes are not used by servers with dependent clients. The advantage is that clients do not need to be configured for a specific server, allowing all operating clients to use the same configuration file. Broadcast mode requires a broadcast server on the same subnet. Because routers do not propagate broadcast messages, only use broadcast servers that are on the same subnet. Broadcast mode is intended for configurations involving one or a few servers and a potentially large client population. A broadcast server is configured using the **broadcast** command

and a local subnet address. A broadcast client is configured using the **broadcast client** command, allowing the broadcast client to respond to broadcast messages that are received on any interface.

Other NTP Configuration Options

NTP will be enabled on all interfaces once NTP configuration is applied. You can use the **ntp disable** interface configuration command on interfaces that connect to external networks, because you do not want to provide clock to those. NTP-disabled interfaces will turn off NTP server functionality, but still allow the interface to act as an NTP client. In addition, use the **ntp max-associations** number command in global configuration mode to limit the number of NTP sessions to avoid overwhelming a switch or router with NTP requests.

Another configuration to keep in mind is the **ntp master** *stratum-number* global configuration command. This command configures the Cisco router or switch to be an authoritative server. This configuration is recommended only when there is no reliable external clock, which is an extremely rare circumstance. Moreover, when using the **ntp master** command, you should choose a high stratum number such as 10. This stratum setting ensures that more trustworthy NTP information is leveraged in the network.

NTP Example

In reference to Figure 7-9, the network topology is set up to run NTP. As illustrated in the figure, the external clock source on the Internet has an IP address of 209.165.200.187. Alternatively, large enterprises may use their own clocking source. Nevertheless, the first configuration step for this example is as follows:

```
ntp server 209.165.200.187
```

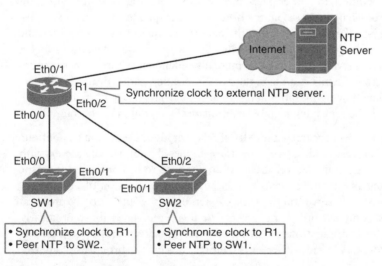

Figure 7-9 *Topology for NTP Example*

When configuring NTP servers, a best practice is to configure more than one NTP server. In this scenario, the network device will associate itself with one server and mark the other one as alternate/backup. To specify a preferred NTP server as the primary NTP server, use the **ntp server** *ip-address* **prefer** command.

Keep in mind that any network management security access lists will need to allow NTP connections. In case there are any access lists in place, an example access list entry to add to the existing access list for NTP is as follows:

```
access-list acl-number permit udp host NTP-host-IP eq ntp
```

acl-number is the access list number, and *NTP-host-IP* is the DNS name or IP address of the NTP server address.

For the example in Figure 7-9 to determine whether the routers clock has been synchronized to the public NTP server, use the **show ntp status** command. Example 7-10 illustrates an example of using the **show ntp status** for the network shown in Figure 7-9.

Example 7-10 *show ntp status Example*

```
R1# show ntp status
Clock is synchronized, stratum 2, reference is 209.165.200.187
nominal freq is 250.0000 Hz, actual freq is 250.0000 Hz, precision is 2**10
ntp uptime is 1500 (1/100 of seconds), resolution is 4000
reference time is D67E670B.0B020C68 (05:22:19.043 PST Mon Jan 13 2014)
clock offset is 0.0000 msec, root delay is 0.00 msec
root dispersion is 630.22 msec, peer dispersion is 189.47 msec
loopfilter state is 'CTRL' (Normal Controlled Loop), drift is 0.000000000 s/s
system poll interval is 64, last update was 5 sec ago.
```

The output of **show ntp status** illustrates whether the device's clock is synchronized with the public NTP server. In addition, the stratum of R1 from Figure 7-9 will be plus one (+1) in comparison to the NTP source. Because the output shows that this device is stratum 2, you can assume that you are synchronizing to a stratum 1 device in this example.

Note that NTP can be slow to synchronize. It can take up to 5 minutes for a device to synchronize with an upstream server, especially considering the NTP poll timer is 64 seconds. In addition, once a device is synchronized to an NTP source or configured to serve as a master, the device will then begin to act as an NTP server to any system that requests synchronization.

To verify NTP associations for R1 in Figure 7-9, use the **show ntp associations** command. An output example of this command based on Figure 7-9 is shown in Example 7-11.

Example 7-11   *show ntp associations Example*

```
R1# show ntp associations

  address          ref clock       st   when   poll reach delay offset   disp
*~209.165.200.187 .LOCL.           1     24     64    17 1.000  -0.500  2.820
 * sys.peer, # selected, + candidate, - outlyer, x falseticker, ~ configured
```

In reference to Example 7-11, the * before the IP address signifies that device is associated with the server listed. If you have multiple NTP servers defined, others will be marked with +, which signifies alternate options. Alternate servers are those that will become associated if the currently associated NTP server fails.

After verification of NTP status and associations, verify the clock is indeed correctly set. By default, IOS-based Cisco devices default to UTC time. You will need to define a local time zone and daylight savings time to complete the NTP configuration.

In addition, NTP will only synchronize the software clock by default on Cisco Catalyst switches running IOS. If you want NTP also to synchronize the hardware clock, you need to issue **ntp update-calendar** in global configuration mode. The **NTP update-calendar** command is only available on specific Catalyst switches; check cisco.com for supported models.

To configure the time zone and to enable daylight savings time, use the **clock time-zone** and **clock summer-time** commands referenced in Table 7-2 earlier in this chapter. To view the current time zone and daylight savings time setting, use the **show clock detail** command. Example 7-12 illustrates an example of this configuration and EXEC commands.

Example 7-12   *Setting and Verifying the Clock Time Zone and Daylight Savings Time*

```
R1(config)# clock timezone EDT -5
R1(config)# clock summer-time EDT recurring

R1# show clock detail
08:01:54.470 EDT Tue Jan 14 2014
Time source is NTP
Summer time starts 02:00:00 EDT Sun Mar 9 2014
Summer time ends 02:00:00 EDT Sun Nov 2 2014
```

Referring back to Figure 7-9 again, Example 7-13 illustrates the commands to configure SW1 to synchronize its clock to R1 via NTP and configure it with the same time zone and daylight savings time configuration as R1. Assume that the interface Eth 0/0 on R1 has an IP address of 10.0.0.1.

Example 7-13 *Downstream NTP Example*

```
SW1(config)# ntp server 10.0.0.1
SW1(config)# clock timezone EDT -5
SW1(config)# clock summer-time EDT recurring
```

SW1 should be a stratum 3 device because R1 is a stratum 2 device. Viewing the output of **show ntp status** from SW1 will verify this behavior. Example 7-14 shows the output for this scenario.

Example 7-14 *Downstream NTP Status Example*

```
SW1# show ntp status
Clock is synchronized, stratum 3, reference is 10.0.0.1
nominal freq is 250.0000 Hz, actual freq is 250.0000 Hz, precision is 2**18
reference time is D67FD8F2.4624853F (10:40:34.273 EDT Tue Jan 14 2014)
clock offset is 0.0053 msec, root delay is 0.00 msec
root dispersion is 17.11 msec, peer dispersion is 0.02 msec
```

NTP Design Principles

With a flat structure, all routers are configured to peer to each other as NTP peers. Each router will act both as a client and server with every other router. Two or three routers should be configured to synchronize their time with external time servers as a best practice to ensure redundancy to external time servers.

This model is very stable because each device synchronizes with every other device in the network. The disadvantages are difficulty of administration, slow convergence times, and poor scalability. If you add a device to the network, it can take you a good amount of time to identify all other devices and peer them with the new device. Because all devices in a peer-to-peer relationship have a say in selecting the best time, it can take some time for the routers to converge on an accurate time.

As a result, a flat NTP structure is not recommended for large networks. For large networks, it is a best practice to implement NTP in a hierarchical manner.

Internet service providers (ISPs) use this kind of hierarchical model to scale time synchronization. Each ISP has multiple stratum 1 servers that synchronize to other ISP devices, and the ISP ultimately provides time synchronization services to customers' devices on the edge of the network. The edge customer device then provides time synchronization to the rest of the internal customer network.

As a result, this tiered model consumes less administrative overhead and time convergence is minimized because every customer edge router is not associated with every other customer edge router. For large enterprise networks, it makes sense to implement a similar hierarchy of NTP synchronization.

A hybrid design of flat and hierarchical is referred to as a *star* structure, where all devices in a network have a relationship with a few time servers in the core. Figure 7-10 shows an example of a star design.

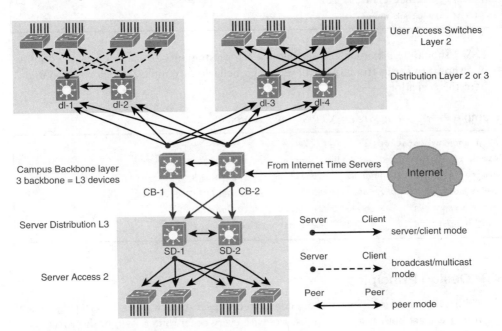

Figure 7-10 *NTP Design Hierarchy*

When designing NTP in campus networks, it is important to consider broadcast association mode. The broadcast association mode simplifies the configurations for the LANs, but reduces the accuracy of the time calculations. Therefore, the trade-off in maintenance overhead must be considered against accuracy in performance measurements.

The high-stratum campus network shown in Figure 7-10 is taken from a standard Cisco campus network design and contains three components. The campus core consists of two Layer 3 devices, labeled CB-1 and CB-2. The server component (data center) that is located in the lower section of the figure has two Layer 3 devices, labeled SD-1 and SD-2. The remaining devices in the server block are Layer 2 devices. In the upper left, there is a standard access block with two Layer 3 distribution devices, labeled dl-1 and dl-2. The remaining devices are Layer 2 switches. In this client access block, the time is distributed using the broadcast option. In the upper right, another standard access block uses a client/server time distribution configuration. Using the peer and broadcast concept reduces the number of full associations in the network.

Looking back at Figure 7-9 and the previous subsection, to configure SW1 and SW2 as peers only requires a single NTP command. Assuming SW1 and SW2 use the IP address 172.16.0.11 and 172.16.0.12 on the interface Eth 0/1, respectively, the NTP commands for SW are **ntp peer 172.16.0.12**, and for SW2, the command is **ntp peer 172.16.0.11**.

In this example, the output of **show ntp associations** with this peering configuration would appear as shown in Example 7-15.

Example 7-15 *show ntp association for Peering NTP*

```
SW1# show ntp association


         address         ref clock     st  when  poll reach  delay  offset    disp
*~10.0.0.1          209.165.200.187    2    22   128  377    0.0    0.02     0.0
+~172.16.0.12       10.0.1.1           3    1    128  376    0.0    -1.00    0.0
 * master (synced), # master (unsynced), + selected, - candidate, ~ configured
```

Securing NTP

As with any open protocol, NTP can be an easy target for hacking in your network. Because device certificates rely on accurate time, securing NTP is a must. You can secure NTP operation using authentication and access lists. Although these are not the strongest methods of security, they are basic best practices.

Note that Cisco devices support only message digest 5 (MD5) algorithm authentication for NTP.

To configure NTP authentication, execute the following steps:

Step 1.   Define NTP authentication key or keys with **ntp authentication-key** command. Every number specifies a unique NTP key.

Step 2.   Enable NTP authentication using the **ntp authenticate** command.

Step 3.   Tell the Cisco device which keys are valid for NTP authentication using the **ntp trusted-key** command. The only argument to this command is the key that you defined in the first step.

Step 4.   Specify the NTP server that requires authentication by using the **ntp server** *ip-address* **key** *key-number* command. You can similarly authenticate NTP peers by using the **ntp server** *ip-address* **key** *key-number* command.

Not all clients need to be configured with NTP authentication. NTP does not authenticate clients; NTP authenticates the source. Because NTP running on a the device will still respond to unauthenticated requests, use access lists to limit NTP access to management networks or peer routers. At a minimum, user VLANs should be restricted from sending NTP frames to the network devices.

Example 7-16 illustrates both a server and client configuration for authentication.

Example 7-16   *NTP Authentication for Server and Client, Respectively*

```
NTPServer(config)# ntp authentication-key 1 md5 MyPassword
NTPServer(config)# ntp authenticate
NTPServer(config)# ntp trusted-key 1
NTPClient(config)# ntp authentication-key 1 md5 MyPassword
NTPClient(config)# ntp authenticate
NTPClient(config)# ntp trusted-key 1
NTPClient(config)# ntp server 10.0.1.22 key 1
```

After implementing authentication for NTP, it is an obvious best practice to use the **show ntp status** command to verify that the clock is still synchronized. If a client has not successfully authenticated the NTP source after authentication has been configured, the clock will be unsynchronized.

As mentioned previously, once a Cisco router or switch has been synchronized to an NTP source, the Cisco router or switch will act as an NTP server to any device that requests NTP synchronization. An earlier subsection highlighted the client/server model for NTP used on Cisco routers and switches. Unfortunately, this behavior is unsecure, and the best method to restrict unauthorized access is to leverage access lists. The use of access lists to restrict unauthorized access is particularly important for routers and switches that synchronize time to external servers on the Internet. It is possible that a hacker could create a denial-of-service (DoS) attack by overwhelming a router with external Internet access with bogus NTP synchronization requests.

In addition, an attacker could use NTP queries to discover the time servers to which your device is synchronized, and then through an attack, such as DNS cache poisoning, redirect your device to a system under its control. If an attacker modifies the time on your devices, any time-based security implementations that you might have may be compromised.

For NTP, you can configure the following four restrictions through access lists:

- **peer:** Time synchronization requests and control queries are allowed. The device is allowed to synchronize itself to remote systems that pass the access list.

- **serve:** Time synchronization requests and control queries are allowed. The device is *not* allowed to synchronize itself to remote systems that pass the access list.

- **serve-only:** Only allows synchronization requests.

- **query-only:** Only allows control queries.

For example, if you have a hierarchical model with two routers configured to provide NTP services to the rest of the devices in your network, you would configure these two routers with **peer** and **serve-only** restrictions. You would use **peer** restriction mutually on the two core routers. You would use **serve-only** restriction on both core routers to specify which devices in your network are allowed to synchronize their information with these two routers.

If your device is configured as NTP master, you must allow access to source IP of 127.127.x.1. This is because 127.127.x.1 is the internal server that is created by the **ntp master** command. The value of the third octet varies between platforms.

After you secure the NTP server with access lists, make sure to check whether clients still have their clocks synchronized via NTP using the **show ntp status** command. You can verify which IP address was assigned to the internal server using **show ntp associations** command.

Example 7-17 illustrates an NTP access list configuration to permit the router to peer only with a specified address. Example 7-18 illustrates an access list configuration to answer synchronization requests only from the 10.1.0.0/16 subnet.

Example 7-17 *NTP Access List to Restrict Peers*

```
Router(config)# access-list 1 permit 10.0.1.0 0.0.255.255
Router(config)# ntp access-group peer 1
```

Example 7-18 *NTP Access List to Restrict Synchronization to a Subnet*

```
Router(config)# access-list 1 permit 10.1.0.0 0.0.255.255
Router(config)# ntp access-group server-only 1
```

NTP Source Address

The source of the NTP packet will be the same as the interface the packet was sent out on. When implementing authentication and access lists, it is good to have a specific interface set to act as the source interface for NTP.

It would be wise of you to choose a loopback interface to use as the NTP source. This is because the loopback will never be down like physical interfaces.

If you configured loopback 0 to act as the NTP source for all communication and that interface has, for example, an IP address of 192.168.12.31, you can write up just one access list that will allow or deny based on one single IP address of 192.168.12.31.

NTP Versions

Currently, NTP Versions 3 and 4 are the only used versions found in the field. Some vendors of operating systems customize and deliver their own versions. In addition, older clients generally can communicate and synchronize with newer versions. This chapter on NTP has focused on NTP Version 3 because that is the most common version found in the campus network today.

NTPv4 is an extension of NTP Version 3. NTPv4 supports both IPv4 and IPv6 and is backward compatible with NTPv3.

NTPv4 provides the following capabilities:

- NTPv4 supports IPv6, making NTP time synchronization possible over IPv6.

- Security is improved over NTPv3. The NTPv4 protocol provides a whole security framework based on public key cryptography and standard X509 certificates.

- Using specific multicast groups, NTPv4 can automatically calculate its time-distribution hierarchy through an entire network. NTPv4 automatically configures the hierarchy of the servers to achieve the best time accuracy for the lowest bandwidth cost. This feature leverages site-local IPv6 multicast addresses.

NTPv3 supports sending and receiving clock updates using IPv4 broadcast messages, as discussed earlier in this chapter. Moreover, many network administrators use this feature to distribute time on LANs with minimum client configuration. For example, Cisco corporate LANs use this feature over IPv4 on local gateways. End-user workstations are configured to listen to NTP broadcast messages and synchronize their clocks accordingly. In NTPv4 for IPv6, IPv6 multicast messages instead of IPv4 broadcast messages are used to send and receive clock updates.

NTPv3 access group functionality is based on IPv4 numbered access lists. NTPv4 access group functionality accepts IPv6 named access lists as well as IPv4 numbered access lists. NTPv4 also adds DNS support for IPv6.

In summary, NTPv4 adds the following capabilities:

- Support for IPv6

- Better security

- Leverages multicast over broadcast for push modes

NTPv4 is an extension of NTP Version 3, which supports both IPv4 and IPv6. NTPv4 support on Cisco Catalyst switches requires specific software and is not supported on all platforms. Check your platform on Cisco.com to verify support for NTPv4. Networking devices running NTPv4 can be configured to operate in a variety of association modes when synchronizing time with reference time sources. A networking device can obtain time information on a network in two ways: by polling host servers and by listening to NTPv4 multicasts.

Configuring of polling host servers is done using the **ntp server** *ipv6-address* **version 4** command. This configuration is also called the *client mode*.

Configuring of synchronization to a peer is done through the **ntp peer** *ipv6-address* **version 4** command. This configuration is also called the *symmetric active mode*.

To configure multicast-based NTPv4 associations, use the **ntp multicast** *ipv6-address* command. You also need to configure the device interface to receive NTPv4 multicast packets. You do that by issuing the **ntp multicast client** *ipv6-address* command in interface configuration mode.

Authentication and access list configuration with IPv6 is similar to that in IPv4. NTP verification and status are similar to those of IPv4.

Example 7-19 shows an IPv6 configuration for NTPv4 example.

Example 7-19   *NTPv4 with IPv6 Example*

```
Switch(config)# ntp server 2001:DB8:0:0:8:800:200C:417A version 4
```

This section only briefly covered NTPv4 enhancements and its use with IPv6. For more information on NTPv4 with IPv6, consult Cisco.com.

SNTP

Simple Network Time Protocol (SNTP) is a simplified, client-only version of NTP supported on select Catalyst switches. SNTP can only receive the time from NTP servers; it cannot be used to provide time services to other systems. Figure 7-11 highlights SNTP at a high level.

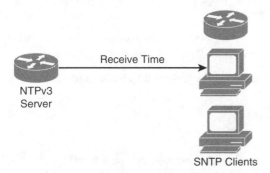

NTPv3 Server

Receive Time

SNTP Clients

Figure 7-11   *SNTP Example*

SNTP typically provides time within 100 milliseconds of the accurate time, but it does not provide the complex filtering and statistical mechanisms of NTP.

You can configure SNTP to request and accept packets from configured servers or to accept NTP broadcast packets from any source. When multiple sources are sending NTP packets, the server with the best stratum is selected. If multiple servers are at the same stratum, a configured server is preferred over a broadcast server. If multiple servers pass both tests, the first one to send a time packet is selected. SNTP will choose a new server only if it stops receiving packets from the currently selected server, or if a better server is discovered.

SNTP and NTP cannot coexist on the same machine because they use the same port. This means that these two services cannot be configured on the system at the same time. SNTP support for IPv6 addresses is available only if the image supports IPv6 addressing.

There is little difference command-wise between SNTP and NTP for end devices. Command **ntp server** *server-ip* gets replaced with **sntp server** *server-ip*. Command **show ntp** gets replaced with **show sntp**. Example 7-20 shows a basic SNTP configuration example.

Example 7-20   *Basic SNTP Example*

```
Switch(config)# sntp server 209.165.200.187
```

To enable SNTP authentication, use the **sntp authenticate** command. To define an authentication key, use the **sntp authentication-key** *number* **md5** *key* command. You can specify one or multiple keys. To mark keys as trusted for SNTP, use the **sntp authentication-key** *number* **md5** *key* command. The last step is to tell the device to which server it should synchronize its time; use the **sntp server** *server-ip* command to accomplish this task.

To verify whether a device has synchronized its time via SNTP, use the **show sntp** command. The output will show you what the IP address is of the SNTP server or servers it uses, what the stratum number is, SNTP version number, when the last synchronization cycle was done, and whether time is synchronized.

If you need to troubleshoot SNTP server selection, use the **debug sntp select** command. Debug will output messages that are related to both IPv4 and IPv6 servers.

If you need to troubleshoot the SNTP process, use the **debug sntp packets** [detail] command.

PTP/IEEE-1588

Precision Time Protocol (PTP) is a similar time synchronization protocol to NTP. However, its accuracy is much greater than the millisecond-accuracy of NTP; PTP supports accuracy to the sub-microsecond level. This time of accuracy is needed for defense systems, seismic analysis, data analytics, application analysis, and algorithmic processing. PTP is defined in the IEEE 1588-2008 standard. Currently, Cisco Catalyst switches do not leverage PTP for clock synchronization. However, Cisco Nexus switches used in data center networks are starting to support PTP. Eventually, PTP support will span outside of the data center to the campus network.

In addition, switches can participate in PTP boundary clock functions. However, that discussion is beyond the scope of this book.

SNMP

Modern communication networks are extremely complex. This is partly due to a combination of different network technologies and techniques that are used to achieve their own specific goals. The trend of transporting different types of traffic (data, voice, and video) over the same IP infrastructure does not help to make your job as a network administrator an easy one. In addition, new technologies such as FabricPath, Dynamic Fabric Automation (DFA), Application Centric Infrastructure (ACI), OpenStack, and so on make today's network even more complex.

In this environment, the need for network monitoring is very important to effectively troubleshoot problems, trend data, and plan for network upgrades.

Simple Network Management Protocol (SNMP) exposes environment and performance parameters of a network device, allowing a network management system (NMS) to collect and process data. All modern NMSs are based on SNMP.

This subsection covers the following topics related to SNMP:

- The role of SNMP

- Different SNMP versions

- Recommended practices for setting up SNMP

- Configuration examples for SNMP Version 3

- Verifying SNMP configurations

SNMP Overview

SNMP has become the standard for network management. SNMP is a simple, easy-to-implement protocol and is thus supported by nearly all vendors.

SNMP defines how management information is exchanged between SNMP managers and SNMP agents. SNMP uses the UDP transport mechanism to retrieve and send management information, such as Management Information Base (MIB) variables that contain information about the platform.

SNMP systems consist of two components, as follows:

- The **SNMP manager** that periodically polls the SNMP agents on managed devices by querying the device for data. Periodic polling has a disadvantage: A delay occurs between an actual event occurrence and the time the SNMP manager polls the data.

- **SNMP agents** on managed devices collect device information and translate it into a compatible SNMP format according to the MIB. MIBs are collections of definitions of the managed objects. SNMP agents keep the database of values for definitions written in the MIB.

Figure 7-12 illustrates these components.

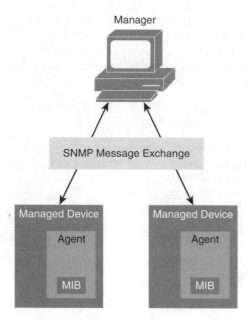

Figure 7-12   *SNMP Overview*

SNMP agents also generate SNMP traps, asynchronous notifications that are sent from agent to manager. SNMP traps are event based and provide almost real-time notification of events.

Figure 7-13 illustrates examples of retrieving data through SNMP, pushing configuration through SNMP, and traps.

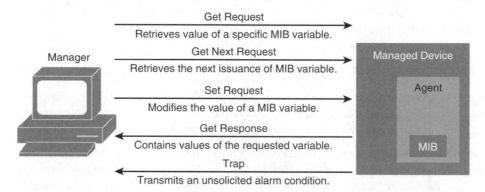

Figure 7-13   *SNMP Processing Examples*

Therefore, SNMP polling is typically used to gather environment and performance data such as device CPU usage, memory usage, interface traffic, interface error rate, and so on. Free and enterprise-level NMS software bundles provide data collection, storage, manipulation, and presentation. An NMS offers a look into historical data, in addition to anticipated trends. An NMS often supports a central view that provides an overview of the entire network to easily identify irregular events, such as increased traffic and devices unavailability due to DoS attacks. These notifications are crucial to responding to attacks quickly. A legacy example of an NMS is Cisco Works. In future networks, orchestration and portal tools may supersede NMS tools.

SNMP Versions

The initial version of SNMP, Version 1, introduced five message types: Get Request, Get Next Request, Set Request, Get Response, and Trap. This version is rarely used nowadays.

SNMP Version 2 introduced two new message types: Get Bulk Request to poll large amounts of data, and Inform Request, a type of trap with expected acknowledgment on receipt. Version 2 added 64-bit counters to accommodate faster network interfaces.

SNMP Version 2 added a complex security model, which was never widely accepted. Instead, a community-based SNMP Version 2, known as *Version 2c, draft standard* was introduced and is now, due to its wide acceptance, considered the de facto Version 2 standard. However, this community-based version of SNMP is very unsecure. Therefore, use of SNMPv3 is required in today's campus network.

In SNMP Version 3, methods to ensure the secure transmission of critical data between the manager and agent were added. It provides flexibility in defining security policy. You can define secure policies per group, and optionally limit IP addresses to which its members can belong. Encryption, hashing algorithms, and passwords are also supported for each user.

To add flexibility while adopting security with SNMP, SNMPv3 supports the following three levels of security:

- **noAuthNoPriv:** No authentication is required, and no privacy (encryption) is provided.

- **authNoPriv:** Authentication is based on Hashed Message Authentication Code (HMAC), MD5, or Secure Hash (SHA). No encryption is provided.

- **authPriv:** In addition to authentication, cipher block chaining - Data Encryption Standard (CBC-DES) encryption is used.

The best practice is to leverage **authPriv** in any campus network.

SNMP Best Practices

NMS systems rarely need SNMP write access, so it is good practice to configure SNMP access as read-only. Separate community/credentials should be configured for systems that require write access for NMS that push configurations and so on. New orchestration tools such as Unified Computing Systems (UCS) Director and Application Policy Infrastructure Controller (APIC) may need configuration write access, but they leverage application programming interfaces (APIs) and other functions aside from SNMP to make changes to network devices.

The **setup snmp view** command can block the user with access limited to only the MIB. By default, there is no SNMP view entry. It works similarly to an access list in that if you have any SNMP view on certain MIB trees, every other tree is implicitly denied.

As another form of security, access lists should be used to limit SNMP access only to known SNMP managers.

SNMPv3 is recommended whenever possible. It provides authentication, encryption, and integrity. Be aware that the SNMPv1 or SNMPv2c community string was not designed as a security mechanism and is transmitted in clear text. Nevertheless, community strings should not be trivial, such as the word *private*, and should be configured similarly to a password. Moreover, community strings should be changed at regular intervals. To avoid these complications, always use SNMPv3.

To recap SNMP best practices, always adhere to the following SNMP recommendations:

- Restrict access to read-only.

- Use write access with separate credentials and careful consideration.

- Set up SNMP views to restrict manager to only access needed sets of MIBs.

- Configure ACLs to restrict SNMP access only by known managers.

- Use SNMPv3 authentication, encryption, and integrity where possible, including upgrading devices to support SNMPv3 if necessary.

SNMPv3 Configuration Example

Configuring SNMPv3 requires several steps. Use the following best practice procedures for configuring SNMPv3:

Step 1.   Configure an access list to be used to restrict subnets for SNMP access.

Step 2.   Configure the SNMPv3 views to limit access to specific MIBs.

Step 3.   Configure the SNMPv3 security groups.

Step 4.   Configure the SNMPv3 users.

Step 5.   Configure the SNMPv3 trap receivers.

Step 6.   Configure ifindex persistence to prevent ifindex changes.

Example 7-21 illustrates an SNMPv3 configuration example applying the SNMPv3 best practice list.

Example 7-21 *SNMPv3 Best Practice Configuration Example*

```
Switch(config)# access-list 99 permit 10.1.1.0 0.0.0.255
Switch(config)# snmp-server view OPS sysUpTime included
Switch(config)# snmp-server view OPS ifDescr included
Switch(config)# snmp-server view OPS ifAdminStatus included
Switch(config)# snmp-server view OPS ifOperStatus included
Switch(config)# snmp-server user userZ groupZ v3 auth sha secretpwd2 priv aes 256
  secondsecretpwd2
Switch(config)# snmp-server enable traps
Switch(config)# snmp-server host 10.1.1.50 traps version 3 priv userZ cpu port-
  security
Switch(config)# snmp-server ifindex persist
```

As shown in Example 7-21 and the best practice list for SNMPv3 configuration, the first step is to configure a standard access list, such as access list 99. This access list is used to limit SNMP access to a local device to SNMP managers with addresses in subnet 10.1.1.0/24 (**permit 10.1.1.0. 0.0.0.255**). This restriction helps secure SNMP from outside networks.

The next step is to configure the restrictions to the MIBs. In Example 7-21, a text label of OPS was configured for both the read and write view for the group groupZ. As in the example, only specific object identifiers (OIDs) are allowed in the view. For the example, the permitted OIDs system uptime, interface status, and descriptions were added.

Continuing with the example, the next step is configuring the SNMPv3 security policy. The SNMPv3 group is configured with the authPriv security level (**snmp-server group groupZ v3 priv**), and the user for that group (**snmp-server userZ groupZ**) with passwords for both authentication (**auth sha itsasecret**) and encryption (**priv aes 256 anothersecret**).

The configuration example then enables SNMP traps with the **snmp-server enable traps** command. Traps are sent to an NMS or equivalent server; therefore, the receiving SNMP manager has to be configured. From the example, SNMPv3 traps will be sent to address 10.1.1.50 (**snmp-server host 10.1.1.50 traps**) using the user with the authPriv security level (**priv**). You can also limit events for which traps are sent. In the example, the traps are limited to CPU and port security-related events (**cpu port-security**).

SNMP does not identify object instances, such as network interfaces, by their names, but rather by their numeric indexes. Whenever a number of instances changes (for instance, when a new loopback interface is configured), index numbers may shuffle. As a consequence, the NMS may mismatch data from different interfaces. To prevent index shuffle, the **snmp-server ifindex persist** configuration command should be applied. This will guarantee index persistence over device reboots and minor software upgrades. Note that Cisco platforms attempt to reserve ifindex values to prevent renumbering.

Table 7-3 reviews the SNMP commands used in this subsection.

Table 7-3   *SNMP Command Reference*

Command	Description
snmp-server enable traps [*notification-type*]	Enables SNMP notification types that are available on your system
snmp-server group *group-name* {**v1** | **v2c** | **v3** {**auth** | **noauth** | **priv**}} [**context** *context-name*] [**read** *read-view*][**write** *write-view*] [**notify** *notify-view*][**access** [*acl-number* | *acl-name*]]	Configures a new SNMP group with specified authentication and optionally with the specified associated SNMP context, read, write, notify view, and associated ACL
snmp-server host {*ip-address*} [**infroms** | **traps**| **version**{**1** | **2c** | **3** {**auth** | **noauth**}}}	Specifies the recipient of an SNMP notification operation
snmp-server ifindex persist	Enable interface index persistence
snmp-server user *username group-name* {**v1** | **v2c** | **v3** [**encrypted**][**atuh** {**md5** | **sha**} *auth-password*]} [**access** [**priv** {**des** | **3des** | **aes** {**128** | **192** | **256**}} *privpassword*]] {*acl-number* | *acl-name*]}	Configures a new user to an SNMP group
snmp-server view *view-name oid-tree*	Creates a view entry

Verifying SNMP Version 3 Configuration

Verification of the administrative and operational state of SNMP is an important step in the overall process of setting up SNMPv3 in your network. The command **show snmp** provides users with basic information about SNMP configuration. Information such as whether the SNMP agent is enabled, whether traps are configured in addition to SNMP traffic statistics, is provided by the **show snmp** output. Example 7-22 shows output from the **show snmp** command.

Example 7-22   *Verifying SNMPv3 Configuration*

```
SW# show snmp
Chassis: FOC1322V1P5
0 SNMP packets input
    ...
    0 Get-request PDUs
    0 Get-next PDUs
    0 Set-request PDUs
    0 Input queue packet drops (Maximum queue size 1000)
476 SNMP packets output
    ...
    0 Response PDUs
    476 Trap PDUs
```

```
SNMP global trap: enabled

SNMP logging: enabled
    Logging to 10.1.1.50.162, 0/10, 476 sent, 0 dropped.
SNMP agent enabled
```

The command **show snmp view** gives the user information about the configured SNMP views. With this command, the user can verify for each group that OIDs are included and allowed. Also, there is a default read view (**v1default**) displayed, which is used if there are no custom read views configured. Example 7-23 shows an example of **show snmp view**.

Example 7-23 *Verifying SNMPv3 Configuration Views*

```
SW# show snmp view
OPS sysUpTime - included nonvolatile active
OPS ifDescr - included nonvolatile active
OPS ifAdminStatus - included nonvolatile active
OPS ifOperStatus - included nonvolatile active
v1default iso - included permanent active
v1default internet - included permanent active
v1default snmpUsmMIB - excluded permanent active
v1default snmpVacmMIB - excluded permanent active
v1default snmpCommunityMIB - excluded permanent active
v1default ciscoMgmt.252 - excluded permanent active
!...output omitted for brevity
```

The command **show snmp group** gives you information about configured SNMP groups. The most important parameters are security model and level, such as SNMPv3 authPriv, displayed as v3 priv in the command output.

Information about read and write views for the group is also displayed. Note that although the notify view was not configured explicitly, it is implicitly defined by a set of allowed SNMP objects for specific trap destination. This is defined at the moment when the trap receiver is configured and tied to a specific user. Access list information is also displayed.

Example 7-24 shows an example of **show snmp group**.

Example 7-24 *Verifying SNMPv3 Group Configurations*

```
SW# show snmp group
groupname:  groupZ                          security model:v3 priv
readview :  OPS                             writeview: OPS
notifyview: *tv.00000000.00000000.10000000.0
row status: active                          access-list: 99
```

The command **show snmp user** provides information about the configured SNMP users. The most important parameters to notice are usernames (userZ) and group names to which users belong (groupZ). In addition, authentication (SHA) and encryption (AES256) algorithms are displayed, which illustrates the security level of the group. Example 7-25 shows an example of **show snmp user**.

Example 7-25   *Verifying SNMP User Configuration*

```
SW# show snmp user
User name: userZ
Engine ID: 80000009030000260AC50201
storage-type: nonvolatile                      active
Authentication Protocol: SHA
Privacy Protocol: AES256
Group-name: groupZ
```

This subsection briefly covered SNMPv3. The goal of this subsection was to provide a quick overview to get started with SNMPv3 configuration. Entire texts have been written on SNMP. Refer to online documentation for a full deep-dive into SNMP, such as the following references:

- **SNMP introduction:** http://www.cisco.com/en/US/tech/tk648/tk362/tk605/tsd_technology_support_sub-protocol_home.html

- **SNMP Object Navigator:** http://tools.cisco.com/Support/SNMP/do/BrowseOID.do

Study Tips

- AAA stands for authentication, authorization, and accounting.

- Authentication identifies users prior to access.

- Authorization controls a user's access level or parameters.

- Accounting tracks users' access and activity.

- 802.1X is an identity-based networking protocol; its main value to Cisco Catalyst switches is providing security and placing users in VLANs based on their identity.

- NTP is a time synchronization protocol that achieves millisecond accuracy in LAN networks and ensures accuracy by using the concept of a stratum (hops away from authoritative clock source).

- RADIUS and TACACS+ are two AAA protocols. TACACS+ supports higher-level of security than RADIUS, but it is Cisco proprietary.

- SNMPv3 provides the necessary security for today's network because it supports securing both authentication and encryption of packets.

Summary

This chapter covered network management, including AAA, identity-based networking, NTP, and SNMP. All of these features are significant to all campus networks and found in all networks everywhere:

- The AAA features include authentication, authorization, and accounting. The use of AAA is required in nearly all campus networks because it secures and provides administrative control and logging of user access to network devices and to the network itself.

- Identity-based networking leverages protocols such as 802.1X to support mobility, security, authentication, and authorization of users to network resources.

- Accurate time is essential for time logging services in campus networks, as are many security features like encryption.

- All Cisco Catalyst switches support NTP for time synchronization.

- NTP generally achieves millisecond accuracy in LAN networks.

- SNMP is a lightweight protocol that not only monitors and controls devices but also supports alerting of events.

- SNMPv3 is the best practice recommendation for SNMP; avoid using SNMPv2 (or v1) if it all possible (because of its lack of security features).

- Security around SNMP must be considered as part of any implementation plan. At a minimum, use authentication and encryption along with restricted write access and IP ACLs to restrict network access.

Review Questions

Use the questions in this section as a review of what you have learned in this chapter. The correct answers are found in Appendix A, "Answers to Chapter Review Questions."

1. Which of the following statements are true? (Choose two.)

   a. Stratum 1 devices have directly attached radio or atomic clock.

   b. A higher stratum number always indicates greater quality and reliability.

   c. The stratum number represents the distance from a reference clock.

   d. Network will always synchronize with NTP server with the highest stratum number.

2. Which of the following SNMP statements are true? (Choose two.)

a. Given SNMP write access, a device can be remotely reconfigured via SNMP.

b. Network management systems (NMSs) include their own SNMP agent.

c. The **snmp-ifindex persist** command exposes interface counters over SNMP.

d. SNMP traps are sent from the SNMP agent to the SNMP manager and are event based.

3. Which of the following SNMP recommendations is not valid?

a. Always use MD5 authentication when SNMPv3 is not available and you are forced to use SNMPv2c.

b. Restrict access to read-only.

c. Set up views to restrict manager to only access needed set of MIBs.

d. Use ACLs to restrict SNMP access only to known managers.

4. What is the role of the switch in a AAA architecture?

a. Authentication server

b. Supplicant

c. Authenticator

d. RADIUS entry point

5. The users in a department are using a variety of host platforms, some old and some new. All of them have been approved with a user ID in a RADIUS server database. Which one of these features should be used to restrict access to the switch ports in the building?

a. AAA authentication

b. AAA accounting

c. AAA authorization

d. 802.1D

e. 802.1X

f. Port security

6. What is the aim of the "sticky" option when used with port security?

a. A learned MAC address must stick to one single port.

b. A dynamically learned MAC address is considered like a statically learned MAC address.

c. For a given MAC address with the sticky option, the port security feature applies to whichever port the MAC address connects to.

d. A router on a stick can bypass the port security feature.

7. At which layer should port security be implemented?

    a. Access layer

    b. Distribution layer

    c. Core layer

    d. All of the above

8. Match each AAA feature to its definition.

    A. Authentication   1. Controls the level of access users have

    B. Authorization   2. Identifies a user before allowing access to a protected resource

    C. Accounting   3. Collects information about the user's activity

9. With authorization, what defines user capabilities?

    a. Source IP address

    b. Login encryption keys

    c. Attribute-value pair

    d. All of the above

10. Leveraging AAA provides which of the following benefits to access control? (Select all that apply.)

    a. Flexibility

    b. Scalability

    c. Standardized Approach

    d. Redundancy

    e. All of the above

11. Which of the following statements are true? (Choose two.)

    a. TACACS+ and RADIUS are industry standard protocols.

    b. TACACS+ differs from RADIUS in that it splits all three AAA functions separately.

    c. TACACS+ encrypts the entire packet and supports bidirectional challenge responses.

    d. RADIUS encrypts the entire packet, but only supports unidirectional challenge responses.

12. Identity-based networks such as implemented in 802.1X allow for which of the following behaviors in the network? (Select all that apply.)

  a. Network access based on user authentication

  b. Mobility

  c. Placement of user into a VLAN based on identity

  d. Security

  e. All of the above

13. Match SNMP versions with their descriptions.

  A. SNMPv1   1. Initial version, rarely used today

  B. SNMPv2   2. Added a complex security model, but was never widely accepted

  C. SNMPv2c 3. Supports authentication and encryption and should be used whenever possible

  D. SNMPv3   4. Community based de-facto standard; widely used, but provides no security features besides a community string.

14. Different NTP restrictions can be configured through a combination of ACLs applying different modes of operation on Cisco devices. Match the restriction keyword with the restriction it applies.

  A. Peer   1. Time synchronization requests and control queries are allowed. Device is allowed to synchronize itself to remote systems that pass an access list.

  B. Query-only 2. Time synchronization requests and control queries are allowed. Device is not allowed to synchronize itself to remote systems that pass an access list.

  C. Serve   3. Only allows synchronization requests.

  D. Serve-only 4. Only allows control queries.

15. With time synchronization, what term describes whether a learned time is to be trusted?

  a. Authoritative

  b. Authenticated

  c. Stratum

  d. Associated

16. From the following list, what are the most authoritative sources for NTP? (Choose three.)

   a. An NTP server sourcing time from GPS

   b. An NTP server sourcing time from an NTP distribution switch

   c. An NTP server sourcing time from a radio clock

   d. An NTP server sourcing time from an atomic clock

   e. None of the above

17. What concept does NTP use to keep accuracy of time when synchronizing time in a network?

   a. NTP time shifting

   b. Stratum

   c. Bidirectional peering

   d. Full-mesh broadcasting

   e. None of the above

18. What level accuracy is generally achieved with NTP in a LAN environment?

   a. Seconds

   b. Milliseconds

   c. Microseconds

   d. Tens of seconds

21. What level accuracy is generally achieved with PTP in LAN environment?

   a. Seconds

   b. Milliseconds

   c. Microseconds

   d. Tens of seconds

Chapter 8

Switching Features and Technologies for the Campus Network

This chapter covers the following Cisco Catalyst switch features:

- Discovery protocols
- Unidirectional Link Detection
- Power over Ethernet
- SDM templates
- Monitoring features
- IP SLA

This chapter explores a variety of extremely useful features of Catalyst switches. The chapter begins with a discussion of Layer 2 discovery protocols, including Link Layer Discovery Protocol (LLDP) and Cisco Discovery Protocol (CDP). Both these features are ideal for verifying network topologies. The chapter continues with an important safety feature, Unidirectional Link Detection (UDLD). This feature is useful for ensuring faulty links do not result in network disasters. Following UDLD is a brief discussion on Power over Ethernet (POE), an extremely common feature in the campus network for powering phones, thin clients, and access points (APs). The next topic discusses Switch Database Management (SDM) templates; SDM templates are useful for configuring Cisco switches to meet specific needs in terms of scale of the campus network where default configurations may not suffice. Switched Port Analyzer (SPAN) and Remote SPAN (RSPAN) are the next features covered; these are common features for network troubleshooting and data analytics. The last section focuses on the Cisco IP Service Level Agreement (SLA); this feature provides feedback on the latency of the network.

Discovery Protocols

Cisco Discovery Protocol (CDP) was the original link layer protocol for the exchange of information. For many years, network operations and troubleshooters used CDP as the first step in building topology, troubleshooting, and so on. Moreover, many network orchestration tools leveraged CDP for neighbor information and mapping.

However, because interoperability between different vendors was needed, a new vendor-neutral link layer protocol was created called Link Layer Discovery Protocol (LLDP). The IEEE specification for LLDP is 802.1AB. Cisco Catalyst and Nexus switches support both these protocols.

This section on discovery protocols covers the following topics:

- Introduction to LLDP and comparison to CDP

- Basic configuration of LLDP

- Discovering neighbors using LLDP

Introduction to LLDP

As mentioned in the previous section, LLDP is an industry standard protocol for neighbor discovery. All current Cisco devices support LLDP, and only legacy and end-of-sale platforms may not support LLDP. Table 8-1 briefly recaps the differences between LLDP and CDP.

Table 8-1 *LLDP Compared to CDP*

	CDP	LLDP
Standard	No, Cisco proprietary	Defined as IEEE 802.1AB
Runs at	Layer 2: Data link layer	Layer 2: Data link layer
Benefits	Lightweight, may contain Cisco-specific information	Highly customizable

Because of the industry standard requirements around network designs, many campus networks are now leveraging LLDP over CDP. By definition, LLDP is a neighbor discovery protocol that is used for network devices to advertise information about themselves to other devices on the network. This protocol runs over the data link layer, which allows two systems running different network layer protocols to learn about each other. LLDP is locally significant, and the switch does not forward LLDP information; the switch only processes the information.

Moreover, LLDP supports a set of attributes that it uses to discover neighbor devices. These attributes contain type, length, and value descriptions and are referred to as TLVs. LLDP-supported devices can use TLVs to receive and send information to their neighbors. This protocol can advertise details such as configuration information, device capabilities, IP address, hostname, and device identity. Although LLDP is used for a plethora of information sharing, it is not architected to send out real-time information such as performance data or counter data.

An advantage of LLDP over CDP is that it allows for customization. LLDP can carry a lot of information that is relevant to your network. One drawback of LLDP in comparison to CDP is that it is not very lightweight.

The following list captures a few important implementation properties of LLDP:

- LLDP is unidirectional.

- LLDP operates only in an advertising mode.

- LLDP does not solicit for information or monitor state changes between LLDP nodes.

- LLDP leverages a Layer 2 multicast frame to notify neighbors of itself and its properties.

- LLDP will receive and record all information it receives about its neighbors.

LLDP uses 01:80:c2:00:00:0e, 01:80:c2:00:00:03, or 01:80:c2:00:00:00 as the destination multicast MAC address. Note that the 01 as the first octet signifies a Layer 2 multicast destination address.

The specification defines mandatory and optional TLVs (device information). The following list defines the most common information exchanged with LLDP (optional and mandatory) with campus switches:

- System name and description

- Port name and description

- Port VLAN and VLAN name

- Management IP address

- System Capabilities (Wi-Fi, routing, switching, and so on)

- Power over Ethernet

- Link aggregation

The next subsection discusses the basic configuration of LLDP.

Basic Configuration of LLDP

CDP is enabled by default on all Cisco devices, but LLDP may be either enabled or disabled by default, depending on the hardware platform and software version. Therefore, to enable LLDP on a device, use the command **lldp run** in global configuration mode. To disable it, use **no lldp run**.

In some cases, you may want to disable LLDP on a specific interface. One such example may be an interface connected to an Internet service provider (ISP). There is no need for the ISP to know details about your connected device, and it may be a security risk.

So, to disable LLDP on a specific interface, you need to disable both LLDP from receiving or transmitting LLDP by issuing both the **no lldp receive** and **no lldp transmit** commands. You can also set the interface to not receive (**no lldp receive**) or to not transmit (**no lldp transmit**) LLDP information individually. The best practice is to configure the interface to only receive on ports where security may be a risk. In this manner, you can learn of the connected device, but they cannot learn about you.

Note   Because LLDP is enabled by default on select platforms and software versions, the **lldp receive** and **lldp transmit** commands will not appear in the configuration by default.

To view the configuration status of LLDP globally, use the **show lldp** command. This command tells you whether LLDP is enabled on the device. In addition, the output will provide you with information like how often LLDP advertisements are sent, how many seconds the hold time is set for, and how the interface reinitialization delay is set. The LLDP advertisement time is the time interval for which an LLDP hello packet is sent; the default time is 30 seconds. The LLDP hold timer tells the device how long it should wait before declaring the neighbor unavailable. By default, the hold time is set to 120 seconds. Therefore, if the device does not hear from a neighbor for 120 seconds, it purges the neighbor entry from the LLDP table. See Example 8-1.

Example 8-1   *Basic Configuration of LLDP*

```
Switch# configure terminal
Enter configuration commands, one per line.  End with CNTL/Z.
Switch(config)# lldp run

Switch# show lldp

Global LLDP Information:
    Status: ACTIVE
    LLDP advertisements are sent every 30 seconds
    LLDP hold time advertised is 120 seconds
    LLDP interface reinitialization delay is 2 seconds

Switch# configure terminal
Enter configuration commands, one per line.  End with CNTL/Z.
Switch(config)# interface GigabitEthernet 0/1
Switch(config-if)# no lldp transmit
Switch(config-if)# lldp receive
```

```
Switch(config-if)# end

Switch# show running-config interface GigabitEthernet 0/1
Building configuration...

Current configuration : 60 bytes
!
interface GigabitEthernet0/1
 duplex auto
 no lldp transmit
end
```

Discovering Neighbors Using LLDP

The **show lldp neighbors** command displays output for the LLDP neighbors. This command provides a concise view of device ID, local interface type and number, hold-time settings, capabilities (device type), and port ID, among other info.

You can investigate the more detailed output of the LLDP neighbors using the **show lldp neighbors detail** command. You can also filter the output to a specific neighbor by specifying the interface to which the neighbor is connected. If the neighbor has a description configured under the interface, it will show up next to "Port id." Example 8-2 shows a practical example of **show lldp neighbor** and **show lldp neighbor detail** output.

Example 8-2 *Displaying LLDP Neighbors and Details About Neighbors*

```
CCNP-Switch1# show lldp neighbors
Capability codes:
    (R) Router, (B) Bridge, (T) Telephone, (C) DOCSIS Cable Device
    (W) WLAN Access Point, (P) Repeater, (S) Station, (O) Other

Device ID           Local Intf      Hold-time  Capability      Port ID
CCNP-Switch2    Fa0             120        B               Eth106/1/14

Total entries displayed: 1

CCNP-Switch1# show lldp neighbor detail
------------------------------------------------
Chassis id: 68ef.bd54.abcf
Port id: Eth106/1/14
Port Description: Ethernet106/1/14
System Name: CCNP-Switch2.cisco.com

System Description:
Cisco Nexus Operating System (NX-OS) Software
```

```
TAC support: http://www.cisco.com/tac
Copyright (c) 2002-2012, Cisco Systems, Inc. All rights reserved.

Time remaining: 118 seconds
System Capabilities: B
Enabled Capabilities: B
Management Addresses:
    IP: 10.1.28.18
Auto Negotiation - not supported
Physical media capabilities - not advertised
Media Attachment Unit type - not advertised
Vlan ID: 46
```

In addition, the **show lldp traffic** command shows you the statistics on exchanged LLDP frames between a device and its neighbors. See Example 8-3.

Example 8-3 *Displaying LLDP Traffic Info*

```
Switch1# show lldp traffic

LLDP traffic statistics:
    Total frames out: 42
    Total entries aged: 0
    Total frames in: 11
    Total frames received in error: 0
    Total frames discarded: 1
    Total TLVs unrecognized: 0
```

In summary, LLDP is a useful mechanism for local switch discovery. It is helpful in troubleshooting and building topology diagrams based on the actual state of the network. In addition, LLDP is commonly used by network management applications for building reports, topologies, and so on. The key takeaways for LLDP are as follows:

- LLDP allows network management applications to automatically discover and learn about network devices.

- LLDP is the industry standard alternative to the CDP.

- LLDP supports enabling or disabling either transmitting or receiving capabilities per port.

- To view LLDP neighbors, use the **show lldp neighbors [detail]** command.

The next section of this book focuses on another link layer protocol, Unidirectional Link Detection.

Unidirectional Link Detection

A unidirectional link occurs when traffic is transmitted between neighbors in one direction only. Most Layer 1 mechanisms built in to the Ethernet specification detect this connection and either prevent the link from ever establishing or bring the link up. However, in some situations, Layer 1 may be operating correctly from a link level but at Layer 2 traffic is unidirectional. Figure 8-1 illustrates this behavior of Unidirectional Link Detection (UDLD).

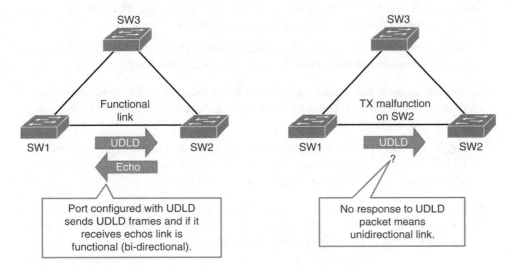

Figure 8-1   *UDLD*

This unidirectional condition at Layer 2 is disastrous for any network because it will lead to either spanning tree not blocking on a forwarding port or a routing black hole. In either of these situations, the network will exhibit a total failure, become instable, and eventually create a complete loss of connectivity for end users.

The conditions where a Layer 1 link is up but Layer 2 is adversely operating are mostly anomalous conditions. For example, although the Cisco switch is designed with the utmost resiliency, it is possible that a transient hardware failure may lead to the described condition. This transient hardware condition may be fixed with a simple reboot, similar to a malfunctioning laptop needing a reboot. The following list summarizes potential cases where UDLD may prevent a complete network meltdown:

- Transient hardware condition

- Hardware failure

- Optic/GBIC (gigabit interface converter) anomalous behavior or failure

- Miswired cabling

- Software defect or condition

- Misconfigured or malfunction of inline tap or sniffer

UDLD Mechanisms and Specifics

UDLD is supported on all current Cisco Catalyst and Nexus switches. UDLD functions by transmitting Layer 2 packets to the well-known MAC address 01:00:0C:CC:CC:CC. If the packets are not echoed back within a specific time frame, the link is flagged as unidirectional, and the interface may be error disabled depending on operating mode. Devices on both ends of the link must support UDLD for the protocol to successfully identify and disable unidirectional links.

UDLD messages are sent at regular intervals. This timer can be modified. The default setting varies between platforms; however, the typical value is 15 seconds.

The behavior of UDLD after it detects a unidirectional link is dependent on its operation mode, either normal mode or aggressive mode. The modes are described as follows:

- **Normal mode:** When a unidirectional link is detected the port is allowed to continue its operation. UDLD just marks the port as having an undetermined state. A syslog message is generated.

- **Aggressive mode:** When a unidirectional link is detected the switch tries to reestablish the link. It sends one message a second, for 8 seconds. If none of these messages are sent back, the port is placed in error-disabled state.

Obviously, the recommended best practice is aggressive mode because normal mode takes no action to prevent a network disaster other than just notification. The authors of this book also consider aggressive mode a highly recommended best practice.

UDLD Configuration

Cisco Catalyst switches support configuration of UDLD on a per-port basis. However, there is an option to enable UDLD on fiber-optic ports globally.

To configure a Cisco Catalyst switch for UDLD normal mode, use the **udld enable** command. Similarly, to enable UDLD in aggressive mode, use the **udld aggressive** keyword.

To display the UDLD status for the specified interface or for all interfaces, use the **show udld** [*interface slot/number*] privileged EXEC command. To view UDLD neighbors, use the **show udld neighbors**.

In addition, use **udld reset** command to reset all the interfaces that were shut down by UDLD. You can also achieve a UDLD reset by first shutting down the interface and then bringing it back up (that is, **shut**, then **no shut**). Example 8-4 illustrates a few example configuration steps of UDLD aggressive mode with status.

Example 8-4   *UDLD Configuration and Status*

```
Switch1(config)# udld aggressive

:

Switch1# show udld neighbors
```

```
Port      Device Name   Device ID    Port ID    Neighbor State
----      -----------   ---------    -------    --------------
Gi1/33    FOX10430380   1            Gi1/33     Bidirectional
Gi1/34    FOX10430380   1            Gi1/34     Bidirectional

Switch# show udld GigabitEthenet1/34
Interface Gi1/34
---
Port enable administrative configuration setting: Enabled / in aggressive mode
Port enable operational state: Enabled / in aggressive mode
 Current bidirectional state: Bidirectional
Current operational state: Advertisement - Single neighbor detected
Message interval: 15000 ms
Time out interval: 5000 ms

Port fast-hello configuration setting: Disabled
Port fast-hello interval: 0 ms
Port fast-hello operational state: Disabled
Neighbor fast-hello configuration setting: Disabled
Neighbor fast-hello interval: Unknown
          Entry 1                        ---
Expiration time: 43300 ms
Cache Device index: 1
Current neighbor state: Bidirectional
Device ID: FOX10430380
Port ID: Gi1/34
Neighbor echo 1 device: FOX104303NL
Neighbor echo 1 port: Gi1/34
          TLV Message interval: 15 sec
No TLV fast-hello interval
TLV Time out interval: 5
TLV CDP Device name: Switch
```

Note the UDLD default behavior and feature support may be different between different Cisco Catalyst switch models and different software versions. Table 8-2 lists the most common default behavior for UDLD.

Table 8-2 *UDLD Default Behaviors*

Feature	Default Behavior
UDLD global state	Disabled
UDLD Per-interface enable state for fiber-optic ports	Enabled on all Ethernet fiber-optic ports
UDLD per-interface enable state for copper ethernet ports	Disable on all copper Ethernet ports

In the event that a unidirectional link is detected by UDLD, the Cisco Catalyst switch will disable the respective port and log the following message as an example:

```
UDLD-3-DISABLE: Unidirectional link detected on port 1/2.
```

Depending on mode, once the port is disabled, it remains disabled until it is manually reenabled or until the err-disable timeout expires (if configured).

The next subsection discusses leveraging UDLD with STP Loop Guard for additional network resiliency.

Leveraging UDLD and STP Loop Guard Together

STP Loop Guard and UDLD both are able to protect against anomalous behavior of Cisco switches that lead to spanning-tree failures. However, they differ in implementation and the situations in which they protect the network. Table 8-3 summarizes the functionality and differences between Loop Guard and UDLD. It is a best practice to use both features together for ultimate network resiliency.

Table 8-3   *Loop Guard and UDLD Functionality Comparison*

Functionality	Loop Guard	UDLD
Configuration granularity	Per-VLAN	Per-Port
Protection against STP failures caused by unidirectional links	Yes, when enabled on all non-designated ports in a redundant topology.	Yes, when enabled on all ports in the topology
Protection against STP failures that are caused by software anomalies, resulting in switches not sending bridge protocol data units (BDPUs)	Yes	No

The next section of this chapter discusses PoE and its uses in the campus network.

Power over Ethernet

Everyday household and commercial devices are beginning to gain IP connectivity, beyond laptops, gaming devices, tables, and cell phones. Some of the devices include refrigerators, microwaves, TVs, washers and dryers, and so on. Soon, billions of devices will be connected to the Internet, even smaller devices (Internet of Everything). Not all these devices will be connected using a wireless connection. If there is a need for high-speed connectivity or a desire to supply power to the device through Ethernet, cabling is a requirement. This is where Power over Ethernet (PoE) becomes important. PoE, also referred to as inline power, supplies power through the same cable as data. This technology reduces the need for power when wired connectivity is needed. Cisco Catalyst switches support PoE on specific models of switches. Figure 8-2 illustrates an example of the converged physical infrastructure PoE offers.

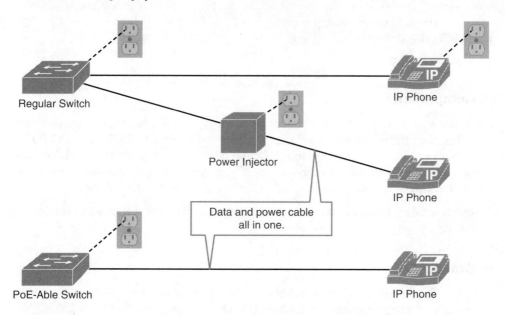

Figure 8-2   *Converged Physical Cabling Associated with PoE*

One example of the use of PoE is for security cameras. Although security cameras can use wireless, wired connections are more stable and provide a method to provide power without a local wall outlet in the same location as the camera.

In the campus network, PoE most commonly uses Cisco Catalyst switches to provide power for wireless access points, IP phones, thin clients, and security cameras. Alternatively, a power injector can provide power inline over a data connection.

In summary, a campus network that leverages Cisco Catalyst switches for PoE benefits from the following:

- PoE switches support remote management where power adapters and injectors do not.

- PoE switches allow for centralized methods of backup power.

- PoE requires less configuration than a local power adapter or injector.

- PoE leverages the data cabling infrastructure, and no additional power cable is required as with the case with power adapters or injectors.

Note   Cisco highly recommends leveraging alternate and backup power sources when deploying PoE such as an uninterruptible backup supply (UPS) backup, generator power, and so on. Without backup power in the case of a power failure, Cisco IP phones will cease to function.

PoE Components

PoE terminology refers to three types of components: power-sourcing devices, powered devices, and Ethernet cabling. Examples of power-source devices (PSE) include Cisco Catalyst switches and power injectors. Powered devices include access points, IP phones, and IP cameras. There are numerous other PoE-capable devices, such as thin clients, sensors, wall clocks, and so on. Even switches can be powered through PoE itself.

As with standard Ethernet, the distance of PoE is limited to 100 meters with Category 5 cabling.

PoE Standards

Because Cisco generally leads in technologies before standards are available, Cisco originally only supported the prestandard Cisco Inline Power standard (circa 2000). Eventually, standards committees released an IEEE standards-based power specification and more recently updated this power specification. The specifics are as follows:

- **IEEE 802.3af (ratified 2003):** This standard provides interoperability between different vendors. Up to 15.4 W of DC power is available for each powered device.

- **IEEE 802.3at (ratified 2009):** This standard is an improvement over the 802.3af standard, and can provide powered devices with up to 25.5 W of power. This number can be increased to 50 W and more with implementations that are outside the standard. This standard is also known as PoE+ or PoE Plus.

PoE Negotiation

The Cisco switches do not supply power to a port unless it specifically detects the need by the end device. This prevents wasting of unnecessary power and so on.

With 802.3af and 802.3at, the switch tries to detect the powered device by supplying a small voltage across the Ethernet cable. The switch then measures the resistance. If the measured resistance is 25K ohm, a powered device is present. The powered device can provide the switch with a power class information. Based on that information, the switch can allocate the powered device with the appropriate maximum power.

IEEE 802.3at power classes are numbered from 0 to 4. The default class of 0 is used if either the switch or the powered device does not support power class discovery. Table 8-4 lists the power classes.

Table 8-4 *PoE Power Classes*

IEEE Power Class	Min. Power Output	Notes
0	15.4 W	Default class
1	4 W	Optional class
2	7 W	Optional class
3	15.4 W	Optional class
4	51 W	Valid for 802.3at devices only (that is, thin clients)

Note The original Cisco Inline Power method has a different method of negotiating power than both of the IEEE standards. The switch sends out a 340-kHz test tone on the Ethernet cable. A tone is transmitted instead of DC power because the switch must first detect the device before supplying it with power. The most appropriate power level is then determined by exchange of CDP information. The switch discovers the type of device (for example, a Cisco IP phone) and the power requirements of the device.

Configuring and Verifying PoE

You can turn on PoE support at the port level. The **power inline auto** command is sufficient to enable PoE and autodetection of power requirements. A device not needing any PoE can still be connected to that port; power is supplied only if the device requires it. The amount of power that is supplied will be automatically detected. You still have to plan for the overall power that is consumed by all the devices that are connected to the PoE switch.

PoE is disabled with the **power inline never** command. Shutting down the port also stops the power supply.

The **show power inline** command displays the configuration and statistics about the power that is drawn by connected powered devices and the capacity of the power supply.

When you are implementing PoE for wireless APs and IP phones, be careful of the switch power budget. The power budget is the total amount of power that a switch can offer to end devices collectively. In Example 8-5, 420 W total is available and the switch has 327.6 W power remaining.

Example 8-5 *Configuring and Verifying PoE*

```
Switch(config-if)# power inline {auto | never}
! Configures the switch port to automatically negotiate inline power levels or to
  turn off PoE
Switch# show power inline
Module      Available                   Used                Remaining
            (Watts)                     (Watts)             (Watts)

---------   ------------                ----------          ------------
1             420.0                       92.4                 327.6
Interface   Admin    Oper    Power    Device            Class    Max
                             (Watts)

-----------  ------   -----   ------   ----------------  ------   -----
Gi1/0/1     auto     off      0.0     n/a               n/a      15.4
Gi1/0/2     auto     on      15.4     AIR-LAP1142N-E-K9    3      15.4
Gi1/0/3     auto     on      15.4     AIR-LAP1142N-E-K9    3      15.4
Gi1/0/4     auto     on      15.4     AIR-LAP1142N-E-K9    3      15.4
Gi1/0/5     auto     on      15.4     AIR-LAP1142N-E-K9    3      15.4
Gi1/0/6     auto     on      15.4     AIR-LAP1142N-E-K9    3      15.4
Gi1/0/7     never    off      0.0     n/a               n/a      15.4
<...output omitted>
! Displays information about PoE on a switch
```

The next subsection covers SDM templates.

SDM Templates

The Switching Database Manager (SDM) templates on specific access layer switches (such as Cisco Catalyst 2960, 3560, or 3750) manages how Layer 2 and Layer 3 switching information is maintained in the ternary content-addressable memory (TCAM). So, different Cisco SDM templates are used for optimal use of system resources for specific features or feature set combination. Although the default SDM is configured for optimal use of all features simultaneously, SDM may be tweaked for those corner-case or specific scenarios.

As an example, the most common SDM default modification action is when deploying a combination of both IPv4 and IPv6 (dual stack) because IPv6 functionality is not supported with the default template. This example is discussed in more detail in upcoming subsections.

Upon completing this section on SDM templates, you will be able to do the following:

■ Describe the typical SDM template types

■ Change the SDM template

■ Describe precautions to take when changing the SDM templates

SDM Template Types

As an example, the architectures of access layer switches were not optimized for Open Shortest Path First (OSPF) or Border Gateway Protocol (BGP) Layer 3 routing even though support exists in the platform for these protocols. Therefore, the default use of resources on the switches focuses on a more common set of tasks where specific model Catalyst switches support reallocation of resources for specific tasks such as Layer 3 routing.

SDM templates modify system resources such as CAM and TCAM. One example may be an SDM template that optimizes the use of access control list (ACL) TCAM. By sacrificing unnecessary features in your network such as IPv6, you may be able to increase the size of the ACLs entries in the switch.

SDM templates vary between Catalyst and Nexus switches and IOS version and NX-OS versions. For example, the following SDM templates from a Cisco Catalyst 3750 switch illustrate a few use cases for SDM templates:

- **Default:** The default template; this template provides for a mix of unicast routes, connected, and host routes.

- **Routing:** As one example, you would enable this template if the device is performing routing in the distribution or core of the network. The device is able to carry numerous routes, but only for IPv4.

- **Access:** You would enable this template if you have many VLANs. In turn, this template reduces the resources that are allocated to routing.

- **VLAN:** When you enable this template, you allocate most of the table space to Layer 2 unicasts. You would use this when you have large subnets with many MAC addresses.

- **Dual IPv4 and IPv6:** You would enable this template if you want to turn on the IPv6 capabilities of the device. When enabling this template, you have to choose between default, routing, and VLAN:

  - **Default:** More space is reserved for IPv6 routing and security. There is less reserved space for Layer 2 unicast.

  - **Routing:** More space is reserved for IPv6 routing than IPv4 routing.

  - **VLAN:** Suitable for when you are running a dual-stack environment with lots of VLANs.

> **Note** If you are attempting to enable IPv6 on a Catalyst switch and the command set is not supported, there may be a need to change the default template to support IPv6.

Example 8-6 illustrates the SDM resource adjustments between a switch with the default template applied and a dual-stack configuration, respectively, after necessary commands have been entered.

Example 8-6   *Displaying SDM Resources*

```
Switch# show sdm prefer
The current template is "desktop default" template.
The selected template optimizes the resources in
the switch to support this level of features for
8 routed interfaces and 1024 VLANs.

  number of unicast mac addresses:                  6K
  number of IPv4 IGMP groups + multicast routes:    1K
  number of IPv4 unicast routes:                    8K
  number of directly-connected IPv4 hosts:          6K
  number of indirect IPv4 routes:                   2K
  number of IPv4 policy based routing aces:         0
  number of IPv4/MAC qos aces:                       0.5K
  number of IPv4/MAC security aces:                 1K

Switch# show sdm prefer
The current template is "desktop IPv4 and IPv6 default" template.
The selected template optimizes the resources in
the switch to support this level of features for
8 routed interfaces and 1024 VLANs.

  number of unicast mac addresses:                  2K
  number of IPv4 IGMP groups + multicast routes:    1K
  number of IPv4 unicast routes:                    3K
  number of directly-connected IPv4 hosts:          2K
  number of indirect IPv4 routes:                   1K
  number of IPv6 multicast groups:                  1.125k
  number of directly-connected IPv6 addresses:      2K
  number of indirect IPv6 unicast routes:           1K
  number of IPv4 policy based routing aces:         0
  number of IPv4/MAC qos aces:                      0.5K
  number of IPv4/MAC security aces:                 1K
  number of IPv6 policy based routing aces:         0
  number of IPv6 qos aces:                          0.625k
  number of IPv6 security aces:                     0.5K
```

Choosing the Right SDM Template

It is a best practice to change the SDM template only if you have a good reason to do so. Before changing the template, investigate whether the change is needed or if it is just a workaround for poor design choices. Ideally for access switches, you should only change the template for IPv6 usage unless directed by a Cisco advisor or architect.

As another best practice, always investigate the amount of systems resources being used prior to considering changes to the SDM template. To verify how much of the system resources are being used, use the command **show platform tcam utilization**. If the TCAM utilization is close to maximum for any of the parameters, check if any of the other template features can optimize for that parameter: **show sdm prefer** {access | default | dual-ipv4-and-ipv6 | routing | vlan}.

Another common reason for changing the SDM template is because you are running out of a specific resource. For example, the use of the switch in a large Layer 2 domain with many ACLs may require a change to the access SDM template. In these kinds of situations, it is important to first investigate whether you can optimize the performance so that you do not need to change the SDM template. It might be that the ACLs that you are using are set up inefficiently such as having redundant entries, the most common entries are at the end of the list, and unnecessary entries. When you change the SDM template, this will not only reserve resources, but will also release other resource reservations. So, while you are solving the problem with ACLs, you might now start running out of resources for unicast routing for example.

System Resource Configuration on Other Platforms

This section on SDM templates introduced you to the concept of managing finite resources on the Catalyst 3750 platform. Other platforms such as the Catalyst 4500, Catalyst 6500, and Catalyst 6800 also have finite TCAM resources where allocation of resources may need to be adjusted. The study of managing these resources on all Catalyst platforms is beyond the scope of CCNP; however, it is important to recognize the mechanism exists on other platforms to tune TCAM usage under different naming conventions.

In brief, SDM templates configure the switch for specific allocation of finite resources. The use of SDM templates is summarized as follows:

- To verify the amount of resources being used, use the command **show platform tcam utilization**.

- To verify the SDM template that is currently in use, use the command **show sdm prefer**.

- To change the template to dual stack, use the command **sdm prefer dual-ipv4-and-ipv6 default**.

- When changing the SDM template, a reload of the switch is required.

■ The concept of SDM templates is applicable to Cisco Catalyst 3750 and other platforms; specific Catalyst platforms such as the Catalyst 6500 that do not use SDM templates have a similar method to adjust allocation of finite resources.

Monitoring Features

Cisco switches provide various useful information to monitor and troubleshoot your campus network. This information includes resource utilization, traffic counts, error counters, and so on. However, certain traffic details for troubleshooting or traffic analytics requires the use of traffic sniffers, taps, probes, and analyzers to capture actual packets. Because switches do not flood traffic on all ports, use of the Switch Port Analyzer (SPAN) feature is necessary to ensure appropriate traffic is fed to these traffic sniffers. This section discusses this feature and its use in the campus network.

Upon completing this lesson, you will be able to meet these objectives:

■ Describe SPAN

■ Describe SPAN terminology

■ Describe different versions of SPAN

■ Configure SPAN

■ Verify local SPAN configuration

■ Configure RSPAN

■ Verify RSPAN configuration

SPAN and RSPAN Overview

The SPAN feature allows you to instruct a switch to send copies of packets seen on one port, multiple ports, or a VLAN to another port on the same switch. As mentioned in the previous subsection, this is an important feature for traffic or application analytics such as traffic sniffers and probes.

Referencing Figure 8-3, to capture and analyze the traffic flowing from PC1 to PC2 on the sniffer, SPAN configuration is required. The first step in configuring SPAN is specifying a source port. For the example in Figure 8-3, you can either configure interface Gigabit Ethernet 0/1 to capture the ingress traffic or interface Gigabit Ethernet 0/2 to capture the egress traffic. Second, you need to specify interface Gigabit Ethernet 0/3 as a destination port. After the configuration is applied, traffic flowing from PC1 to PC2 will then be copied to the SPAN destination of the Gigabit Ethernet 0/3 interface where it can be analyzed with a traffic sniffer.

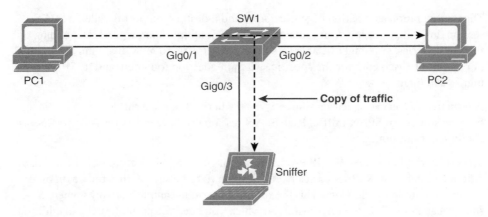

Figure 8-3 *Example Use of SPAN*

SPAN also supports monitoring traffic from an entire VLAN. In a single switch, this feature may be useful. However, in a large network, the sniffer may not have the processing power to capture traffic for all the communication on a VLAN. Traffic sniffers can filter traffic; however, you still cannot send 40 Gbps of SPAN traffic out to a 10-Gbps port. In other words, plan for the use of sniffers and problems carefully and ensure that they can handle the amount of traffic that is sent to them.

SPAN features two different port types. The source port is a port that is monitored for traffic analysis. SPAN can copy ingress, egress, or ingress and egress traffic from a source port. Both Layer 2 and Layer 3 ports can be configured as SPAN source ports. Traffic is copied to SPAN destination (monitor) port. Figure 8-4 illustrates these port designations where the goal is to capture traffic sourced from PC1.

- **SPAN session:** An association of a destination port with source ports.
- **Source VLAN:** VLAN monitored for traffic analysis.

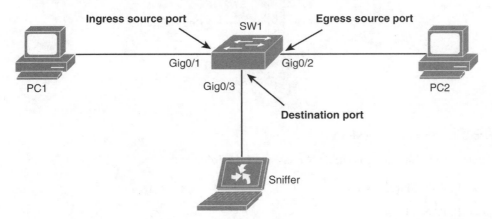

Figure 8-4 *SPAN Terminology*

The configuration association of source ports and a destination port is called a SPAN session. In a single session, you can monitor one or multiple source ports. Depending on the switch series, you might be able to copy session traffic to more than one destination port. Consult Cisco.com for the specific switch in question to understand its SPAN capabilities and limits.

Alternatively, you can specify a source VLAN, where all ports in the source VLAN become sources of SPAN traffic. Each SPAN session can have either ports or VLANs as sources, but not both.

Moreover, the Remote SPAN (RSPAN) feature takes the SPAN feature beyond a single switch to a network. RSPAN basically enables you to remotely capture traffic on different switches in the network. This is extremely useful in campus networks where a sniffer may not be located on a switch on which you need to capture traffic. In addition, this allows you to also place a sniffer permanently attached to the campus network to SPAN traffic as necessary or when troubleshooting situations arise. Figure 8-5 shows an example of RSPAN.

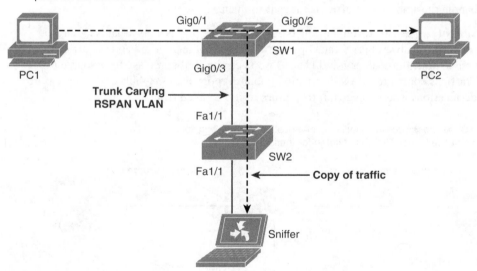

Figure 8-5   *Example of RSPAN*

In terms of configuration, RSPAN consists of the following:

- RSPAN source session
- RSPAN VLAN
- RSPAN destination session

You separately configure RSPAN source sessions and destination sessions on different switches. Your monitored traffic is flooded into RSPAN VLAN that is dedicated for the RSPAN session in all participating switches. RSPAN destination port can then be anywhere in that VLAN.

On some of the platforms, a reflector port needs to be specified together with RSPAN VLAN. A reflector port is a physical interface that acts as a loopback and reflects the traffic that is copied from source ports to an RSPAN VLAN. No traffic is actually sent out of the interface that is assigned as the reflector port. The need for a reflector port is caused by hardware design limitations on some platforms. A reflector port can only be used for one session at a time. The next section goes into detail about configuration specifics of SPAN and then RSPAN.

SPAN Configuration

The capabilities of SPAN are platform dependent. Some Catalyst switches support multiple source and destination ports, multiple sessions, and so on. In addition, there are hardware limitations on SPAN in terms of placement of ports and so on. There are many enhancements and restrictions that are platform specific; an entire book could be written on SPAN. Nevertheless, in general, SPAN adheres to the following caveats, especially on lower-end switches such as the Catalyst 2900, 3500, and 3750 family of switches:

- A destination port cannot be a source port or vice versa.

- The number of destination ports is platform dependent; some platforms allow for more than one destination.

- Destination ports do not act as normal ports and do not participate in spanning tree and so on. Normal traffic flows through a destination. Be careful not to connect anything besides an end device to a SPAN destination port.

In the example shown in Figure 8-6, the objective is to capture all the traffic that is sent or received by the PC connected to port Gigabit Ethernet 0/1 on the switch. A packet sniffer is connected to port Gigabit Ethernet 0/2. The switch is instructed to copy all the traffic that it sends and receives on port Gigabit Ethernet 0/1 to port Gigabit Ethernet 0/2 by configuring a SPAN session.

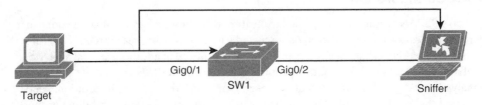

Figure 8-6 *Example SPAN Configuration*

The SPAN session is identified by a session number (in this example, 1). The first step is then that you associate SPAN session with source ports or VLANs by using the following command:

```
monitor session number source interface/vlans
```

Similarly, you associate destination port with SPAN session number by using the following command:

```
monitor session number destination interface/vlans
```

To verify the SPAN session configuration, use the **show monitor** command. The **show monitor** command returns the type of the session, source ports for each traffic direction, and the destination port.

Example 8-7 illustrates a basic configuration of SPAN for Figure 8-6.

Example 8-7   *Sample Local SPAN Configuration*

```
Switch1(config)# monitor session 1 source interface GigabitEthernet 0/1
Switch1(config)# monitor session 1 destination interface GigabitEthernet 0/2

Switch1# show monitor

Switch# show monitor
Session 1
---------
Type                   : Local Session
Source Ports           :
    Both               : Gi0/1
Destination Ports      : Gi0/2
    Encapsulation      : Native
            Ingress    : Disabled
```

The next section discusses RSPAN, taking SPAN beyond a local switch.

RSPAN Configuration

Cisco's RSPAN feature is a revolutionary feature that allows creating SPAN sessions that cross physical switch boundaries. As discussed earlier, this feature is extremely useful when placing sniffers and analyzers in a strategic location. In addition, several analytic software packages and trading floor applications leverage RSPAN for remote traffic analysis. RSPAN configuration requires a few extra steps than SPAN. In addition, keep in mind that different models of Catalyst switches support different capabilities around RSPAN. This section discusses RSPAN in general support as found on the Catalyst 3750.

With RSPAN, because the source and destination ports are on different switches, a special and unique VLAN is required to transport the traffic from one switch to another. You configure this VLAN as any other VLAN, but in addition, you enter the **remote-span** keyword in VLAN configuration mode. You need to define this VLAN on all switches in the path and allow the VLAN on trunk ports between the source and destination.

Remote SPAN uses two sessions, one session as the source and one session to copy or receive the traffic from a VLAN.

As an example with Figure 8-7, RSPAN needs to be set up for the sniffer attached to SW2 and needs to be configured to view the traffic to and from the PC attached to SW1.

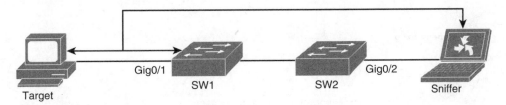

Figure 8-7   *RSPAN*

From SW1 perspective, the first step is configuring the RSPAN VLAN. The commands are as follows:

```
SW1(config)# vlan 100
SW1(config-vlan)# name RSPAN-VLAN
SW1(config-vlan)# remote-span
SW1(config-vlan)# exit
SW1(config)# monitor session 2 source interface GigabitEthernet0/1
SW1(config)# monitor session 2 destination remote vlan 100
```

The monitor session commands configure SPAN from and to Gigabit Ethernet 0/1 on the RSPAN VLAN 100.

Subsequently, from the SW2 perspective, the configuration is as follows:

```
SW2(config)# vlan 100
SW2(config-vlan)# name RSPAN-VLAN
SW2(config-vlan)# remote-span
SW2(config-vlan)# exit
SW2(config)# monitor session 2 destination interface GigabitEthernet 0/2
SW2(config)# monitor session 2 source remote vlan 100
```

These monitor session commands configure the sniffer (SPAN destination) as Gigabit Ethernet 0/2 and the source VLAN as 100.

When verifying the configuration, the output of the **show monitor** command SW1 and SW2 is as follows, respectively:

```
SW1# show monitor


Session 2
---------

Type                        : Remote Source Session
Source Ports                :
    Both                    : Gi0/2
Dest RSPAN VLAN             : 100



SW2# show monitor



---------

Type                        : Remote Destination Session
Source RSPAN VLAN           : 100
Destination Ports           : Gi0/2
    Encapsulation           : Native
          Ingress           : Disabled
```

In addition to verifying the correct configuration, it is also important that you verify that the VLAN is configured correctly as RSPAN VLAN on both switches. You can verify this by using the **show vlan remote-span** command.

In summary, SPAN and RSPAN are useful tools for monitoring and capturing network traffic. These features may be used for simple PC performance debugging or leveraged for traffic analytics in trading floor environments. RSPAN allows for SPAN configuration beyond a single switch and allows for centralized placed sniffers.

The next section journeys into a completely orthogonal feature to SPAN and RSPAN, IP SLA.

IP SLA

The Cisco IOS IP SLA (Service Level Agreement) feature can be used to gather realistic information on how specific types of traffic are being handled when they flow across the network. An IP SLA device generates traffic destined to a far-end device. When the far-end device responds, the IP SLA device gathers data about what happened to the traffic along the way. Upon completion of this section, you will understand the following:

- Basic use cases of IP SLA

- What an IP SLA source and responder are

- Basic example of an ICMP IP SLA configuration and a UDP configuration

Introduction to IP SLA

Because campus networks and data centers have become increasingly critical for customers, any downtime or degradation of these networks can adversely affect company revenues. Therefore, companies need some form of predictability with IP services. An SLA (service level agreement) is a contract between the network provider and its customers, or between a network department and internal corporate customers. It provides a form of guarantee to customers about the level of user experience.

SLA may contain specifics about connectivity and performance agreements for an end-user service from a service provider. An SLA typically outlines the minimum level of service and the expected level of service. The networking department can use the SLAs to verify that the service provider is meeting its own SLAs or to define service levels for critical business applications. An SLA can also be used as the basis for planning budgets and justifying network expenditures.

Typically, the technical components of an SLA contain a guaranteed level for network availability, network performance in terms of round-trip-time (RTT), and network response in terms of latency, jitter, and packet loss. The specifics of an SLA vary depending on the applications that an organization is supporting in the network.

A simple example of an IP SLA test is the ICMP echo test. IP SLA uses ICMP Echo Request and Response packets to test availability of far-end devices. The far-end device can be any device with IP capabilities such as router, switch, PC, or server. Figure 8-8 illustrates an ICMP echo test.

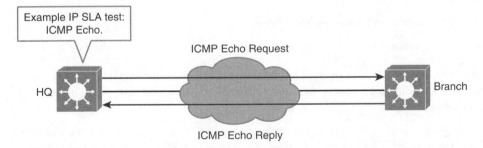

Figure 8-8 *IP SLA ICMP Echo Test Example*

Overall, the IP SLA feature provides real-time feedback about network reachability. For features such as voice and video, network availability with stable jitter and latency are important. The IP SLA provides the feedback necessary to ensure the network can sustain real-time applications as well as mission-critical applications such as web portal or ordering. Additional functions and uses for IP SLA are as follows:

- Edge-to-edge network availability monitoring.

- Network performance monitoring and network performance visibility

- Voice over IP (VoIP), video, and virtual private network (VPN) monitoring

- SLA monitoring

- IP service network health

- MPLS network monitoring

- Troubleshooting of network operation

Consult Cisco.com for any specific details about these functions you are not familiar with. From a network perspective, IP SLA provides feedback on these functions (among others):

- Gather information of VoIP quality.

- Track interfaces to influence behavior of first-hop redundancy protocols (Hot Standby Router Protocol [HSRP], Virtual Router Redundancy Protocol [VRRP], Gateway Load Balancing Protocol [GLBP]).

- When thresholds are breached, schedule further IP SLA tests that will tell you more about your network.

- When a threshold is breached send an SNMP trap.

Going even future into the details, IP SLA measures various operation characters via actively generated traffic probes. These probes gather statistics such as the following:

- Network latency and response time

- Packet-loss statistics

- Network jitter and voice quality scoring

- End-to-end network connectivity

Moreover, multiple IP SLA operations (measurements) can be running in a network at any given time. Reporting tools then can use SNMP to extract the data into a database and then report on it.

The supported probes or tests that IP SLA supports varies significantly between platform and software versions. Example 8-8 illustrates the supported configurations options for IP SLA on a Catalyst 3750 switch.

Example 8-8   *IP SLA Options Available on a Catalyst 3750*

```
Switch(config-ip-sla)# ?
IP SLAs entry configuration commands:
  dhcp              DHCP Operation
  dns               DNS Query Operation
  exit              Exit Operation Configuration
  ftp               FTP Operation
  http              HTTP Operation
  icmp-echo         ICMP Echo Operation
```

```
path-echo          Path Discovered ICMP Echo Operation
path-jitter        Path Discovered ICMP Jitter Operation
tcp-connect        TCP Connect Operation
udp-echo           UDP Echo Operation
udp-jitter         UDP Jitter Operation
```

IP SLA Source and Responder

The IP SLA source is where all IP SLA measurement probe operations are configured either by the command-line interface (CLI) or through an SNMP tool that supports the IP SLA operation. The source is also the Cisco IOS device that sends probe packets. The destination of the probe may be another Cisco device or another network target such as a web server or IP host.

Although the destination of the majority of the tests can be any IP device, the measurement accuracy of some of the tests can be improved with an IP SLA responder. An IP SLA responder is a device that runs Cisco IOS Software. The responder adds a time stamp to the packets sent so the IP SLA source can take into account any latency that occurred while the responder is processing the test packets. For this test to work properly, both the source and responder clocks need to be synchronized through Network Time Protocol (NTP).

In review, the IP SLA source is the Cisco IOS Software device that sends data for operation/analysis. The target device may or may not be a Cisco IOS Software device; however, some operations require an IP SLA responder.

Subsequently, the IP SLA responder is a Cisco IOS Software device that is configured to respond to IP SLA packets and supports more accurate measurement than a non-IP SLA responder.

IP SLA Configuration

To implement IP SLA network performance measurement, you need to perform the following tasks:

Step 1. Enable the IP SLAs responder, if required.

Step 2. Configure the required IP SLA's operation type.

Step 3. Configure any options available for the specified operation type.

Step 4. Configure threshold conditions, if required.

Step 5. Schedule the operation to run, and then let the operation run for a period of time to gather statistics.

Step 6. Display and interpret the results of the operation using the Cisco IOS CLI or a network management system (NMS) with SNMP.

There are many options and different measurements for IP SLA as discussed in the previous subsections. Example 8-9 illustrates the configuration of leveraging ICMP echoes for IP SLA.

Example 8-9 *IP SLA ICMP Echo Configuration Example*

```
Switch(config)# ip sla 12
Switch(config-ip-sla)# icmp-echo 192.168.139.134
Switch(config-ip-sla-echo)# frequency 30
Switch(config-ip-sla-echo)# exit
Switch(config)# ip sla schedule 5 start-time now life forever
Switch(config)# end
```

The **ip sla** *operation-number* command creates the IP SLA instance and enters the IP SLA configuration mode. The **icmp-echo** command has many options. The full command syntax is as follows: **icmp-echo** {*destination-ip-address* | *destination-hostname*} [**source-ip** {*ip-address* | *hostname*} | **source-interface** *interface-id*]. In Example 8-9, the destination IP address is explicitly defined; however, the command does support hostnames and sourcing the echo from specific IP addresses or interfaces. The command has a default of 60 seconds and configures the rate at which IP SLAs are repeated. In this case, the echoes will occur every 30 seconds.

The **ip sla schedule** global schedule command controls the scheduling parameters of the individual IP SLA operation. The full syntax of the command is as follows: **ip sla schedule** *operation-number* [**life** {**forever** | *seconds*}] [**start-time** {*hh:mm* [*:ss*] [*month day* | *day month*] | **pending** | **now** | **after** *hh:mm:ss*] [**ageout** *seconds*] [**recurring**]. In Example 8-8, the IP SLA will start immediately after the command is issued and will run **forever**. As indicated in the command options, IP SLA supports specific start times, end times, age out, and reoccurrence.

To verify the configuration of IP SLA, leverage the **show ip sla configuration** *operation-number* command. Example 8-10 illustrates the use of this command

Example 8-10 *Show IP SLA Configuration Example*

```
Switch# show ip sla configuration 22
IP SLAs, Infrastructure Engine-II.

Entry number: 12
Owner:
Tag:
Type of operation to perform: echo
Target address: 192.168.139.134
Source address: 0.0.0.0
Request size (ARR data portion): 28
Operation timeout (milliseconds): 5000
Type Of Service parameters: 0x0
```

```
Verify data: No
Vrf Name:
Schedule:
    Operation frequency (seconds): 60
    Next Scheduled Start Time: Pending trigger
    Group Scheduled : FALSE
    Randomly Scheduled : FALSE
    Life (seconds): 3600
    Entry Ageout (seconds): never
    Recurring (Starting Everyday): FALSE
    Status of entry (SNMP RowStatus): notInService
Threshold (milliseconds): 5000
Distribution Statistics:
    Number of statistic hours kept: 2
    Number of statistic distribution buckets kept: 1
    Statistic distribution interval (milliseconds): 20
History Statistics:
    Number of history Lives kept: 0
    Number of history Buckets kept: 15
    History Filter Type: None
Enhanced History:
```

Lastly, the **show ip sla statistics** command provides feedback on the operation status of the IP SLA. Example 8-11 shows an example output.

Example 8-11   *Show IP SLA Statistics Output*

```
HQ# show ip sla statistics
IPSLAs Latest Operation Statistics

IPSLA operation id: 22
        Latest RTT: 1 milliseconds
Latest operation start time: 13:31:26 EST Mon Aug 11 2014
Latest operation return code: OK
Number of successes: 32
Number of failures: 0
Operation time to live: Forever
```

IP SLA Operation with Responder

Specific IP SLA measurements, such as ICMP echo, Telnet, or HTTP can be performed against a destination device running standard network services. As noted previously, the accuracy of the measurements can be greatly improved with the use of an IP SLA responder. The IP SLA responder is a component embedded in the destination Cisco device that allows the system to anticipate and respond to IP SLA request packets.

Switches and routers can take tens of milliseconds to process incoming packets due to other high-priority processes; this behavior is ideal to ensure stability of the network. This delay often affects the response times because the test packet reply might be in a queue while waiting to be processed. In this situation, the response times would not accurately represent true network delays. IP SLA minimizes these processing delays on the source device and on the target device (if the responder is being used) to determine true round-trip times. IP SLA test packets use time stamping to minimize the processing delays.

A good example of this behavior is sending ICMP echoes directly to the management IP address of a Catalyst switch. The Catalyst switch will place the lowest priority on these ICMP echoes, and you will observe much higher-than-expected latency and jitter. This behavior is as expected (see Figure 8-9).

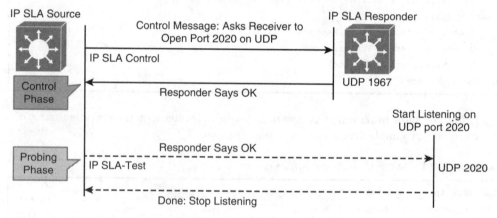

Figure 8-9   *IP SLA Operations with a Responder*

Referring to Figure 8-9 and specifically looking at the details of how IP SLA works, the following sequence of events occurs for each IP SLA operation that requires a responder on the target:

1. At the start of the control phase, the IP SLA source sends a control message with the configured IP SLA operation information to IP SLA control port UDP 1967 on the target router. The control message carries information such as protocol, port number, and duration.

   ■ If MD5 authentication is enabled, message digest 5 (MD5) algorithm checksum is sent with the control message.

   ■ If the authentication of the message is enabled, the responder verifies it; if the authentication fails, the responder returns an authentication failure message.

   ■ If the IP SLA measurement operation does not receive a response from a responder, it tries to retransmit the control message and eventually times out.

2. If the responder processes the control message, it sends an OK message to the source router and listens on the port that is specified in the control message for a specified duration. If the responder cannot process the control message, it returns an error. In the figure, UDP port 2020 is used for the IP SLA test packets.

Note   The responder is capable of responding to multiple IP SLA measurement operations that try to connect to the same port number.

3. If the return code of the control message is OK, the IP SLA operation moves to the probing phase, where it will send one or more test packets to the responder for response time computations. The return code is available with the **show ip sla statistics** command. In Figure 8-9, these test messages are sent on control port 2020.

4. The responder accepts the test packets and responds. Based on the type of operation, the responder may add an "in" time stamp and an "out" time stamp in the response packet payload to account for CPU time that is spent in measuring unidirectional packet loss, latency, and jitter to a Cisco device. These time stamps help the IP SLA source to make accurate assessments on one-way delay and the processing time in the target routers. The responder disables the user-specified port after it responds to the IP SLA measurements packet or when a specified time expires.

IP SLA Time Stamps

Figure 8-10 illustrates the use of IP SLA responder time stamps in round-trip calculations. The IP SLA source will use four time stamps for accurate calculation of the RTP.

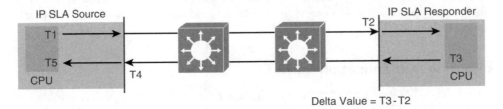

Figure 8-10   *IP SLA Time Stamps*

When the IP SLA process sends a test packet, it is marked with a time stamp, denoted T1. The IP SLA responder records a time stamp when it receives the frame, denoted T2, and when it transmits the response, denoted T3.

The time stamps at T2 and T3 are important because the IP SLA responder may take a few milliseconds to process the incoming test packet because of other higher-priority packets such as spanning tree or routing protocol updates. Therefore, using T2 and T3 time stamps the IP SLA source will calculate the time it takes for the IP SLA responder to reply to the frame as T3-T2. The result of T3-T2 gives a delta value that is subtracted from the overall RTT.

The IP SLA source also may be busy processing other high-priority packets in the queue when it receives the response to the test packet. So, a fourth time stamp and fifth time stamp, T4 and T5 respectively, are recorded when the frame is received on the IP SLA source and when it is processed.

T4 is marked by the IP SLA source via specialized processing. This concept is often referred to as "at interrupt level." The specialized process is outside the topic of CCNP. Figure 8-11 shows an example.

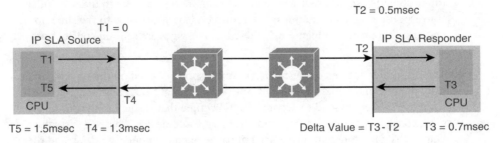

Figure 8-11   *Example of SLA Timestamps*

In Figure 8-11, time is marked from 0 in milliseconds for simplicity. The RTT in this example is calculated as RTT = T5 – (T5-T4) = (T3-T2) = 1.5msec – (1.5msec-1.3msec) – (1.7msec -1.5msec) = 1.1msec.

Another important detail for this calculation to work accurately is the clocks on both the IP SLA source and responder must be synchronized. The best approach to synchronizing the clock is with NTP.

Moreover, the IP SLA responder supports additional capabilities outside the context of this discussion that aid in accuracy of measurements and are vital to providing a plethora of statistics.

Configuring Authentication for IP SLA

One brief configuration point is that key chains are supported with IP SLAs to ensure authentication of control messages. Key chains must be configured on both IP SLA source and responder as a first step. Example 8-12 details a brief configuration.

Example 8-12   *IP SLA Authentication*

```
Switch(config)# key chain MYKEY
Switch(config-keychain)# key 1
Switch(config-keychain-key)# key-string SuperSecretPWD
Switch(config)# ip sla key-chain MYKEY
```

IP SLA Example for UDP Jitter

The IP SLAs UDP jitter operation was primarily designed to diagnose network suitability for real-time traffic applications such as VoIP, video over IP, or real-time conferencing. It provides a much more accurate depiction of the network than an Internet Control Message Protocol (ICMP) test, especially in networks applying quality of service (QoS) for voice.

Jitter refers to the variance in interpacket delay or RTT. For normal data applications such as web browsing, jitter is not an issue. Jitter is an issue for time-sensitive applications such as voice, video, and algorithmic trading applications. Jitter is an issue with voice and video type applications, because jitter makes the network unpredictable. Jitter may result in suboptimal performance of voice and video applications from the user-perspective.

For example, when multiple packets are sent consecutively from source to destination (for instance, 10 ms apart), and the network is behaving ideally, the destination should be receiving them 10 ms apart. But if there are delays in the network (like queuing, arriving through alternate routes, and so on), the arrival delay between packets might be greater than or less than 10 ms. Using this example, a positive jitter value indicates that the packets arrived more than 10 ms apart. If the packets arrive 12 ms apart, positive jitter is 2 ms; if the packets arrive 8 ms apart, negative jitter is 2 ms. For delay-sensitive networks like VoIP, positive jitter values are undesirable, and a jitter value of 0 is ideal.

Nonetheless, IP SLA is useful for discovering the User Datagram Protocol (UDP) jitter of the network for applications such as voice, video, and analytics that leverage UDP. It is not uncommon for ICMP and UDP jitter to vary as QoS features may be applied in the network that differentiate the traffic. Example 8-13 illustrates a configuration example using a UDP test.

Example 8-13   *IP SLA UDP Jitter Example*

```
Switch(config)# ip sla 1
Switch(config-ip-sla-jitter)# udp-jitter 192.168.1.2 65000 num-packets 20
Switch(config-ip-sla-jitter)# request-data-size 160
Switch(config-ip-sla-jitter)# frequency 30
Switch(config-ip-sla-jitter)# exit
Switch(config)# ip sla schedule 1 start-time after 00:05:00
Router(config)# ip sla responder
```

To configure UDP jitter SLA, simply enter IP SLA configuration mode and define UDP jitter test, as illustrated in Example 8-13:

```
Switch(config-ip-sla)# udp-jitter dest-ip-add dest-udp-port [source-ip src-ip-add]
   [source-port src-udp-port] [num-packets num-of-packets] [interval packet-interval]
```

With UDP jitter IP SLA configurations, you can specify IP source and destination IP addresses and also specify the port numbers that are used for the packet stream. By default, 10 packets, spaced at 20 ms, will be sent. You can override this behavior by specifying the **num-packets** and **interval** keywords.

After defining the basic UDP jitter test, you can specify additional parameters. In the provided example, these additional parameters are the frequency of test execution and number of bytes in payload.

In summary, IP SLA is a useful feature for gathering detailed information about your network to ensure that it meets specific requirements. The following list reviews the key details of the IP SLA:

- The Cisco IP SLA provides information for analysis of traffic as it traverses the network.

- IP SLA optionally supports triggering events such as SNMP traps.

- The IP SLA source is the Cisco device that sends data for analysis.

- The IP SLA responder is a network device specifically configured to respond to IP SLA packets from the source.

- The IP SLA feature supports generic network devices that can respond to packets from the source for analysis; however, the use of a specific IP SLA responder is best practice for accurate information.

Study Tips

- The LLDP feature displays topology information and details about directly connected neighbors.

- The UDLD aggressive mode feature ensures additional resiliency in campus networks by ensuring that links that are connected and in the UP state are forwarding traffic correctly. UDLD will take measures to disable links that it determines are not operating correctly.

- The SPAN feature is leveraged to copy traffic to specific ports for analysis

- Use the **monitor session** command to configure SPAN sessions.

- The RSPAN feature enables use of the SPAN feature across multiple switches.

- The RSPAN feature requires the use of an RSPAN VLAN which must be present on source and destination switches and configured across applicable trunk ports.

- The Cisco IP SLA feature gathers network information on how specific types of traffic are being handles across the network; the information gathered includes latency, RTT, and so on.

- The IP SLA destination may be a generic IP device or an IP SLA responder.

Summary

This chapter branched into discussions on specific Catalyst features that are useful for an optimal campus network deployment. In today's network, these features are used extensively and should be considered best practices. In review of the high-level concepts, this chapter is summarized as follows:

- LLDP and the legacy CDP features are useful for discovering neighbor adjacencies and their details.

- The UDLD aggressive mode feature is useful in adding resiliency to networks to avoid disasters in case of anomalous behaviors.

- SPAN and RSPAN are common debugging and traffic capture features that are also leveraged to capture traffic for network analytics.

- The IP SLA features provide useful information about traffic and how it flows in the network.

Review Questions

Use the questions in this section as a review of what you have learned in this chapter. The correct answers are found in Appendix A, "Answers to Chapter Review Questions."

1. Which of the following statements are true about LLDP?

   a. It is an industry standard protocol.

   b. It runs at the data link layer.

   c. When the LLDP feature is enabled, the switch will forward all received LLDP frames on all ports except the port the frame was received.

   d. To verify neighbors, use the **show cdp neighbors** command.

2. Which of the following statements is true about both CDP and LLDP?

   a. When a switch receives a CDP frame, it forwards it out to all other ports on the switch.

   b. Older-generation switches may support CDP and not LLDP because LLDP was ratified as a standard long after CDP was supported on Cisco devices.

   c. CDP nor LLDP pose any type of security risk and should be enabled everywhere for ease of us.

   d. CDP and LLDP may be enabled at the same time and can share information between each other.

3. LLDP is defined as which of the following standards?

   a. 802.1ac

   b. 802.1ab

   c. 802.1X

   d. 802.1c

4. What type of information may LLDP send out? (Choose more than one answer)

   a. Hostname

   b. IP address

   c. Software version

   d. Device capabilities

   e. Performance data from an MIB

   f. All of the above

5. What types of frames do CDP and LLDP use?

   a. Layer 2 unicast

   b. Layer 2 multicast

   c. Layer 3 unicast

   d. Layer 3 multicast

6. What is the global command to enable LLDP on a Cisco Catalyst switch?

   a. CDP enable

   b. LLDP run

   c. LLDP enable

   d. Feature LLDP

7. Which of the following statements is true regarding UDLD? (Hint: There is only one correct answer, although at first read you might believe there are two correct answers.)

   a. UDLD detects physical one-way links for fiber pairs connected only on one end.

   b. UDLD, by default, will disable links it detects as unidirectional.

   c. UDLD detects unidirectional behavior on links that are link up but not passing traffic in one direction.

   d. UDLD is enabled by default on all copper ports.

8. UDLD aids in detection of which of the following types of anomalous conditions? (Choose more than one.)

   a. Transient hardware condition

   b. Hardware failure

   c. Optic/GBIC failure

   d. Expired frame TTL

   e. Miswired copper cabling

   f. Software defect or condition

   g. Misconfigured or malfunctioning of a sniffer

   h. Routing loops

9. True or False? UDLD in normal mode will detect and shut down a unidirectional link in about 60 seconds. UDLD aggressive mode will detect the link in a shorter time and attempt to reestablish the link every 8 seconds.

10. Which two statements are true about the IEEE 802.3at standard?

    a. It can provide your powered devices with more than 15 W of power.

    b. It is not backward compatible with 802.3af.

    c. It is an improvement over the 802.3af standard.

    d. It is a method that was developed by Cisco.

11. Which two statements are true about the PoE negotiation process?

    a. The PoE switch keeps the power on a disabled port up, just in case a device that needs PoE will be connected.

    b. With 802.3af and 802.3at, the switch tries to detect the powered device by supplying a small voltage across the Ethernet cable.

    c. IEEE 802.3af power classes are numbered from 0 to 4.

    d. Cisco Inline Power has the same method of negotiating power as both of the IEEE standards.

12. Which of the following are reasons for leveraging PoE in a campus network?

    a. Support for remote power management

    b. Centralized method of backup power

    c. Simplified configuration

    d. Re-use existing cabling infrastructure

    e. All of the above

13. Which of the following statements best describes SDM templates?

    a. SDM templates are useful for applying a standard configuration on initial boot.

    b. SDM templates define a basic management configuration.

    c. SDM templates are pre-defined templates used to configure scarce hardware resources of a Catalyst switch for optimal use in specific environments.

    d. SDM templates are necessary port layout configurations.

14. Which of the following statements is true about SDM templates?

    a. All Catalyst switches support SDM templates.

    b. The resources that SDM templates manage are exactly the same on all Catalyst switches.

    c. Although only the low to mid-range campus network switches support SDM templates, all Catalyst switches support mechanisms to manage scarce hardware resources.

    d. SDM templates are not persistent on reboot of the Catalyst switch.

15. Which of the following are examples of SDM template use cases? (Choose multiple answers.)

    a. Default, the standard template optimized for broad set of use cases

    b. VLAN, the template optimized for large-scale Layer 2 designs with large number of MAC addresses

    c. PoE optimized template to ensure power to phones

    d. Routing, the template optimized for routing

    e. Access, the template optimized for large number of VLANs

    f. Dual-stack IPv4 and IPv6

16. Why is the SPAN feature necessary on today's switches?

    a. Switches do not flood traffic on all ports, they switch traffic based on destination MAC address.

    b. Switches flood data traffic on all ports, overloading probes and traffic sniffers.

    c. Switches flood control traffic on all ports, overloading probes and traffic sniffers.

17. Which of the following are uses of SPAN and RSPAN?

   a. Troubleshooting a networking problem

   b. Network traffic analytics

   c. Congestion control

   d. Policy enforcement

   e. A, B, and C

   f. A and B

   g. All of the above

18. Which of the following RSPAN statements are true? (Choose three.)

   a. RSPAN requires a dedicated RSPAN VLAN.

   b. RSPAN supports source and destination ports on different switches.

   c. RSPAN sessions require inter-VLAN routing

   d. A reflector port forwards all traffic to connected device.

   e. Switches may need to be configured on the interconnecting trunk port with the RSPAN VLAN.

19. What responder device from the following list provides the most accuracy for IP SLA?

   a. Cisco IOS router

   b. Cisco IOS switch

   c. Cisco Nexus switch

   d. PC or server

   e. Cisco IOS Software with IP SLA responder

20. Which statement about an IP SLA responder is true?

   a. The responder can respond to multiple IP SLA measurement operations that try to connect to the same port number.

   b. IP SLA operation with responder has two phases: control and management.

   c. IP SLA source and responder communicate over TCP.

   d. All IP SLA tests will work only if IP SLA responder is used.

21. Which of the following IP SLA statements are true? (Choose two.)

    a. IP SLA guarantees the service level of a network link.

    b. Results of the IP SLA tests can be polled from device using SNMP.

    c. An IP SLA responder can improve the accuracy of the test by subtracting the time spent to process a packet on the destination device.

    d. Under no condition can IP SLA measurement take into account the processing delay of an IP SLA test.

22. In the following figure, which of the following sets of commands is valid to configure SPAN to monitor traffic to and from PC1 to the sniffer on Gig 1/1/1?

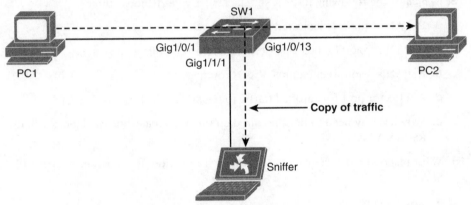

    a. Monitor session 1 source interface Gig1/0/1

       Monitor session 2 destination interface Gig1/1/1

    b. Monitor session 1 source interface Gig1/0/13

       Monitor session 1 destination interface Gig1/0/1

    c. Monitor session 2 source interface Gig1/0/1

       Monitor session 2 destination interface Gig1/1/1

    d. Monitor session 1 source interface Gig1/0/13

       Monitor session 1 destination interface Gig1/0/1

23. In the following figure, which of the following sets of commands is valid to configure RSPAN on SW2?

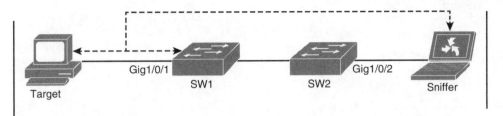

a. VLAN 100

    Monitor session 1 source interface Gig1/0/2

    Monitor session 1 destination remote vlan 100

b. VLAN 100; remote-span

    Monitor-session 1 source interface Gig1/0/2

    Monitor-session 1 destination remote vlan 100

c. VLAN 100; remote-span

    Monitor-session 1 source vlan 100

    Monitor-session 1 destination interface Gig1/0/2

d. VLAN 100; remote-span

    Monitor session 1 source remote vlan 100

    Monitor session 1 destination interface Gig1/0/2

Chapter 9

High Availability

This chapter covers the following topics:

- The need and basic idea behind switch stacking and VSS

- StackWise

- The benefits of StackWise

- Verifying StackWise

- VSS

- VSS benefits

- Verifying VSS

- Supervisor redundancy

- Supervisor redundancy modes

A network with high availability provides an alternative means that enables constant access to all infrastructure paths and key servers. High availability (HA) is not just about adding redundant devices. It implies planning to understand where the points of failure occur and designing the network so that an alternative solution exists to compensate for the loss of these points of failure, especially single point of failures.

HA can be divided into two categories. One is focused on networking devices, and a second one is focused on first-hop gateway redundancy. In the case of networking devices, redundant topologies often introduce overhead in terms of management, resiliency, and performance. To reduce the number of logical network devices and simplify Layer 2 and Layer 3 network topology, some of the switch virtualization technologies are discussed with regard to the two switch virtualization technologies: StackWise and Virtual Switching System (VSS). This chapter also covers supervisor redundancy options such as route processor redundancy (RPR), route processor redundancy plus (RPR+), stateful switchover (SSO), and nonstop forwarding (NSF).

For a complete HA solution, we need to look into not only the network devices' HA but also first-hop gateway redundancy protocols like the Hot Standby Router Protocol (HSRP), Virtual Router Redundancy Protocol (VRRP), and Gateway Load Balancing Protocol (GLBP), which are discussed in detail in Chapter 6, "First-Hop Redundancy."

The Need for Logical Switching Architectures

Figure 9-1 shows a typical switch topology on the access and the distribution layer. Two (or more) access switches are sitting next to each other in the same rack to provide enough access ports for all the network devices, each one with two redundant connections to each of the distribution switches.

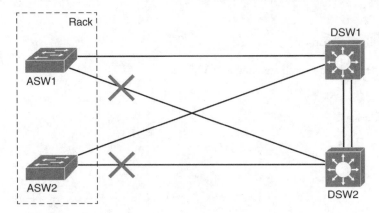

Figure 9-1   *The Need for Logical Switching Architecture*

As shown in Figure 9-1, this topology introduces certain overhead in terms of management, resiliency, and performance. Every switch demands its own configuration and management, even though you can clearly identify only two different roles: access and distribution. Every access switch needs its own uplink to each of the distribution switches to satisfy the redundancy requirements, but one of the uplinks has to be blocked by the Spanning Tree Protocol (STP) to prevent a loop, thus cutting the bandwidth in half. Configuring the Per-VLAN STP (PVSTP) will unequally utilize both uplinks, but with additional management overhead. Hosts connected to ASW1 can only communicate with hosts in the same VLAN connected to ASW2 via one of the distribution switches.

To overcome some of these limitations, Cisco proposes the following virtualization solutions.

- **StackWise:** Focused on the access layer module

- **VSS:** Focused on the aggregation layer module

In addition to providing virtualization solutions, you can add supervisor redundancy to help mitigate some of the effects of switch failure, especially the aggregation and core switches.

What Is StackWise?

Cisco StackWise technology provides a method for collectively utilizing the capabilities of a stack of switches. Configuration and routing information is shared by every switch in the stack, creating a single switching unit. Switches can be added to and deleted from a working stack without affecting performance.

Figure 9-2 shows some pictures of the StackWise solution.

Figure 9-2 *StackWise Solution*

As shown in Figure 9-2, the switches are united into a single logical unit, using special stack interconnect cables that create a bidirectional closed-loop path. This bidirectional path acts as a switch fabric for all the connected switches. Network topology and routing information is updated continuously through the stack interconnect. All stack members have full access to the stack interconnect bandwidth. The stack is managed as a single unit by a master switch, which is elected from one of the stack member switches. Up to nine separate switches can be joined.

Each stack of switches has a single IP address and is managed as a single object. This single IP management applies to activities such as fault detection, VLAN creation and modification, security, and quality of service (QoS) controls. Each stack has only one configuration file, which is distributed to each member in the stack. This allows each switch in the stack to share the same network topology, MAC address, and routing information. In addition, it allows for any member to become the master if the master ever fails.

Catalyst 3750-E, 3750-X, and 3850 series switches support StackWise and StackWise Plus. StackWise Plus is an evolution of StackWise. StackWise Plus supports local switching, so locally destined packets need not traverse the stack ring. In addition, it supports spatial reuse, the ability to more efficiently utilize stack interconnect, thus further improving its throughput performance. Catalyst 3850 series supports StackWise-480 with improved 480-Gbps stacking. Catalyst 2960-S series supports FlexStack, a

StackWise-based feature tailored for Layer 2 switches. FlexStack is limited to four stacked switches.

StackWise Benefits

Uniting switches into a stack, as shown in Figure 9-3, provides several benefits.

StackWise is typically used to unite access switches mounted in the same rack. Multiple switches are used to provide enough access ports. The stack, up to nine switches, is managed as a single unit, reducing the number of units that you have to manage in your network. Switches can be added to and removed from a working stack without affecting stack performance. When a new switch is added, the master switch automatically configures the unit with the currently running IOS image and the configuration of the stack. You do not have to do anything to bring up the switch before it is ready to operate.

The switches are united into a single logical unit using special stack interconnect cables that create a bidirectional closed-loop path. This bidirectional path acts as a switch fabric for all the connected switches. When a break is detected in a cable, the traffic is immediately wrapped back across the remaining path to continue forwarding.

Multiple switches in a stack can create an EtherChannel connection. STP can thus be avoided, doubling the available bandwidth of the existing distribution switches uplinks.

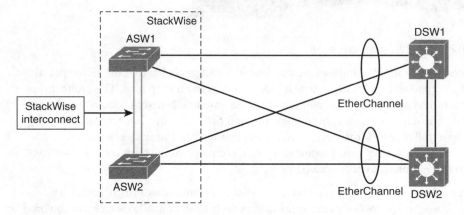

Figure 9-3 *StackWise Benefits*

Verifying StackWise

You can verify the status of your stack by using the **show switch** command with different parameters. Example 9-1 demonstrates how to verify stack members.

Example 9-1 *Stack Member Verification*

```
Switch1# show switch
Switch/Stack Mac Address: 0013.6075.7280


Switch#  Role     Mac Address     Priority H/W  Version  Current State
*1       Master   0013.6075.7280     1            0       Ready
2        Member   0013.60e1.1800     1            0       Ready
```

Example 9-2 demonstrates how to verify stack interconnect ports.

Example 9-2 *Stack Member Verification*

```
Switch1# show switch stack-ports
Switch #        Port 1          Port 2
---------       ------          ------
1               Ok              Ok
2               Ok              Ok
```

As shown in Example 9-1, the **show switch** command without additional parameters returns the shared stack MAC address and lists all the switches in a stack with their stack number, stack role, MAC address, hardware priority, hardware version, and current state. Hardware priority is used in stack master election and can be configured. Hardware version number is associated with the switch model. Different switch models can have the same hardware version if they support the same system-level features. Hardware version number is not used in the stack master election.

Each stack switch uses two ports to connect to other stack switches to form a bidirectional ring. To verify the state of stack port, use the **show switch stack-ports** command, as shown in Example 9-2.

The **show platform stack manager all** command offers an in-depth view into StackWise status. It reveals the stack status, stack ports status, stack manager version, different counters, and so on.

What Is VSS?

Virtual Switching System (VSS) is a network system virtualization technology that combines a pair of Catalyst 4500 or 6500 series switches into one virtual switch, increasing the operational efficiency, boosting nonstop communications, and scaling the system bandwidth capacity. The VSS simplifies network configuration and operation by reducing the number of Layer 3 routing neighbors and by providing a loop-free Layer 2 topology. In the campus switched architecture, VSS is usually deployed in the aggregation layer to avoid the redundancy to the access layer switches in case of the switch failure.

As illustrated in Figure 9-4, VSS is made up of two Catalyst switches and a virtual switch link (VSL) between them. The VSL is made of up to eight 10 Gigabit Ethernet connections bundled into an EtherChannel. VSL carries the control plane communication between the two VSS members, in addition to regular data traffic.

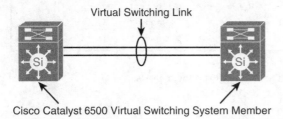

Figure 9-4 *VSS*

Once the VSS is formed, only the control plane of one of the members is active. The data plane and switch fabric of both members are active. Both chassis are kept in sync with the interchassis SSO mechanism, along with NSF to provide nonstop communication even in the event of failure of one of the member supervisor engines or chassis.

VSS Benefits

VSS increases operational efficiency by reducing switch management overhead and simplifying the network. It provides a single point of management, IP address, and routing instance.

VSS can be managed with single management point from which you configure and manage the VSS. Neighbors see the VSS as a single Layer 2 switching or Layer 3 routing node, thus reducing the control protocol traffic. VSS provides a single VLAN gateway IP address, removing the need for the first-hop redundancy protocol (HSRP, VRRP, GLBP), as shown in Figure 9-5 and as discussed in Chapter 6. Multichannel EtherChannel (MEC) allows you to bundle links to two physical switches in VSS, creating a loop-free redundant topology without the need for STP.

Interchassis stateful failover results in no disruption to applications that rely on network state information (for example, forwarding table info, NetFlow, Network Address Translation, authentication, and authorization). VSS eliminates Layer 2 / Layer 3 protocol reconvergence if a virtual switch member fails, resulting in deterministic subsecond virtual switch recovery.

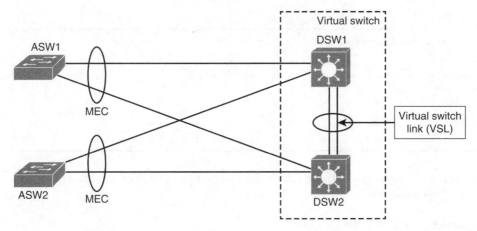

Figure 9-5 *VSS Benefits*

Verifying VSS

To verify the status of VSS configuration, use the following **show switch virtual** commands with various parameters:

- **show switch virtual**

- **show switch virtual link**

- **show switch virtual role**

- **show switch virtual link port-channel**

To display configuration and status information for a VSS, use the **show switch virtual** command as shown in Example 9-3. Active and standby switches will be displayed, together with a virtual switch domain number.

Example 9-3 *Verifying VSS*

```
Switch1# show switch virtual
Switch mode                  : Virtual Switch
Virtual switch domain number : 1
Local switch number          : 1
Local switch operational role : Virtual Switch Active
Peer switch number           : 2
Peer switch operational role  : Virtual Switch Standby
```

To verify the status of a switch virtual link and the status of its up time, use the **show switch virtual link** command as shown in Example 9-4.

Example 9-4 *Verifying VSL*

```
Switch1# show switch virtual link
VSL Status : UP
VLS Uptime : 7 weeks, 4 days, 31 minutes
VSL SCP Ping : Pass
VSL ICC Ping : Pass
VSL Control Link : Tel/5/5
VSL Encryption : Configured Mode - Off, Operational Mode - Off
```

By adding the **role** keyword, you can display more detail, such as priority, as demonstrated in Example 9-5.

Example 9-5 *Verifying the VSS Status*

```
Switch1# show switch virtual role
RRP information for Instance 1


-----------------------------------------------------------------
Valid   Flags   Peer        Preferred   Reserved
                Count       Peer        Peer


-----------------------------------------------------------------
TRUE    V       1           1           1

Switch  Switch   Status      Priority    Role    Local   Remote
        Number               Oper(Conf)          SID     SID
-----------------------------------------------------------------
LOCAL   1        UP          200(200)    ACTIVE  0       0
REMOTE  2        UP          100(100)    STANDBY 1730    5394


Peer 0 represents the local switch


Flags : V - Valid



In dual-active recovery mode: No
```

Use the **show switch virtual link** command to display virtual switch link status. More information, such as EtherChannel used for VSL, can be obtained by adding the **port-channel** keyword, as demonstrated in Example 9-6.

Example 9-6 *Verifying the VSS Port Channel Status*

```
Switch1# show switch virtual link port-channel
Flags:  D - down         P - bundled in port-channel
        I - stand-alone s - suspended
        H - Hot-standby (LACP only)
        R - Layer3       S - Layer2
        U - in use       N - not in use, no aggregation
        f - failed to allocate aggregator

        M - not in use, no aggregation due to minimum links not met
        m - not in use, port not aggregated due to minimum links not met
        u - unsuitable for bundling
        d - default port

        w - waiting to be aggregated


Group  Port-channel  Protocol    Ports
------+-------------+-----------+-------------------
2      Po2(RU)         -          Te1/5/4(P)     Te1/5/5(P)
3      Po3(RU)         -          Te2/5/4(P)     Te2/5/5(P)
```

Redundant Switch Supervisors

The Cisco supervisor engine module is the heart of the Cisco modular switch platforms. The supervisor provides centralized forwarding information and processing. All software processes of a modular switch are run on a supervisor.

Redundant supervisors are highly recommended for the aggregation and core layer so that they might help provide faster convergence in case of the primary supervisor failure.

Platforms such as the Catalyst 4500, 6500, and 6800 series can accept two supervisor modules that are installed in a single chassis, thus removing a single point of failure. The first supervisor module to successfully boot becomes the active supervisor for the chassis. The other supervisor remains in a standby role, waiting for the active supervisor to fail.

The active supervisor provides all switching functions. The standby supervisor, however, is allowed to boot and initialize only to a certain level. When the active module fails, the standby module can proceed to initialize any remaining functions and take over the active role.

Supervisor Redundancy Modes

Redundant supervisor modules can be configured in several modes. The redundancy mode affects how the two supervisors handshake and synchronize information. In addition, the mode limits the standby supervisor's state of readiness. The more ready the standby module is allowed to become, the less initialization and failover time will be required. Table 9-1 illustrates modes of the redundant supervisor and its failover time.

Table 9-1   *Supervisor Redundancy Modes*

Redundancy Mode	Behavior When Active Module Fails	Failover Time
RPR	The standby module reloads every other module, initializes all supervisor functions.	> 2 minutes
RPR+	The standby module finishes initializing without reloading other modules.	> 30 seconds
SSO	The standby module is already initialized.	> 1 second

Redundant supervisor modules can be configured in several modes.

Redundancy mode limits the standby supervisor's state of readiness.

SSO allows for NSF.

Use the following redundancy modes on Catalyst switches:

- **Route processor redundancy (RPR):** The redundant supervisor is only partially booted and initialized. When the active module fails, the standby module must reload every other module in the switch and then initialize all the supervisor functions.

- **Route processor redundancy plus (RPR+):** The redundant supervisor is booted, allowing the supervisor and route engine to initialize. No Layer 2 or Layer 3 functions are started. When the active module fails, the standby module finishes initializing without reloading other switch modules. This allows switch ports to retain their state.

- **Stateful switchover (SSO):** The redundant supervisor is fully booted and initialized. Both the startup and running configuration contents are synchronized between the supervisor modules. Layer 2 information is maintained on both supervisors so that hardware switching can continue during a failover. The state of the switch interfaces is also maintained on both supervisors so that links do not flap during a failover.

The following subsection discusses SSO in more detail because it is the most commonly deployed mode.

Stateful Switchover

RPR and RPR+ recover the traffic forwarding of the switch from 30 seconds to 2 minutes after a switchover of the supervisor engine; however, RPR and RPR+ disruptions are not transparent to the end user. For example, if the user were using an IP phone, the call would be dropped. Even though a minute-long outage might not be significant to a typical Internet user, it is critical for IP phone users or database applications; therefore, this poses the need for a better redundancy protocol to minimize the disruption of traffic. The Catalyst 4500 and Catalyst 6500 families of switches support SSO to provide minimal Layer 2 traffic disruption during a supervisor switchover.

In SSO mode, the redundant supervisor engine starts up in a fully initialized state and synchronizes with the startup configuration and the running configuration of the active supervisor engine. The standby supervisor in SSO mode also keeps in sync with the active supervisor engine for all changes in hardware and software states for features that are supported via SSO. Any supported feature interrupted by failure of the active supervisor engine is continued seamlessly on the redundant supervisor engine.

The following list details the current protocols and features that SSO modes support for Layer 2 redundancy. For a complete and current list, refer to Cisco.com:

- 802.3x (Flow control)

- 802.3ad (Link Aggregation Control Protocol [LACP] and Port Aggregation Protocol [PagP])

- 802.1X (Authentication and port security)

- 802.3af (Inline power)

- VTP

- Dynamic ARP inspection / DHCP snooping / IP Source Guard

- IGMP snooping (Versions 1 and 2)

- DTP (802.1Q and ISL)

- MST/PVST+/Rapid-PVST

- PortFast / UplinkFast/ BackboneFast/ BPDU Guard and Filtering

- Voice VLAN

- Unicast MAC filtering

- Access control lists (ACLs; VLAN ACLs, port ACLs, router ACLs)

- QoS (Dynamic buffer limiting [DBL])

- Multicast storm control / broadcast storm control

In SSO mode, ports that were active before the switchover remain active because the redundant supervisor engine recognizes the hardware link status of every link. The neighboring devices do not see the link-down event during the switchover, except for the link to the previous active supervisor. On the Catalyst 4500 switches, the uplink on the previous active supervisor engine is also retained even though that supervisor engine might be rebooting. In such a case, no spanning-tree topology changes occur because no link states change.

On the Catalyst 6500 family of switches, the time it takes for the Layer 2 traffic to be fully operational following a supervisor failure is between 0 and 3 seconds.

On the Catalyst 4500, subsecond switchover can be achieved for Layer 2 traffic. Layer 3 information, however, needs to be relearned after a supervisor engine failover with just the SSO mode of redundancy, but the newly active supervisor engine continues to use existing Layer 2 switching information to continue forwarding traffic until Layer 3 information is relearned. This relearning involves rebuilding Address Resolution Protocol (ARP) tables and Layer 3 Cisco Express Forwarding (CEF) and adjacency tables. Until the routing converges and CEF and adjacency tables are rebuilt, packets that need to be routed are dropped.

Nonstop Forwarding

You can enable another redundancy feature along with SSO. NSF is an interactive method that focuses on quickly rebuilding the Routing Information Base (RIB) table after a supervisor switchover. The RIB is used to generate the Forwarding Information Base (FIB) table for CEF, which is downloaded to any switch modules that can perform CEF. Both the Catalyst 4500 and 6500 family supports this feature.

NSF with SSO redundancy includes the standard SSO for Layer 2 switching; however, it also minimizes the amount of time that a Layer 3 network is unavailable following a supervisor engine switchover by continuing to forward IP packets using CEF entries built from the old active supervisor. Zero packet loss or near-zero packet loss is achieved with NSF with SSO redundancy mode.

When using the NSF with SSO feature, reconvergence of supported Layer 3 routing protocols (Border Gateway Protocol [BGP], Enhanced Interior Gateway Routing Protocol [EIGRP], Open Shortest Path First [OSPF] Protocol, and Intermediate System-to-Intermediate System [IS-IS] Protocol) happens automatically in the background while packet forwarding continues. The standby supervisor engine maintains the copy of the CEF entries from the active supervisor engine, and upon switchover, the new active supervisor engine uses the CEF entries while the routing protocol converges without interruption to user traffic. When the routing protocol has converged and the RIB has been built fresh on the route processor, any stale CEF entries are removed, and packet forwarding is fully restored.

Changes have been made to the routing protocols so that upon switchover an NSF-enabled router sends special packets that trigger routing updates from the NSF-aware neighbors without resetting the peer relationship. This feature prevents route flapping and routing changes during a supervisor failover. NSF-aware routers understand that a neighboring NSF router can still forward packets when a route processor (RP) switchover happens. NSF-aware routers are not required to be NSF routers themselves.

> **Note** For information about the NSF operations for each of the routing protocols, refer to the "Configuring NSF with SSO Supervisor Engine Redundancy" configuration section of the Catalyst 6500 configuration guide at Cisco.com.

In summary, Cisco NSF provides the following benefits:

- **Improved network availability:** NSF continues forwarding network traffic and application state information so that user traffic is not interrupted after a supervisor switchover.

- **Overall network stability:** Network stability is improved by maintaining routing protocol neighbor relationships during supervisor failover.

Study Tips

- Cisco StackWise technology provides a method for collectively utilizing the capabilities of a stack of switches. It also provides ease of management by having a single master switch controlling all the switches.

- Using VSS technology available on the Catalyst 6500 and 4500 series families, two physical switches act as a single virtual switch. In addition, VSS provides a single VLAN gateway IP address, removing the need for the first-hop redundancy protocol.

- Redundant supervisors are highly recommended for the aggregation and core layer because they can help provide faster convergences in case of the primary supervisor failure.

- Redundant supervisors work in three modes: RPR, RPR+, and SSO.

- NSF with SSO redundancy includes the standard SSO for Layer 2 switching; however, it also minimizes the amount of time that a Layer 3 network is unavailable following a supervisor failover, using CEF.

Summary

This key points discussed in this chapter include the following:

- Redundant network topology introduces management overhead and complicates the network.

- Unification of physical switches into one virtual switch simplifies management and network efficiency using VSS or StackWise.

- VSS combines a pair of distribution/core switches into a single virtual unit.

- StackWise stacks up to nine access switches into a single virtual unit.

- Adding the redundant supervisor to the module switches provides an extra layer of redundancy and resiliency to the network.

- SSO, RPR, RPR+ are various modes for redundant supervisors.

References

For additional information, refer to these references:

- **StackWise and StackWise Plus whitepaper:** http://www.cisco.com/en/US/prod/collateral/switches/ps5718/ps5023/prod_white_paper09186a00801b096a.html

- **StackWise creation and management:** http://www.cisco.com/en/US/products/hw/switches/ps5023/products_configuration_example09186a00807811ad.shtml

- **FlexStack description and usage:** http://www.cisco.com/en/US/prod/collateral/switches/ps5718/ps6406/white_paper_c11-578928.html

- **SSO configuration guide:** http://www.cisco.com/en/US/docs/switches/lan/catalyst6500/ios/12.2SY/configuration/guide/stateful_switchover.html

- **VSS configuration guide:** http://www.cisco.com/en/US/docs/switches/lan/catalyst6500/ios/12.2SX/configuration/guide/vss.html

- **VSS Q&A:** http://www.cisco.com/en/US/prod/collateral/switches/ps5718/ps9336/prod_qas0900aecd806ed74b.html

Review Questions

Use the questions in this section as a review of what you have learned in this chapter. The correct answers are found in Appendix A, "Answers to Chapter Review Questions."

1. Which of the following routing protocols is not supported as part of NSF?

   a. BGP

   b. OSPF

   c. IS-IS

   d. EIGRP

   e. RIP

2. What is the expected failover time for SSO mode for Layer 2 switching on the Catalyst 4500 family of switches?

a. 2 to 4 minutes

b. 30 to 60 seconds

c. Less than 3 seconds

d. Subsecond

e. None of the above

3. Match switch virtualization terms with their descriptions.

a. StackWise

b. Virtual switch link (VSL)

c. Virtual Switching System (VSS)

d. StackWise interconnect cable

1. Joins up to 9 individual switches in a single logical switching unit.

2. Network system virtualization technology that pools two multichassis switches into one virtual switch.

3. Connects switches to create a bidirectional closed-loop path.

4. Carries regular data traffic in addition to the control plane communication between the two virtual switch members. It consists of multiple 10 Gigabit Ethernet connections bundled in an EtherChannel.

4. Which of the following is *not* a technology used to join Cisco switches in a stack?

a. StackWise

b. StackWise Plus

c. StackWise-480

d. StackPower

e. FlexStack

Chapter 10

Campus Network Security

This chapter covers the following topics:

- Overview of switch security issues

- Required best practices for basic security protection on Catalyst switches

- Campus network vulnerabilities

- Port security

- Storm control

- Mitigating spoofing attacks

- DHCP snooping, IP Source Guard, and dynamic ARP inspection

- Securing VLAN trunks

- Private VLANs

Much attention focuses on security attacks from the Internet, but securing the campus network from the inside is just as important. Viruses, malicious behavior by employees, and malfunctioning devices can bring down an entire network unless security is put into place to limit and prevent vulnerabilities.

In this chapter, inherit switch security issues are covered. The chapter then continues with discussions about Catalyst security measures to address campus network security requirements by first exploring port security, which limits port access, in addition to storm control. Following the section on storm control, you will learn about spoofing prevention levering Dynamic Host Configuration Protocol (DHCP) snooping, IP Source Guard, and dynamic ARP inspection (DAI), in addition to VLAN access lists, which aid in building secure networks. Private VLANs are then covered as another means to limit the reachability of ports in the campus network.

Overview of Switch Security Issues

Most of the industry attention focuses on security attacks from outside the walls of an organization and at the upper OSI layers. Network security often focuses on edge routing devices and the filtering of packets that are based on Layer 3 and Layer 4 headers, ports, stateful packet inspection, and so on. Most of this filtering occurs on high-end firewalls such as the Cisco Adaptive Security Appliance (ASA). Campus access devices and Layer 2 communication are largely unconsidered or an afterthought in most security discussions, which potentially leaves the campus network vulnerable to internal attacks.

The default state of networking equipment highlights this focus on external protection and internal open communication. Firewalls, placed at the organizational borders, arrive in a secure operational mode and allow no communication until they are configured to do so. Routers and switches that are internal to an organization and that are designed to accommodate communication, delivering needful campus traffic, have a default operational mode that forwards all traffic unless they are configured otherwise. Their function as devices that facilitate communication often results in minimal security configuration, and they become targets for malicious attacks. If an attack is launched at Layer 2 on an internal campus device, the rest of the network can be quickly compromised, often without detection. Figure 10-1 illustrates the increasing security risk found with switches in the access layer.

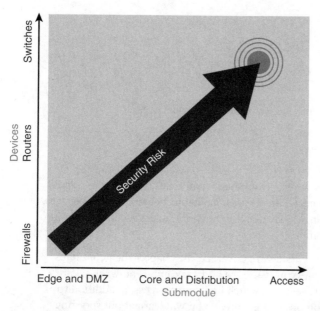

Figure 10-1   *Heighten Security Risk of Campus Networks*

Many security features are available for switches and routers, but they must be enabled to be effective. As with Layer 3 routers, where security was enhanced because malicious activity that compromised this layer increased, security measures must be taken to guard against malicious activity at Layer 2. A new security focus on attacks that are launched maliciously using normal Layer 2 switch operations is emerging. Fortunately, security features exist to protect switches and Layer 2 operations in an effort to prevent such attacks. However, as with access control lists (ACLs) for upper-layer security, a policy must be established, and appropriate features must be configured, to protect against these potential malicious acts while maintaining daily network operations and to ensure minimal operational overhead.

Moreover, the new Application Centric Infrastructure (ACI) paradigm leverages default states of protection where devices cannot communicate without explicit authorization. At the time of publication, ACI is a new feature for data centers; however, the concept will quickly migrate to campus networks. In the future, campus network switches from Cisco will not be configured for open communication by default, but will deploy features as discussed in this chapter as a means to restrict communication unless explicitly defined.

In review of switch security issues, several reasons exist for strong protection of the enterprise campus infrastructure, including security functions in each individual element of the enterprise campus network. These reasons are as follows:

- Relying on the security that has been established at the enterprise edge fails as soon as security there is compromised. Having several layers of security increases the protection of the enterprise campus, where the most strategic assets usually reside.

- If the enterprise allows visitors into its buildings, an attacker can potentially gain physical access to devices in the enterprise campus. Relying on physical security is not enough.

- Very often, external access does not stop at the enterprise edge. Applications require at least an indirect access to the enterprise campus resources, which means that strong campus network security is also necessary.

- Public and hybrid cloud architectures pose new risks. Even if the cloud is secure, attacks from the inside can ultimately compromise the cloud.

The next section of this chapter focuses on standard security configuration recommendations that are standard best practices for all Cisco network devices.

Cisco Switch Security Configuration Best Practices

From a Cisco switch configuration perspective, there is a minimal set of required configurations necessary to provide basic security. These requirements are often called *best practices*; however, *requirements* is a better term because the network is unsecure without them. These configuration requirements are also found on many Cisco routers and other Cisco devices.

Table 10-1 outlines the required basic security configurations for any campus network switch.

Table 10-1   *Required Basic Security Configuration for Campus Network Switches*

Security Configuration	Configuration notes
Secure passwords	The **enable password** command employs weak encryption. Use **enable secret** whenever possible.
	Use the **service password-encryption** global configuration command to encrypt all passwords that cannot be encrypted using strong authentication. Even though this is weak, easily broken encryption, it can prevent casual passers-by from seeing clear-text passwords.
	Having external AAA (authentication, authorization, and accounting) servers means that you do not need to manage and maintain user credentials on individual devices. Use of external AAA authentication is a requirement of any large enterprise.
Leverage system banners	After users successfully access a device, they need to be made aware of access policies of your organization. The goal is to warn unauthorized users that their activities could be grounds for persecution.
	Use the **banner login** command to configure text that is displayed to authenticated users.
Secure console access	Even though switches usually reside in locked cabinets and access-controlled data centers, it is a best practice to configure authentication on any console. It is acceptable to use the same passwords for both the vty and console lines.
Secure vty access	Always secure all vty lines on a device.
	Configure access lists to limit access from source IP addresses of potential administrative users who try to access the device remotely.
	Example configuration: **access-list 1 permit 10.0.0.234** **access-list 1 permit 10.0.0.235** **line vty 0 15** **access-class 1 in**

Security Configuration	Configuration notes
Secure the embedded web interface	If you are not using web interface to manage a switch, disable its web interface using **no ip http server** command.
	If you do decide to use the switch's web interface, use HTTPS (if it is supported). With standard HTTP, traffic is not encrypted. To enable HTTPS, use the **ip http secure server** global configuration command.
	If you do decide to use the switch's web interface, use access lists to limit source addresses that can access the HTTPS interface.
	Example configuration: **ip http secure server** **access-list 1 permit 10.100.50.0 0.0.0.255** **ip http access-class 1**
	HTTP is disabled by default on later IOS versions.
Always leverage Secure Shell (SSH) and ensure that the Telnet server is disabled	Telnet is easy to use but not secure. All text that is sent through a Telnet session is passed in clear text. It is easy to eavesdrop on Telnet sessions and observe usernames and passwords with a simple sniffer.
	SSH uses strong encryption to secure session data. You should use the highest SSH version available on the device.
Secure SNMP access	If you do not need the write access through SNMP, disable it. This will prevent unauthorized users from making changes to the configuration. It is always recommended to exclusively use SNMPv3, which leverages secure authentication.
Secure STP operation	You should always enable the BPDU Guard feature on any access switch ports. This way, if an unexpected BPDU is received, the port will be automatically disabled.
	Do not ever configure BPDU Guard and BPDU Filter on the same port. If you do, only BPDU Filter will take effect. BPDU Filter ignores BPDUs when enabled on an interface; and if you enable it on access ports, this can be a great opportunity for a Layer 2 loop to occur.
Secure Cisco Discovery Protocol (CDP)	As a rule, all Cisco devices have CDP enabled on all ports by default. CDP by itself is very useful to discover network topology. However, you should disable CDP on ports that connect to outside networks. This will prevent advertising unnecessary information about your switch to listening attackers. CDP advertisements are sent in clear text, and you cannot configure authentication.
	In addition, always disable CDP on end-user access ports.

Security Configuration	Configuration notes
Secure unused switch ports	All unused switch ports should be shut down to prevent unauthorized users from connecting to your network.
	All user ports should be configured with **switchport mode access** command. If user ports are configured to Dynamic Trunking Protocol's (DTP) dynamic or auto mode, a malicious user might connect and attempt to negotiate trunking mode on a port.
	For ports that remain enabled, alternatively place all other unused ports into an isolated or bogus VLAN. If malicious users succeed in accessing an unused port, they will only have access to a VLAN that is isolated and will be prevented from accessing the rest of the network.

The next section discusses specific campus network vulnerabilities that all network engineers should be familiar with.

Campus Network Vulnerabilities

Aside from the common vulnerabilities with networks in general, the campus network has specific vulnerabilities that warrant additional scrutiny. The most common vulnerability in the campus network is unauthorized rogue access.

Rogue Access

Rogue access comes in several forms. For example, because unauthorized rogue access points (APs) and wireless routers are inexpensive and readily available, employees sometimes plug them into existing LANs and build ad hoc wireless networks without IT department knowledge or consent, as illustrated in Figure 10-2. These rogue APs can be a serious breach of network security because they can be plugged into a network port behind the corporate firewall. Because employees generally do not enable any security settings on the rogue AP, it is easy for unauthorized users to use the AP to intercept network traffic and hijack client sessions.

Deliberate and malicious rogue APs, although much less common than employee-installed rogue APs, are also a security concern. These rogue APs create an unsecured wireless LAN connection that puts the entire wired network at risk. Malicious rogues present an even greater risk and challenge because they are intentionally hidden from physical and network view.

APs are not the only rogue access. Rogue access can be achieved via physical access as well. In addition, running malicious software on a desktop or server may also grant rogue access to the networks. Rogue access itself does not cause issues, but unauthorized access allows someone to attempt malicious attacks on the network to disable or disrupt operation and to attempt to gain access to protected data.

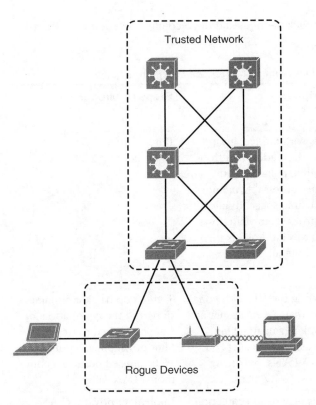

Figure 10-2 *Unauthorized Access by Rogue Devices*

Switch Vulnerabilities

After rogue access has been achieved, attacks may be generated in an effort to disrupt the network. The attack may also come from an external intrusion that takes control of, and launches attacks from, a trusted device. In either case, the network sees all traffic as originating from a legitimate connected device.

Attacks that are launched against switches and at Layer 2 can be grouped as follows:

- MAC layer attacks

- VLAN attacks

- Spoofing attacks

- Attacks on switch devices

Significant attacks in these categories are discussed in more detail in subsequent subsections of the chapter. Each attack method is accompanied by a standard measure for mitigating the security compromise.

Table 10-2 describes common attack methods and the recommended best practices for mitigation.

Table 10-2   *Command Switch Attacks and Recommended Steps to Mitigate*

Attack Method	Description	Steps to Mitigate
MAC Layer Attacks		
MAC address flooding	Frames with unique, invalid source MAC addresses flood the switch, exhausting the content-addressable memory (CAM) table space, disallowing new entries from valid hosts. Traffic to valid hosts is then flooded out all ports.	Port security. MAC address VLAN access maps.
VLAN Attacks		
VLAN hopping	By altering the VLAN ID on packets that are encapsulated for trunking, an attacking device can send packets on various VLANs, bypassing Layer 3 security measures.	Tighten up trunk configurations and the negotiation state of unused ports. Shut down unused ports. Place unused ports in a common VLAN.
Attacks between devices on a common VLAN	Devices may need protection from one another, even though they are on a common VLAN. This is especially true on service provider segments that support devices from multiple customers.	Implement private VLANs (PVLANs).
Spoofing Attacks		
DHCP starvation and DHCP spoofing	An attacking device can exhaust the address space available to the DHCP servers for a time period or establish itself as a DHCP server in man-in-the-middle attacks.	Use DHCP snooping.
Spanning-tree compromises	Attacking device spoofs the root bridge in the Spanning Tree Protocol (STP) topology. If successful, the network attacker can see various frames.	Proactively configure the primary and backup root devices. Enable Root Guard.

Attack Method	Description	Steps to Mitigate
MAC spoofing	Attacking device spoofs the MAC address of a valid host currently in the CAM table. The switch then forwards to the attacking device any frames that are destined for the valid host.	Use DHCP snooping, port security.
Address Resolution Protocol (ARP) spoofing	Attacking device crafts Address Resolution Protocol (ARP) replies intended for valid hosts. The MAC address of the attacking device then becomes the destination address that is found in the Layer 2 frames that were sent by the valid network device.	Use DAI. Use DHCP snooping, port security.
Switch Device Attacks		
Cisco Discovery Protocol (CDP manipulation)	Information sent through CDP is transmitted in clear text and unauthenticated, allowing it to be captured and to divulge network topology information.	Disable Cisco Discovery Protocol on all ports where it is not intentionally used.
SSH protocol and Telnet attacks	Telnet packets can be read in clear text. SSH is an option, but it has security issues in Version 1.	Use SSH Version 2. Use Telnet with vty ACLs.

The next subsection discusses the first type of attack listed in Table 10-1, MAC address flooding attacks.

MAC Flooding Attacks

A common Layer 2 or switch attack is MAC flooding, which results in an overflow of the CAM table of a switch. The overflow causes the flooding of regular data frames out all switch ports, black-holing, or intermittent loss of traffic. This attack can be launched for the malicious purpose of collecting a broad sample of traffic or as a denial-of-service (DoS) attack where the switch does not function correctly. Figure 10-3 illustrates a MAC flooding attack.

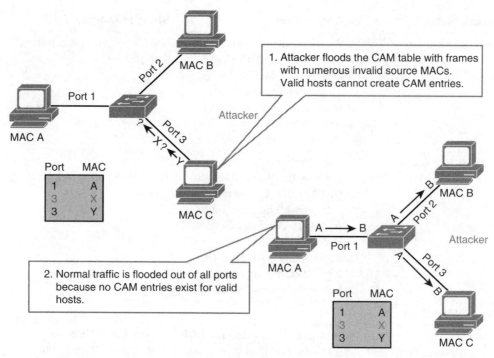

Figure 10-3   *MAC Flooding Attack*

The CAM tables of a switch are limited in size and therefore can contain only a limited number of entries at any one time. A network intruder can maliciously flood a switch with many frames from a range of invalid source MAC addresses. If enough new entries are made before old ones expire, new and valid entries will not be accepted. Then, when traffic arrives at the switch for a legitimate device that is located on one of the switch ports that was not able to create a CAM table entry, the switch must flood the frames to that address out all ports. This scenario has the following two possible adverse effects:

■ The switch traffic forwarding is inefficient and voluminous.

■ An intruding device can be connected to any switch port and can capture traffic that is not normally detected on that port.

If the attack is launched before the beginning of the day, the CAM table would be full when most devices are powered on. Then frames from those legitimate devices are unable to create CAM table entries as they power on. If this represents many network devices, the number of MAC addresses that are flooded with traffic will be high, and any switch port will carry flooded frames from many devices.

If the initial flood of invalid CAM table entries is a one-time event, the switch will eventually age-out older, invalid CAM table entries, allowing new, legitimate devices to create entries. Traffic flooding will cease and may never be detected, even though the intruder may have captured a significant amount of data from the network.

To mitigate MAC flooding attacks, configure port security to define the number of MAC addresses that are allowed on a given port. Port security can also specify which MAC address is allowed on a given port. Let's now turn the discussion to port security.

Introducing Port Security

A common misconception is that port security only supports a specific allowed MAC address for each port. Although this functionality is supported, port security supports many other capabilities.

In brief, port security restricts a switch port to a specific set or number of MAC addresses. Those addresses can be learned dynamically or configured statically. The port will then provide access to frames from only those addresses. If the number of addresses is limited to three but no specific MAC addresses are configured, however, the port will allow any three MAC addresses to be learned dynamically, and port access will be limited to those three dynamically learned addresses. Figure 10-4 illustrates this behavior, with a hacker creating many bogus MAC addresses.

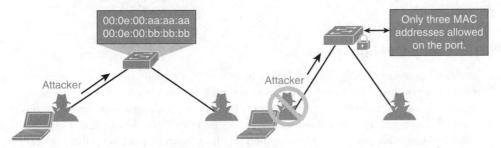

Figure 10-4   *Port Security Example*

Moreover, a port security feature called *sticky learning*, available on some switch platforms, combines the features of dynamically learned and statically configured addresses. When this feature is configured on an interface, the interface converts dynamically learned addresses to *sticky secure* addresses. This feature then adds the learned MAC addresses to the running configuration as if they were configured with the **switchport port-security mac-address** command. Sticky learning is a powerful and useful security tool because it reduces the overhead of managing MAC addresses.

Table 10-3 describes the actionable behavior associated with port security.

Table 10-3   *Port Security Process*

Step	Action	Notes
1.	Configure port security.	Configure port security to allow only the desired number of connections on the port. Configure an entry for each of these allowed MAC addresses. This configuration, in effect, populates the MAC address table with new entries for that port and allows no additional entries to be learned dynamically.

Step	Action	Notes
2.	Allowed frames are processed.	When frames arrive on the switch port, their source MAC address is checked against the MAC address table. If the frame source MAC address matches an entry in the table for that port, the frames are forwarded to the switch to be processed like any other frames on the switch.
3.	New addresses are not allowed to create new MAC address table entries.	When frames with a nonallowed MAC address arrive on the port, the switch determines that the address is not in the current MAC address table and does not create a dynamic entry for that new MAC address, because the number of allowed addresses has been limited.
4.	Switch takes action in response to non-allowed frames.	The switch will disallow access to the port and take one of these configuration-dependent actions: The entire switch port can be disabled, access can be denied for that MAC address only and a log error can be generated, or access can be denied for that MAC address but without generating a log message.

Port Security Configuration

Interfaces configured on a Catalyst switch must first be configured in access interface mode. The command for this configuration is **switchport mode access**. Enabling port security is only one command; however, port security supports many different options based on Cisco Catalyst model and software version through optional commands. The command to enable port security on an interface is **switchport port-security**. Table 10-4 highlights the optional parameters found on most Cisco Catalyst switches.

Table 10-4   *Port Security Configuration Options*

Command	Purpose
switchport port-security maximum *value*	Optionally sets the maximum number of secure MAC addresses for the interface. The range is 1 to 3072; the default is 1.
switchport port-security violation {restrict | shutdown}	Optionally sets the violation mode, the action to be taken when a security violation is detected, as one of these: **restrict** A port security violation restricts data and causes the SecurityViolation counter to increment and send an SNMP trap notification. **shutdown** The interface is err-disabled when a port-security violation occurs.
switchport port-security limit rate invalid-source-mac	Sets the rate limit for bad packets.

Command	Purpose
switchport port-security mac-address *mac-address*	Optionally enters a secure MAC address for the interface. You can use this command to enter the maximum number of secure MAC addresses. If you configure fewer secure MAC addresses than the maximum, the remaining MAC addresses are dynamically learned.
switchport port-security mac-address sticky	Optionally enables sticky learning on the interface.

Two useful commands to verify configuration of port-security are **show port-security address** and **show port-security address interface** *interface-id*.

Example 10-1 shows how to enable port security on Gigabit Ethernet port 3/12 and how to set the maximum number of secure addresses to five. The violation mode is the default, and no secure MAC addresses are configured.

Example 10-1 *Port Security Example*

```
Switch# configure terminal
Enter configuration commands, one per line.  End with CNTL/Z.
Switch(config)# interface gigabitethernet 3/12
Switch(config-if)# switchport mode access
Switch(config-if)# switchport port-security
Switch(config-if)# switchport port-security maximum 5
Switch(config-if)# switchport port-security mac-address sticky
Switch(config-if)# end

Switch# show port-security interface gigabitethernet 3/12
Port Security              :Enabled
Port Status                :Secure-up
Violation Mode             :Shutdown
Aging Time                 :0
Aging Type                 :Absolute
SecureStatic Address Aging :Enabled
Maximum MAC Addresses      :5
Total MAC Addresses        :0
Configured MAC Addresses   :0
Sticky MAC Addresses       :11
Last Source Address        :0000.0000.0401
Security Violation Count   :0
```

Example 10-2 shows how to configure a secure MAC address on Gigabit Ethernet port 5/1 and verify the configuration.

Example 10-2 *Port Security Configuration with Secure MAC Addresses*

```
Switch# configure terminal
Enter configuration commands, one per line.  End with CNTL/Z.
Switch(config)# interface gigabitethernet 5/1
Switch(config-if)# switchport mode access
Switch(config-if)# switchport port-security
Switch(config-if)# switchport port-security maximum 10
Switch(config-if)# switchport port-security mac-address 0000.0000.0003
Switch(config-if)# switchport port-security mac-address sticky
Switch(config-if)# switchport port-security mac-address sticky 0000.0000.0001
Switch(config-if)# switchport port-security mac-address sticky 0000.0000.0002
Switch(config-if)# end
Switch# show port address
Secure Mac Address Table
-------------------------------------------------------------------------

Vlan    Mac Address       Type            Ports     Remaining Age
                                                    (mins)

----    -----------       ----            -----     -------------
  1     0000.0000.0001    SecureSticky      Gi5/1       -
  1     0000.0000.0002    SecureSticky      Gi5/1       -
  1     0000.0000.0003    SecureConfigured  Gi5/1       -


-------------------------------------------------------------------------
Total Addresses in System (excluding one mac per port)     : 2
Max Addresses limit in System (excluding one mac per port) : 1024
```

Port Error Conditions

Loosely tied to security principles is the concept of port error conditions. This concept is covered here because it is important to port security. The switch places a port into an *err-disabled* state and shuts down the interface when it detects error conditions or takes action based on specific effect. Examples include port security violations, duplex mismatches, and excessive link flapping.

Ideally, this behavior of error-disabling a port is a best practice because a malfunctioning port or a major misconfiguration of spanning tree could cause a major network outage.

The following list highlights the most common situations where a port will go into the err-disabled state:

■ **Port security violation:** When an invalid MAC address is learned on a port or too many MAC addresses, the switch can optionally place the port into the err-disabled state.

- **Spanning-tree BPDU guard violation:** When you have PortFast configured in combination with BPDU Guard, the port will switch to the err-disabled state if a BPDU is received on the port.

- **EtherChannel misconfiguration:** All parameters have to be the same for all ports on both sides of the bundle; otherwise, the port will switch into the err-disabled state.

- **Duplex mismatch:** Duplex mode has to be the same on both sides of the link; otherwise, the ports switch into the err-disabled state.

- **UDLD condition:** Unidirectional Link Detection (UDLD) ensures that the link is bidirectional at all times; so when it detects a unidirectional link, it places the port into the err-disabled state.

- **Spanning-tree Root Guard:** If a Root Guard-enabled port receives a superior BPDU from those sent by the current root bridge, the port is moved into the err-disabled state.

- **Link flapping:** When link state is flapping between the up and down states, the port is placed into the err-disabled state.

- **Other reasons:** Other reasons include late collision detection, Layer 2 Tunneling Protocol Guard, DHCP snooping rate-limit, incorrect gigabit interface convert (GBIC), and ARP inspection.

Err-disabled detection is enabled for all of these causes by default. You can configure other reasons to trigger the port being disabled. Use the following command to specify the causes:

```
Switch(config)# errdisable detect cause [all | cause-name]
```

Err-Disabled Automatic Recovery

Once the root cause of the err-disabled state is removed, an err-disabled port can become operational after a **shut/no shut**. Because the error condition is no longer present, the trigger for err-disable will not occur. Therefore, to reduce the administrative overhead, the switch port can be configured to be automatically reenabled after a specified time. Of course, if the error condition is still present, the port will immediately go back to the err-disabled state.

A good example of the use of this behavior is in conference rooms. Often people plug downstream switches into corporate Ethernet connections in conference rooms to gain additional port access. The switches are considered rogue because the corporate IT group does not manage them. If configured, BPDU Guard will immediately err-disable once it receives a BPDU from one of these rogue switches. Once the conference room users realize they created a problem, they often remove the rogue switch. The port they accidentally disabled will eventually be reenabled for the next group to use the conference room.

In terms of configuration, the **errdisable recovery** command enables the automatic attempt to reenable the port after a specified period of time. Example 10-3 shows the use of this configuration command.

Example 10-3   *Err-Disable Autorecovery Configuration*

```
Switch(config)# errdisable recovery cause psecure-violation
Switch(config)# errdisable recovery interval 60
```

The default time interval for err-disable autorecovery is 300 seconds, and the minimum is 30 seconds. You can verify where you have autorecovery enabled by using the command **show errdisable recovery**. By default, the autorecovery feature is disabled.

Port Access Lists

Port access lists (PACLs) are yet another way to apply security in the campus network. Standard access control lists (ACLs) are applied to traffic passing through the Layer 3 interface (for instance, a switch virtual interface [SVI] used to route from one VLAN to another VLAN on a Layer 3 switch). The PACL feature provides the ability to perform access control on a specific Layer 2 port.

Of note, PACLs are not supported on all Cisco Catalyst switch platforms. In addition, the supported parameters and scale of the supported access lists vary per platform and per Catalyst software version. Consult cisco.com for specifics about the platform you are working with before configuring PACLs.

A Layer 2 port is a physical access or trunk port that belongs to a VLAN. The port ACL feature is supported only in hardware. (Port ACLs are not applied to any packets routed in software.) The PACL feature does not affect Layer 2 control packets, such as CDP, VTP, DTP, and STP, received on the port.

There are two types of PACL:

- **IP access list** filters IPv4 and IPv6 packets on a Layer 2 port.

- **MAC access list** filters packets that are of an unsupported type (not IP, ARP, or MPLS) based on the fields of the Ethernet frame. A MAC access list is *not applied* to IP, MPLS, or ARP messages. You can define only named MAC access lists.

PACLs interaction with other types of ACLs depends on the configured mode:

- In **prefer port mode**, the PACL takes effect and overrides the effect of other ACLs. This mode is the only mode that is allowed when applying PACL on a trunk.

- In **merge mode**, PACLs, VACLs, and standard ACLs are merged in the ingress direction. This is the default mode.

PACLs can be configured on an EtherChannel interface, but not on its port members.

IP and MAC ACLs can be applied to Layer 2 physical interfaces. Standard (numbered, named) and extended (numbered, named) IP ACLs and extended named MAC ACLs are supported.

In terms of configuration, the commands to configure a MAC ACL and apply it to a Layer 2 interface are as follows:

```
SW(config)# mac access-list extended acl-name
SW(config-ext-macl)# permit host [source-mac | any] [destination-mac | any]
SW(config-ext-macl)# interface interface-slot/number
SW(config-if)# mac access-group acl-name in
```

In addition, the commands to configure a standard or extended IP ACL and apply it to a Layer 2 interface are as follows:

```
SW(config)# ip access-list acl-type acl-name
SW(config-ext-nacl)# permit protocol [source-address | any] [destination-address | any]
SW(config-ext-nacl)# interface interface-slot/number
SW(config-if)# ip access-group acl-name in
```

Note   The command-line interface (CLI) syntax for creating a PACL is identical to the syntax for creating a Cisco IOS ACL. An instance of an ACL that is mapped to a Layer 2 port is called a *PACL*. An instance of an ACL that is mapped to a Layer 3 interface is called a *Cisco IOS ACL*. The same ACL can be mapped to both a Layer 2 port and a Layer 3 interface.

To configure the access group mode on a Layer 2 interface, perform this task:

```
SW(config)# interface interface-slot/number
SW(config-if)# access-group mode [prefer port | merge]
```

Note that access mode command is not supported on all platforms.

For additional information on configuring PACLs, reference the Catalyst 6500 port-security document as a starting point: http://www.cisco.com/c/en/us/td/docs/switches/lan/catalyst6500/ios/12-2SY/configuration/guide/sy_swcg/port_acls.html.

Storm Control

Network or host misconfigurations, host malfunctions, or intentional denial-of-service attacks may flood the network with traffic storms. Cisco IOS switches provide the storm control feature to limit the impact of traffic storms and, if necessary, take appropriate actions.

Upon reading this subsection, you will be able to do the following:

- Describe what a traffic storm is and how to control it

- Configure and verify storm control

Introduction to Storm Control

A traffic storm occurs when packets flood the LAN, creating excessive traffic and degrading network performance. The storm control feature prevents LAN ports from being disrupted by a broadcast, multicast, or unicast traffic storm on physical interfaces and is used to protect against or isolate broadcast storms caused by STP misconfigurations. Storm control also protects against unicast storms created by malfunctioning hosts or denial of service attacks.

To combat this traffic storm situation, the switch runs a process called *traffic storm control* (also called *traffic suppression*) that monitors incoming traffic levels over a 1-second traffic storm control interval. During the interval, it compares the traffic level with the traffic storm threshold level that you configure. The traffic storm control level is either an absolute number of bits or packets per second or a percentage of the total available bandwidth of the port. Two thresholds can be configured. When traffic exceeds the rising threshold level, storm control blocks the port. Once the traffic falls under the falling threshold, storm control removes the block. Configuration of a falling threshold is optional. Figure 10-5 illustrates the behavior of storm control.

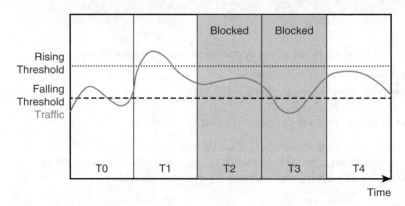

Figure 10-5 *Storm Control Behavior*

Each T slot in Figure 10-5 represents a 1-second interval. In T0, ingress traffic stays below the rising threshold. In T1, traffic breaches the rising threshold, and consequently the port is blocked in the next interval, T2. In T2, traffic falls below the rising threshold, but it is still above the falling thresholds, so the port block is kept until T3. Finally, traffic falls under falling threshold in T3, and the port block is removed in T4.

Note   The behavior of storm control differs between Catalyst software versions and hardware models. On several Cisco Catalyst switches, the port is blocked as soon as the storm control threshold is breached and is kept blocked until the end of the 1-second interval. Consult Cisco.com for specifics about the switch you are configuring for storm control.

Optionally, an interface can be shut down if a threshold level is breached or an SNMP trap is sent. In addition, storm control is configured per interface for each traffic type (unicast, multicast, broadcast) separately, with the caveat that some Catalyst switches consider multicast traffic as broadcast traffic. Consult cisco.com for details about the Catalyst switch you are configuring and how multicast traffic is treated. The next subsection discusses how to configure storm control.

Configuring and Verifying Storm Control on an Interface

Storm control configuration is done per interface for each type of traffic separately. Storm control is typically configured on access ports, to limit the effect of traffic storm on access level, before it enters the network. Storm control can be configured on trunk ports and this configuration may be used as a secondary control.

In terms of configuration, the first step is to configure a rising threshold. Configuration of a falling threshold is optional. Both thresholds can be configured either in percent of the total interface bandwidth, bits per second (bps), or packets per second (pps). The command for configuring storm control is as follows:

```
Switch(config)# interface interface-slot/int
Switch(config-if)# storm-control [broadcast | multicast | unicast] level {rising-
percent | bps rising-bps | pps rising-pps} [falling-percent | falling-bps |
falling-pps]
```

Networks differ from one another, so do the traffic patterns. To configure an effective threshold level, interface traffic monitoring over a longer period is advised to establish a baseline. Monitoring of storm control events, either with remote syslog server or an SNMP trap receiver, will allow you to effectively adjust the thresholds when needed. Incorrectly configuring storm control for your network can have negative impact on production applications. In the campus network, applications generally do not use excessive amounts of traffic per port. Data centers are an exception where steady-state monitoring and leveling is required before configuring storm control.

Another noted caveat is that although storm control can be configured on the port channel interface of an EtherChannel, do not configure it on ports that are members of an EtherChannel because it is an unsupported configuration.

Note The configured percentage thresholds of storm control are only approximations; actual enforced level might differ. On some platforms, setting percentage thresholds under 0.33 percent may suppress all traffic, and some platforms round thresholds.

When storm control reaches thresholds, additional actions can be taken, such as putting the interface in an err-disabled state or sending an SNMP trap. Use the following commands to configure these options:

```
Switch(config)# interface interface-slot/int
Switch(config-if)# storm-control action {shutdown | trap}
```

Example 10-4 illustrates a sample storm control configuration. In this configuration, storm control is configured for the following:

- 0 percent rising and 25 percent failing thresholds of port bandwidth for broadcast traffic

- 50,000 packets per second (pps) rising and 25,000 packets per second (pps) failing thresholds for multicast

- 20,000,000 bits per second (bps) for unicast traffic.

- Switch to place ports into err-disable that exceed thresholds

- Send an SNMP trap when thresholds reached

Example 10-4 *Sample Storm Control Configuration*

```
Switch(config)# interface GigabitEthernet 0/0/1
Switch(config-if)# storm-control broadcast level 40 25
Switch(config-if)# storm-control multicast level pps 50k 25k
Switch(config-if)# storm-control unicast level bps 20m
Switch(config-if)# storm-control action shutdown
Switch(config-if)# storm-control action trap
```

The **show storm-control** command without an additional parameter displays the **broadcast** filter state. In Example 10-5, the rising threshold is set to 40 percent of interface bandwidth, the falling threshold is configured for 25 percent, and the current broadcast traffic is currently around 3.5 percent of the bandwidth. Because the traffic is below threshold, the filter state is in forwarding:

Example 10-5 *Display Storm Control for Broadcast Traffic*

```
Switch# show storm-control
Interface  Filter State   Upper        Lower        Current
---------  ------------   -----------  -----------  ----------
Gi0/1      Forwarding     40.00%       25.00%        3.50%
```

When using **show storm-control**, the additional **multicast** keyword displays only multicast information. In Example 10-6, the output shows a rising threshold set to 50,000 packets per second and falling threshold set to 25,000 packets per second.

Example 10-6 *Display Storm Control for Multicast Traffic*

```
Switch# show storm-control multicast
Interface  Filter State  Upper        Lower        Current
---------  ------------  -----------  -----------  ----------
Gi0/1      Blocking      50m pps      25m pps      34m pps
```

Moreover, when using **show storm-control**, leverage the **unicast** filter to view only unicast output. In Example 10-7, the rising threshold is set to 20 Megabits per second. The falling threshold is not configured and is thus equal to the rising threshold. The current unicast traffic exceeds the threshold with 37 Mbps. Because the threshold was already breached in the previous 1-second interval, the filter is set to blocking.

Example 10-7 *Display Storm Control for Unicast Traffic*

```
Switch# show storm-control unicast
Interface  Filter State  Upper        Lower        Current
---------  ------------  -----------  -----------  ----------
Gi0/1      Blocking      20m bps      20m bps      37m bps
```

Note Traffic generation tools such as iPerf are useful in testing storm control in a lab environment.

In review of this section, storm control is a useful and handy tool to help limit excessive traffic of unicast, multicast, and broadcast. Storm control can help reduce the impact of an anomalous behavior or security attack. Unfortunately, many anomalous events and security attacks often go well beyond flooding of traffic, such as in the case of spoofing. Storm control is useful, but it is just one of many necessary security features. The next subsection starts discussion of security measures to protect against spoofing.

For additional information, consult the following documents on Cisco.com for the Catalyst 3560, 4500, or 6500; Consult Cisco.com for other switch models:

- **Configuring storm control on Catalyst 3560 series:** http://www.cisco.com/c/en/us/td/docs/switches/lan/catalyst3560/software/release/15-0_2_se/configuration/guide/scg3560/swtrafc.html#wp1063295

- **Configuring storm control on Catalyst 4500 series:** http://www.cisco.com/c/en/us/td/docs/switches/lan/catalyst4500/12-2/15-02SG/configuration/guide/config/bcastsup.html

■ **Configuring storm control on Catalyst 6500 series:** http://www.cisco.com/c/en/us/
td/docs/switches/lan/catalyst6500/ios/15-0SY/configuration/guide/15_0_sy_swcg/
traffic_storm_control.html

Mitigating Spoofing Attacks

Hackers often attempt to spoof (pretend to be another machine) in an attempt to create
network chaos or gain access to secure data. Most commonly, spoofing attempts redirect part or all of the traffic coming from, or going to, a predefined target such as a web
server. After the attack, all traffic from the device under attack flows through the attackers device and then to its destination.

Spoofing attacks can affect devices that are connected to your Layer 2 network by
sending false information to devices that are connected to the same broadcast domain.
Spoofing attacks can also intercept traffic that is intended for other hosts in the same
domain. In all cases, spoofing attacks always attempt to undermine network security and
create network instability or service interruption.

Several features available on Cisco Catalyst switches can help mediate common spoofing
attacks such as DHCP, MAC, and ARP spoofing features. These features include DHCP
snooping, IP Source Guard, and dynamic ARP inspection (DAI).

After reading this subsection, you will have an understanding of the following topics:

■ How can a rogue DHCP server harm your network

■ DHCP spoofing

■ Configuring and verifying DHCP snooping

■ What IP Source Guard is and why you need it

■ Configuring IP Source Guard

■ ARP spoofing

■ How DAI works

■ Configure DAI

DHCP Spoofing Attacks

DHCP servers support dynamic IP assignment, including subnet mask, default gateway,
DNS servers, and so on to any host, server, or any other IP-enabled device on request.
One of the ways that an attacker can gain access to network traffic is to bring a rogue
DHCP server in the same subnet as DHCP clients in an attempt to break DHCP services
or gain malicious access to resources.

The most common example of a rogue DHCP server is when a PC is configured as a
DHCP server in the campus network as shown in Figure 10-6.

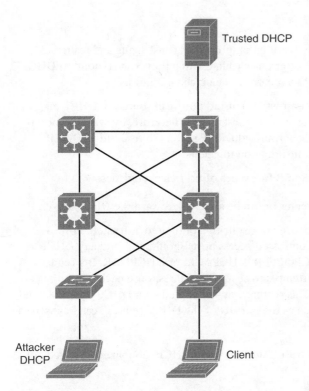

Figure 10-6   *DHCP Spoofing Attacks*

DHCP clients send initial DHCP requests as broadcasts. Therefore, both the legitimate and the rogue DHCP servers will see the request and both will respond. If the rogue DHCP server's reply arrives at the DHCP client first, the client will use this response. Because this first response from the rogue server is bogus, the client will not be able to gain the correct network connectivity and may have its traffic redirected to a bogus default gateway. The most common sequence of events created by a rogue DHCP server is as follows:

1. Attacker hosts a rogue DHCP server off a switch port to the same subnet as the clients.

2. Client broadcasts a request for DHCP configuration information.

3. The rogue DHCP server responds before the legitimate DHCP server, assigning attacker-defined IP configuration information.

4. Host packets are redirected to the attacker's address because it emulates a default gateway for the erroneous IP address that is provided to the client via DHCP.

To combat DHCP spoofing attacks, switches deploy a feature known as *DHCP snooping,* which is introduced in the next subsection.

DHCP Snooping

DHCP snooping is a Cisco security feature that protects against rogue and malicious DHCP servers. The feature simply determines which switch ports can respond to DHCP requests and prevent rogue DHCP servers from seeing client requests.

Ports are identified as trusted and untrusted. Trusted ports can source all DHCP messages, whereas untrusted ports can source requests only. Therefore, by switch configuration, DHCP snooping allows only authorized DHCP servers to respond to DHCP requests and to distribute network information to clients.

In review, the DHCP feature configures two types of port characteristics:

- **Trusted ports** host a DHCP server or can be an uplink toward the DHCP server.

- **Untrusted ports** are those that are not explicitly configured as trusted. From a DHCP snooping perspective, untrusted access ports should not send any DHCP server responses, such as DHCPOFFER, DHCPACK, or DHCPNAK. If a rogue device on an untrusted port attempts to send a DHCP response packet into the network, the port is shut down. This feature can be coupled with DHCP option 82, in which switch information, such as the port ID of the DHCP request, can be inserted into the DHCP request packet.

Figure 10-7 displays an example of trusted and untrusted DHCP snooping configured ports.

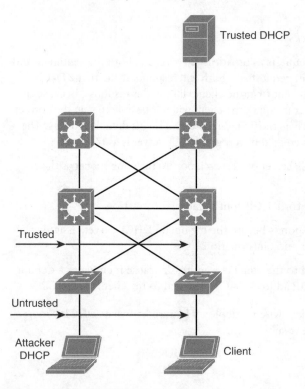

Figure 10-7 *DHCP Snooping*

DHCP Option 82

As mentioned in the previous section, DHCP option 82 provides additional security when DHCP is used to allocate network addresses. This feature enables the DHCP relay agent, to include information about itself and the attached client in the DHCP request frames when forwarding DHCP requests from a DHCP client to a DHCP server.

The DHCP server can then use this information to assign IP addresses, perform access control, and set quality of service (QoS) and security policies (or other parameter-assignment policies) for each subscriber of a service provider network. Some cable providers use DHCP option 82 with cable modems to ensure access control and quality of server for business class users among residential users. Alternatively, if the information is not present or incorrect, the DHCP server could choose to ignore the request.

DHCP option 82 along with DHCP snooping are both best practices for campus networks as an additional security measure.

DHCP Snooping Example Configuration

Figure 10-8 illustrates a sample topology where DHCP snooping is to be applied.

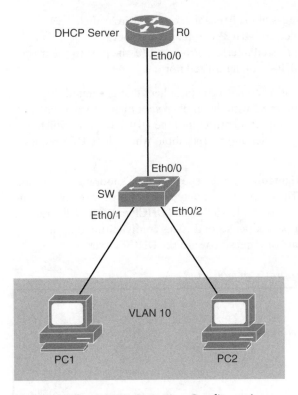

Figure 10-8   *DHCP Snooping Configuration*

The steps to enable DHCP snooping for VLAN 10 with a DHCP server on Ethernet 0/0 are as follows:

Step 1. Enable DHCP snooping globally.

Step 2. Enable DHCP snooping on selected VLANs.

Step 3. Configure trusted interfaces, since untrusted is default.

Step 4. Configure rate-limit of DHCP requests on untrusted ports.

Step 5. Configure information option using DHCP option 82.

Example 10-8 demonstrates the configuration associated with this simple example.

Example 10-8 *Sample DHCP Snooping Configuration*

```
SW(config)# ip dhcp snooping
SW(config)# ip dhcp snooping VLAN 10
SW(config)# interface Ethernet 0/0
SW(config-if)# ip dhcp snooping trust
```

With Example 10-8, DHCP snooping is globally enabled on the switch labeled SW as a first step. Then, VLAN 10 is enabled for DHCP snooping. Next, because the default configuration is that all ports are untrusted interface Ethernet 0/0, the port to the trusted DHCP server is configured as a DCHP snooping trusted port.

If you want to provide more information about the actual client that generated the DHCP request, configure DHCP option 82 with the **ip dhcp snooping information option** command. This adds the switch port identifier into the DHCP request, which provides additional information to switches and routers about where the DHCP request was initiated.

To verify the DHCP snooping configuration, use the **show ip dhcp snooping** command, as demonstrated in Example 10-9. The output shows only trusted ports or the ports configured with optional rate limits. Refer to Table 10-5 to see DHCP rate limits that restrict DHCP requests to a specific rate of packet per seconds. This configuration option thwarts attacks that launch a high rate of requests toward the DHCP server.

Example 10-9 *Verifying DHCP Snooping Configuration*

```
SW# show ip dhcp snooping
Switch DHCP snooping is enabled
DHCP snooping is configured on following VLANs:
10
DHCP snooping is operational on following VLANs:
10
DHCP snooping is configured on the following L3 Interfaces:
```

```
Insertion of option 82 is enabled
   circuit-id default format: vlan-mod-port
   remote-id: 0024.f9c6.1a80 (MAC)
Option 82 on untrusted port is not allowed
Verification of hwaddr field is enabled
Verification of giaddr field is enabled
DHCP snooping trust/rate is configured on the following Interfaces:

Interface               Trusted     Allow option    Rate limit (pps)
---------------------   -------     ------------    ----------------
Ethernet0/0               yes         yes             unlimited
```

To display all the known DHCP bindings that have been learned on a switch, use the **show ip dhcp snooping binding** command. In Example 10-9, there are two PCs connected to the switch in VLAN 10, so there is a binding for each of them in the table, as shown in the output in Example 10-10.

Example 10-10 *IP Snooping Binding*

```
SW# show ip dhcp snooping binding
MacAddress          IpAddress         Lease(sec)   Type            VLAN  Interface
------------------  ---------------   ----------   -------------   ----  ----------
----------
00:24:13:47:AF:C2   192.168.1.4       85858        dhcp-snooping   10    Ethernet0/1
00:24:13:47:7D:B1   192.168.1.5       85859        dhcp-snooping   10    Ethernet0/2
Total number of bindings: 2
```

Table 10-5 reviews all the commands associated with DHCP snooping.

Table 10-5 *DHCP Snooping Command Review*

Command	Comments
ip dhcp snooping	Enables DHCP snooping globally. By default, the feature is not enabled.
ip dhcp snooping information option	Enables DHCP option 82. This is optional for the forwarded DHCP request packet to contain information on the switch port where it originated. The option is enabled by default.
ip dhcp snooping vlan *vlan-id[vlan-id]*	Identifies VLANs that will be subject to DHCP snooping.
ip dhcp snooping trust	Configures trusted port. Use the **no** keyword to revert to untrusted. Use this command in the interface configuration mode.

Command	Comments
ip dhcp snooping limit rate *rate*	Configures the number of DHCP packets per second that an interface can receive. This ensures that DHCP traffic will not overwhelm the DHCP servers. Normally, the rate limit applies to untrusted interfaces. Use this command in the interface configuration mode.
show ip dhcp snooping	Verifies the configuration.

IP Source Guard

All IP-enabled devices use IP addresses to communicate. One common malicious attack method is to hijack an IP address of a valid host or server. This hijacking is also referred to as *IP spoofing*. This type of spoofing is difficult to mediate; however, Catalyst switches support a featured called *IP Source Guard* (IPSG) that helps protect against IP address spoofing attacks.

In brief, IPSG operates by dynamically maintaining per-port VLAN ACLs based on learned IP-to-MAC-to-switch-port bindings.

From a detailed perspective, when IPSG is enabled, the switch blocks all IP traffic into the port except for DHCP packets captured by the DHCP snooping process.

After the DHCP process is complete and the client receives a valid IP address from the DHCP server (or when a static IP source binding is configured by the user), a per-port and VLAN access control list (PVACL) is installed on the port dynamically.

This process restricts the client IP traffic ingress on the respective port to the source IP address that is configured in the binding. Any IP traffic with a source IP address other than that in the IP source binding will be filtered out. As such, this dynamic filtering capability limits the ability of a host to attack the network by claiming the IP address of a neighbor host.

Note   If IPSG is enabled on a trunk port with a large number of VLANs that have DHCP snooping enabled, the switch might not have enough ACL hardware resources to accommodate this configuration. Consult Cisco.com for ACL limitations before enabling IPSG on trunk ports. Nevertheless, the best practice is to enable IPSG on access ports.

In terms of configuration, IPSG is only supported on Layer 2 ports, including both access and trunk ports. IPSG labels untrusted ports as those needing the dynamic filtering capability and trusted ports as those that need no IPSG filtering. Figure 10-9 illustrates a simple topology with trusted and untrusted ports.

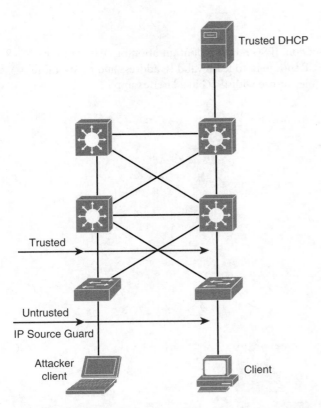

Figure 10-9 *IPSG Topology Layout*

For each untrusted port, there are two possible levels of IP traffic security filtering:

■ **Source IP address filter:** IP traffic is filtered based on its source IP address. Only IP traffic with a source IP address that matches the IP source binding entry is permitted.

An IP source address filter is changed when a new IP source entry binding is created or deleted on the port. The PVACL will be recalculated and reapplied in the hardware to reflect the IP source binding change. By default, if the IP filter is enabled without any IP source binding on the port, a default PVACL that denies all IP traffic is installed on the port. Similarly, when the IP filter is disabled, any IP source filter PVACL will be removed from the interface.

■ **Source IP and MAC address filter:** IP traffic is filtered based on its source IP address in addition to its MAC address; only IP traffic with source IP and MAC addresses that match the IP source binding entry are permitted.

IPSG Configuration

As mentioned in the previous section, IPSG requires configuration of DHCP snooping because IPSG leverages DHCP snooping to learn valid IP address and MAC address pairs. Figure 10-10 shows a sample for use with IPSG in a later example.

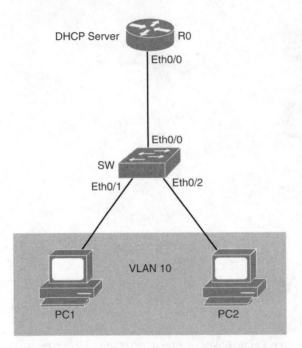

Figure 10-10 *IPSG Example*

IPSG configuration is brief and straightforward. To enable IPSG on the port use the **ip verify source** interface command for enabling IP address filters. To enable MAC address filtering and IP filters, add the **ip verify source port-security** interface command. The configuration example for Figure 10-10 for both IP and MAC address filtering is as follows:

```
SW(config)# interface Ethernet 0/1
SW(config-if)# ip verify source
SW(config-if)# ip verify source port-security
SW(config-if)# interface Ethernet0/2
SW(config-if)# ip verify source
SW(config-if)# ip verify source port-security
```

To verify the IPSG configuration, use the **show ip verify source** command. In the example, switch access ports are configured with IPSG, so both Ethernet 0/1 and Ethernet 0/2 are listed in the output in Example 10-11. In addition, each interface has one valid DHCP binding.

Example 10-11 *IPSG Configuration and State Verification*

```
SW# show ip verify source
Interface  Filter-type  Filter-mode  IP-address       Mac-address         Vlan
---------  -----------  -----------  ---------------  ------------------  ----
Et0/1      ip           active       192.168.1.4                          10
Et0/2      ip           active       192.168.1.5                          10
```

ARP Spoofing

ARP spoofing is yet another attack mechanism used by hackers to disrupt networks. Recall from basic networks that IP-enabled devices use ARP to resolve MAC addresses for IP addresses. When an IP-enabled device sends an ARP request, the device with the corresponding IP address replies with an ARP reply. The origination device stores the MAC-to-IP mapping in an ARP table that is cached for future use for up to 4 hours.

ARP spoofing works by spoofing an ARP reply from a legitimate device with an invalid MAC. For example, an attacker may opt to spoof an ARP reply from a router. In this manner, the requested IP-enabled device will receive an ARP reply with a spoofed MAC address and direct further communication to this device instead of the intended router. At minimum, traffic from the IP-enabled device to the router will be disrupted. It is also possible the attacker could intercept some critical data.

Figure 10-11 provides a more detailed example.

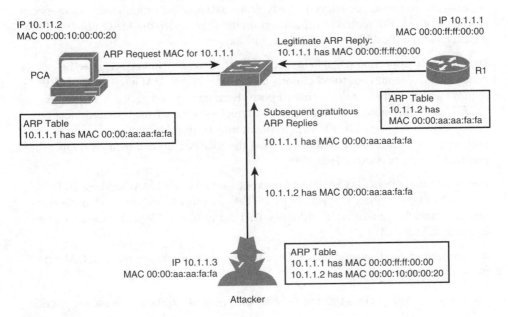

Figure 10-11 *ARP Spoofing*

The following steps occur when the attacker ARP spoofs:

Step 1.   PCA sends an ARP request for MAC address of R1.

Step 2.   R1 replies with its MAC and IP address. It also updates its ARP cache.

Step 3.   PCA binds MAC address of R1 to R1's IP address in its ARP cache.

Step 4.   Attacker sends its ARP reply to PCA, binding its MAC address to the IP of R1.

Step 5.   PCA updates ARP cache with MAC address of attacker bound to IP address of R1.

Step 6.   Attacker sends its ARP reply to R1, binding its MAC address to the IP of PCA.

Step 7.   R1 updates ARP cache with MAC address of attacker bound to IP address of PCA.

Step 8.   Packets are diverted through attacker.

The next section discusses a feature on Catalyst switch that aids in preventing ARP snooping.

Dynamic ARP Inspection

To prevent ARP spoofing or poisoning, a switch must ensure that only valid ARP requests and responses are relayed. In a typical ARP spoofing attack, malicious users can send unsolicited ARP replies to other hosts on the subnet with the MAC address of the attacker and the IP address of the default gateway.

Dynamic ARP inspection (DAI) helps prevent such attacks by not relaying invalid or gratuitous ARP replies out to other ports in the same VLAN. DAI intercepts all ARP requests and all replies on the untrusted ports. Each intercepted packet is verified for valid IP-to-MAC binding similar to IPSG. ARP replies coming from invalid devices are either dropped or logged by the switch for auditing so that ARP poisoning attacks are prevented. You can also use DAI to rate-limit the ARP packets and then err-disable the interface if the rate is exceeded.

DAI determines the validity of an ARP packet based on a valid MAC-address-to-IP-address bindings database that is built by DHCP snooping. In addition, to handle hosts that use statically configured IP addresses, DAI can validate ARP packets against user-configured ARP ACLs.

In review, to ensure that only valid ARP requests and responses are relayed, DAI performs these tasks:

■ Forwards ARP packets that are received on a trusted interface without any checks

■ Intercepts all ARP packets on untrusted ports

■ Verifies that each intercepted packet has a valid IP-to-MAC address binding before forwarding packets that can update the local ARP cache

■ Drops, logs, or drops and logs ARP packets with invalid IP-to-MAC address bindings

It is best practice to configure all access switch ports as untrusted and all switch ports that are connected to other switches as trusted, as shown in Figure 10-12. In this case, all ARP packets that are entering the network would be from an upstream distribution or core switch, bypassing the security check and requiring no further validation.

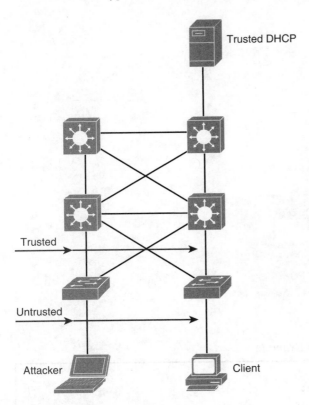

Figure 10-12 *Trust Boundaries with DAI*

DAI Configuration

The DAI configuration is straightforward and relies on DHCP snooping configuration similar to IPSG. The following steps are the recommended practice for configuring DHCP spoofing:

Step 1.   Implement protection against DHCP spoofing:

a. Enable DHCP snooping globally.

b. Enable DHCP snooping on selected VLANs.

Step 2. Enable DAI: Enable ARP inspection on selected VLANs.

Step 3. Configure trusted interfaces for DHCP snooping and ARP inspection (untrusted is default).

Figure 10-13 shows a DAI topology example, and Example 10-12 shows the applied configuration.

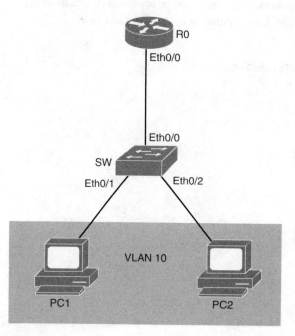

Figure 10-13 *DAI Topology*

Example 10-12 *DAI Configuration Example*

```
SW(config)# ip dhcp snooping
SW(config)# ip dhcp snooping vlan 10
SW(config)# ip arp inspection vlan 10
SW(config)# interface Ethernet 0/0
SW(config-if)# ip dhcp snooping trust
SW(config-if)# ip arp inspection trust
```

In Example 10-12, the configuration enables DHCP snooping globally. DHCP snooping and ARP inspection are then enabled for the PC's VLAN, VLAN 10. In addition, the uplink, interface Ethernet 0/0, is configured as trusted for DHCP snooping and ARP inspection.

Table 10-6 reviews the commands application to DAI.

Table 10-6 *DAI Commands*

Command	Description
ip arp inspection vlan *vlan-id* [, *vlan-id*]	Enables DAI on a VLAN or range of VLANs
ip arp inspection trust	Sets the interface as a trusted interface
ip arp inspection validate {[*src-mac*] [*dst-mac*] [*ip*]}	Configures DAI to drop ARP packets when the IP addresses are invalid, or when the MAC addresses in the body of the ARP packets do not match the addresses that are specified in the Ethernet header

In summary, this section discussed DHCP snooping and IPSG and DAI. These features are summarized as follows:

■ Use DHCP snooping to mitigate DHCP spoofing attacks.

■ Leverage IPSG to protect against spoofed IP addresses.

■ Use DAI to aid in mitigation of ARP spoofing attacks.

The next section discusses a more common configuration: securing VLAN trunks.

Securing VLAN Trunks

Creating trunk links on Cisco switches requires administrative configuration access, and therefore is considered secured. Unfortunately, it is possible that physical access to fixed or dynamic trunk ports may expose vulnerability to some types of attacks. In this section of the book, you will be exposed to some of the possible attacks against truck ports and learn how to prevent them.

Upon completing this section, you will be able to do the following:

■ Describe the switch spoofing attack associated with VLAN trunks

■ Protect your network against switch spoofing

■ Describe the VLAN hopping attack

■ Protect your network against the VLAN hopping attack

■ Describe the need for VLAN access lists

■ Describe how VLAN access lists interact with standard and port access lists

■ Configure the VLAN access lists

Switch Spoofing

For Layer 2 connections and designs, interconnected switches are often linked via a trunk, which generally carries traffic from multiple VLANs. A trunk link can be either manually configured on both sides of a link, or automatically negotiated using the Dynamic Trunking Protocol (DTP), as discussed in earlier chapters. Although use of DTP simplifies switch administration, it may lead to configuration errors and switch port exposure.

Depending on the switch IOS version running on a Catalyst switch, switch ports default to either the *dynamic desirable* or the *dynamic auto* DTP mode. The default setting of dynamic auto is convenient because when a switch is connected to a dynamic port, a trunk is formed after a DTP negotiation and no additional configuration is needed. When a workstation is connected, no DTP negotiation occurs, and the switch port is turned into an access port with a single access VLAN.

Although difficult and complex, an attacker might exploit the DTP and negotiate a trunk with the switch port. It is possible that the attacker will attempt to leverage a PC or server to present itself as a switch to the connected switch. If the attacker is able to negotiate DTP, the attacker could gain access to any VLAN, perhaps secured VLANs for critical data transfers. Figure 10-14 illustrates this attack method.

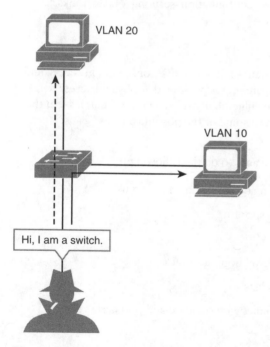

Figure 10-14   *Switch Spoofing*

There are several mechanisms or best practices to minimize authorized access to trunk ports and switch spoofing, including the following

- Manually configure access ports
- Shut down unused interfaces
- Restrict VLANs on trunk ports

Manually configuring access ports prevents trunks from being dynamic. This configuration is a best practice for ports that are deemed to be only access ports. Recall that depending on mode, the default behavior on a specific Catalyst switch may be set to negotiate trunk mode, and this configuration will prevent dynamic configuration to a trunk operation. It is best practice to always configure determined access ports with the access port configuration. The configuration for manually configuring access ports is as follows:

```
SW(config)# interface interface-slot/number
SW(config-if)# switchport mode access
SW(config-if)# switchport access vlan vlan-id
```

Shutting down unused ports is a simple practice. This is a best practice regardless of security configuration around switch spoofing, and it aids in preventing connection of wrong ports, incorrect cabling, and so on. The command to shut down a port is as follows:

```
SW(config)# interface interface-slot/number
SW(config-if)# shutdown
```

Lastly, a final configuration to aid in securing trucks is to limit the VLANs on the trunk ports to VLANs needed to pass on the trunk. In a large network, not all VLANs will pass on every trunk port. Reducing the number of VLANs to only interested VLANs helps limit the impact of switch spoofing. The configuration for limiting VLANs on a trunk is as follows:

```
SW(config)# interface interface-slot/number
SW(config-if)# switchport trunk allowed vlan vlan-list
```

Example 10-13 illustrates a sample configuration for manually configuring access ports, and shutting down interfaces and restricted VLAN access lists, respectively.

Example 10-13 *Securing VLAN Trunks*

```
Switch(config)# interface GigabitEthernet 1/1
Switch(config-if)# switchport mode access
Switch(config-if)# switchport access vlan 100

Switch(config)# interface GigabitEthernet 2/1
Switch(config)# shutdown
```

```
Switch(config)# interface GigabitEthernet 3/1
Switch(config)# switchport trunk allowed vlan 2-10
```

The next section discusses another vulnerability: VLAN hopping.

VLAN Hopping

Another switch inherit vulnerability, although uncommon, is VLAN hopping. VLAN hopping is where an attacker modifies particular frames to be sent into the network on an access port with spoofed 802.1Q tags. The spoofed 802.1Q can trick the switch into sending frames on a different VLAN than the access VLAN of the port. This attack method is also called *double tagging*.

This VLAN hopping vulnerability occurs only in very specific circumstances, as illustrated in Figure 10-15.

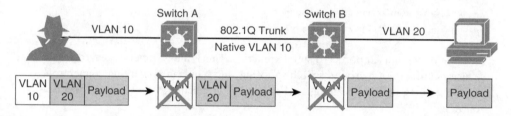

Figure 10-15 *VLAN Hopping*

The circumstances are as follows:

- The IP-enabled device the attacker is using must be connected to an access port.
- The IP-enabled device must send a double-tagged frame.
- The first-hop switch must be configured to accept 802.1Q frames.
- The first-hop switch must be connected to another switch with an 802.1Q truck, and its native VLAN must match the attackers outer VLAN tag.

In Figure 10-15, the attacker is connected to an access port of Switch A. All traffic between a workstation and an access port would normally be untagged, but the attacker prepends its payload with two 802.1Q tags, the outer one with the native VLAN of the access port (VLAN 10 in the figure) and the inner one with the VLAN the attacker wants to hop into (VLAN 20 in the figure).

A switch then accepts frames if the outer VLAN tag matches the VLAN in which the access port is put into. The 802.1Q tag (VLAN 10) is removed, and the payload, together with the inner tag (VLAN 20), is forwarded.

The frame is then forwarded to an adjoining trunk. For the attack to succeed, the trunk's native VLAN must match the attacker's access port VLAN (10 in the figure). Only then is the frame sent over a trunk without the additional VLAN tag prepended.

Switch B receives a frame, which now only has one tag in the header, so it considers the frame as a part of a VLAN the attacker wants to hop into (VLAN 20). Switch B forwards the frame to the destination workstation, which is located in VLAN 20. The attacker has thus successfully hopped from VLAN 10 to VLAN 20.

Obviously, this attack requires knowledge of the configuration of the switches, and it is not simple to execute. Moreover, the attack traffic flow is one way, and this attack is generally only useful for DoS types of attacks where bogus data would be flooded on a VLAN. The next subsection discusses how to prevent this attack.

Protecting Against VLAN Hopping

As discussed in the previous section, VLAN hopping attacks are not easy to pull off because they require specific native VLAN settings on a trunk. They also have limited usability because VLAN hopping only works in one direction, thus preventing the attacker from establishing a TCP session. Nevertheless, protection against VLAN hopping attacks is simple and should be considered a best practice.

Because an attacker's port VLAN must match the native VLAN of a trunk, the simple solution is to configure the native VLAN of all trunk ports to an unused VLAN. A command VLAN number associated with a nontraffic VLAN is 999. This configuration does not effect the behavior of trunk port in any manner.

In review, the configuration for configuring the native VLAN on the trunk is a follows:

```
SW(config)# interface interface-slot/number
SW(config-if)# switchport trunk native vlan vlan-id
```

An alternate method is to prune the native VLAN from the trunk. The configuration to prune VLANs from a trunk port is as follows:

```
SW(config)# interface interface-slot/number
SW(config-if)# switchport trunk native vlan vlan-id
SW(config-if)# switchport trunk allowed vlan remove vlan-id
```

Yet another option is to tag all frames on trunk ports by default. The command to configure this option is as follows:

```
SW(config)# vlan dot1q tag native
```

Note, maintenance protocols, such as CDP and DTP, are normally carried over the native VLAN. Native VLAN pruning will not affect the functionality of these protocols because they will use the native VLAN regardless of configuration.

Example 10-14 illustrates the native VLAN secure configuration options, configuring the native VLAN to an unused VLAN, pruning Native VLAN from trunk ports, and tagging the native VLAN, respectively.

Example 10-14   *Securing the Native VLAN on Trunks*

```
SW(config)# interface gigabitEthernet 1/1
SW(config-if)# switchport trunk native vlan 999
SW(config)# interface gigabitEthernet 1/1
SW(config-if)# switchport trunk native vlan 999
SW(config-if)# switchport trunk allowed vlan remove 999
SW(config-if)# vlan dot1q tag native
```

The next section discusses a brute-force method of filtering traffic: VLAN access lists.

VLAN Access Lists

VLAN access lists (VACLs) on Catalyst switches serve the following two distinct purposes:

- With certain limitations, filter traffic at Layer 2

- Overcome VLAN Switch Port Analyzer (SPAN) limitations via use of the Capture Port feature

VACLs can provide access control for all packets that are bridged within a VLAN or packets that are routed into or out of a VLAN or a WAN interface. Unlike Cisco IOS ACLs that are applied on routed packets only, VACLs apply to all packets and can be applied to any VLAN or WAN interface.

You can configure VACLs for IP or MAC layer traffic with some limitations depending on platform and software version.

Each VLAN access map can consist of one or more map sequences; each sequence has a match clause and an action clause. The match clause specifies IP or MAC ACLs for traffic filtering, and the action clause specifies the action to be taken when a match occurs. When a flow matches a permit ACL entry, the associated action is taken, and the flow is not checked against the remaining sequences. When a flow matches a deny ACL entry, it will be checked against the next ACL in the same sequence or the next sequence. If a flow does not match any ACL entry and at least one ACL is configured for that packet type, the packet is denied.

Beyond traffic filtering, the VACL Capture Port feature can help overcome some limitations of VLAN SPAN. VACLs are primarily not designed to monitor traffic. However, with a wide range of capability to classify the traffic, the Capture Port feature was introduced so that network traffic analysis can become much simpler. These are the advantages of VACL Capture Port usage over VSPAN:

- **Granular traffic analysis:** VACLs can match based on source IP address, destination IP address, Layer 4 protocol type, source and destination Layer 4 ports, and other information. This capability makes VACLs very useful for granular traffic identification and filtering.

- **The number of sessions:** VACLs are enforced in hardware. The number of access control entries (ACEs) that can be created depends on the ternary content-addressable memory (TCAM) available in the switches.

- **Destination port oversubscription:** Granular traffic identification reduces the number of frames to be forwarded to the destination port and thereby minimizes the probability of their oversubscription.

- **VACLs are enforced in hardware:** There is no performance penalty for the application of VACLs to a VLAN on the Cisco Catalyst 6500 series switches.

As with PACLs, there are two types of VACL configurations:

- **IP access list:** Filters IPv4 and IPv6 packets on a Layer 2 port.

- **MAC access list:** Filters packets that are of an unsupported type (not IP!) based on the fields of the Ethernet datagram. A MAC access list is *not applied* to IP messages.

Note   VACLs have an implicit deny at the end of the map; a packet is denied if it does not match any ACL entry and at least one ACL is configured for the packet type.

VACL Interaction with ACLs and PACLs

VACLs, Layer 3 ACLs on routed interfaces, and PACLs work together seamlessly; however, care must be taken when engineering these filtering techniques together.

As illustrated in Figure 10-16, for an incoming packet on a physical port, the PACL is applied first. If the packet is permitted by the PACL, the VACL on the ingress VLAN is applied next. If the packet is Layer 3 forwarded and is permitted by the VACL, it is filtered by the Cisco IOS ACLs on the same VLAN. The same process happens in reverse in the egress direction. However, there is currently no hardware support for output PACLs.

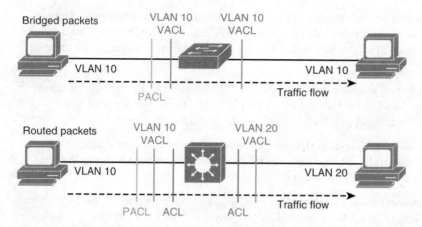

Figure 10-16   *VACL Interaction with ACLs and PACLs*

The PACLs override both the VACLs and Cisco IOS ACLs when the port is configured in prefer port mode. The one exception to this rule is when the packets are forwarded in the software due to an exception to hardware forwarding. The route processor then applies the ingress Cisco IOS ACL regardless of the PACL mode. Two examples where the packets are forwarded in the software are as follows:

- Packets that are egress bridged (due to logging or features such as NAT)

- Packets with IP options

The next section discusses configuring VACLs; the configuration principles are similar to Cisco IOS ACLs.

Configuring VACLs

VLAN ACLs are configured through the VLAN access maps and than applied to a VLAN. Two types of ACLs can be configured as VACL, MAC access lists, and IP access lists. There is an implicit deny at the end of each list:

```
SW(config)# mac access-list extended acl-name
SW(config-ext-macl)# permit host [source-mac | any] [destination-mac | any]
SW(config)# ip access-list acl-type acl-name
SW(config-ext-nacl)# permit protocol [source-address | any] [destination-address
| any]
```

Configured ACLs are then used as a matching ACL inside a VLAN access map. When the traffic is matched against a configured ACL, **action** is taken. The action clause in a VACL can be forward, drop, capture, or redirect. Traffic can also be logged. There is an implicit drop at the end of the map:

```
SW(config)# vlan access-map map-name
SW(config-access-map)# match [mac | ip] address acl-name
SW(config-access-map)# action [drop | forward | redirect] [log]
```

VLAN access map can be applied to one or multiple VLANs, but only one VLAN access map can be applied to each VLAN:

```
SW(config)# vlan filter map-name vlan-list [vlan-list | all]
```

Example 10-15 shows some VACL examples, starting with the access list creation, followed by the access map created for the VACLs, and then an application of the VACL to a VLAN.

Example 10-15 *VACL examples*

```
SW(config)# mac access-list extend simple-mac-acl
SW(config-ext-macl)# permit host 0000.001c.2014 any
SW(config-ext-macl)# exit
SW(config)# ip access-list extended simple-ip-acl
SW(config-ext-nacl)# permit ip host 192.168.1.1 any
SW(config-ext-nacl)# exit
SW(config)#
SW(config)# vlan access-map simple-vlan-map
SW(config-access-map)# match mac address simple-mac-acl
SW(config-access-map)# match ip address simple-ip-acl
SW(config-access-map)# action forward
SW(config-access-map)# exit
SW(config)# vlan filter simple-vlan-map vlan-list 2-10

SW(config)# end
```

For additional information on VACLs, consult the following reference:

http://www.cisco.com/c/en/us/td/docs/switches/lan/catalyst6500/ios/15-0SY/configuration/guide/15_0_sy_swcg/vlan_acls.html

Private VLANs

There are cases when Layer 2 communication inside a single VLAN needs to be limited. The PVLAN features support this ability by partitioning the Layer 2 broadcast domain of a VLAN into subdomains, isolating ports on the switch from each other, while keeping them in the same subnet.

This section covers the following topics related to PVLANs:

- Introduction to private VLANs
- Describe the private VLAN feature
- Describe the private VLAN port types
- Configure private VLANs

- Verify private VLAN configuration

- Describe private VLANs across multiple switches

- Describe the protected port feature

Introduction to PVLANs

Private VLANs fit a specific requirement often found in public networks. PVLANs also have usefulness in enterprise and campus networks. Essentially, PVLANs restrict end-user devices such as PCs and mobile devices from communication between each other, but still allow communication to router ports and network services. In this manner, the end-user devices will behave as normal but cannot communicate to other devices in the same Layer 2 domain. This mechanism provides a level of security. Examples of the security is when an end-user device is infected with port scanners or viruses, the end-user cannot communicate with other devices on the same network to either infect the end-user devices or scan open ports for other vulnerabilities.

Of course, assigning every single end device its own VLAN would accomplish the same security method as PVLANs; however, switches have a limit on the number of VLANs supported, and a large number of VLANs creates scalability issues. Figure 10-17 illustrates this behavior. The left of the diagram illustrates private VLANs, and the right illustrates port isolation via using multiple VLANs.

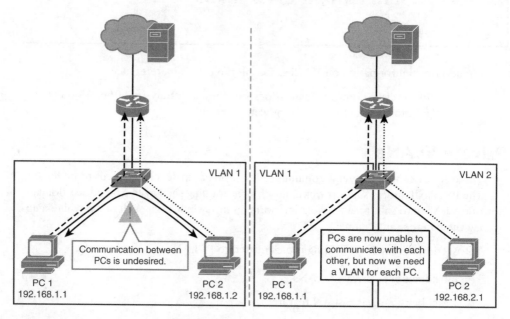

Figure 10-17 *The Need for PVLANs*

To restate, PVLANs are essentially VLANs inside a VLAN. Different VLANs are not allowed to communicate directly; a Layer 3 device is needed to route packets between different VLANs. PVLANs follow the same concept: A Layer 3 device is needed to route packets between different PVLANs. However, there is a difference between VLANs and PVLANs. A VLAN typically corresponds to an IP subnet. When a VLAN is partitioned into PVLANs, devices in different PVLANs still belong to the same IP subnet. They are, however, unable to communicate with each other on Layer 2; all traffic has to be routed through a Layer 3 device, where additional security techniques, such as ACLs, can be applied.

PVLANs are an elegant solution when you need to keep multiple devices in the same IP subnet yet provide port isolation on Layer 2. The next subsection discusses PVLAN port types.

PVLAN Port Types

A PVLAN domain has one primary VLAN. Each port in a private VLAN domain is a member of the primary VLAN; the primary VLAN is the entire private VLAN domain.

Secondary VLANs are subdomains that provide isolation between ports within the same private VLAN domain. There are two types of secondary VLANs: isolated VLANs and community VLANs. Isolated VLANs contain isolated ports, which cannot communicate between each other in the isolated VLAN. Community VLANs contain community ports that can communicate between each other in the community VLAN.

Figure 10-18 illustrates these concepts; they are not easy to understand without visual aid. Note that the primary VLAN is 100, which contains all the ports in the topology. Within VLAN 100, there are two secondary VLANs: 101 and 102. VLAN 101 is an isolated VLAN. PC 1 and PC 2 are isolated and cannot communicate between each other. VLAN 102 is a community VLAN. PC 3 and PC 4 can communicate between each other. PC 3 and PC 4 cannot communicate with PC 1 and PC 2, and vice versa, because they are in different secondary VLANs.

For the PCs to be able to communicate with shared devices or communicate beyond the Layer 2 VLAN, the PVLAN feature supports configuration of promiscuous ports. Promiscuous ports are usually uplink connections to the rest of the network and thus a router port. In Figure 10-18, the router uplink is the promiscuous port.

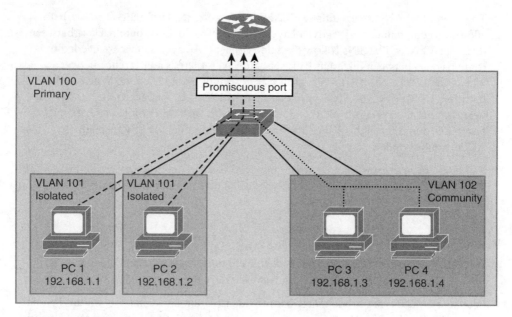

Figure 10-18   *PVLAN Port Types*

In review, the three types of private VLAN port types are as follows:

- **Promiscuous:** A promiscuous port belongs to the primary VLAN and can communicate with all mapped ports in the primary VLAN, including community and isolated ports. A port that provides uplink connection to a router is configured as a promiscuous port, because all hosts need to communicate with the router. There can be multiple promiscuous ports in a primary VLAN.

- **Isolated:** An isolated port is a host port that belongs to an isolated secondary VLAN. An isolated port has complete isolation from other ports, except with associated promiscuous ports. You can have more than one isolated port in a specified isolated VLAN. Each port is completely isolated from all other ports in the isolated VLAN.

- **Community:** A community port is a host port that belongs to a community secondary VLAN. Community ports communicate with other ports in the same community VLAN and with associated promiscuous ports. They are isolated from all ports in other community VLANs and all isolated ports.

The next subsection discusses private VLAN configuration.

PVLAN Configuration

PVLAN configuration is straightforward; however, the primary and secondary VLANs must be configured first. In addition, because the PVLANs feature is not compatible with VTP, VTP must be set to transparent or off.

The command to configure VTP mode to transparent is **vtp mode transparent.**

As mentioned, the first step in the PVLAN configuration is to configure the primary VLAN by using the following commands:

```
SW(config)# vlan vlan-id
SW(config-vlan)# private-vlan primary
```

The next step is to configure the secondary VLANs and apply the configuration of these PVLANs as isolated or community by using the following commands:

```
SW(config)# vlan vlan-id
SW(config-vlan)# private-vlan isolated
SW(config)# vlan vlan-id
SW(config-vlan)# private-vlan community
```

After the secondary VLANs have been created and configured, the secondary VLANs need to be associated with the primary VLAN. The configuration command for this step is as follows:

```
SW(config)# vlan primary-vlan-id
SW(config-vlan)# private-vlan association secondary-vlan-id {, secondary-vlan-id}
```

Example 10-16 illustrates a sample configuration of the PVLAN creation and associations based on the example PVLAN in Figure 10-18.

Example 10-16 *Sample PVLAN Configuration*

```
SW(config)# vlan 100
SW(config-vlan)# private-vlan primary
SW(config)# vlan 101
SW(config-vlan)# private-vlan isolated
SW(config)# vlan 102
SW(config-vlan) private-vlan community
SW(config-vlan) vlan 100
SW(config-vlan) private-vlan association 101, 102
```

Now that the PVLANs are configured and associated, the individual ports must be configured.

All promiscuous ports are assigned to a single primary VLAN and may be configured with multiple secondary VLANs. In addition, the feature supports associating a secondary VLAN to more than one promiscuous port, as long as the promiscuous port and secondary VLANs are within the same primary VLAN. The configuration commands for configuring promiscuous ports are as follows:

```
SW(config)# interface interface-slot/number
SW(config-if)# switchport mode private-vlan promiscuous
SW(config-if)# switchport private-vlan mapping primary-vlan-id add secondary-vlan-id {, secondary-vlan-id}
```

Following the promiscuous port configuration, the next step is configuring the end-user ports into the primary and secondary VLANs. Using the **range** command is useful when configuring multiple continuous ports.

Keep in mind that if a secondary VLAN is isolated, all ports in that secondary VLAN will be isolated. If a secondary VLAN is a community VLAN, all ports in that PVLAN will be community. A host (end-user) port can only be a part of one secondary VLAN. The commands to configure host ports into a PVLAN are as follows:

```
SW(config)# interface range interface-range
SW(config-if-range)# switchport mode private-vlan host
SW(config-if-range)# switchport private-vlan host-association primary-vlan-id
secondary-vlan-id
```

Example 10-17 illustrates a sample configuration of the PVLAN port assignments based on the example PVLAN in Figure 10-18. This example is a continuation of Example 10-16.

Example 10-17 *Sample PVLAN Port Assignment Configuration*

```
SW(config)# interface GigabitEthernet 0/1
SW(config-if)# switchport description Interface-to-Router
SW(config-if)# switchport mode private-vlan promiscuous
SW(config-if)# switchport private-vlan mapping 100 add 101, 102
SW(config-if)# interface range GigabitEthernet 0/2-3
SW(config-if-range)# switchport description End-User-Ports-In-Isolated-PVLAN
SW(config-if-range)# switchport mode private-vlan host
SW(config-if-range)# switchport private-vlan host-association 100 101
SW(config-if)# interface range GigabitEthernet 0/4-5
SW(config-if-range)# switchport description End-User-Ports-In-Community-PVLAN
SW(config-if-range)# switchport mode private-vlan host
SW(config-if-range)# switchport private-vlan host-association 100 102
```

PVLAN Verification

PVLAN verification is straightforward using the **show vlan private-vlan** command. Example 10-18 illustrates a verification based on Figure 10-18 and the previous examples in this section.

Example 10-18 *PVLAN Verification*

```
Switch# show vlan private-vlan

Primary  Secondary  Type                  Ports
-------  ---------  --------------------  ------------------------
100      101        isolated              Gi0/1, Gi0/2, Gi0/3
100      102        community             Gi0/1, Gi0/4, Gi0/5
```

```
Switch# show interfaces gigabitEthernet 0/1 switchport | include private-vlan
Administrative Mode: private-vlan promiscuous
Administrative private-vlan host-association: none
Administrative private-vlan mapping: 100 (VLAN0100) 101 (VLAN101) 102 (VLAN102)
Administrative private-vlan trunk native VLAN: none
Administrative private-vlan trunk Native VLAN tagging: enabled
Administrative private-vlan trunk encapsulation: dot1q
Administrative private-vlan trunk normal VLANs: none
Administrative private-vlan trunk associations: none
Administrative private-vlan trunk mappings: none
Operational private-vlan: 100 (VLAN100) 101 (VLAN0101) 102 (VLAN0102)
```

The next section discusses PVLANs across multiple switches.

PVLANs Across Multiple Switches

PVLANs can span multiple switches. Different trunk port types can be used, depending on the type and ability of a device on the other side of a trunk. The different PVLAN trunk port types are as follows:

- Standard trunk port
- Isolated PVLAN trunk port
- Promiscuous PLVAN trunk port

Leveraging a standard trunk port to carry the primary VLAN and secondary VLANs to a neighboring switch is the same as the trunk carrying any VLAN. To maintain the security of your PVLANs and to avoid other use of the VLANs configured as PVLANs, the configuration of PVLANs must match on all intermediate switches, including devices that have no private VLAN ports.

An isolated PVLAN trunk port is used when connecting a PVLAN-enabled switch to a switch with no PVLAN support, such as Catalyst 2950. Normal VLAN traffic is treated the same as on a standard trunk port. Traffic tagged with a VLAN that is configured as isolated, however, is treated the same as the traffic from an isolated port; it is isolated from other isolated and community ports. A switch with an isolated trunk port can thus isolate between the traffic from the isolated trunk and directly connected hosts, but not between hosts connected to the non-PVLAN switch.

A promiscuous PVLAN trunk port is used in a situation where a PVLAN promiscuous host port would normally be used but where it is necessary to carry multiple normal VLANs or PVLAN domains. An upstream router without PVLAN support can be connected to a promiscuous trunk port. A router on a subinterface, just like any other VLAN traffic, receives traffic that is sent out through a promiscuous trunk port.

In review of PVLAN trunk ports, always select the PVLAN trunk port type that best fits your design. Ideally, using standard trunk ports is easiest to manage when all switches in the network support PVLANs.

Using the Protected Port Feature

The PVLAN feature is not available on all switches; for instance, the Catalyst 2950 does not support it. However, the protected port feature provides a similar functionality to PVLAN on a wider range of Catalyst switches.

Protected port, also known as the PVLAN edge, is a feature that (unlike PVLANs) has only local significance to the switch. Protected ports do not forward any traffic to protected ports on the same switch. This means that all traffic passing between protected ports (unicast, broadcast, and multicast) must be forwarded through a Layer 3 device. Protected ports can forward any type of traffic to nonprotected ports, and they forward as usual to all ports on other switches.

Configuration of a protected port is simple:

```
SW(config)# interface interface-slot/number
SW(config-if)# switchport protected
```

Essentially, the protected port feature is a shortcut method of PVLANs, without having to configure promiscuous and isolated ports.

In summary, PVLANs isolate ports from each other while keeping them in the same VLAN and subnet. This characteristic is useful in large campus networks. Moreover, there are three types of PVLAN ports: promiscuous, isolated, and community. Each has its special behavior useful for building a network with PVLANs.

For additional information about PVLANs, consult the following documentation on Cisco.com:

- **Configuring isolated PVLANs on Catalyst switches:** http://www.cisco.com/c/en/us/support/docs/lan-switching/private-vlans-pvlans-promiscuous-isolated-community/40781-194.html

- **Configuring PVLANs:** http://www.cisco.com/c/en/us/td/docs/switches/lan/catalyst4500/12-2/54sg/configuration/guide/config/pvlans.html

Study Tips

- PVLANs allow for ease of configuration when securing Layer 2 VLANs.

- Promiscuous PVLAN ports allow all traffic from the primary VLAN; this configuration is commonly used on router ports.

- Isolated VLANs are PVLANs where hosts cannot communicate with one another.

- Community VLANs are PVLANs that allow communication within the PVLAN, but not to other secondary VLANs.

- DHCP snooping is a useful feature to prevent DHCP snooping attacks by ensuring only valid DHCP servers assign addresses to end users.

- DAI and IPSG prevent ARP and IP spoofing attacks, respectively. Both leverage DHCP snooping to function.

- VACLs are ACLs that support bridge filtering and filtering in and out of VLANs.

- Port security is useful in limiting and filtering MAC addresses per port.

Summary

This chapter covered the most important topic when designing or implementing campus networks: security. The security principles in this chapter are more than best practices (and instead are near requirements) for today's campus networks. Campus network security is often belied by the fact that most security efforts focus on the edge of the network and not inside the network. However, attackers and hackers only need physical access to the network to create a plethora of network security risks by attacking the basics of Layer 2 networks. In summary, this chapter covered the following features useful for securing campus networks:

- Configure port security to limit and filter MAC addresses on ports; port security supports features that reduce the overhead of assigning MAC addresses per port.

- Use PVLANs to restrict traffic within a VLAN with simple configuration.

- Leverage DHCP snooping, DAI, and IPSG to prevent spoofing attacks.

- Consider VACLs when appropriate to block unnecessary traffic and known traffic attacks.

- Always adhere to basic security configurations such as AAA on all Cisco devices.

- Stay current on all vulnerabilities and security notices from Cisco.

- Keep current on Cisco Catalyst software versions because new software versions address known vulnerabilities.

Review Questions

Use the questions in this section as a review of what you have learned in this chapter. The correct answers are found in Appendix A, "Answers to Chapter Review Questions."

1. Which feature that is supported on Cisco switches restricts a switch port to a specific set or number of MAC addresses?

    a. DHCP snooping

    b. Private VLANs

    c. Access lists

    d. VACLs

    e. Port security

    f. None of the above

2. The storm control feature controls which type of traffic?

    a. Unicast

    b. Multicast

    c. Broadcast

    d. None of the above

    e. Not enough information provided on model switch and software version under consideration, but generally storm control supports unicast, multicast, and broadcast.

3. With DHCP snooping, which port is configured as trusted?

    a. The port to the DHCP client is always trusted.

    b. The port to the DHCP server is always trusted.

    c. With DHCP snooping, all ports are trusted.

    d. Trust ports have no context in DHCP snooping.

    e. Any port to the client and to the server can become trusted as soon as a DHCP transaction is secured.

    f. A and B

4. Which two of the following does a switch use to detect spoofed addresses when IP Source Guard is enabled?

  a. ARP entries

  b. DHCP database

  c. DHCP snooping database

  d. Static IP source binding entries

  e. Reverse path-forwarding entries

  f. VACLs

5. By default, Cisco IOS switch ports are put in one of the two DTP modes. Which two?

  a. Dynamic desirable

  b. Access

  c. Dynamic auto

  d. Off

  e. Non-negotiate

  f. Trunk

6. What is the aim of the "sticky" option when used with port security?

  a. A learned MAC address must stick to one single port.

  b. A dynamically learned MAC address is considered like a statically learned MAC address.

  c. For a given MAC address with the sticky option, the port security feature applies to whichever port the MAC address connects to.

  d. A router on a stick can bypass the port security feature.

7. At which layer should port security be implemented?

  a. Access layer

  b. Distribution layer

  c. Core layer

  d. All of the above

8. Which statements about VLAN hopping are correct? (Choose two.)

    a. A Catalyst switch discards VLAN tagged packets ingressing an access port.

    b. A Catalyst switch accepts VLAN-tagged packets ingressing an access port if VLAN tag matches the VLAN of the access port.

    c. A VLAN hopping attack with double tagging is possible only when attacker's access port is in the same VLAN as the native VLAN of a trunk port.

    d. A VLAN hopping attack with double tagging is bidirectional; traffic can hop from the attacker's VLAN to the target VLAN and vice versa.

    e. Native VLAN pruning disables maintenance protocols, such as CDP and DTP.

9. There are two types of secondary private VLANs. Which two?

    a. Promiscuous

    b. Primary

    c. Transparent

    d. Isolated

    e. Community

    f. RSPAN

10. Which statements about PVLAN promiscuous mode are correct? (Choose two.)

    a. Promiscuous ports can be mapped to a single primary VLAN.

    b. Promiscuous ports can be mapped to multiple primary VLANs.

    c. Promiscuous ports can always communicate with all ports in the same primary VLAN.

    d. Promiscuous ports can only communicate with ports in the second VLAN it is mapped to.

    e. Promiscuous ports do not participate in spanning tree.

11. Which of the following reasons describes why configuring campus network security is so important?

    a. Current-generation campus network switches' default mode of operation is to allow all traffic through the network.

    b. Hackers may gain physical access to the campus network to launch attacks.

    c. Viruses may effect corporate laptops at home and then cause havoc when connected at the office.

    d. Bring your own devices (BYOD) is common in today's workplace and these devices are more easily compromised because security of the device is placed mostly in the hands of the owner and not corporate IT.

    e. The emergence of public and private clouds creates even more opportunity for hackers to gain malicious access to the network.

    f. All of the above

    g. None of the above

12. Which of the following statements are generally true about firewalls, routers, and switches? (Choose two.)

    a. Firewalls come preconfigured to deny all traffic, and specific traffic must be permitted.

    b. Routers and switches come preconfigured to deny all traffic, and specific traffic must be permitted.

    c. Routers and switches come preconfigured to allow all traffic, and specific traffic must be denied.

    d. Firewalls come preconfigured to allow all traffic, and specific traffic must be denied.

13. With MAC flooding attacks, what are the two possible malicious outcomes?

    a. Switch resource overflows, such as the MAC address table, which may result in traffic loss.

    b. The switch detecting MAC flooding and shutting down all ports by default.

    c. The switch signaling the DHCP server not to give out new DHCP addresses.

    d. The switch flooding traffic, which may result in an intruding device intercepting traffic.

14. Which statement describes the err-disabled state on a switch?

    a. The err-disabled state of a port is the default state of a port during initial configuration.

    b. The err-disabled state of a port is when the port is up but nothing is connected.

    c. The err-disabled state of a port describes a condition when the switch has disabled the port due to an error condition to prevent any further issues on the network.

    d. The err-disabled state of a port describes the condition when the spanning-tree state is not forwarding.

15. Which of the following conditions will a switch place a port into an err-disabled state? (Choose all that apply.)

    a. Duplex mismatch

    b. UDLD condition

    c. Spanning-tree BPDU Guard

    d. Spanning-tree UplinkFast

    e. HSRP duplicate MAC

    f. Excessive link flapping

    g. Port security Violation

16. What is the difference between a PACL and an ACL?

    a. ACLs are applied to ports, whereas PACLs are applied to physical interfaces on routers.

    b. ACLs and PACLs are the same feature, just applied to different types of interfaces.

    c. ACLs are used for Layer 3 interfaces, whereas PACLs are used for Layer 2 interfaces.

17. If the failing threshold for storm control is not set, what is the default value used for the failing threshold.

    a. 50 percent of the total bandwidth

    b. 50 percent of the rising threshold

    c. 0 packets per second

    d. 100 percent of the rising threshold

18. What is the purpose of DHCP option 82?

  a. DHCP option 82 provides information that allows the host to request a static IP address assignment.

  b. DHCP option 82 allows the use of virtual machines on the attach host, such as VMWare ESX.

  c. DHCP provides additional information in the DHCP request to inform the DHCP server of additional specifics about the locality and details about the DHCP request.

  d. DHCP option 82 is a required feature for IPv6.

  e. All of the above

  f. None of the above

19. Which statement best describes how IP Source Guard works?

  a. IP Source Guard works by building dynamic PACVLs and VACLs by leveraging DHCP snooping to ensure that the frames entering the switch port are only from an IP address assigned by a trusted DHCP server.

  b. IP Source Guard works by building dynamic PACLs and VACLs by leveraging the ARP table to ensure the frames entering the switch port are only from a valid IP address.

  c. IP Source Guard works by building dynamic PACVLs VACLs by leveraging the preconfigured ACLs to ensure that the frames entering the switch port are only from a valid IP address.

  d. IP Source Guard works by directly acting as a DHCP server.

  e. None of the above

20. Which statement describes ARP spoofing?

  a. ARP spoofing is when a host assumes the IP address of a legitimate host in the network.

  b. ARP spoofing attacks networks by spoofing an ARP reply from a legitimate device with an invalid MAC address.

  c. ARP spoofing works by flooding a bogus ARP request at the next-hop router in a DoS attempt.

  d. None of the above

21. Which statement best describes how dynamic ARP inspection (DAI) works?

   a. DAI uses the ARP table of the first-hop router to ensure only valid ARP enter the network.

   b. DAI leverages custom, statically configured ACLs to ensure that only ARPs from valid MAC addresses enter the switch.

   c. DAI uses LLDP to communicate with the attach host to put an authoritative MAC table.

   d. DAI prevents attacks by filtering ARP requests that are not valid by referencing the MAC-to-IP address bindings built from DHCP snooping.

22. What is the main difference between ACLs on Cisco routers and VACLs on Cisco Catalyst switches?

   a. Router ACLs can provide access control for routed and bridged frames in the VLAN, and switch VACLs can access control only bridged frames.

   b. Router ACLs can provide access control for routed frames across VLANs, and switch VACLs can access control only bridged frames in a VLAN.

   c. Router ACLs can provide access control for routed frames, and switch VACLs can access control routed frames out of VLAN and bridged frames.

   d. Both router ACLs and switch VACLs provide the same function.

   e. None of the above

23. What are five best practices recommendations associated with securing VLAN trunks?

   a. Restrict MAC addresses on VLAN trunks

   b. Configure all trunks as DHCP snooping untrusted

   c. Manually configure all host ports as access ports instead of dynamic modes of DTP

   d. Restrict VLANs on trunk ports to necessary VLANs

   e. Do not use valid native VLANs on trunk ports

   f. Configure all trunks ports statically

   g. Shut down all unused interfaces

24. Match each port type to its definition.

A. Standard trunk port   1. Leveraged to enable private VLANs across multiple switches

B. Isolated port   2. Connects a PVLAN-enabled switch with an upstream router with subinterfaces but with no PVLAN support

C. Community port   3. Maintains complete isolation from other ports, except promiscuous ports

D. Protected port   4. Communicates with ports in same PVLAN and promiscuous ports, but not other PVLANs

E. Promiscuous PLVAN trunk port   5. Restricts traffic between protected ports on the local switch

25. Put the ACLs in order of operation (1–5 or not applied) for an incoming routed packet through the switch.

a. Egress VLAN ACL

b. Egress SVI standard ACL

c. Ingress port ACL

d. Ingress SVI standard ACL

e. Ingress VLAN ACL

f. Egress port ACL

Answers to Chapter Review Questions

Chapter 2

1. B
2. B
3. B
4. A, B, C, D
5. B
6. B
7. C
8. A, B, C, E, F, G
9. False
10. A and C
11. B and C
12. E
13. C
14. C
15. A, B, D, E, F
16. A
17. F
18. A, B, E
19. E
20. A
21. B and C
22. C
23. D

Chapter 3

1. False
2. False
3. False
4. False
5. False
6. A
7. D
8. A
9. B
10. C
11. A
12. B
13. A and C
14. D
15. A

16. A

17. B

18. C

19. D

20. A and E

21. C

22. D

23. D

24. B, C, D

25. A

26. D

27. True

28. A and B

29. C

30. a. 5

  b. 1

  c. 6

  d. 4

  e. 3

  f. 2

31. A and C

32. B

33. D

34. C

Chapter 4

1. A

2. B

3. C

4. B

5. C

6. B and C

7. A

8. B and D

9. A

Chapter 5

1. False

2. True

3. True

4. A

5. B

6. C

7. B and E

8. a. 2

  b. 4

  c. 5

  d. 1

  e. 3

9. C and E

10. B

11. D

12. C

13. C

14. A

15. DHCP is a client/server application, in which the DHCP client contacts a DHCP server for configuration parameters using a broadcast request. If a client is in a different subnet than a server, the broadcast is forwarded using the DHCP relay agent feature by the local router or multilayer switch.

16. B and C

17. A

18. B and C

19. A

20. B

21. C

22. False

Chapter 6

1. D

2. D

3. B

4. C

5. B

6. B

7. B

8. C

9. E

Chapter 7

1. A and C

2. A and D

3. A

4. C

5. E

6. B

7. A

8. A-2

B-1

C-3

9. C

10. E

11. B and C

12. E

13. A-1

B-2

C-4

D-3

14. A-1

B-4

C-2

D-3

15. A

16. A, C, D

17. B

18. B

21. C

Chapter 8

1. B

2. B

3. B

4. A, B, C, D

5. B

6. B

7. C

8. A, B, C, E, F, G

9. False

10. A and C

11. B and C

12. E

13. C

14. C

15. A, B, D, E, F

16. A

17. F

18. A, B, E

19. E

20. A

21. B and C

22. C

23. D

Chapter 9

1. E

2. D

3. a. 1

b. 4

c. 2

d. 3

4. D

Chapter 10

1. E

2. E

3. B

4. C and D

5. A and C

6. B

7. A

8. B and C

9. D and E

10. A and C

11. F

12. A and C

13. A and D

14. C

15. A, B, C, F, G

16. C

17. D

18. C

19. A

20. B

21. D

22. C

23. C, D, E, F, G

24. A-1

B-3

C-4

D-5

E-2

25. a. 5

b. 4

c. 1

d. 3

e. 2

f. not applied

Index

D

T

W

X-Y-Z